# Studies in Immigration and Culture
Royden Loewen, series editor

# HOLOCAUST SURVIVORS IN CANADA

Exclusion, Inclusion, Transformation, 1947–1955

## ADARA GOLDBERG

University of Manitoba Press

University of Manitoba Press
Winnipeg, Manitoba
Canada R3T 2M5
uofmpress.ca

Printed in Canada
Text printed on chlorine-free, 100% post-consumer recycled paper

19  18  17  16  15      1  2  3  4  5

Cover image: Eating a meal outside at the Mothers' and Babes' Summer Rest Home, 1948.
Ontario Jewish Archives, fonds 52, series 1-7, file 5, item 2.
Cover design: David Drummond
Interior design: Jess Koroscil

**Library and Archives Canada Cataloguing in Publication**

Goldberg, Adara, 1983–, author
Holocaust survivors in Canada : exclusion, inclusion,
transformation, 1947-1955 / Adara Goldberg.

(Studies in immigration and culture ; 14)
Includes bibliographical references and index.
Issued in print and electronic formats.
ISBN 978-0-88755-776-7 (pbk.)
ISBN 978-0-88755-496-4 (pdf)
ISBN 978-0-88755-494-0 (epub)

1. Jews—Canada—History—20th century. 2. Jews—Cultural
assimilation—Canada—History—20th century. 3. Jews, Canadian—
History—20th century. 4 . Holocaust survivors—Canada—Biography.
5. Immigrants—Canada—Biography. 6. Canada—Emigration and
immigration—History—20th century. I. Title. II. Series: Studies in
immigration and culture ; 14

FC106.J5G63585 2015       971.004'924       C2015-903498-1
                                            C2015-903499-X

The University of Manitoba Press gratefully acknowledges the financial support
for its publication program provided by the Government of Canada through the Canada
Book Fund, the Canada Council for the Arts, the Manitoba Department
of Culture, Heritage, Tourism, the Manitoba Arts Council,
and the Manitoba Book Publishing Tax Credit.

FSC
www.fsc.org
MIX
Paper from
responsible sources
FSC® C016245

*To my father, David Goldberg, whose high standards and strong moral code I strive to live up to. I hope that I've made you proud.*

# CONTENTS

# LIST OF ILLUSTRATIONS

# INTRODUCTION

In October 1949, at the request of the Canadian Jewish Congress (CJC), Miss Mary Palevsky, a former caseworker with the United Nations Relief and Rehabilitation Administration (UNRRA) and deputy director of the New York Association of New Americans, produced a survey report on Jewish refugee settlement work in Montreal and Toronto, two metropolises representing 85 percent of Canadian Jews. The investigation shed a disheartening, unflattering light on communal efforts to effectively serve the first wave of postwar Holocaust survivors to reach Canada: "The settlement of thousands of immigrants is essentially a large-scale welfare operation. The resources for an operation of such scope were lacking in Canada. Canadian communities are not well organized to serve the normal demands of even the native population. Confronted by the need to extend its limited resources to meet the urgent and almost unlimited needs of the immigrants, the program collapsed at pressure points and emergency measures had to be improvised from day to day."[1] Miss Palevsky reported that lack of communication, coordination, funding, staffing, services, and psychological help were responsible for the poor quality of practical support for "new" Jewish Canadians. The only commendation referred to the reasonably well-orchestrated and applied care and protection of dependent and unattached young persons. While Palevsky acknowledged the reactive nature of the service agencies—many of which developed only immediately prior to the arrival of their clients—and applauded their efforts, her diagnosis remained bleak.[2] In her eyes, the CJC and its affiliated organizations had failed the survivors.

And, yet, Holocaust survivors entered and integrated into Canada's Jewish communities, and in the process, they affected and transformed various aspects of Canadian Jewish life. Possessing limited political agency or power, in addition to the lingering physical and psychological effects of wartime abuses, survivors collectively navigated the resettlement process with varying degrees of savvy. And, in spite of legal, social, political, and economical obstacles, most survivors became engaged "new Canadians" by the latter part of the 1950s. They spearheaded the development of Hassidic and ultra-Orthodox communities, contributed to and rejuvenated Yiddish culture and the arts, and helped enact legislative change relating to refugee laws and human rights. Although financially poor, the newcomers brought with them energy, expertise, and a commitment to re-establishing their lives.

Canadian Jewry was dramatically reshaped by the arrival of approximately 35,000 survivors of Nazi persecution, plus their dependents, from 1947 to 1955. A small but well-established community of 170,000 persons in the 1930s, Canadian Jews had maintained close ties with Eastern Europe prior to and during the first years of the Second World War, and pioneered campaigns to deliver money, food, and resources to suffering relatives and friends. As the war progressed and the Final Solution unrolled, however, these ties withered. Knowledge about the destruction of their European co-religionists arrived through various sources, including press coverage, public demonstrations, and military reports. Unprecedented accounts of mass, state-sponsored, anti-Jewish violence challenged comprehension. Few Canadians could begin to fathom, or believe, the extent to which Nazi Germany decimated Jewish life in Europe.

When surviving remnants of European Jewry, the She'erith Hapleitah, began to trickle into Canada two years after liberation, Canadian Jews were ill-prepared to attend to all but their most basic needs. Joseph Kage, director of social services of the Jewish Immigrant Aid Society (JIAS), understood that the incoming refugees required special treatment because of the conditions under which they lived prior to immigration.[3] In practice, however, such special treatment was rarely available or delivered. The absorption and treatment of refugee trauma victims was uncharted territory for the social work profession. As such, caseworkers attended to their clients in an ad hoc manner without sufficient experience or expertise in meeting the psychological needs of trauma victims. Social service agencies also operated on miniscule budgets.[4] But despite the inadequacies of the system, as well as the unprecedented nature of this immigrant population and the bureaucratic service limitations, Jewish agencies responded to the newcomers to the greatest of their professional capability.

If the official Jewish service agencies understood their task, the role of the average Canadian Jew was not clearly defined. Synagogue bulletins, community papers, the *JIAS Record*, and *JIAS News* encouraged citizens to donate their time and money to the refugee cause, and many showed great generosity. However, beyond an initial meet-and-greet at train stations and YMHAs, and donations of second-hand clothing, Canadian Jews received the newcomers reluctantly. The latter were expected to behave like any other group of immigrants: find work, settle down, and move forward. Local co-religionists' responsibilities did not include the provision of emotional or psychological support.

This study highlights the experience of immigration, resettlement, and integration from the perspective of Holocaust survivors and those who sought to assist them in the years 1947 to 1955. It explores the relationships between the survivors, Jewish social service organizations, and local Jewish communities, and considers how those relationships—strained by mammoth disconnects in experience, language, culture, and world view—both facilitated and impeded survivor adaptation. Were refugees well received by Canadian Jews (or more established immigrants)? Or were they treated as inferior foreigners, that is, as "greenhorns" or "greeners"? What factors influenced their reception by members of local Jewish communities and social service providers? How did relational roles and power imbalances, in combination with postwar middle-class values—amongst survivors, and between survivors and caseworkers, males and females—affect this process? And how did the survivors respond to the welcome they received? Comprising a total of approximately 35,000 persons nationwide (and some one-fifth of Jewish homes in 1950s Montreal),[5] the survivors and their dependents imparted new cultural, linguistic, and religious perspectives. They also contributed to the postwar national labour boom and had significant influence on the important revisions to Canada's immigration and, later, refugee policy. Although focusing on the largest Jewish centres in the country—Montreal, Toronto, Winnipeg, Calgary, and Vancouver—the research undertaken in support of this study also looks at small communities in the Maritime provinces and other towns across Canada.

The following chapters lay out the nuanced history of survivors chronologically and thematically. Canadian Jewish history, the country's binational English-French experience, and the national emphasis on cultural plurality loom large in "A Door, Slightly Ajar." This initial chapter follows desperate European Jewish refugees and the attempts of Canadian Jews to bring them to safety in the interwar and early wartime years. Religious and politically driven anti-Semitism prevented the rescue of more than 900 German-Jewish refugee passengers on the *St. Louis*, and cemented Canada's anti-refugee stance for the duration of the war. At the same time, the experiences of the 5,000 refugees who did enter during this period are explored. These included German, Austrian, and Czech Jews who immigrated to Canada predominantly as farmers in 1938 and 1939, interned "enemy aliens" sent from Britain in 1940, and the Iberian refugees who entered Canada on temporary permits in 1944.

If a few hundred Jewish refugees managed to enter the country during the Second World War, their numbers were trumped by the mass influx of Holocaust survivors in the postwar period. The stories of the "ordinary survivors," the predominantly young and healthy refugees who immigrated between late 1947 and 1950, are taken up in Chapter 2. These refugees came to Canada under the official auspices of the CJC and the Jewish Labour Committee, in partnership with various labour unions, as garment industry workers, or through the close relatives program, which permitted the sponsorship of first-degree relatives.

Chapters 3 and 4—"The War Orphans Project" and "'I Remain Its Reluctant Child'"—explore two groups: participants in the War Orphans Project, a CJC-sponsored program, and child survivors who immigrated under other auspices, with or without their parents. Some, like Hungarian Jew Susan Garfield, were placed in small farming communities with tiny Jewish populations and no Hungarian speakers, and suffered great hardships in adaptation in spite of kind treatment by foster families.[6] Other child survivors, like Melvin Goldberg, who had a loving extended family of Polish speakers to receive him in Toronto, faced an entirely different set of challenges.[7] Demographics, language, educational opportunities, and the availability of social services are some of the factors that shaped the integration of child and youth survivors.

Issues surrounding religious observance and affiliation accompanied many survivors across the Atlantic. Chapter 5, "Keeping the Faith," follows the establishment and furious development of Hassidic and ultra-Orthodox communities in Montreal by European-trained yeshiva students and rabbis who arrived in Canada during and immediately after the war. These groups and their respective institutions broadened the spectrum of Jewish religious possibilities for Canadian Jews and survivors alike, and reaffirmed the role of faith in spiritual and emotional rehabilitation among this subgroup of newcomers. The experiences of religious functionaries trained in European yeshivas and Orthodox newcomers follow. Chapter 6, "Moving Forward: Survivor Shuls," considers the creation of two survivor synagogues in Toronto: Clanton Park Synagogue-Kahal Machzikei Hadas, a traditional shul founded largely in part by survivors from across Europe, and Congregation Habonim, a liberal synagogue established by Czech-, German-, and Austrian-Jewish survivors. Chapter 7, "Abandoning Tradition: Atheism and Converts," explores the largely neglected narratives of survivors who shed their Jewish identity by cutting ties with the organized Jewish community or formally converting to Christianity.

Not all survivors came to Canada directly from European displaced persons (DP) camps. Chapter 8, "The Final Movement: Israeli Transmigrants and Other 'Late Arrivals,'" focuses on those who migrated to Canada in the early to mid-1950s from other countries. They tended to be older than the original wave of newcomers, and had larger families. Many arrived to relatives, themselves only recently established, and many among this subgroup were arriving from the newly minted Israeli state. Among the "Israeli transmigrants"—survivors who travelled to Canada as immigrants, not refugees—were those who had served in Israel's War of Independence, and maintained a strong affinity for the Jewish state and the Hebrew language. Other Holocaust survivors who arrived in Canada during this second wave as refugees or immigrants (depending on their point of departure and citizenship status) had already experienced the resettlement process at least once since liberation. The languages, cultures, and identities formed during the intervening years accompanied the survivors to Canada.

All survivors, whether they arrived in Canada in 1947 or 1955, from DP camps, Israel, or another country, encountered trying circumstances during the process of integration. The final chapter, "Mothers and Misters: Parenting, Work, and Gender," examines the impact of gender roles and relationships on survivor adaptation and integration. Parenting presented significant challenges for young men and women whose childhood and adolescence had been cut short by the Holocaust. Robbed of their formative years, they had limited opportunities to attain emotional maturity or witness healthy marital relationships, never mind practical education about child rearing. Young mothers faced substantial obstacles to education, employment, and childcare supports. The unorthodox nature of survivor families did not match the societal attitudes and gendered expectations reflective of North American middle-class ideals and led to challenging relationships between survivors and service workers. Discussions of single fatherhood, and role reversals in homes with female breadwinners, ignite questions about the significance of gender roles in postwar Canada. An examination of the obstacles faced by professional female survivors for entry into the workforce, and case studies of those who succeeded in breaking the barriers imposed by traditional gender values and certification requirements, bring this study to a close.

The history of Holocaust survivors in early postwar Canada has garnered relatively little attention.[8] Irving Abella and Harold Troper authored the seminal book on Canadian immigration and refugee policy in relation to the Holocaust. Where that study tapers off in 1948, Franklin Bialystok's critical analysis of the impact of survivors on the cultural formation of Holocaust memory and memorialization continues. Although survivor integration and acculturation are not central themes in the above narratives, these texts nonetheless provide the theoretical framework for the book. Historians Paula Draper, Richard Menkis, and Jean Gerber, as well as social workers Myra Giberovitch, Ben Lappin, and Fraidie Martz, address questions of identity, belonging, and interaction with the

Canadian Jewish populace. While they offer insight into Holocaust survivor life, none take a national approach to their analysis, instead providing regional or subgroup-specific accounts. Joseph Kage's examination of Canadian Jewish immigration history and communal aid work with newcomers merits attention, but it is now dated and lacks primary sources. Jack Lipinsky's study of Jewish Toronto's organizational history between 1933 and 1948 provides a thorough and rich account ripe with primary sources, but is regionally specific and offers scant insight into neighbouring communities' challenges and successes.[9]

Holocaust survivors' foray into American citizenship has, in comparison, been the focus of substantial scholarly research. William Helmreich and Dorothy Rabinowitz's studies glamourize the success and acquired wealth and status of U.S. survivor immigrants superficially, while minimizing the early years of hardship experienced by this very cohort. Leonard Dinnerstein's work also addresses survivors in the United States, but focuses more on the nation's restrictive immigration and refugee policies than the survivors themselves.

Notwithstanding such contemporary reports, scholars and journalists glamorized the successes of Holocaust survivors and elided failures and discontent until Beth Cohen's groundbreaking book, *Case Closed: Holocaust Survivors in Postwar America*. A social history of Holocaust survivors who immigrated to the United States in the fifteen years following the Second World War, *Case Closed* is the sole account to thoroughly address the immediate postwar resettlement and adjustment of approximately 140,000 Jewish DPs between 1946 and 1954, and the newcomers' relationships to the organized Jewish community. Cohen's study concluded that American Jewry was unaware of, and largely unresponsive to, the needs of Holocaust survivors. Hasia Diner's *We Remember with Love and Reverence* asserts an opposing and problematic perspective, namely that postwar American Jews demonstrated compassionate awareness of the recent tragedy to have befallen European Jews, and were committed to educating U.S.-born Jews on recent events. Yet these outwardly proactive individuals represented only a small fragment of the population. While American Jews—and, by extension, Canadian Jews—and service professionals certainly expressed outrage by the war, few native Jews felt it their obligation to remember *and* care for the surviving remnants. Most preferred to support the plight of the nascent Jewish state of Israel and celebrate the heroics of partisan and resistance fighters.[10]

The study of survivors in Israel (British-mandated Palestine until 1948) in the decade following the Second World War occupies a central space in Holocaust historiography, studies of the nascent state, and, more recently, scholarship on the legacy of the Holocaust looming large in Israeli memory and society. An estimated 170,000 Jewish DPs immigrated to Israel by 1953. While thousands illegally entered Palestine through the Jewish Brigade's Bricha movement, the number of survivor refugees increased exponentially with the declaration of the Jewish state in May 1948. Unlike the ethnocultural service agencies of Canada and the United States, survivors to Israel first fell under the directive of the American Jewish Distribution Committee and international aid groups and re-settled in refugee camps and on *kibbutzim*. Sharon Kangisser Cohen and Hanna Yablonka's research represent but two key English-language works on survivor adjustment and postwar life, while Judith Tydor Baumel-Schwartz focuses on one group of refugees' efforts to establish a *kibbutz*. Abram Leon Sachar and Idith Zertal tackle the position of survivors in relation to the emerging state of Israel, and noted Holocaust historian Dina Porat explores the status of the Holocaust, and its survivors, in contemporary Israeli society.[11]

Canadian immigration and post–Second World War social history has been of great scholarly interest. A small sampling of these studies leads to the works of Gerald E. Dirks, Ninette Kelley and Michael J. Trebilcock, and Valerie Knowles, who attempt to explain the nation's pre- and post-Confederation immigration history over a stretch of upward of 500 years. Simon Belkin's research speaks to Jewish immigration and immigration aid work in Canada. Social historian Franca Iacovetta's studies on gentile internees during the Second World War, the postwar Italian-Canadian experience, and Cold War Canadian immigration represent some of the finest research in the field. So too does Sonia Cancian's thoughtful examination of Italian postwar migration, and Hans Werner's investigations into the lives of Soviet German immigrants who settled in postwar Winnipeg.[12]

Literature citing early relationships between refugees and Canadian Jews contains multiple gaps. The most glaring of these is the exclusion of subgroups of Holocaust survivors whose histories fall outside the boundaries of the grand narrative: multiple waves of Hassidic and ultra-Orthodox survivors from 1941 through 1950 and the establishment of now-flourishing religious communities; survivors who rejected Jewish life, including those who did and did not convert to another faith; the complicated immigration process and absorption of Is-raeli transmigrants who entered Canada as Israeli citizens, not refugees; and the particular obstacles faced by elderly new Canadians. The experiences of young survivor women as mothers and active contributors to the postwar workforce are also marginalized.

Any examination of survivors' first years as new Canadians, and any chal-lenge to the accepted narratives of triumphalism, must be seen through the eyes of the newcomers themselves. This research fuses a wide range of archival materials, including case files prepared by agency social workers, correspondence between coordinating organizational bodies and survivors, oral testimonies, and contemporary interviews. The Canadian Jewish Congress Charities Committee (CJCCC) National Archives, as well as the Ontario Jewish Archives (OJA), house rich, undermined collections from Canadian Jewish Congress, Jewish Immigrant Aid Society, Jewish Family and Child Services (JF&CS), the Baron de Hirsch Society, the United Jewish Relief Agencies (UJRA), and the Vaad Hatzair. The Jewish Historical Society of Southern Alberta, the Manitoba Holocaust Heritage Project, the Canadian Museum of Immigration at Pier 21, Archives of Ontario, and Library Archives Canada (LAC), among others, house passenger lists, oral histories, and community financial records. Published and unpublished theses offer insights into the plights of interned enemy aliens and those who entered Canada as part of the Iberian refugee movement. And the value of oral history collections cannot be overestimated; more than 125 interviews conducted solely for this study—as well as testimonies from the University of Southern California Shoah Foundation Institute for Visual History and Education, Fortunoff Video Archives (Yale University), the CJC Holocaust Documentation Project, the Vancouver Holocaust Education Centre, and other repositories—provide key information about lives built by survivors in postwar Canada. A critical synthesis of these variant sources reveals the complex and nuanced relationships between survivors, social service providers, and the lay community. Holocaust survivors emerge as nuanced and diverse immigrants, expressing variant beliefs and agendas, and sharing but one fate: they represent a tiny remnant of European Jewry that had been slated for extinction.

This book explores the daily lives of Holocaust survivors who entered the country during the Second World War and in the immediate postwar period until 1955. It does so through several veins and, in the process, raises questions about intra-ethnic relationships, economic and social conditions, gender, age, and faith as factors in the acculturation and absorption processes. Driving this research are some core concepts: the role and function of the organized Canadian Jewish community and social agencies charged with helping to resettle and integrate survivors; survivor-driven support networks, religious groups, and family re-creation; and the influence of personal agency and power on adaptation techniques.

There was no singular, monolithic experience of resettlement, integration, and acculturation among the Holocaust survivor community in Canada. And there was significant diversity within the cohort of survivors who entered the country at different times and through divergent methods during the historical period under consideration. Moreover, among the survivors, differing degrees of "success" were experienced in the integration process. Reflecting upon one ethnic immigrant group's response to resettlement at a moment of national growth and postwar developments gleans insight into a broader conversation about Canadian identity, the contemporary role of ethnic social service organizations, and immigration and refugee policy. This study shines light too on the Holocaust and the survivor as "witness," as well as the history of Canada's Jews. The pages that follow focus primarily on these discussions.

# CHAPTER ONE

# A DOOR, SLIGHTLY AJAR

The ascendance to power of Adolf Hitler and the National Socialist German Workers (Nazi) Party in 1933 exacerbated a European Jewish refugee crisis that had begun with the close of the First World War. Jews living in Germany and German-occupied territory were faced with few options. Some, especially youth in the tens of thousands, had the good fortune to find new homes abroad. A paltry number were able to immigrate to Canada, which accepted fewer Jewish refugees than any other nation in the western hemisphere, including the Dominican Republic.[1] Canadian immigration policy and policy makers had a distinct anti-Jewish bias, and allowed only 5,000 Jews to enter the country between 1933 and 1947.

This chapter tells the story of the earliest European Jewish refugees admitted to Canada and their experiences of resettlement and integration. Those experiences later established the framework for the subsequent absorption, resettlement, and integration of the waves of postwar Holocaust refugee survivors to embark upon Canadian shores.

## Canadian Jewish Life

Canadian soil gained its first permanent Jewish settlers in the latter part of the eighteenth century, more than one century before Confederation. Comprising primarily German- and British-Jewish immigrants abandoning the United States for professional opportunities in the underdeveloped North, small Jewish hubs sprouted up in Lower and Upper Canada (present-day Quebec and Ontario), typically in close proximity to water with quick access to the larger and more established American Jewish communities. Communal institutions, including synagogues and cemeteries, sparingly followed. In 1882, an estimated 1,300 Jews permanently resided in Canada. This figure rose dramatically between 1882 and 1914, owing to a mass exodus of Jewish immigrants from the Pale of Settlement, a region of Imperial Russia occupying much of present-day Poland, Lithuania, Ukraine, Belarus, and western Russia. Jewish residents in the Pale, the largest ghetto in recorded history, experienced economic, social, and legal restrictions, living according to 1,400 legal statutes and regulations that controlled all aspects of Jewish life. Laws dictated Jewish occupations, places of residence, and movement; obscene taxes on religious life, down to Sabbath candles, contributed to the debilitating poverty under which much of the population subsided. As a further assault on Jewish traditional life, community leaders were mandated to present young male recruits, aged twelve to twenty-five years, for twenty-five-year military terms.

Life deteriorated further following the March 1881 murder of Czar Alexander II in St. Petersburg by revolutionaries belonging to the *Narodnaia Volia*, or the "People's Will." Despite the fact that only one Jewish woman revolutionary—Gesia Gelfman—participated, Jews were blamed for the assassination. Reprisals began immediately. Jewish communities across the Pale lived in fear of pogroms, or orchestrated acts of anti-Jewish violence, for sixteen months. Jewish homes, businesses, and synagogues were destroyed, men were beaten and slaughtered, and women subjected to public rapes.[2] Anti-Jewish regulations known as the May Laws, enacted in 1882 in response to the pogroms, coupled with utter poverty and lack of opportunity, prompted the migration of nearly two million Jews to Western Europe and North America, including Canada. In 1914 alone, approximately 20,000 Eastern European Jews arrived in Canada primarily from present-day Poland, Russia, Romania, and Galicia—the single largest number of immigrants from one ethnic group in Canadian history. More than 150,000 Jews called Canada home by 1929.[3]

Immigration of "undesirables" came to a halt after the First World War. A newly instated emphasis on immigrant applicants' ethnic backgrounds challenged the prevailing policy, which had supported immigration as a means to populate and till the Prairie provinces. While British and Northern European candidates were preferred, the previous policy emphasized numbers, not creed. Post–First World War policy suggested that non-British immigrants possessed inferior moral and ethnic characters, posed a literal risk to Canada's economy, and challenged the nation's health.[4] Immigration officers and the Canadian public made no efforts to mask their racist attitudes.[5] By the mid-1920s, ideology transformed into action with the official instatement of ethnically selective immigration restrictions.

And yet despite these restrictions, Canada's Jewish population continued to grow, reaching 155,614—or 1.5 percent of the country's total population—in 1931. With the exception of agricultural colonies in the Prairies, Jews were concentrated primarily in the urban centres of Toronto, Montreal, and Winnipeg. Montreal counted 48,724 Jews in its 1931 census, representing 5.9 percent of the city's total, while Toronto ranked slightly behind with 45,305 persons, or 7.2 percent of the total. Winnipeg represented the third-largest Jewish centre, counting approximately 17,000 Jewish residents in 1941.[6] The Jewish community grew slowly over the ensuing decade, to 165,000 in 1939. Canadian Jews were loosely divided into two groups: those who were well established and integrated, having migrated prior to 1900; and the masses of working-class, Yiddish-speaking Jews who had emigrated from Europe only a generation earlier.[7]

German, British, and American Jews who had immigrated to Canada prior to, or separate from, the Pale Jews represented a numerical minority among interwar Jews. Through linguistic, cultural, and ideological differences, prosperous Jews and their newly arrived co-religionists were separate entities with limited overlap.[8] Eastern European transports observed laws of *kashrut* and Orthodox observance to varying degrees.[9] Conservative synagogues gained momentum only in the 1930s, and Canada did not share the dominant German-Jewish tradition of Reform Judaism present in the United States. Younger generations' commitment to traditional and seemingly insular ways of life declined. Devotion to religiosity waned due to practical factors, such as the need to work on Shabbat and high cost of kosher food, as well as the influence of political ideology and contemporary attitudes about integration and secularism.[10]

Integration efforts aside, Jews experienced increasingly insidious forms of anti-Semitism through the 1930s. Discriminated against in education, employment, and housing, and subject to stringent immigration restriction, their capacity to sponsor relatives and *landsleit* in politically unstable Europe collapsed.[11] Anti-Semitic fervour reigned in Quebec, home to the most sizeable Jewish community in the interwar years.[12] Quebec Catholics' hatred was rooted in Jewish theology, while French nationalists recognized Jews as the "embodiment of the anti-French."[13] Both parties considered Jews inherently threatening. Interwar Jewish life in Quebec was most often conducted in English. Quebec Jews were perceived as aligned with Protestant English Canada, whose language, culture, and political ideologies challenged that of the French.[14]

Québécois anti-Semitism was fostered by community leaders and absorbed by the masses. The "father of French Canadian nationalism," Roman Catholic priest Lionel Groulx, also an active political leader and intellectual, regarded himself a rabid anti-Semite.[15] Abbé Groulx founded the journal *L'Action Française* in the early 1920s to increase awareness of provincial politics among francophone youth. He also acted as the public face of L'Action Nationale, a nationalist organization promoting French Catholic independence from English Canada's social, economic, and political arenas. Groulx publicly blamed English Canada, and particularly its Jewish actors, for all societal woes affecting Quebec, applying a lethal combination of Catholic anti-Jewish liturgy and contemporary Judeo-Bolshevik ideology to denounce the Jewish presence in Canada.[16]

Beyond Groulx's manipulation of Catholicism's anti-Jewish doctrine, French Canada was also gripped by popular Nazism and fascist ideologies transported from Europe. Montreal-based journalist turned rabble-rouser and Hitler-enthusiast Adrien Arcand established the anti-communist and anti-Jewish Christian National Social Party (Parti National Social Chrétien) in the mid-1930s. In 1938, Arcand took the helm of the National Unity Party of Canada, an amalgamation of his Québécois party and the Nationalist Party of Ontario, itself a product of the "swastika clubs," minor Nazi-inspired anti-Semitic groups that arose across the country. Arcand espoused his racist and anti-refugee sentiments through several weekly French-language newspapers and magazines, including *L'Action Française*, *Le Goglu*, and *Le Patriote*. Images of the "savage Jew" participating in the blood libel, and more contemporary conspiracy theories of world domination by the "Jewish race," abounded in the papers' pages.[17] Arcand's party achieved nominal success in provincial (Quebec) elections and held seats in the national assembly. The leader's 1941 arrest as a Nazi sympathizer, and subsequent detention in a New Brunswick internment camp, dictated the collapse of the National Unity Party.[18] Arcand's legacy persisted, continuing to influence anti-refugee and nationalist sentiments into the postwar period.[19]

Anti-Semitism and nativism in Canada were never limited to Quebec. The Social Credit Party of Alberta operated as an expression of the die-hard nationalism of the anti-foreigner beliefs of its British founder and engineer, Major Clifford Hugh (C.H.) Douglas.[20] During the Great Depression, Albertans suffered from a dramatic decline in agricultural production (its primary economic market) and mounting farm debts. The virulently anti-Semitic Social Credit's popularity was enmeshed in the regional and national political, social, and economic landscape of financial woes, and traditional nativist ideologies. Banking systems purportedly managed and owned by wealthy capitalist Jews became the party's focus of all criticism. The party's first leader, Baptist pastor William Aberhart, presented an identifiable scapegoat for their political and economic ills: the international Jewish conspiracy.[21]

Aberhart instructed party officials to disseminate anti-Semitic sentiment in newspapers and especially through radio broadcasts—practices similarly employed in the Nazi state. Aberhart and his peers distributed copies of the *Protocols of the Elders of Zion*, the most famous fabrication of anti-Semitic propaganda produced in turn-of-the-century Russia, in civic centres and churches. The party's popular newspaper, the *Canadian Social Crediter,* featured hateful serials like *The Land for the (Chosen) People Racket,* which blamed Jews for nationalization of land, and the *Programme for the Third World War,* which posited that international Jewish conspirators were planning world domination.[22] The distribution of racist literature ended only with Ernest Manning's restructuring of the Social Credit Party in the postwar decade.

Communities in English-speaking Canada faced more genteel but equally damaging anti-Jewish sentiment. Prejudicial messages streamed through media and spiritual congregations. Quotas on Jewish enrolment in university faculties persisted into the postwar period, limiting the professional aspirations for those with the intellect and financial means to meet institutional standards.[23] Jews who successfully penetrated the walls of academia encountered obstacles on the path to professional lives. Most recognized the social prejudices and ventured toward self-employment in medicine, law, dentistry, and mercantilism in an effort to avoid the omnipresent "gentiles only need apply" advertisements.[24] Few bothered considering careers in politics, engineering, or academia. But discrimination did not stop with employment. Legislated racial profiling deterred Jews from purchasing land in desirable Anglo-Saxon upper-middle-class neighbourhoods.[25] Socially, Jews were also unabashedly excluded from enjoying "gentile only" beaches, country clubs and other recreational facilities, and hotel properties.[26] Such restrictions protected gentiles from unnecessary social interaction with Jews while simultaneously, if unintentionally, strengthening Canadian Jewry's internal organization and infrastructure.

Despite the ubiquitous anti-Jewish prejudices and nativist undercurrents plaguing interwar Canada, anti-Semitism  rarely culminated in violence in English-speaking provinces. The riot at Toronto's Christie Pits the night of 16 August 1933 constituted an infamous exception to this rule. Fighting exploded at a baseball game when youth members of the local swastika club unveiled a flag bearing a swastika. The predominantly Jewish opposition team responded to the provocation. Italian Canadians stood alongside their Jewish neighbours. Extreme acts of violence took to the streets, and continued throughout the night. Miraculously, no one died.[27] The riot served as a warning: while Canadian Jews did not live under the oppression of Hitler's Germany, their presence and livelihood stood under an omnipresent shadow of anti-Semitism.[28] Canadian Jews needed a central representative body to speak on their behalf.

1. Gentiles only sign, Forest Hill Lodge at Burleigh Falls, Ontario, 28 January 1940. Ontario Jewish Archives, fonds 17, series 5-3, file 64, item 1.

## Organizational Life

The interwar period saw an exponential growth in Jewish organizational life. There were three central forms of organization: *landsmanshaftn*, Zionist parties, and Jewish labour unions. *Landsmanshaftn*, or benevolent societies, composed of individuals originating from a town or region in Eastern Europe, flourished across North America in the first half of the twentieth century.[29] *Landsmanshaftn* assisted newcomers in practical matters and most frequently conducted operations in Yiddish. Groups served as free loan societies and provided members' access to physicians, cemetery plots, and emergency aid. Zionist organizations also abounded in the early 1900s; the arrival of European Jewish immigrants brought both traditional and radical versions of Zionism to Canada, serving as a response to both the ascendance of extreme nationalism in Europe and to the centuries-old "Jewish question."[30] Labour unions like the Arbeter Ring (Workmen's Circle) promulgated socialist demands for better working conditions and liveable wages.[31] With the exception of anti-Zionist fringe organizations, Canadian Jews overwhelmingly supported the 1917 Balfour Declaration and rallied behind Great Britain to pursue the creation of a Jewish national home in Palestine.[32]

Jewish communal groups shared frustrations when their efforts to open Canada's doors to co-religionists seeking asylum from authoritarian regimes failed miserably. Canadian Jewry at the time was largely fragmented, with myriad organizations performing ineffectively. Recognized leaders, or *shtadlan* (a Yiddish term denoting a traditional European Jewish community's emissary to the court, based on wealth and influence), including Lyon Cohen, the former president of the Montreal Clothing Manufacturers Union, and Michael Garber and Clarence DeSola, former presidents of the Zionist Organization of Canada, realized that a single unified pressure group to represent the causes and concerns of the community would be more effective than small, unstable groups. In early 1919, the Canadian Jewish Congress (CJC) was born.

The major issues on the table at the Congress's first plenary session included the plight of Jewish refugees displaced by the First World War, the pogroms that ravaged Eastern European Jewish towns, the threats to Jewish survival posed by communism, and the question of a Jewish state in British-mandated Palestine. The CJC was free to conduct advocacy activities and protest policies and anti-Semitic parliamentarians, but as a voice for a minority ethnic group, it possessed no authority to enforce constitutional change.[33] Despite the promise of unity and consensus on the issues tabled, the CJC failed to entrench itself as a national entity after the plenary, the momentum of the monumental session dissipating quickly. Yet the demands for an immigrant resettlement organization, managed by one coordinating body operating on national and regional levels, rang loud. The North American social work profession developed out of a religious tradition of charity. Ethnocultural traditions dictated communal responses to social and economic issues, including poverty and immigrant resettlement throughout the interwar period. Canadian Jewry's solution to a single coordinating resettlement and support body emerged with the creation of the Jewish Immigrant Aid Society (JIAS) in 1919. The agency vaulted to the forefront in the settlement and assistance of new Jewish immigrants. Relative instability, coupled with limited funds and minimal organization, temporarily dissolved interest in all other agenda items, leaving regional divisions in Montreal, Toronto, and Winnipeg to continue minimal operations within their own jurisdictions for one decade.[34]

The stock market crash of Wall Street of October 1929 launched the Great Depression, which erupted into an economic downturn and unemployment crisis. Immense pressure fell on communal organizations such as JIAS to provide provisions to the Jewish needy. The new economic state also gave rise to an increase in overt anti-Semitism in Quebec and bore witness to rising nativist thought in western Canada. With the country bowing to historical precedent, and the more recent example of the rise of National Socialism in Germany, the years 1929 to 1935 found Canada's Jews in a perilous state.

The CJC reconvened, this time as a permanent body, at its second plenary session in January 1934. Leadership pledged to create a strong and forceful voice in Parliament, and employed the services of influential Jews to give an authoritative affect to their demands. Samuel Jacobs, Member of Parliament for the Montreal-area riding of Cartier, was appointed president of the Congress, and with the support of two other Jewish Members of Parliament, Sam Factor and A.A. Heaps, the men were expected to enhance the community's political influence by encouraging non-Jewish politicians to advocate on behalf of Jewish interests. While Jacobs was rather unsuccessful in influencing policy changes, he did succeed in acquiring a small number of entry permits for European Jews.[35] Samuel Bronfman, a wealthy Jewish businessman and philanthropist, began his twenty-year presidential tenure with the CJC following Jacob's death in 1938. Although it was widely assumed that Bronfman's influence and status in non-Jewish society would facilitate great progress, he produced mediocre results, especially with regard to the facilitation of entry visas for Jewish asylum seekers.

All proposals for immigrant sponsorship by the CJC and prominent non-Jewish Canadians failed to influence policy makers, despite many opportunities to interact with senior government officials and Cabinet ministers, including the prime minister.[36] Canadian immigration policy remained inflexible and offered no room for negotiation. Nowhere was this fact made clearer than at the Evian Conference of 6 to 15 June 1938 in Evian-les-Bains, France. The conference was announced as an international gathering of delegates from the Western world for the purpose of discussing the mounting refugee crisis of German and Austrian Jews.[37] Prime Minister William Lyon Mackenzie King opposed Canadian attendance at the conference, fearful that the country's official presence could be misinterpreted as a willingness to take in refugees. Mackenzie King defended his position in a diary entry dated 29 March 1938:

> A very difficult question has presented itself in Roosevelt's appeal to different countries to unite with the United States in admitting refugees from Austria, Germany etc. That means in a word, admitting numbers of Jews. My feeling is that nothing is to be gained by creating an internal problem in an effort to meet an international one.... So far as Canada is concerned, with our great open spaces and small population, we must nevertheless seek to keep this part of the Continent free from unrest and from too great of an intermixture of foreign strains of blood.... I fear we would have riots if we agreed to a policy that admitted numbers of Jews. Also we would add to the difficulties between the Provinces and the Dominion.[38]

The prime minister only conceded to send representation after persistent pressure by the United States and Britain, and with reassurance that no country at the conference would be forced into any action.[39] At the time, Canada had no refugee policy to speak of. Instead, refugee applicants for asylum were evaluated by the same criteria as immigrants, whose quota numbers were increasingly slim owing largely to the economic downturn and high unemployment sired by the Wall Street crash of 1929.

Racist and nativist ideology also influenced immigration policy. Based on the regulations that ranked persons by nationality, as well as the large capital required for admission as a manufacturer, or demonstrated successes in agricultural planning, Jewish refugees stood virtually no chance of gaining entry. Rather than treating Jewish applicants as persons belonging to European national groups and linking them to existing quotas, Jewish applicants faced the stigma of identification as a distinct religious and ethnic group irrespective of their country of origin. A Gallup poll taken in mid-1943 asked Canadians to identify groups deemed least desirable as immigrants. Jews were listed third after Japanese and Germans, members of the Axis and "enemy" states. A year after the war's end, Jews rose in undesirability, coming in second only after the Japanese, demonstrating Canadians' deeply ingrained anti-Jewish sentiment.

The Evian Conference presented a perfect opportunity for Canada to stake a position on the refugee crisis.[40] The Canadian Jewish community had already declared its unconditional willingness and ability to support the newcomers financially. At the conclusion of the ill-fated conference, only one country—the Dominican Republic—agreed to receive a limited number of European refugees. As for Canada, the immigration gates remained tightly shut to German and Austrian Jews.[41]

Following the disappointing Evian Conference, few Jewish community leaders harboured hope that the government would change its immigration policy. M.A. Solkin, JIAS national director, summed up his progress with immigration officers: "From my frequent conversations with the high Department of Immigration officials," Solkin wrote to a colleague, "I know only too well that the government is as far from admitting refugees as they ever were and that any attempt to obtain a general relaxation in immigration is doomed to certain failure."[42] Jewish leaders' commitment to influencing political will did not waver, despite the bleak outlook.

Another opportunity for Canada to effect positive change in its attitude toward European Jewish refugees presented itself with the so-called *St. Louis* affair. In May and June 1939, a chartered ship carrying 937 Jewish refugee passengers out of Hamburg, Germany, found itself literally out to sea. Although the passengers possessed legitimate Cuban entry visas, they were denied admittance to the country at the port of Havana, with Cuban government officials citing invalid papers. The ship's captain tried to persuade the United States to permit the refugees—many of whom were waiting for their U.S. quota numbers to be called—to land. But the United States refused. Jewish and non-Jewish community leaders and members of Canada's Parliament pressured the Mackenzie King government to help the stranded refugees, among them women, young children, and seniors, all running low on food, fresh water, and medical supplies. A telegram from George M. Wrong and other leading non-Jewish intellectuals called on the prime minister to show "true Christian charity" and offer the homeless exiles sanctuary in Canada.[43] By granting entry visas, Canada would prevent the refugees from being returned to Nazi-occupied territory.

Prime Minister Mackenzie King expressed mixed emotions in response to the pleas for asylum, recording deep personal empathy with the refugees' plight, as well as his hesitancy citing political expediency. The *St. Louis* affair, he wrote in his diary, was "much less our problem than the U.S. and Cuba."[44] Owing to his personal reluctance and busy schedule hosting the visiting British royal family, Mackenzie King assigned responsibility for the affair to his most trusted and dedicated advisors, Frederick Charles Blair and Ernest Lapointe.

Director of the Immigration Branch of the Department of Mines and Resources Frederick Charles Blair controlled all immigration matters. The blatantly anti-Semitic bureaucrat expressed personal distaste for Jews and opposed any special considerations for Jewish refugee applicants. Blair's personal anti-Jewish agenda spilled over into his political will. He recognized all Jews, Canadian-born or foreign, as inassimilable, selfish, and calculating. Citing requests for immigration sponsorship of relatives and friends as overtly demanding, the director accorded no sympathy for the plight of European Jews. Unreasonable conditions, including a required proof of $15,000 in capital for prospective Jewish applicants, made the application process nearly impossible. Simply put, the refugee problem belonged to the Jews and the Jews alone. Blair's mission as gatekeeper was to uphold the letter of the law.[45]

Justice Minister Ernest Lapointe shared Blair's outlook on the Jewish refugee crisis. On several occasions, Lapointe stressed to Mackenzie King that the entire Quebec caucus was "emphatically opposed" to any liberalization of immigration policy, and the admission of Jewish refugees to Canada and Quebec, in particular. He suggested that rash moves would result in a severe dip in popular support for Mackenzie King and the Liberals among the majority of French-Canadian voters.[46] And Mackenzie King was, above all else, a consummate politician fixated on placating public opinion. Canada's prime minister's concern over his political popularity—especially in Quebec, a heartland of support for the federal Liberal Party, where polls indicated the majority French voters—overshadowed any humanitarian sentiments.[47] Assuming responsibility for the *St. Louis* debacle, Blair remained steadfast in his resolve: since the ship's passengers did not meet Canadian immigration requirements, the ship could not enter Canadian territorial waters. "No country," he publicly declared, could "open its doors wide enough to take in the hundreds of thousands of Jewish people who want to leave Europe: the line must be drawn somewhere."[48] Canada would not become Europe's dumping ground. Without any hope for asylum, the *St. Louis* was forced to return to Europe. The 937 refugee passengers were distributed among the Netherlands, England, France, and Belgium; 254 were murdered in the Holocaust.[49]

Despite the rising European Jewish refugee crisis, Canadian immigration policy did not bend. But the *St. Louis* incident left an indelible stain on the country and provided an argument for changes to policy, and a driving force behind governmental actions, in the postwar period.

*The Fortunate Few*

On 19 October 2011, an obituary memorialized the life of a recently deceased Canadian Jewish couple of German heritage. Accompanied by a photo of what looked like two awkward but content farmhands was the following entry: "Walter and Jeanny [Bick] survived the horrors of the Holocaust by posing as Christian farmers—they were neither Christian nor farmers—but that was the only way they could get into Canada in 1939. They put their heart and muscle into their 160-acre farm next to what is now the Scarborough Town Centre. The farm was not only their refuge but became their salvation."[50] The couple, as well as Walter's brother and parents, immigrated to Canada via Amsterdam as farming refugees. Abiding by the conditions of their labour contract, the elder Bicks purchased the farm and raised cattle, chickens, and pigs for their first five years in the country. Later, the family became the proprietors of a hugely successful pickling empire, Bick's Pickles. Despite the knowledge that they had been saved only because they had hidden their religion from Canadian Pacific Railway (CPR) recruiters, the Bicks were generous philanthropists and contributed vast sums to Canadian culture and civil life, both in the Jewish and gentile spheres.[51]

Although the gates to Canada were officially closed to Jewish refugees, approximately 5,000 managed to enter the country between 1933 and 1947. A handful trickled in through close relatives' sponsorships in the mid-1930s. But, of the remainder, the first (though relatively undetected) group to arrive immediately prior to the onset of the Second World War were central European Jews like the Bicks, who posed as farmers to gain inclusion in the CPR's land settlement program. Officially, Jews were automatically rejected by recruiting officers according to rigid criteria set by Director of Immigration F.C. Blair, who stressed Jews' racial unsuitability to farming.[52] However, human errors, deliberate oversights (precipitated, in some cases, by generous bribes), and falsification of religious identity helped several hundred Jewish refugees immigrate as farmers and farm hands in the late 1930s into the country.

Marianne Echt's childhood in Broesen, a small town of 4,000 persons in the Free City of Danzig (present-day Gdansk, Poland), was charmed. Her father, Otto, was a pharmacist and her mother, Meta, was a homemaker; though among only a few Jewish residents, they were prominent leaders and were active in Broesen's charitable organizations. The entire Echt family participated in all aspects of Jewish and non-Jewish community life until Hitler's rise to power in 1933. Although Danzig was an independent region, since the Treaty of Versailles, it had remained under the nominal authority of both Poland and Germany. And since

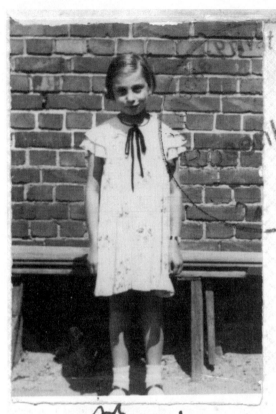

Berechtigt zur Fahr-
preisermässigung
auf den Staatsbah-
nen gemäss den ta-
rifarischen Ermässi-
gungen für die
Schuljugend.

Uprawnia do ulgo-
wych przejazdów
kolejami państwo-
wemi według ulg
taryfowych dla mło-
dzieży szkolnej.

Unterschrift des Inhabers des Ausweises
podpis właściciela legitymacji

Gültig bis zum
30. September 19 36

Ważna do dnia
30. września 19 .......... r.

Stempel der Schule
Pieczęć szkoły.

Gültig bis zum
31. März 19 ..........

Ważna do dnia
31 marca 19 ..........

Stempel der Schule
Pieczęć szkoły.

2. Immigration identification card issued to Marianne Echt Ferguson, 1932. Canadian Museum of Immigration at Pier 21 (DI2013.1018.23).

much of the city's population was ethnically German, anti-Semitic legislation and discriminatory treatment of its Jewish citizens was readily enacted.[53]

When conditions for Jews living in Danzig became unbearable, Otto Echt initiated emigration plans for his family. He met with travelling recruiters from the CPR's department for colonization and agriculture, a colonization program mandated by the Canadian government to promote land settlement. His limited experience as a hobby farmer sufficed and Echt passed theoretical and practical exams. With a small amount of capital and a contract declaring their intention to work the land for five years, the Echts were granted entry visas for Canada. Discussion of religious affiliation apparently did not surface in the interview process and the Echts, for their part, certainly had no intention of raising the issue. On 7 March 1939, the family—which included the parents, Marianne and her two younger sisters, and Mrs. Echt's elderly mother—docked at Halifax's Pier 21, a central port for transatlantic transports and immigration processing centre.[54]

The Echts were warmly received at the dock by the local designated "greeter" for JIAS, Mrs. Sadie Fineberg, and were settled temporarily in a hotel. Mrs. Fineberg took it upon herself to introduce the family to Halifax's small but close-knit Jewish community, helped them locate a homestead, and aided in English-language instruction. The significance of this welcome was long lasting. After five years on the farm just outside of the city, the Echts chose to settle permanently in Halifax, abandoning their earlier ambitions of moving on to Montreal. Cementing her status as a contributing community member, Mrs. Echt officially took over Sadie's function of greeting Jewish immigrants at Pier 21 in 1951, after serving as a volunteer greeter for five years. As Marianne, who often assisted her mother, recalled, "Having been treated so well when we arrived, we did the same for people who came over [after the Holocaust], many of whom were pitiful human beings."[55] In 1946, Marianne married Sadie Fineberg's nephew, Lawrence Ferguson, with whom she raised three children in Halifax.

Other refugees succeeded in slipping through the door just prior to the onset of the Second World War as the result of poor screening—or deliberate oversight—on the part of the CPR recruiters. The Waldsteins fell into this category. Having lived in Sudetenland, the German-speaking portion of then-Czechoslovakia annexed by Nazi Germany, the Waldsteins received exit visas just days before the occupation of Prague on 15 March 1939.

According to Helen Waldstein Wilkes, the family lore was that "someone was asleep at the switch" when her aunt and uncle were permitted to enter Canada through the CPR program. The Abeles, cousins of Ludwig Ekstein— brother-in-law to Mrs. Waldstein—had been prominent cattle-dealers in interwar

Czechoslovakia and had invited a CPR representative to visit their facilities. Reportedly impressed by their industriousness, the representative agreed to forward a special recommendation to Canadian immigration authorities. Shortly thereafter, the Abeles were granted permission to buy land in Canada and to immigrate as Czech farmers—evidently, with no reference to their Jewish identity. The cousins applied for the Eksteins to join them. Canadian immigration authorities were presumably asleep again when Anne Ekstein was permitted to sponsor her sister and brother-in-law, Gretl and Edmund Waldstein, and their two-year-old daughter, Helen. Reflecting several decades later on the circumstances of her family's entry to Canada, Helen suggested that an early form of racial profiling might have worked to their advantage: "Immigration officials likely did not realize that the leader of the Czechoslovak group [of cattle dealers] was Jewish. [Uncle] Ludwig's cousin Karl Abeles was far from the stereotypical Jew that Canada's newspapers of the day portrayed as dark, hunched, and hook-nosed. Karl Abeles was a big, blond man with a handlebar moustache...robust and outgoing, with a jovial manner that would fit into a contemporary beer commercial."[56]

3. Echt family in Poland, 1930s. Canadian Museum of Immigration at Pier 21 (DI2013.1018.4).

The family's case was also anomalous in that Helen was one of only a handful of Jewish children to escape with her parents to Canada, and one of even fewer to enter before the onset of war. Gretl, Edmund, and Helen arrived at a New Brunswick port on 16 April 1939, and travelled west toward Ontario. The extended family unit began their lives as new Canadians on a collective farm in southern Ontario for several months before the Waldsteins and Eksteins jointly purchased an inexpensive farm several miles outside of Mount Hope. The nearest city was Hamilton. With no farming experience, they reluctantly but dutifully fulfilled their five-year labour contracts. These years were lonely and miserable ones for the whole family, entirely foreign from their former lives in Czechoslovakia. As Helen Waldstein Wilkes recalled, "It was a big leap. My mother needed to go from being the belle of the village ball to plucking and disembowelling chickens, milking large, ungainly cows, and feeding slop to pigs that disgusted her. My father needed to say farewell to a life that was all he'd ever wanted, and step into a life that he hated. He was completely unsuited to farming.... Worse, he was ashamed. He lived in daily humiliation at what he had done. He had reduced to a life of drudgery his Gretl. The beautiful bride to whom he had promised the world."[57]

The Waldsteins' style of dress, cooking, and accented speech identified them as foreigners. The adults were aware of, and shamed by, still-enforced anti-Semitic practices imposed on Jewish employment and property ownership in Ontario, including university quotas and restricted beaches, which heightened their distrust of the Canadian government. All applications for visas to rescue relatives stranded in Czechoslovakia were denied, and their entire extended family was murdered in the Holocaust. With no private telephone, no car, and few friends, Edmund, feeling far removed from his comfortable European middle-class surroundings, suffered from deep sadness and loneliness, and feared for his wife and daughter's growing isolation on the farm. When they had repaid their debt to Canada following five years of tilling the land, the Waldsteins sold the farm at a loss to the first buyer and purchased an old house in Hamilton, where they regained some downgraded semblance of their former urbane cosmopolitan lifestyle.

Despite their move to town and integration into the workforce as a shipper (Edmund) and pieceworker in a garment factory (Gretl), according to Helen the Waldsteins never fully connected with what they referred to as "real" Canadians, nor did they fully align themselves with postwar refugee Jews.[58] They lived out their lives feeling both blessed and cursed because they survived "it," while none of their overseas relations did.[59] Unlike the Echts, whose integration efforts met with success through organizational engagement and leadership roles, as well as Marianne's marriage into an established Canadian Jewish family, the Waldsteins

4. Refugee farmer with his horse on an agricultural settlement, c. 1930s. Courtesy of the Canadian Jewish Congress Charities Committee National Archives.

remained forever on the periphery of community life.[60] Ludwig Ekstein died young, leaving Anne widowed and childless. She lived out her remaining years in Brantford, Ontario, where she maintained a strained relationship with Gretl.

## Wartime Arrivals

Only a handful of Jews immigrated to Canada between 1939 and 1945. The few who successfully penetrated the country's iron-clad gates were either the recipients of special Cabinet orders-in-council (due to international pressures), or settled in Canada by chance. The largest group of approximately 2,300 German and Austrian Jewish male refugees to arrive came in 1940 as "potentially dangerous enemy aliens" via Britain. The men, many of whom had only recently spent time in Nazi concentration camps prior to the outbreak of war, had been identified as potential fifth columnists following Britain's entrance into the war. Doubly displaced, the men were arrested in spring of 1940 and initially detained on the Isle of Man in the Irish Sea alongside genuine threats in the form of Nazi prisoners of war and Italian fascists.

In the summer of 1940, more than 3,000 refugees—including some 2,300 German and Austrian Jewish refugee males, many between the ages of sixteen and twenty years—were transported to Canada and interned in guarded camps in Ontario, Quebec, and New Brunswick.[61] The "accidental immigrants," as the Jews in the group came to be known, were initially interned in camps as prisoners of war alongside bona fide Nazis, Italian fascists, and genuine enemies of the state. This deplorable situation was protested loudly by the internees, as well as the CJC and the Canadian National Committee on Refugees and Victims of Persecution (CNCR), an agency headed by Senator Carine Wilson that was formed at a meeting of the League of Nations, Canada.[62] British and Canadian parliamentarians soon realized that the Jewish refugees—not threats to British or Canadian society—were not safe living among Nazis, and separate camps were established in Canada. This realization did not transform the refugees' legal status; even once the men's prisoner-of-war status was lifted and replaced by that of "refugees of Nazi oppression," complete freedom from barbed wire took years to achieve.

---

Life in the internment camps was difficult but bearable for the Jewish refugees, who ranged in age from sixteen to sixty and represented a cross-section of central European Jewish life. They included everyone from yeshiva students to philosophers, and from self-identifying Jews to converts with no connection to Jewish life. The internees were identified as enemy aliens who posed security risks and therefore were permitted limited communication with the outside world. All able-bodied men participated in manual labour and worked as lumberjacks, in the camp kitchens, and on farms, for which they earned nominal wages. In June 1941, the internees' status officially changed to "refugees," and all were offered the opportunity to return to England and serve in the non-combat Auxiliary Pioneer Corps. Over half of the group accepted this proposal. The others chose interned status until the opportunity to remain permanently in Canada arose.[63] In this group was Erwin Schild, then a twenty-one-year-old former yeshiva student from Mülheim, Germany, interned at the Île-aux-Noix camp in Quebec. Schild spoke for many of his fellow internees when he offered the following rationale for staying in the camps rather than returning to Britain: "I was not inclined to re-enter a country that might still be invaded by Germany. Moreover, Canada was closer to the United States. If given a choice, most European Jews would have preferred to relocate in the New World, and that meant America. At the time, it would certainly have been my choice. Though immigration to the United States was ruled out for the time being, Canada was, at least, as close as I could get."[64]

For those internees like Schild who remained in camps, the situation became not only tolerable, but also intellectually stimulating. Academics offered lectures, religious leaders led prayer services and taught the yeshiva students, and artists gave performances. Some men later recalled their time in the camps as a productive period during which they learned English and became acquainted with Canadian culture and values. Through concerted efforts by the refugees and local Jewish organizations, youth whose studies had been disrupted received permission to sit McGill University matriculation examinations. These men applied for entry into nearby universities. Religious life blossomed within the camp walls, too. After protests from Orthodox internees for the right to preserve Jewish tradition, kosher kitchens and designated prayer rooms were established at camp through the intervention of Montreal's Rabbinical Society. Rabbis and their students organized camp-wide services for holy days, observed the Sabbath and laws of *kashrut*, and made available prayer books and religious items, such as menorahs at Chanukah, phylacteries, and prayer shawls.[65]

Once the interned refugees' status was revised, advocacy groups turned their attention toward achieving their release. The Canadian Central Committee for Interned Refugees (a united venture of the United Jewish Refugee and War Relief Agencies and the National Committee on Refugees) pressured the government to turn the refugees into the custody of Canadian citizens, industries, and institutions.[66] Internees with first-degree relatives in Canada began to be released in

5. Forestry work at Acadia Forestry Station, Camp B (Ripples, New Brunswick). Courtesy of the Vancouver Holocaust Education Centre Archives, Gunter Bardeleben Collection.

February 1941. After this, Frederick C. Blair grudgingly processed applications from would-be sponsors within the Jewish community, including business owners, farmers, and heads of yeshivas. Despite Blair's concerted efforts, loopholes in the national immigration policy, coupled with immense pressures from British parliamentarians, the CNCR, and the CJC, along with financial guarantees that shielded the state from financial responsibility toward the refugees, signalled the internees' eventual release. By the end of 1943, the internment camps for Jewish refugees closed and 972 men were admitted into Canada.[67] Although permitted to enter the workforce and enrol in school, they were not entirely free. They were subject to travel restrictions, had to apply for permission to change jobs (if they were released from the camps to professional sponsors), and were required to report to the police periodically.[68]

Exiting the internment camps proved traumatizing for some former internees-cum-refugees. If youngsters who went to schools and yeshivas had a plan for the immediate future, those older men released on work contracts secured by strangers, often only to appease the pleas of the refugee relief committees, had seemingly little idea about life outside the camps. Michael Guggenheim, a native of Munich, Germany, was thirty-six years old when he left the internment camp in November 1942 and travelled to Montreal with his own money. Guggenheim arrived with eighty dollars that he had earned performing forced labour at the camp and a small parcel of belongings. An accounting firm in Montreal had arranged a contract on Guggenheim's behalf as a humanitarian gesture; the refugee possessed no training in the field. Guggenheim turned to JIAS and requested assistance in finding housing and money to keep him afloat until he began work. The representative's response shocked Guggenheim: "Well, you have 80 dollars. You don't need any help from us, you can manage yourself."[69] Without the agency's support, Guggenheim rented a room in a boarding house and went to work. He survived on fifty dollars per month for his first several months in freedom.

Other middle-aged refugees, like Julius Pfeiffer, a former superior court judge from Düsseldorf, Germany, were released to relatives and employment sponsors. Pfeiffer's release from internment was arranged by a brother-in-law in Montreal, with whom he lived briefly before finding his bearings and setting up his own home. Although he wished to return to the legal profession, that move would have necessitated his taking additional costly training to meet Canadian standards. Instead, Pfeiffer went to work as a chartered accountant.[70] He was among the fortunate ones: his wife and sons, still in Europe, survived the Holocaust. The family was reunited in Montreal on 12 February 1946 and together they rebuilt their lives.[71] The Pfeiffers' reunification was an exception, not the rule, among

6. Internment Camp A (Farnham, Quebec) school matriculation photo with instructors, 1941. Back row, left to right: Fred (David) Hoeniger, Ulrich Steinfeld, Peter Harisch, Dr. Einsiedeln, Helmut Jakobi, Peter Fokschaner, Peter Zappler, Carl Amberg, Rudi Meyer, Peter Neurath, Kurt Haiblen, Gerd (Gregory) Baum, Walter Hitschfeld, Dr. von Harrer.

Front row, left to right: Heinz Matzdorff, Schneider, Goetz Weiss, Werner Bruck (Vernon Brooks), Dr. Philipp Koller, George Liebel, Dr. Willy Heckscher, Alois Zoechling, Charles Kahn, Ulrich Weil, Sturm, Paul Mandl, Pater Hartmann, Pater Haring, Rudolf Hirsch. Courtesy of the Vancouver Holocaust Education Centre Archives, Gunter Bardeleben Collection.

wartime refugees. Few men lived to witness the return of surviving relatives; fewer still among older refugees remarried and established new Canadian families.

Things appeared slightly easier for the thirty young men who transitioned into the custody of the heads of yeshivas in Montreal and Toronto, and were placed in local homes and boarding houses at the schools' expense. Erwin Schild was among the students who returned to Torah study in Toronto at Rabbi Abraham Price's Yeshiva Torath Chaim. Within the confines of the yeshiva, Schild and his peers were assisted by Rosh Yeshiva Rabbi Price—recalled by Schild as a type of surrogate father—and kindness from yeshiva supporters and alumni. Schild also undertook secular education at the University of Toronto while preparing for the rabbinate.[72] Other youthful refugees followed suit and entered the academe, acclimatizing to both the Canadian Jewish traditions and the professional playing field.

Life in wartime Canada presented challenges for the refugees as they struggled to develop relationships with the existing Jewish community. Some newcomers felt that the disconnect stemmed from Canadian Jewry's perception of the refugees as suspicious persons, combined with the community's inability to comprehend the refugees' reports of the deteriorating conditions in Nazi Germany, throughout occupied Europe, and of life inside Canadian internment camps. Others felt that they faced discrimination as German and Austrian Jews and "greenies," ignorant newcomers in an unfamiliar foreign environment. According to Schild, "[T]hat most of the 'yeshiva boys' were well-educated, from refined, respected families, that we spoke better English than most of the locals, who were Yiddish-speakers, that we had a better understanding of the contemporary world than many long-term members of Toronto Jewry, went unnoticed."[73]

Rather than forcing their way into Jewish communities consisting of first- and second-generation immigrants, the newcomers often found themselves situated among the "uptowners" of Canadian Jewish society. As an aggregate, the refugees achieved professional successes and enjoyed illustrious careers disproportionate to the general Jewish population. Among the 972 former internees who remained in wartime Canada were numerous academics, politicians, musicians, writers, and candidates to the North American rabbinate.[74] Many, through their strong educational and cultural backgrounds, became highly respected community leaders alongside Canadian-born and European-born peers.[75] They went from objects of curiosity into marriages with Canadian-born women from the middle class, and thus enlarged their kinship and social circles while cementing their links with the upper echelon of established Jews. These German-speaking refugees enriched Canadian-Jewish life and contributed greatly to secular society at large. Members of this illustrious group included many notable names: winner of the Nobel Prize in Chemistry, Professor Walter Kohn; Order of Canada recipients, the Honourable Fred Kaufman, judge in Quebec Court of Appeal, and the late Peter Oberlander, professor of urban and regional planning at the University of British Columbia; Catholic theologian Gregory Baum; and philosopher Emil Fackenheim.

Jewish refugees who immigrated to Canada during the war faced barriers to communal belonging and integration similar to those the German and Austrian refugee internees endured. Among this wartime cohort were the Hechts, natives of Brno, Czechoslovakia (present-day Czech Republic). Eugene Hecht owned a successful pharmaceutical marketing and distribution business while his wife, Sidonie, cared for their children, Madeleine and Thomas. Eugene took a "business trip" to Paris in May 1939. The rest of the family fled to Slovakia that September, bribing a border guard to allow them into Hungary. Eugene arranged for French entry visas, and the family reunited in Paris. The Hechts then fled south with the goal of crossing the Pyrenees and reaching Portugal.[76]

The family's first step toward freedom involved disguising themselves as Hungarian Roman Catholics who had lost their documents in a bombing raid. Persuaded by their tale, the Honorary Consul of Hungary in Marseilles granted four legitimate Hungarian passports. These documents afforded legal protection to the Hechts, but did not guarantee their safety. Fortuitously, Madeleine discovered that a friend's cousin had been named the Slovak ambassador to Spain.

She prevailed upon him to provide documents to help her family enter Portugal, via Spain. After much discussion and many monetary transactions, they received new papers stating that they were Roman Catholic Czechs and "good fascists" who had to get to Madrid to obtain new Slovakian passports. With documents in hand, the family landed in Lisbon on 10 January 1941.[77]

The Hechts had applied years earlier for U.S. visas but were far down on the list. Canada, however, glimmered as a possible haven. With the help of the Czech consul and intervention of the Czech government-in-exile—which paid for the immigrants' transatlantic passages and served as guarantor—Ottawa had been persuaded to accept a handful of refugees.[78] The Hechts benefited from this arrangement and were issued visas to enter Canada as Czech nationals, not as Jews. Armed with tickets and $400, the Hechts boarded the *Serpa Pinto* and arrived at Montreal's Bonaventure Station on 31 December 1941.

According to Thomas Hecht, the family's initial contact with the organized Jewish community was neither pleasant nor productive. This discontent can be addressed on two levels relating to expectations and values. Coming from a well-connected and successful urban existence in Brno, the Hechts were unaccustomed to financial hardships or country living. When a JIAS official wanted to place the family with a Jewish farmer in Repentigny, east of Montreal, the refugee family reportedly balked at the suggestion. The family sought placement in the city; life on a farm did not meet their perhaps unreasonable expectations. Thomas reminisced years later about the agency's perceived attitudes toward the newcomers. "Later, in the postwar years, empathy and services would improve greatly. But in 1942, some community leaders feared that Jewish immigrants from Europe would 'rock the boat.'"[79] Against their JIAS settlement worker's advice, the Hechts insisted on remaining in Montreal. In turning down the agency's offer of shelter, work, and a paycheque unmatchable in wartime Montreal, the Hechts surrendered any claim to JIAS support and elected to apply their $400 savings— an enormous sum in comparison to other wartime arrivals—to rent a flat. Eugene accepted a job in a shoe factory and later in a knitting mill; Madeleine found work in the needle trade. Paranoid that Thomas would face double discrimination in the English school board as a Jew and refugee, Eugene insisted on enrolling his son as a Protestant, despite settling in a largely Jewish neighbourhood.

The Hechts adapted quickly to the workplace conditions. Their greatest challenges were the English language and social adjustments. Although they were multilingual and spoke French, they knew no English, the lingua franca of the street and of most of Montreal's Jewish community. Through night school classes and intensive self-education, they conquered English rapidly. Socially, things were more challenging. Like other Jewish refugee children who found refuge in wartime Canada and those who arrived post-liberation, Thomas recalled being a very unhappy teenager who experienced difficulty befriending his peers. Having been forced to accept adult responsibilities and anxieties prematurely, Thomas' world view looked entirely different than those of his Canadian-born cohorts. He was bullied and beaten up, and claims that classmates described him as "a strange man in a strange land."[80] Foreign clothing, traditions, and languages exacerbated these differences. So too, perhaps, did the religious label of "Protestant" in a predominantly Jewish neighbourhood. In a time of unrest, entering the classroom as a young Jewish refugee might have earned Thomas allies among his co-religionists. The elder Hechts undertook a different approach to integration. As self-identifying Jews displaced by war, the couple found acceptance at Temple Emanu-El, a Reform synagogue that operated a small refugee social club and welcomed them as non-paying members. Engagement with the congregation and refugee club yielded meaningful friendships for the middle-aged couple as well as critical contacts that supported the upwardly mobile family's re-entry into communal leadership roles.

This family stood among only a handful of refugees to enter the developing Jewish social service infrastructure. In the eyes of the Hechts, Canadian Jews seemingly possessed no comprehension of the atrocities being committed against their European brethren, and thus could not empathize or commiserate with the few newcomers. Decades after the event, Thomas Hecht inferred that, "the Canadian government and, specifically, the organized Jewish community services, showed no particular interest in, or outreach to, impoverished new immigrants. The leadership of the organized Jewish community neither had any understanding of our needs, nor any policies in play to assist the plight of refugees from Nazi-dominated Europe.... They just did not know us, nor did they care."[81] In retrospect, while the Hechts perceived themselves as having received the short end of the stick, a more realistic conclusion relates to social service agencies' unpreparedness and limitations in receiving this unprecedented group of refugees. While the government failed to roll out the red carpet in greeting wartime refugees who, against all odds, secured asylum in Canada, the organized Jewish community did care about the newcomers' well-being. The perceived poor response and neglect by agency employees who refused to accommodate all refugee requests pertaining to work and housing might be better chalked up to the circumstances and expectations, combined with limited training or historical precedent. JIAS and its affiliated institutions focused on placing refugees in secure housing and jobs where they became available. Refugees' preferences did not necessarily factor into these decisions.

Eugene Hecht travelled to postwar Europe in search of survivors and to try to salvage his business assets. He succeeded on both counts, returning to Montreal with an orphaned niece, Ruthie, some money, and papers from his former company. Madeleine, too, returned to Europe to marry her long-time beau. The family reunion and re-establishment of Eugene's pharmaceuticals company helped the Hechts regain some semblance of their pre-Holocaust universe.

Thousands of other Jewish refugees fleeing Nazi-occupied Europe had, by the outbreak of the Second World War, found asylum in the Iberian Peninsula. Some, like the Hecht family, enjoyed temporary stays. The vast majority, however, had nowhere to go and lingered for years under uncertain circumstances. European Jewish refugees, rendered stateless by the war, held no official status in their sites of temporary asylum. Their lack of immigrant status (due to their surreptitious entrées to freedom) and inability to legally undertake work rendered the refugees completely dependent on the largesse of the international aid organizations. Founded in 1914, the humanitarian assistance organization American Jewish Joint Distribution Committee (AJDC), also known as the Joint, provided significant aid to Jewish asylum seekers who reached neutral territory. The Joint supplied food, clothing, and household goods to the refugees; American Jewish donations paid for shelter; and Joint caseworkers attended to the refugees' day-to-day needs, alleviating the financial hardships of unemployment and helping to facilitate emigration from the European continent. Despite their minimal reliance on the host Iberian governments, the Jewish refugees faced an insecure situation. No one knew if Spain and Portugal would maintain neutrality or transfer their loyalty to the Axis. Frequent complaints by Madrid and Lisbon about overcrowded conditions caused panic, too. Rumours abounded that future refugees would be denied entry if the countries were not relieved of the existing refugee migrant population. Britain received the bulk of complaints, and pressured the member states of the empire to do their part in alleviating the strain. Canada reluctantly agreed to offer temporary asylum to a small number of the Iberian refugees.[82]

Canadian immigration authorities laid out clear guidelines as to the refugees' status. Legally, the refugees' status was to be that of visitors granted temporary asylum until the cessation of hostilities in Europe, at which time they would return to their countries of origin. Participants in this last-ditch rescue mission were advised that they should not anticipate offers of permanent residency as bona fide immigrants.[83] Conditions for inclusion in this program were strict.

7. Iberian refugees arriving in Montreal via the *Serpa Pinto*, c. April 1944. Courtesy of the Canadian Jewish Congress Charities Committee National Archives.

Only complete family units, including all first-degree relatives (parents, children, grandparents), were admissible. Missing relatives, such as a son serving in the military, made the family automatically ineligible. This was based on Canada's fears that the refugee families would try to play on the heartstrings of the Canadian public and, citing humanitarian factors, attempt to reunite with loved ones in Canada. The quota was set for 200 families, but stringent conditions caused the project to fall short of this goal.[84] In the end, 455 persons, representing a total of 153 families, arrived from the Iberian Peninsula (as well as one movement from Morocco) between 10 April and 1 October 1944 in four shifts.

The groups arrived at the port of entry in Philadelphia where Hebrew Immigrant Aid Society (HIAS) and JIAS representatives assigned to support the registration process met them. Intervention at border patrols by these officials was a necessity to ensure that the refugees' extraordinary status as temporary residents was not contested. Then, the newcomers travelled to Canada in sealed train cars. Montreal absorbed a total of 297 individuals (eighty-nine families); the remaining 158 individuals (sixty-four families) were transferred to Toronto. Members of this movement were mostly Jews of Polish and German descent, followed by Austrian and Hungarian Jews, and a handful of other European nationals. The majority of heads of household were skilled workers, manufacturers, and merchants. Many arrived with vast linguistic prowess, energy, and a yearning to reactivate their professional and family lives long placed on hold.[85]

The resettlement process in both Montreal and Toronto was administered through JIAS offices and jointly funded by two Jewish organizations: the United Jewish Refugee and War Relief Agencies of Canada (later known as United Jewish Relief Agencies, or UJRA) and the CJC. Established in 1938 with the support of whisky magnate and philanthropist Samuel Bronfman, the UJRA worked to support Jewish refugees in Europe and Canada on multiple levels. Initially, organizational activities centred on providing material and diplomatic aid to Jewish refugees interned in Canada from 1940 to 1943. Following the cessation of hostilities, the UJRA collected and transported goods, including kosher provisions, to displaced persons camps overseas, aided Canadian Jews in locating surviving relatives, and helped facilitate the testing, transportation, and eventual resettlement of thousands of skilled labourer refugee families. JIAS and the Jewish Vocational Service (JVS) oversaw housing arrangements and work placements for the refugees.

Volunteer groups also turned their attention to those in need. Throughout the war, Jewish women's organizations took active roles in the war effort, raising funds for refugee relief organizations and protesting restrictive immigration quotas. These women, many of whom directly experienced the impact of war with husbands and sons serving in the military, felt obliged to do their part. The arrival of wartime refugees signalled great change and presented new opportunities for collaboration and cooperation between the factional groups. The Council for Jewish Women's Refugee Committee, representing women from the National Council of Jewish Women, Hadassah-WIZO, Pioneer Women, and the Dinah Lily Caplan Social Service Group in Montreal, bonded for this purpose. The Committee greeted the refugees upon their arrival, and worked alongside JIAS to arrange accommodations, many of which they acquired gratis.[86] An informal division of labour was struck between the volunteer National Council of Jewish Women (NCJW) and the professional agency, JIAS, whereby the NCJW organized teas and holiday parties, as well as house visits, while JIAS took responsibility for distributing maintenance checks and loan guarantees.

Follow-up visits by NCJW volunteers in the fall of 1945 suggested that sufficient assistance had been provided. Of the 89 Iberian refugee families resettled in Montreal, only twenty-five were still receiving financial support from JIAS. Of this group, eight units had been referred to the Family Welfare Department of the Baron de Hirsch Institute for ongoing social support. All families reported speaking English well enough to manage in economic and social spheres. And nearly all of the newcomers, now holders of permanent immigrant status, planned to remain in Canada. Only three wished to return to Europe.[87] The report also noted one specific suggestion to better help postwar survivors: "That people, upon arrival, be treated more individually and be given more help in finding suitable work, that they may thus become independent sooner."[88] Similar outcomes were reflected anecdotally in Toronto.

Among the Iberian refugees who found safe haven in 1944 Canada were Hungarian Jews Solomon Alexander and Irene Kohn, and their Italian-born daughter, Magda. As a young man, Solomon left his family outside of Budapest and set out to travel Europe, in the early 1920s, falling in love with Italy and its people. Around the same time, Irene joined family in the United States, but grew homesick. On the way home, she stopped in Italy to visit her sister, and met her future husband. The pair and their daughter enjoyed a comfortable life in Milan until Mussolini signed the Pact of Steel with Hitler on 22 May 1939 and became Germany's ally. This collaboration signalled a subsequent rise in state-sponsored anti-Semitism.[89] Fearful of a complete German takeover, the Kohns abandoned their furniture factory and fled to Tangiers, Morocco, in August 1939. It would be their home for the next five years.

Solomon jumped at the chance to relocate his family to North America. "Miraculously," Magda recalled, "we all had clear bills of health, no missing relatives. We were one of the few families to be accepted."[90] On 1 October 1944, the Kohns arrived in Canada, as part of the final wartime transfer, with one suitcase each. Following a brief stopover in Montreal, the family settled in Toronto. They knew nobody, spoke little English, and knew nothing about the city. JIAS and community groups tried to alleviate some of the refugees' stress by linking them with a host family which would help the newcomers navigate the housing and employment markets, and act as translators. A host family, JIAS believed, would support families' acculturation processes and churn out active, engaged new Canadians at rapid speeds. Rather than accepting their responsibilities as a support network, the Kohns' hosts neglected their three charges. Instead of providing short-term accommodations, guidance, and translation services, they planted the new arrivals in a hotel, leaving no forwarding number. After that, the Kohns located a suitable flat and took out a loan to purchase furniture, struggling to communicate with assigned caseworkers.

Solomon, a well-known proprietor of his former furniture factory, found work quickly at a downtown store and then joined the ranks at a paper factory as a dye maker. Irene undertook employment for a short time repairing costume jewellery. Sixteen-year-old Magda registered at Harbord Collegiate Institute, a predominantly Jewish public high school in downtown Toronto, on 19 October 1944, and was placed in grade eleven. Magda enjoyed a positive learning environment and experience at the school, recalling no incidents of anti-Semitism or ill treatment. "The teachers were lovely and the kids were helpful. I had one English teacher who went out of her way to make me feel welcome and brought me up to speed in the English language and our lessons," Magda recalled. "[The teacher] asked girls from the class to work with me for one hour after school each day, and they agreed. Thanks to them, I was able to graduate on time."[91]

Although the Kohns made acquaintances at work and at English night classes, they mostly befriended the small group of central European refugees, including Jews who had come as farmers, who frequented the New World Club, a social venue in Toronto catering to German- and Czech-speaking Jews. It was there, and not through social service agencies, that Solomon and Irene learned the ins and outs of life in Canada, gained access to religious services, and developed new communal bonds. The Kohns' reliance on and gravitation to individuals with shared common traits for support, as opposed to official communal bodies like JVS and JIAS, does not suggest a systemic failing by said organizations. Rather, it highlights how more acclimatized refugees' provisions of support to their brethren, socially and professionally, relieved pressure on poorly resourced

8. Group Passover seder in Montreal, 4 April 1944. Courtesy of the Canadian Jewish Congress Charities Committee National Archives.

communal agencies. Refugees at the New World Club appreciated the Kohns' knowledge of culture and languages, despite their diminished social status within their new circumstances. The postwar arrival of survivors completed the family's social circle and allowed them, to a small but crucial degree, to reconnect with their Hungarian roots, which had previously been absent from the New World Club and most of Canadian Jewish society. Within this wave of immigrants was one Andrew Klein, a young Hungarian man who had survived forced Hungarian and Nazi labour battalions before being sponsored by his sister as an immigrant. In 1953, Magda and Andrew were married in Toronto, increasing the number of the small Kohn family.[92]

Not all of the Iberian refugees who arrived during the war years adapted as well as the Kohns. Some, despite employment opportunities, encouraging living conditions, and available social supports, made a conscious decision to remain on the periphery and resist integration. Steven B, a Hungarian-born civil engineer and professional violinist, and his Austrian-born political-scientist wife, Edith, arrived in Canada on 8 April 1944 via Lisbon, Portugal. The pair had met and married in Berlin before immigrating with their two young sons to Belgium in 1935, followed by safety in neutral Lisbon in 1939. Mr. and Mrs. B travelled across the Atlantic alone, their sons having been taken nearly two years earlier by the United States Committee for the Care of European Children and placed in separate foster homes in New England. They settled in a room in a Toronto boarding house at the expense of the CJC, which paid for their housing and meals for several weeks.[93]

The Bs met with a JVS counsellor right away. Mr. B refused to accept factory work, which, he claimed, would destroy his hands. The counsellor made an exception to the rule that stressed applying the same criteria to all cases to avoid setting an unsustainable precedent: since Mr. B spoke English, German, French, and Hungarian, he should be able to undertake work in his field, especially owing to the country's manpower shortage. Mr. B found a position at Ontario Hydro Electric without agency intervention. Even with these early signs of positive integration, the Bs had no intention of setting up a permanent home, as they did not plan to remain in Canada. They hoped to join their sons in the United States, a plan that never materialized. According to the JIAS report, "The Bs are not liked by other refugees and there are unflattering reasons for [the] FBI's refusal to give them admission to U.S.A."[94] No reasons were offered as explanation.

Instead, the family was reunited in Toronto in the fall of 1944. At that time, Mrs. B rejected any aid from the UJRA or JIAS, even though she had expressed earlier that she would require support in placing her children in a room in their boarding house (the couple's space was too small for four people) and in arranging lunchtime meals for the boys while she worked in an unspecified job.[95] By December of that year, the family's case was closed. Nothing more is known about their lives, or whether they did in fact leave Canada. Neither JIAS, nor the UJRA, undertook any vigorous attempts to follow up with the family, or to offer administrative support in arranging the parental Bs' reunification with their sons.

Aside from thin organizational documentation and oral histories, primarily relating to the internment of Jewish wartime refugees at the CJCCC and LAC, there is little information about the few thousand late-interwar and wartime refugees who were able to penetrate Canada's closed immigration gates. And, in comparison to the experiences of Holocaust survivors who immigrated in the postwar period, little attention has been paid to their extraordinary, and rare, stories. With the notable exception of Irving Abella and Harold Troper's research on Canadian immigration policy, and Paula Draper's work on the internees, Canadian historians have not documented the lives of these refugees from Nazi-occupied lands as distinct from, yet as important as, survivors who arrived from the late 1940s onward.

This lack of interest could relate to the scant documentation. Unlike the mass movement of survivors in the late 1940s, whose early experiences were carefully recorded, social service workers did not pay much attention to refugees who entered Canada immediately prior to or during the war. Several explanations could account for this. These early refugees were few in number and many immigrated either as a family unit or joined relatives in Canada. Service providers might have assumed that these persons did not require substantial support beyond the initial meet-and-greets and housing placements. Whereas postwar survivors frequently immigrated as single persons or small, young families, making their need for support obvious to service providers, interwar and wartime arrivals frequently arrived with relatives who provided emotional or practical supports. Other explanations lie with the fact that early arrivals were reluctant to request assistance, or even turned outside the Jewish community for support.

A lack of knowledge about these newcomers is due to JIAS caseworkers' scant records. The immigration agency's social service departments emerged only following the quick and steady influx of survivor refugees in 1948. Unlike the small numbers of wartime migrants who were absorbed with little fuss or resource expenditure, the scale of the early postwar refugee resettlement process proved vast and unprecedented. So, too, did their need for intensive care and ongoing support. While caseworkers frequently recorded survivors' failures to attain independence swiftly and cited psychological distress, there is little evidence to suggest that workers sufficiently applied "special treatment"—as recommended by executive director Joseph Kage—to their clients' cases, nor investigated the root of the survivors' inability to adapt to their new lives. Recognition of post-traumatic stress disorder, which many clients surely experienced, surfaces rarely. And limited human and material resources dictate that, with few exceptions, psychological counselling fell secondary to employment counselling. This trend of applying band-aid solutions to treat psychological ailments resulting from wartime trauma persisted into the 1950s.

While the late-interwar and wartime immigrants failed to elicit the interest of most Canadian Jews or to help broaden the infrastructure of social service networks, the mass movements of thousands of Holocaust survivors into Canada from the latter half of the 1940s through the early 1950s led to further changes. Members of this wave entered the country through industrial labour schemes and close relatives' sponsorship, and dramatically altered the composition of Canadian Jewish life and culture. The following chapters consider these movements, and the early experiences of survivors in postwar Canada.

# CHAPTER TWO

# "ORDINARY SURVIVORS"

As a young child growing up in the industrial city of Lodz, Poland, Anna Szczercowska worried little about the future. Born in 1927 and the youngest of four children—two girls and two boys—Szczercowska was raised in a traditional Jewish home where she received both secular and religious schooling. Lodz's collapse, and the subsequent establishment of the Litzmannstadt Ghetto in 1940, obliterated her and her family's fates forever. One brother escaped to Russia during the German occupation of 1939, where he survived the war deep in Soviet Asia. The rest of the family was trapped. By the time Szczercowska was deported to Auschwitz in 1944, her mother had died of starvation, and her father and other brother had been murdered under Nazi occupation. She and her sister-in-law survived slave labour, first at Auschwitz III (Monowitz) and, later, Bergen-Belsen. One sister, Mania, also survived a separate series of camps. The sisters reunited in postwar Germany.

Young Anna began to rebuild her life first at Braunschweig, a women's-only DP camp in Germany, then in the Bergen-Belsen DP camp. There, Anna reluctantly accepted financial aid from the AJDC; after this, she conclusively decided to never again accept monetary assistance from anybody. While working in the latter DP camp's nursery school teaching music, Anna met and married a fellow Polish survivor, Oscar Holtzman. Like many of her contemporaries, the young wife took Hebrew lessons in the hopes of making *aliyah* (moving "up") to the newly established state of Israel:

> We never thought about coming to Canada. We had nobody there, or in Israel. Then one day, union representatives from Canada came to the camp looking for tradespeople. We had very little at the time but my husband was working as a tailor. He took their [skill] test, and passed; they offered to bring us to Canada. Since we had decided to go to whichever country gave us visas first, we went to Canada. And on

18 June 1948, we landed in Toronto with no money to our names, just some food preserves that we had rationed throughout the journey.[1]

Upon their Friday arrival in Toronto, a union representative loaned the Holtzmans twenty dollars and assigned the couple a temporary room in a boarding house. Oscar began work the following Monday; the twenty-dollar loan was repaid to the union within weeks. The young couple welcomed their son Sam, the first "true Canadian," to their family in 1949, and then Willy in 1951. They also moved three times, engaged in a series of degrading employment opportunities, and studied English at night school. True to her word, neither Anna nor Oscar accepted organizational support during this transitional period. Young and impoverished, but fiscally responsible and determined to succeed in a "very, very hard life," the couple jumped feet first into their new community and created a safe and loving environment for their sons.[2]

Sidney (Sichum) Cyngiser faced Holocaust ordeals similar to those of Anna Szczercowska. Born in 1924 in Lodz, and raised in Radom, Poland, Sidney spent approximately a year and a half trapped in that city's ghetto with his parents, maternal grandmother, and three sisters. All of his female relatives were deported and killed. Sidney and his father were sentenced to slave labour at a munitions factory and then Auschwitz, where the senior Cyngiser perished. Having nearly died himself in camp, Sidney was barely alive when liberated while on a death march in 7 April 1945. Saved only by surgery performed by a Jewish prisoner doctor that left the young man with a lung condition, Sidney was placed in a French-run hospital. There he met the tuberculosis-ridden Bronia, a woman eight years his junior and a fellow survivor of the Radom Ghetto and Auschwitz, in addition to a death march to Bergen Belsen. In hospital, the couple began a love affair that would straddle two continents.

During his convalescence, Sidney investigated the possibility of immigrating to the United States to obtain an American visa. When his application was repeatedly rejected due to a chronic lung condition, the memory of a great-aunt in Canada, one Mrs. Bella Singer, popped into his mind. Bella Switzer Singer was a highly respected community leader who had helped more than 200 members of her extended family immigrate to Calgary during the 1920s. To prepare for his imminent movement to bilingual Canada, the tenacious young man took French lessons every morning, followed by English studies in the afternoon. With her sponsorship, Sidney arrived in Calgary in 1949: "All these relatives—who did not know me from a hole in the wall—came out in droves to meet me. They were all warm, and it was nice to know that I was in a free country."[3] When the newcomer failed to secure work as a farmer (his official visa designation) due to a lack of agricultural skills, relatives found him work at a clothing store. Sidney lived with Bella Singer until finding his bearings, a total of eleven months. Two years later, Bronia and her aged father, Pinchas Karafiol, who had settled in New Jersey, travelled to western Canada on a visitor's visa. They never left. The young couple was married in Calgary. Bronia undertook English studies at Western Canada High School one evening per week, and developed linguistic confidence by engaging with native English speakers. Her father, Pinchas, operated a small store entirely in Yiddish and Polish. All three survivors stuck mostly with other newcomers in the early years. With few options and limited professional experiences or formal education, the Cyngisers jumped into an unknown career of small-hotel management. With four children in tow, the young family—with their loved ones' support—forged ahead.[4]

Thousands of Holocaust survivors immigrated to Canada from Europe between 1947 and 1950. These newcomers arrived via one of two vehicles. Anna and Oscar Holtzman were but two survivors who immigrated to Canada as contracted labourers for the garment industry as tailors, furriers, milliners, and the like, on various schemes. With respect to immigration guidelines, gentile DPs also entered the country through these schemes and their immediate border registration, and the Jewish community attended to housing needs. All refugees signed contracts agreeing to undertake employment in their particular trade for a minimum of eleven months. These contracts were processed and the situations monitored by the country's Labour Department and sponsored according to agreements between the Canadian Jewish Congress and the garment industry and unions. The sponsoring bodies were determined to increase the stagnated flow of survivors into Canada who were cleared by the Department of Immigration and Citizenship, which required an increase in manpower to fill the demand of the country's rapidly expanding postwar economy.[5] Other survivors, such as Sidney Cyngiser, availed themselves of the sole alternative, the Department of Mines and Resources' (later the Department of Immigration) "close relatives" sponsorship scheme. Members of this early migration of "ordinary survivors" were young and healthy, and carried with them little but their few worldly goods. They entered the workforce immediately upon arrival. This chapter considers the first few years of those survivors' lives in Canada.[6]

## Changing Tides

For two years following the end of the Second World War, Canada's gates remained closely guarded against most immigrants and European refugees. Only a handful of prospective candidates—specifically, some first-degree relatives of Canadian citizens, some single (non-Jewish) labourers, and war brides—were permitted to enter the country. Moves toward the liberalization of the Canadian government's approach toward immigrants and refugees took hold on 28 May 1946, when the Cabinet passed Privy Council Order 2071. The gradual liberalization permitted Canadian residents, not strictly citizens, to sponsor the admission of first-degree European relatives, as well as orphaned nieces and nephews less than sixteen years of age, assuming they were financially capable of accepting responsibility for them.[7]

The postwar immigration of refugees to Canada, however, began en masse only after Prime Minister William Lyon Mackenzie King's announcement on 1 May 1947 of Canada's newly amended immigration policy (the first change in declarative policy in several years). The aging prime minister reported that his government had adopted new criteria that would permit the admission of relatives of persons already living in Canada and assist with the resettlement of DPs in Europe. The revised policy's announcement fell nearly two years to the day after the German army's unconditional surrender and cessation of the Second World War on the European continent, 7 May 1945. During those two intervening years, the world awoke to the event later referred to as the Holocaust. Newsreels depicting human skeletons and mass graves, as well as bereaved survivors and despondent civilians forced to march through former concentration camp sites, found eager audiences on international screens; reports of captured Nazis and military tribunals graced newspaper covers as well while Canadian soldiers returned home to their loved ones. The harsh, undeniable reality of Nazi terror in Europe, and against Jews in particular, became an unavoidable reality for all Canadians.

A liberalized immigration policy served two ends. First, the amendment fulfilled a political aim. While the postwar economy boomed and industries flourished, the demand for cheap labour rose at unprecedented rates. The native Canadian workforce could not support the demands. A reasonable alternative presented itself in the form of displaced person workers—men and women presumably willing to accept menial wages in exchange for immigration papers. International aid organizations supported the immigration process and loaned refugees money for transportation costs while Canadian unions and industries guaranteed jobs. This tactic proved a win-win situation for the Canadian government: it relieved itself of international pressures to expand immigration quotas while receiving thousands of skilled labourers at no cost. The second end served by the policy amendment is more difficult to quantify. In light of the tragedy that befell European Jews, the Canadian government experienced a failure of conscience, epitomized in its inactive refusal to accept Jewish refugees during the war. This shame of inaction filtered down to the Canadian public. In receiving displaced workers, Jewish and non-Jewish, Canada aimed to right the wrongs of its past and to posit itself as a just nation in opposition to fascism. Regardless of the motivation, the amended policy officially intended "to foster the growth of the population of Canada by the encouragement of immigration. The government will seek by legislation, regulation, and vigorous administration to ensure the careful selection and permanent settlement of such numbers of immigrants as can advantageously be absorbed in our national economy."[8] To ensure the admission of only healthy, able-bodied, and skilled refugees who would not burden the country, immigration officers were deployed to assist in the selection process.

Chagrin at having been unable to influence policy change a decade earlier, which might have resulted in the rescue of a greater number of Jewish victims of the Holocaust, was a driving factor in the Canadian Jewish community's determination to help survivors immigrate. The garment industry (in which Jews were disproportionately represented at all levels) and the CJC campaigned for manufacturers, factory owners, and independent operators to provide contracts in sponsorship of refugee workers badly needed in the growing economic market.[9] Requests for skilled labourers, particularly tailors, furriers, and milliners, were then directed toward government authorities for approval. Schemes for the admission of survivors who might find work as domestics, lumber workers, miners, and farmers were also devised. One request to the Labour Department, made by the Cloak Manufacturers' Association and the International Ladies' Garment Workers Union of Toronto (which represented nearly 100 percent of all employers and employees in the city's predominantly Jewish cloak and suit industry), claimed that they were in desperate need of workers to supplement the current ranks of aging employees, and to keep up with the skyrocketing demand for domestic and export production. Supporting a "growing industry of great importance," the unions asked for a minimum of 200 skilled workers.[10] Permission to sponsor 200 refugee workers from DP camps was granted.

Representatives of the Canadian Overseas Garment Commission (COGC), on behalf of predominantly Jewish manufacturers considering sponsorship opportunities, and CJC representatives travelled to Europe to recruit refugees for the various labour schemes. Competition for inclusion on labour schemes was fierce.

9. Atlantic Fur Company, c. 1941. Ontario Jewish Archives, fonds 12, item 1.

Young, single men were the ideal candidates. Single, skilled women followed, while couples (all admissible refugees were entitled to bring their families with them) with one or more infant children came next.[11] More mature individuals in exceptional health—or with desired professional portfolios—rounded out the bunch. All would-be contract workers were required to provide evidence of experience in their respective trades, and they strove to impress upon interviewers their ability through practical skill-testing exams, which took place at AJDC facilities. They were also expected to demonstrate in interviews how they could contribute to Canada—that is, not become a burden on the state, and be physically fit and mentally sound. Any noticeable physical conditions (a limp, missing limbs) or lung problems, including evidence of tuberculosis, were grounds for rejection.

Perhaps most difficult for refugees to meet were the deadlines and conditions of settlement of the International Refugee Organization (IRO), a temporary agency operating under the UNRRA. These organizations were established in response to the refugee crisis resulting from the Nazi occupation, and shouldered international responsibility for the care and repatriation of millions of displaced Europeans. Established in 1943, UNRRA received billions of dollars from fifty-two member states (the United States at the helm) for three purposes: 1) to distribute emergency aid, including food provisions and medication to DPs in Europe and, later, war-ravaged China; 2) to support the restoration of public services and functions, including industry and agriculture; and 3) to facilitate the repatriation of millions of Europeans. Another critical function of UNRRA was the establishment and temporary oversight of DP camps to house the more than one million Europeans—Jewish refugees included—unable or unwilling to repatriate to their country of birth.[12] The IRO managed the legal work of refugee repatriation and the resettlement project, and provided direct legal aid and monetary allocations to displaced Jews seeking asylum outside of European borders in the war's aftermath. The agency paid for both the operating costs in Europe and the ocean passes for vetted refugees to travel to Canada as loans, not gifts. To qualify for the IRO's official DP status, survivors needed to be in the country of initial resettlement (i.e., DP camps in Germany or Austria) and living under the jurisdiction of Allied powers by 1946. Newcomers were expected to begin to repay the loans immediately. Individuals sponsored through the close relatives scheme that met IRO guidelines, and whose families could not afford the steep transportation fees, also had their transatlantic fares covered. Their sponsors were responsible for remunerating the agency.[13]

Selected refugee workers were part of a three-way contract involving the sponsoring employers or unions, the Canadian government, and the survivors themselves. The COGC represented the garment industry manufacturers who sponsored thousands of Jewish and non-Jewish labourers between 1947 and 1950. As a contracting body accountable to the Department of Labour and the Department of Mines and Resources, the industry outlined three primary obligations to its workers. The first indicated that the industry represented employers sponsoring individuals and was responsible for ensuring that tailors' and other labourers' contracts were implemented and fulfilled. It accepted responsibility for providing accommodation facilities, with the assistance of the CJC. And finally, the industry committed to pay the transportation costs of the newcomers and their dependents from Halifax to their destination in Canada. Refugees were expected to pay back all expenses at their earliest opportunity, and within two years. The COGC persistently made it clear that it was not a welfare organization and did not undertake long-term responsibility for the refugees, Jewish or non-Jewish; this was the legal responsibility of its contracting partner, the CJC.[14]

The mass movement of refugees to Canada resulted in much confusion. The CJC placed an announcement in its "Inter-Office Information Bulletin" that broke down issues of transportation, payment, and government intervention on newcomers' behalf. The IRO was responsible for handling the transportation of persons on work and close relatives schemes, paying for their ocean passage and overseas processing. Canada's Labour Department issued entry permits following the signing of employment contracts and the CJC's guarantee of maintenance for all refugee workers. As the official operating bodies under the surveillance of the CJC, the UJRA, and by extension, JIAS, shouldered responsibility for placing newcomers in homes, ensuring they had employment and granting assistance when necessary. Family members were responsible for maintaining and housing their relatives.[15]

According to the Department of Mines and Resources, 1,866 Jews entered Canada in 1947. The following year, the number jumped exponentially to 9,386, the majority of whom originated in Europe.[16] This represented the largest migration of Jews to the country in over two decades.[17] Of the 1948 newcomers, 3,332 persons arrived under the tailors and furriers schemes, 250 immigrated as milliners, and the remaining 6,054 came by way of close relatives sponsorships. Those who migrated via industrial or garment workers schemes met with Jewish representatives the moment their ships docked at one of several ports in Canada, usually at Halifax or Montreal. Less frequently, newcomers arrived at U.S. ports, including

New York and Philadelphia, where they were, again, greeted by Canadian Jewish representatives, who shepherded them to their destinations north of the border.

In Halifax, Noa Heinish and members of the local Jewish community met incoming Jewish DPs at Pier 21. Meta Echt, a native of Danzig who immigrated to Canada with her family as farmers in 1939, was named the mayor's representative at Pier 21 and held the title of official JIAS "greeter."[18] Responsibilities for this paid position entailed ensuring that community representatives (preferably multilingual) were present upon the arrival of all registered Jewish refugees and that the newcomers received assistance during processing by immigration and customs officers. Confusion over baggage, such as missing pieces and enforced tariffs that the newcomers could not yet pay, also fell within the greeters' jurisdiction. In the immediate postwar years, JIAS expended minimal resources hiring professional social service workers, relying primarily on volunteers and unskilled workers to absorb the first wave of refugees. The agency elected to spend its modest resources on items such as food or clothing. Occasionally, refugees found shelter in local Jewish homes, especially when ships docked immediately prior to or during High Holidays, and synagogues opened their doors for services. Meta Echt and her teenage daughter Marianne distributed kosher food, provided by Jewish merchants, as well as money to sustain the survivors as they continued to travel by train toward their final destinations.

These early meetings at ports of entry by local Jewish communal greeters had a tremendous impact on some newcomers. Nathan Wasser, a teenaged survivor from Sandomierz, Poland, and his father came to Canada through the furriers scheme in 1948. En route from Germany, Wasser lost the few dollars he had earned on the black market and which he had planned to use to help get settled in Montreal. Years later, Wasser recalled feeling overwhelmed by the situation, without a clear sense of his own identity:

> Everything began to swirl in his mind when two women helped him up to a counter at Pier 21, began feeding him candy, and told him that now, in Canada, everything was going to be all right.... One of the women gave him twenty dollars. He could not accept such generosity, how could he ever pay it back? Her words, "We trust you, we have faith in you, you are going to be a good Canadian citizen," hit him like a ton of bricks.[19]

10. Jewish immigrants on board the *General Sturgis*, Halifax, Nova Scotia, 6 February 1948. Ontario Jewish Archives, item 628.

After boarding the train, Wasser watched as the pair of women, Meta Echt and her daughter, Marianne, blew him kisses and waved goodbye. This personal relationship between the immigrant and local Jews, themselves former refugees from Nazism, proved significant. He never forgot the kindness and humanity shown to him. More than fifty years later, Wasser returned to Pier 21 to thank Marianne in person, and return the $20 tenfold.

## Housing and Employment

Social workers operating inside the private sector suffered from debilitating shortcomings, foremost among them being a lack of education or training. Social work had historically been heralded as a "helping profession," work relegated to faith-based communities and volunteers.[20] The first bachelor's degrees in social work were conferred only at the University of Toronto, McGill University, and the University of British Columbia in 1947.[21] Individuals employed in the field prior to this stemmed from a range of backgrounds. A study conducted in November 1930 by the National Committee of Social Workers found that out of a total of 228 registered social workers, seventy possessed no social work training or university education. Another eighty received at least one university course, while forty-nine others reported non-specific "basic training."[22] Many social workers relied on gut instincts and a fine-tuned moral code, not psychological or sociological theories and approaches in their practices. This pattern proved most detrimental in cases of clients experiencing the equivalent of post-traumatic stress disorder (PTSD), specifically genocide survivors. In a female-dominated field, social workers accepted unreasonably heavy workloads, routinely clocked long hours without remuneration or benefits, and received low wages. Such detriments affected the service outcomes of worker–client relationships.

Similar deficiencies plagued Jewish social service agencies that, as private community-based operations, were not required to comply with professional guidelines dictated by the National Committee of Social Workers. JIAS Montreal's social service department began operations in January 1948 with only one professional social worker and a handful of agency-trained (but not accredited) caseworkers. In its nascent year, it was poorly equipped to handle emotionally intensive or "chronic" cases. Holocaust survivors, suffering from a host of psychological and physical ailments, proved difficult and sometimes unmanageable clients. Persons suffering from emotional disturbances or those released from sanatoria were referred to Jewish family-welfare agencies and social workers that could best meet their needs. JIAS Toronto's department, modelled on Montreal's, opened in the fall of 1948. With time, operations improved as JIAS hired additional social workers and gained expertise on how to handle emotional clients better. In 4,429 of the close relatives cases recorded in 1948, JIAS employees assisted families on the Canadian side locate survivors in Europe and file immigration applications on their behalf. The agency also helped local clients secure the necessary funds for travel on their relatives' behalf. It could therefore be said that, although newcomers who arrived through family sponsorships did not officially fall under JIAS responsibility, many benefited from its assistance at all stages of the resettlement process.

JIAS addressed three basic challenges faced by all immigrants, and in the case of survivors, exacerbated by their Holocaust trauma: financial insecurities (including accommodations and employment), language difficulties, and the social adjustment necessitated by entry into a new environment.[23] In tending to these matters, the agency was careful to maintain its status as a social organization, not a charity. For instance, any money extended to newcomers came in the form of a loan requiring repayment in full. The goal was to help survivors maintain their dignity and feelings of self-worth, while simultaneously acquiring financial stability and save as quickly as possible.[24]

Education and training varied among the caseworkers employed by the privately operated JIAS and other immigrant and refugee aid agencies, with the workers' credentials correlated closely with professional standards of the era. Few agency employees possessed university degrees in any subject, let alone social work. Caseworkers assigned to "new Canadians" were no exception. Until JIAS opened its social service departments in 1948 in response to the mass influx of Holocaust survivors, there was little recognized need for professional social workers at the agency. Staffers were instead employed for practical reasons—specifically for their multilingualism, which would enable them to communicate with a gamut of newcomers. Oftentimes, persons selected for employment had lived through the refugee experience themselves. These employees shared knowledge of wartime trauma, and often language and traditions, with clients, increasing their ability to respond to resettlement issues with greater immediacy, empathy, and understanding than Canadian-born workers.

Benjamin Schlesinger, a native of Poland who had arrived in Montreal with the Iberian refugee movement in 1944, joined the JIAS staff straight out of high school in 1948 as an alternative to pursuing a university education, the cost of which was prohibitive.[25] Schlesinger was fluent in Polish, Yiddish, English, and French, and could communicate with fellow JIAS officials and newcomers alike. The teenager learned the ropes by shadowing social service department director Joseph Kage, self-educating with social work literature, and observing caseworkers in action. Perhaps of greater importance than his linguistic skills or ability to grasp organizational behaviours was Schlesinger's sensitivity toward the survivors and his personal awareness and experiences of wartime trauma. Schlesinger would relocate to Toronto to gain professional accreditation as a social worker.

For Schlesinger and his colleagues at JIAS and affiliated groups, the never-ending search for housing for survivor refugees posed a major challenge. Campaigns to encourage Canadian Jews to offer rooms in their homes drummed up placement possibilities between housing committees and landlords.[26] Housing should not have posed any problems in the cases of close relatives sponsorship. According to their applications, family members accepted legal responsibility for providing accommodations and pledged to cover any maintenance costs for their survivor relatives for at least their first month in Canada. But, good intentions did not always suffice, and sponsors were often unable to follow through with their guarantees, usually because they themselves were recent arrivals living in modest dwellings in rundown boarding houses. In such circumstances, survivors were referred to JIAS and assigned a caseworker who interviewed the sponsors, viewed their bank statements and employment records, and submitted an application for aid to the executive committee. JIAS routinely made its temporary shelters available while a decision concerning applications for support was pending. Newcomers with successful verdicts continued to receive financial assistance. Those denied monetary aid were returned to their sponsors' responsibility, but were offered vocational training as a means of enhancing their prospects for self-sufficiency. Sponsors who failed to adequately provide for their charges were not reported to governmental authorities.[27]

Moritz and Irene G and their teenage daughter Agata arrived in Canada on 19 May 1950 and travelled directly to Irene's niece, Lilly L, a participant on the War Orphans Project, a scheme which helped more than 1,200 Jewish youth migrate to Canada between 1947 and 1952.[28] Residing in Montreal, Lilly had only recently arrived in Canada. Eager to reunify her family, Lilly persuaded a second cousin (another recent immigrant) who was employed full-time to help her file the appropriate immigration papers for her aunt, uncle, and their young daughter. With $2,000 in his bank account, much of it borrowed from his employer and friends, the cousin's sponsorship was nevertheless accepted. But upon their arrival in Montreal, the Gs found themselves sharing cramped quarters with the second cousin, his wife, and young children in a two-room house. The Gs and their sponsors visited JIAS a few days later to request new accommodations. Owing to the circumstances, the agency took on the close relatives' case, placed the Gs in an affordable two-room apartment, covered several months' rent, and provided job counselling in cooperation with JVS.[29]

Such happy outcomes tended to be the exception, as there existed a major housing crisis for newcomers in most large Jewish population centres across Canada.

Garment industry employers were urged by Jewish community organizations like JIAS to provide housing support for their sponsored DP workers. If refugee workers lived in the residences of their employers or other employees, spaces would be freed up for other new arrivals, particularly those with young children, routinely refused accommodations.[30]

Unfortunately for the placement committees, these recommendations rarely culminated in action. With the exception of the absorption of Jewish war orphans, insufficient numbers of Toronto Jews opened their homes to incoming refugees. This failure to provide shelter contributed to a housing crisis in the city. Jewish women's communal groups took an active role in remedying this situation and facilitating housing options for survivors. Temporary shelters were set up at a reception centre at 150 Beverley Street (centralized home to the CJC, JIAS, and other Jewish communal organizations) and at the Council for Jewish Women's community house on nearby St. George Street. In 1948, two houses on Beverley Street were purchased by the CJC with financing from UJRA; by the early 1950s, an additional fifteen homes had been bought, and another three leased. The cost expenditure exceeded $100,000. These homes were later sold to survivors, and the costs recuperated.[31]

Montreal Jewish aid agencies and the CJC did not purchase buildings for the newcomers despite the tight housing market. Instead, they relied on temporary housing for refugee workers eighty kilometres away from the city at a DP reception centre at St. Paul L'Ermite, at the Montreal JIAS reception house, and in local hotels. The Montreal agencies took a different approach from that of their Toronto counterparts for providing long-term housing solutions, too. Rather than having the CJC buy homes for survivors, Montreal agencies helped to facilitate loans with the cooperation of the Hebrew Free Loan Association. Newcomers were granted low-interest loans with the help of the agency; such loans helped them obtain and afford flats and apartments.[32]

Operating under the guidance of JIAS, women's groups supplied much of the refugees' basic necessities. The Council of Jewish Women in Toronto accepted the task of looking after the comforts of the new immigrants, providing transportation, furniture, utensils and other domestic necessities. Montreal's Dinah Lily Caplan Social Service group likewise "adopted" several DP families, supplying them with clothing, linens, medical assistance, and food. And across the country,

11. Hattie Bloom of the National Council of Jewish Women, c. 1955. Ontario Jewish Archives, fonds 38-1, series 1, file 1, item 1.

Canadian Jewish women facilitated the collection and distribution of clothing donations. The National Council of Jewish Women in Montreal single-handedly ran the JIAS Clothing Centre three times weekly for more than two years, with fundraising efforts extending well into the 1950s. Members garnered donations of new items, including undergarments and furniture, from local industries to supplement second-hand donations. Many financially secure women dipped into their own closets to clothe the newcomers in "Canadian" styles, and convinced hairdressers to offer refugee ladies discounted appointments. While these philanthropic gestures ensured a minimum level of sustenance among the impoverished refugees, women's communal organizations bore little responsibility for housing or work assignments, jobs being left to professional agencies.[33]

While the majority of survivors were resettled in Montreal and Toronto, other Jewish communities reported a plethora of unique challenges in placing refugee workers and their accompanying family members. Winnipeg, home to the third-largest Jewish population in the country, warmly received several hundred newcomers in the latter half of the 1940s. These arrivals, including more than 200 sponsored skilled labourers for the fur and garment industry, led to a conflict of interests between national demands and the reality of organizational staffing and financial limitations. Where the will existed, adequate professional staffing and funding lagged. With a geographical reach and resettlement oversight stretching hundreds of kilometres beyond city limits, CJC's western branch expressed its desire to do its part in absorbing survivors, and a willingness to possibly exceed its quota (approximately 15 percent of the national total) of garment workers. But, to take on this burden, Winnipeg needed greater financial assistance from the COGC or CJC national headquarters to offset costs associated with the hiring of additional placement service workers and the locating and subsidizing of safe housing. Winnipeg's rental market was small and few landlords were willing to accept newcomer families with children, thus forcing most survivor families to live indefinitely in the city's former Jewish orphanage and in rundown hotels. The sole solution for permanent and stable arrangements for this refugee survivor cohort appeared to be the purchase of an apartment house, which occurred in 1949.[34]

Conditions were not much better in Vancouver, a geographically smaller city that received several dozen refugee workers and families during the latter half of the 1940s. Local CJC leadership and garment manufacturers expressed disappointment with the region's resettlement process. In a letter to CJC executive director Saul Hayes, Charles Walfish of the Congress's B.C. branch addressed the issue that was of greatest concern in his community: "Congress has not made sufficient provisions for their [survivor] accommodations, especially in a city like Vancouver, where housing is so scarce."[35] Walfish recommended the joint purchase of a temporary shelter and clearing centre for newcomers, with financial support from local sponsoring employers who could not afford to undertake such a venture on their own. In the final analysis, no funds were allocated to this proposal, and the struggle for affordable and safe accommodations for newcomers to Vancouver continued through the 1940s, limiting resettlement options for displaced persons, and delaying the acculturation process.

Housing was not the only major challenge facing those involved in survivor resettlement in Canada. According to the contractual agreements involving the refugees, the COGC (representing the garment industry), and the federal government's National Employment Service (NES), all refugee workers, Jewish or gentile, were to enter the workforce in their respective fields within days of their arrival. Industry sponsors were responsible for placing skilled labourers in the appropriate trade positions, while the NES took responsibility for non-skilled workers, including domestics and manual labourers. The problem arose when survivors could not be placed by the industry because they did not have the necessary skill, even though they were still included on labour schemes, due to poor judgment or humanitarian screeners who recognized the survivors' limited opportunities for migration and included them on the schemes despite their lack of ability. It fell to JIAS to refer such newcomers to JVS for assistance in finding work in a more suitable field so as to work for at least eleven months, and thereby uphold their contractual obligations and maintain their immigrant status. Survivors who arrived through relatives' sponsorships were also directed to JVS and encouraged to seek employment through their sponsors' work, social, or religious contacts.

Although JIAS did not place newcomers in jobs, immigrants turned to the agency for help in cases of workplace conflict and with loan requests. Most significantly, JIAS counselled survivors on the "American tempo of work"—which the caseworkers considered more strenuous than the European model, and helped newcomers accept the realities of immigrant employment (mainly that some would be forced to take jobs beneath their educational standing) and create a liveable budget on low wages.[36] JIAS caseworkers aimed to transform the newcomers into culturally aware and law-abiding Canadians who would blend into existing Jewish communities. In maintaining a low profile and avoiding drawing attention to themselves as distinct, foreign groups, agency workers aimed to prove the refugees' suitability for life in Canada. Respectful and self-sufficient refugees were better positioned to contribute positively economically; poorly adjusted and mischievous survivors' could jeopardize future immigration schemes proposed by the organized Jewish community.[37]

JIAS oversaw the social welfare of all newcomers and was actively engaged in ensuring that the refugee workers fulfilled their contractual obligations. On occasion, the agency received refugees who faced alleged discrimination or mistreatment at their place of employment. Aron H was twenty-five, single, and ready for adventure when he encountered representatives from the CPR at a DP camp in Germany. Desperate to escape Europe, Aron embarked on a series of physical examinations before being deemed healthy enough to work as a lumberjack and to help construct new railway tracks in northern Ontario.

Upon his arrival in Halifax on 15 November 1947, Aron was directed to a lumber site in White River, Ontario, and joined Gang Camp 433.[38] After one month at the campsite, however, Aron used his earnings to travel to Toronto, where he presented himself at the JIAS office, declaring to the intake worker that he would not, under any circumstances, return to camp. "He claimed that the other workers were extremely unfriendly to him and that he feared for his life," the intake report recalled. "He was the only Jewish person there and was unable to speak to any one at the camp.... He stated that he would rather return to Germany than go back to White River."[39] Ignoring the usual protocol that dictated neutrality in contractual conflicts between DP employees and the NES, the JIAS worker intervened.[40] In a rare display of outreach and genuine empathy for her client's situation, the worker convinced one Mr. Sharrer of the NES that, as a Jew, Aron's emotional and physical well-being were under attack at the camp. She successfully secured the young refugee's reassignment to the CPR yard in Toronto. Aron's relationship with his caseworker ceased to exist following this transfer. Nothing more is known about his experience at the CPR yard, nor his integration into the local Jewish community.

Aron H's professional relationship with his empathetic and proactive JIAS caseworker produced positive results. Sioma and Rebeka Bialystok's interactions with the social service agency concerning work opportunities yielded less constructive outcomes than Aron's. The Polish survivor couple and their infant son, Franklin, took a circuitous route on their way to Toronto. After purchasing Mexican visas in Lodz, they travelled first to visit with Sioma's brother in Buffalo, New York. When their papers turned out to be phoney and their travel permits came close to expiring, Sioma's brother insisted that the family attempt to enter Canada. Although Rebeka wanted nothing to do with Canada—all she knew was that "it was a very cold country"—a positive meeting with a Canadian immigration officer sealed the family's fate.[41] On 7 April 1948 the Bialystoks arrived in Toronto as contract farmers.

*Official Receipt* № 6559

**CANADIAN JEWISH CONGRESS**
CENTRAL DIVISION   150 BEVERLEY STREET

*re Shanghai Refugees*

TORONTO, *Sept - 16* 194*9*

To *U. J. R. A., Montreal*

Your kind payment of *Forty-Two Sixty-two* XX Dollars
is gratefully acknowledged.     100

$ *4,262* 00

*P. Nichols*
FOR TREASURER

---

*Official Receipt* № 6560

**CANADIAN JEWISH CONGRESS**
CENTRAL DIVISION   150 BEVERLEY STREET

| J.F.+C.S. | 10,000 | Refunds to Tailors | |
| Tailors | 2,000 | for September | 1,300 |
| Furriers | 400 | J.V.S. - | 300 |

TORONTO, *Sept - 16* 194*9*

To *U. J. R. A., Montreal*
*Expenditures for September*

Your kind payment of *Fourteen Thousand* XX Dollars
is gratefully acknowledged.     100

$ *14,000* 00

*P. Nichols*
FOR TREASURER

12. Reimbursement receipt issued by the Canadian Jewish Congress, Central Division, to the United Jewish Relief Agencies, Montreal, for needle-trade workers and Shanghai Jewish refugees' expenditures, 16 September 1949. Courtesy of the Canadian Jewish Congress Charities Committee National Archives.

The couple barely eked out a living in their first year in the country. Sioma went to work as a manual labourer on his sponsor's farm near Hamilton, Ontario, while his wife and son rented a single room in Toronto. In his first position, Sioma performed back-breaking and mediocre work for one dollar a day, and was constantly hungry. His second job—cleaning and preparing a summer camp in Pickering, Ontario, at the rate of twenty-five dollars a week until the camp opened, and fifty dollars a week for the duration of the summer—fared little better. The facility could not accommodate Rebeka and Franklin, so the family rented a room on a nearby Polish-owned farm, paying for two months in advance. The camp directors refused to uphold their promise of a raise, and when the immigration officer visited the site to check on Sioma, the directors arbitrarily fired him without cause. The family forfeited the forty-dollar advance rent paid on the room and returned to Toronto to seek new accommodations and employment opportunities.

Desperate for more suitable working conditions, Sioma turned to JIAS for help. After describing what he regarded as exploitative treatment by his original sponsor and subsequent employers, a JIAS employee offered a disheartening response, as recalled by Rebeka: "You came to work on a farm and if the contract is over you have to find another farm and you have to stay a whole year, otherwise they won't let another Jew to [sic] come to Canada as a farmer."[42] Sioma found work in Niagara-on-the-Lake, Ontario, where he chopped down trees, picked bushels of tomatoes and peaches, and worked in a junkyard for little to no money. After suffering a spinal injury on the job and landing himself in hospital, Rebeka broke down and approached JIAS for the second time. Only then did the agency provide them with one month's rent. Despite future challenges, including debilitating illness and surgeries, the memory of perceived maltreatment by the organized Jewish community deterred the Bialystoks from seeking agency support. Instead, the burgeoning community of *landsmen* from the Zaglembie region to resettle in the Greater Toronto Area helped sustain this survivor immigrant family during their formative years as new Canadians.

### Education and Socialization

For JIAS director Joseph Kage, education and socialization went hand-in-hand. He believed adamantly that education was key to helping transform Holocaust survivors from refugees into informed and productive Canadians. Competency in the country's national languages was of utmost importance. "Language," Kage argued, "is the medium of interaction without which social life could not develop, and is the only effective force in helping the person to become part of a group. Much of the opposition that a newcomer may encounter can be explained by the fact that the old Canadian and the new Canadian cannot understand one another."[43] In Montreal, Toronto, and Winnipeg, JIAS (with the cooperation of provincial school boards) ran language and citizenship classes twice weekly on a year-round basis according to standards set by Canada's Ministries of Immigration and Citizenship and Education. Elsewhere, including Calgary and Winnipeg, Jewish refugees typically attended English-as-a-second-language and citizenship classes through non-sectarian institutions and school boards or at YMCAs and public libraries. Those programs did not cater specifically to survivors, but rather served new Canadians of all faiths and ethnicities.

JIAS evening classes, which were open to all newcomers regardless of age, educational background, or religious affiliation, focused on two specific goals: to teach newcomers basic English skills, as well as basic Canadian history, politics, and citizenship. The assigned texts in the uniform curriculum—"English for Newcomers" (produced by Canada's Ministry of Immigration and Citizenship and used by all ethnic groups across the country) and "History of Canada" (by Kage)—were indicative of the agency's goals. Each school was staffed by certified teachers and the education provided was consonant with students' abilities. Supplementary material on other subjects, such as geography and Jewish studies, was included at instructors' discretion. Above all, the classes tried to transform the survivors into Canadians first, Jews second. Educators believed that indoctrinating newcomers into Canadian customs and languages, and instilling Canadian values, would produce more well-rounded, law-abiding "new Canadians." Instruction and initiation into the Canadian Jewish community constituted a secondary, and private, priority. By the end of 1948, nearly 1,000 newcomers had registered in Montreal JIAS schools; numbers in Toronto were only slightly lower at JIAS and UJRA organized schools. Countless others received unofficial lessons from private teachers within and outside the Jewish community, Canadian-born student tutors and relatives, and on job sites.[44]

While survivors received language and citizenship instruction through JIAS-run evening classes and community-sponsored lectures and events, other venues served to educate and integrate the newcomers as well. Following the belief that "education and assimilability go hand in hand,"[45] Jewish communities organized formal and informal programming that covered a gamut of topics and recreational activities at libraries—most notably Montreal's Jewish Public Library (JPL), Young Men's-Women's Hebrew Associations (YM-WHAs), the Arbeter Ring, and synagogues. Survivors attended lectures on Yiddish poetry, Israel's War of Independence, or *tanach,* or joined in pick-up soccer games. YM-WHAs across the country offered free one-year memberships to all new immigrants. Mary Palevsky, the New York Association for New Americans worker who surveyed the efficiency and effectiveness of Canadian Jewry's response to the newcomers, recognized the value of this free membership. According to her report, "The YMHA has taken cognizance of the need for increased cultural, recreational, and social opportunities for adults. Other agencies have also recognized this need such as the JPL. In the main it is felt that the resources are available and are well-known in the community and it is up to the newcomer to fit in as soon as he is able to join and desirous of doing so."[46] Palevsky also recommended strengthening professional and budgetary resources allocated to gender-specific services, making a strong case for mothers' clubs for education in practical parenting matters such as nutrition, childcare, and budgeting, in addition to unregimented activities for all adults to create lasting ties to the existing community.[47]

Acting on their own agency, displaced persons also frequented established "survivor clubs" like the New World Clubs in Montreal and Toronto; in their rare moments of leisure, survivors across the country convened get-togethers with fellow "greeners" for card playing and to celebrate holidays and special occasions. Others preferred to meet with other newcomers in immigrant hubs, such as on The Main or Plateau in Montreal, and in the Spadina Avenue and College Street neighbourhoods in downtown Toronto. In Winnipeg, survivors found *landsmen* and created social networks in the city's North End, frequenting local restaurants and the nearby Winnipeg Beach; similar initiatives took place in Vancouver. Survivors gossiped about new arrivals, met potential love matches and old friends, and reminisced about the past. Untrusting relationships between refugees and the organized Jewish communal institutions charged with providing professional guidance and information drove many newcomers to seek support though survivor-based networks. These unofficial associations provided practical advice about which businesses were hiring, which stores carried the best (and least expensive) produce, and which landlords would accept families with children. They advised and sought out loans for needy newcomers to obtain "key money" (an exorbitant fee to gain access to rental units charged by landlords) and purchase household goods.

In regions with substantial survivor populations, many newcomers preferred to approach other recent arrivals for ad hoc support, as opposed to relying on what they perceived as unkind or ignorant service organizations. Many of the survivors experienced what they interpreted as rejection when they tried to share stories of their pasts with agency workers and Canadian Jews, and found solace among other newcomers in survivor enclaves who had shared similar pasts.[48] Sioma and Rebeka Bialystok, for one, helped establish the Toronto branch of the Zaglember Society, an organization of survivors from southern Poland. Societies and alternate venues contributed to newcomers' well-being and provided lifelines in a sea of uncertainty and confusion. Fellow survivors—especially the elders among them—represented the last links to refugees' former lives and communities, and provided emotional support and connections for individuals establishing new lives on their own.

There was minimal interaction between survivors and Canadian gentiles, both on personal and social levels. The Canadian populace remained resolute in its anti-immigration attitudes throughout the cessation of the Second World War, likening Jewish refugees as especially abhorrent applicants. Where knowledge of the mass destruction of European Jewry certainly elicited compassion and the liberalization of immigration policy on a bureaucratic level, a long tradition of anti-Semitism and nativist thought proved more difficult to purge. The broader gentile community remained uninterested in newcomers of any background, let alone Jewish, and dealings between the groups were largely limited to business transactions and placements (i.e., National Employment Service and Canadian Pacific Railway) and not socialization. As a result, private, survivor-driven initiatives and official communal organizations became all the more important to successful integration.

The most significant and influential of all infrastructures for survivor integration and reestablishment were *landsmanshaftn*, or mutual benefit and aid societies composed of individuals from a particular city or region in Eastern Europe. Through their shared histories and similar perspectives, society members experienced a sense of comfort and belonging; they also enjoyed interest-free loans, access to physicians and emergency funds, burial plots, and social activity.[49] Like the CJC and community leadership, in addition to international Jewish relief agencies such as the American Joint Distribution Committee, *landsmanshaftn* in Canada raised funds and collected relief packages to send to DP camps in postwar Europe, called on the Canadian government to increase immigration, and arranged affidavits on behalf of those *landsmen* who had survived the Holocaust. Molly Harrendorf Bainerman, a JIAS Toronto employee from 1944 to 1946, recalled working intensively with such groups. One of Harrendorf Bainerman's primary responsibilities involved processing lists of survivors compiled at liberated camps and helping to locate relatives residing in Ontario to facilitate reunions. "Each time I came across a person and their hometown," she said, "I would write to that *landsmanshaft* to tell them there was a survivor from their community. Then, they could either find their relatives—if they had any—or help get them to Canada through another means."[50]

The societies worked diligently to bring survivors to Canada and distribute meagre provisions as per sponsorship arrangements. Among the many sponsored as relatives (irrespective of blood relations) or through employment guarantees were Polish survivors Moniek and Lola Olmer, and their infant daughter Sharon, whose 1948 immigration was facilitated by Toronto's Ostrovtzer Mutual Benefit Society. The Olmers' impression of Canada, and Canadian Jewish society on the whole, was initially grim. "We were not welcomed by [Canadian] Jews; they looked down on us and they called us *greenies*," Lola recalled sixty years after making the journey to her *goldene medina*. "They thought they were better than us, even though their own families had come from the old country just like us.... When my daughter was married into a Canadian Jewish family, the only person to really accept me and make me feel welcome was Jackie [a Canadian-born aunt of Lola's daughter's husband]. Other than her, no one cared."[51]

The only place where the Olmers felt welcome was with the *landsmanshaft*, into which the couple was immediately incorporated.[52] They moved into a room near the Ostrovtzer Synagogue on Cecil Street, in the heart of Toronto's Spadina district and, with other newcomers, became involved in all aspects of Ostrovtzer Society life. According to Bainerman, whose husband belonged to the society and was a distant relative of Lola Olmer, "The whole society became survivors. They gave it life, and helped it last when fewer and fewer Canadians were joining."[53] The Olmers' membership extended throughout their entire lives, their *landsmen* filling the role of missing aunts, uncles, and grandparents for their children.

Although the Canadian Jewish Congress held a great deal of sway over communal Jewish life, *landsmanshaftn* stridently maintained their autonomy. By the late 1940s, nearly fifty such groups were registered with the Societies Division, a body loosely affiliated with the CJC that aspired to operate democratically with representatives from each group, to form policies about societal administration and mutual relations. Formal efforts among the groups to assist survivors coalesced at this level. In February 1949, at an executive meeting of the Societies Division of the CJC, Toronto branch, the "Program to Help Integration of Newcomers into Community" was tabled for consideration. A key recommendation was that all societies, as an extension of their goodwill and compassion, grant free six-month memberships to interested newcomers.[54] Most groups accepted this recommendation.

Abe Zukerman took advantage of the membership opportunity. The sole survivor of his immediate family when he immigrated to Canada at the age of thirty-five, Zukerman was in a self-described fog, his life at a standstill, "half paralyzed by my struggle to survive, and by my constant loneliness."[55] A native of the Polish city of Wierzbnik, Zukerman received an invitation from his *landsleit* at Toronto's Wierzbnik Society. Membership provided him with the social interaction he was missing. But Zukerman's connection to the society was cemented when he joined its *Chevra Kadisha* (burial society): "To me, this was such holy work, so significant—ensuring the proper burial, with dignity and with respect for our laws and traditions. At last no more burnings, no more murders, no more unspeakable indignities that claimed the lives of 6 million of our people. And I was so pleased to participate in such a noble mitzvah."[56] When Abe Zukerman passed away at the age of ninety-five, his obituary noted that he was a "proud senior executive member of the Wierzbniker Society for over fifty years."[57]

*Landsmanshaftn* capitalized on newcomers' talents and experiences by including them in organizational programming.[58] Lawyer Emil Kingsley had escaped Nazi occupation to serve in the Polish army-in-exile. In postwar Toronto, Kingsley—now an affiliate with the law firm Rosenberg & Smith—expressed his willingness to address societies and share his experiences of life under the Nazis and as a soldier stationed in the Middle East. An announcement at an executive meeting of the CJC's Societies Division noted that Kingsley was "thoroughly informed on European Jewish affairs and fluent in Yiddish and English," and that Canadian Jews would benefit from his insight.[59] B'nai Brith lodges in Toronto and Vancouver were among the community organizations that took the veteran up on his offer. Kingsley was particularly active in B'nai Brith's Lion's Gate Vancouver Lodge 668, which he joined, and to which he offered his legal expertise and wartime recollections from 1948 to 1951, when he relocated to the United States.[60]

Artist survivors also drew the attention of societies. Painter Henry Weingluck was a prominent artist in interwar Europe whose Jewish-themed works had been displayed across the continent. After surviving both the German occupation of France and imprisonment in eight concentration camps, Weingluck joined a surviving brother in Canada.[61] Soon after arrival, the young artist was approached by the Societies Division to arrange for an exhibition of his art in Toronto in 1948; later, the CJC helped orchestrate a national tour.[62] Weingluck married a Canadian Jewish woman in 1950, and together they opened and operated Weingluck's Art Gallery in Toronto's downtown core. To fulfil his spiritual needs, he became an official at Congregation Habonim, a liberal synagogue established in Toronto by central European survivors, serving as its Torah reader and second cantor.[63] The combination of spiritual- and ethnic-based communities served to blend Weingluck's dual position as a displaced Holocaust survivor as well as a Canadian Jew, making artistic and spiritual contributions to his adopted homeland.

On the whole, survivors' early experiences of Canada and their new lives were mixed. The process of integration began with a rocky start for Miss Y, a single female sponsored to work in the needle trade. Shortly after arriving in Montreal, Miss Y fell into a deep depression and lost her job, placing her in the dangerous position of possibly having her visa withdrawn. To avoid this fate, JIAS reviewed its Volunteer Case-work Aid Committee and selected a suitable volunteer to support the agency's plan of treatment for the young woman. According to the *JIAS Record*, the National Council of Jewish Women volunteer was a "mature, sympathetic, warm-hearted person, well established in the community with a European background and a knowledge of languages."[64] The two women forged a mother-daughter-like bond. Through the volunteer worker's vested interest and wide network of contacts, Miss Y went on to secure permanent work in a Montreal office, and begin to rebuild a meaningful life in her adopted country.

Where Miss Y experienced grave uncertainty during her initial period of acclimatization, others, like Polish survivor Joseph Riesenbach, recalled feeling absolute joy: "When I arrived in Canada, I kissed the ground. I knew I was a free man, a free person, and that the opportunity was there. Whatever happened, at least I was safe."[65] The Riesenbach family, consisting of parents, two daughters, and one son, Joseph, originated in a large village in Galicia (interwar Polish territory) where they owned three plots of land (which provided them with much of their sustenance) and a small, successful business run out of their home. In the spring of 1943, two local Polish police officers warned the family of an *aktion* (an "action," an organized round-up by the Nazis or their collaborators and mass arrest in public spaces that usually transported Jews to concentration camps or death) and recommended that they abandon their home. Mr. Riesenbach buried their Torah at once and the family of five fled. They spent six weeks hiding in open fields and ditches before finding safe haven with a tiny, devout Catholic woman, Julia Barr, her husband Joseph, and daughter, Janina. For the next two years, the Riesenbachs resided in the Barrs' attic, with Joseph, a member of the Polish underground, keeping them abreast of the war's progress. Liberated in 1945, they recovered the Torah and made their way to the DP camp at Linz, Austria.

The Riesenbachs hoped to join relatives in the United States or Argentina. When those plans did not materialize, all hopes turned to a gentile acquaintance from interwar Poland who now operated a farm outside of Winnipeg. He agreed to sponsor the family as agricultural labourers. Distant relatives of the Riesenbachs already in Canada, who were unable to act as sponsors as a result of conflicting obligations, helped finance their costly transportation. On the eve of Yom Kippur, 10 October 1948, the Riesenbachs began their lives anew in Winnipeg. The refugees zealously leapt into the workforce. "After the yom tovim," Joseph recalled, "I immediately went to work in a candy store. My parents and older sister found jobs in garment factories and my younger sister went to school. I had several different jobs over the next few years and later went into the cattle business with my father."[66]

At the candy store, Joseph worked under a foreman, whom he described as "a mean character who did not care much about the newcomers, but was ready to take advantage of them."[67] When Joseph complained to the owner, one Mr.

Schwartz, a Canadian Jew, about the foreman's mistreatment of the newcomers, the young man was removed from the post and placed on a machine. In his
second job at a fur factory, Joseph struggled to breathe amidst all the animal hair.
The Riesenbach men's venture into cattle trading (a popular profession among
new immigrants to western Canada) was initiated in response to the poor opportunities for fair employment in Winnipeg. They purchased a truck with financing
from a Canadian-born Jew, Mr. Levine of Globe Motors. Joseph attested to
Levine's character, remembering him as "a true friend of survivors, unlike most
'Aboriginal Jews'"—who had themselves been in Canada for perhaps only one
generation longer than the new immigrants, "who were [purportedly] jealous of
the [older] immigrants' achievements." With his assistance, the senior Riesenbach
attempted to carve out a niche in the cattle trade.[68] Despite their experience with
livestock, the initiative collapsed within a year and a half. Joseph then embarked
on a journey of self-discovery. After a short stint in Toronto, he returned to Winnipeg and in 1952 married the Canadian-born Ruth. With loans from a cousin,
they purchased a grocery store, and raised three children.

The process toward integration came about with minimal turmoil and distress for the Riesenbachs. Although they were not immune to exploitation, and
initially struggled with work, they were fortunate to arrive through a sponsoring
acquaintance and a handful of relatives, both survivors and established Canadians, who were ready and willing to help the family get their feet on the ground.
Joseph and the older of his sisters took evening classes at St. John's High School in
Winnipeg's North End, and they quickly learned English. They, in turn, taught
their parents the particularities of the English language, thus helping to ease the
path toward social and cultural integration and confidence. Their resettlement
experience represents a true success story made possible through the support of
multiple parties, including relatives, Canadian-born colleagues and friends, and
the educational system.

Others' memories were less positive. In close relatives sponsorships, relatives (and those posing as such) provided the necessary paperwork and funds
for survivors to immigrate to Canada. However, in many cases the parties
were complete strangers in all but name, with those in Canada determined
to help the surviving remnants of their extended families leave Europe. Their
well-intended actions were driven by conflicting, often overlapping, motiva-
tions. These included humanitarian inclinations to help their relatives rebuild
their lives in a free country, and a sense of responsibility and powerlessness
at not having been able to rescue them before the Shoah. Many Canadian
Jews showed genuine interest in their survivor relatives, and tended to their

physical well-being. Still, like much of the population, they showed little interest in hearing about, or the ability to holistically comprehend, the survivors' experiences during the war. This reluctance of even close family members to listen had less to do with insensitivity on the part of Canadian relatives and more to do with a misguided sense of protecting the newcomers from reliving their trauma.[69] Inviting conversations about wartime suffering necessitated Canadian Jews' willingness to bear witness to memories of mass violence, and learn about the fates of murdered relatives and *landsmen*. Even the most caring and compassionate among the Canadian sponsors were recalled by newcomers and Canadians alike as ill-prepared to handle intimate details. A misguided assumption that survivors' silence was indicative of moving onward and upward trumped dialogue that might have, in actuality, prompted emotional healing. Meaningful and open conversations between survivors and their Canadian hosts about the Holocaust typically occurred only after the advent of the Holocaust as a topic of public consciousness from the 1960s forward. Until then, polite, socially acceptable encounters were absent from most wartime narratives.

Other relatives possessed no such social graces. While prepared to sponsor survivors, some people harboured no desire to greet or show compassion toward their relatives upon their arrival. Pola C and her family (husband and two children) were confronted with such a response. "When we got to Toronto, my uncle was there, my auntie was there, and two daughters [resided in the city]. I was thinking, at least they're going to give us a night to sleep over," Pola remembered. "At the station my uncle was not there, my auntie was not there, my cousins, maybe they were scared they'd have to take us to sleep over."[70] The refugee family spent the few dollars they had on a taxi to drive them to their sponsors' home. When they arrived to an empty house and locked door, a neighbour informed them that the family was on vacation in Florida and would not return for two weeks. The newcomers thus turned to JIAS, which placed them in one room of a CJC-owned rooming house with four other families. The couple scrimped and saved, purchasing a house on Euclid Street in 1951; they rented nearly every room to boarders.

The survivor family felt deeply affected by what could only be understood as their relatives' rejection of them. They were disappointed at their relatives' refusal to assist them (as per the terms of their sponsorship contract) by accommodating them, helping them find work, and providing maintenance until they could get on their feet. But Pola C was most upset by her relatives' utter lack of interest in the emotional well-being of her and her family, the sole survivors of the Holocaust from a once large family. The Canadian relatives, who had immigrated during the interwar period, never once asked about their murdered loved ones, or seemed to consider the grave importance the surviving remnant placed on familial ties for support and belonging. Faced with this perceived lack of compassion on the part of even their closest relatives, many survivors reluctantly entered a cone of silence about their wartime experiences.[71]

Perceived ignorance and a lack of interest among Canadian Jews was not limited to the familial sphere. A Hungarian survivor of several concentration camps, Judy Weissenberg Cohen was nineteen years old when she and her older sister Eva arrived at Halifax's Pier 21 on 10 June 1948, with no more than a few family pictures and the clothes they wore. They spoke no English but a little French and settled promptly in Montreal. Weissenberg Cohen described everything as a bitter struggle to be endured without any guidance or compassion from the Jewish community beyond the payment of their first month's rent. Both sisters believed that the Organization for Rehabilitation through Training (ORT) professional certifications that they had earned in the DP camps would make them valuable employees in Canada's booming economy, thus facilitating swift integration into their new community. "I planned on gaining employment as a [dental] technician," she recalled, "and was upset to learn that I could not work in Quebec in that medium for five years. That was the law."[72] So instead, the girls each bought one cotton dress in an attempt to look right, and went out to find work: "My first job in Montreal was in the garment industry, alongside many other immigrants lacking the necessary language skills to gain better employment. I was a terrible dressmaker earning eight dollars a week. In an attempt to normalize my life, I enrolled in the free English classes offered by the Jewish community, and learned French by working with the French Canadians. By that August, Eva and I had saved enough money to buy material to make new skirts. That was an exciting day!"[73]

The next few years were a blur for Weissenberg Cohen, filled with seemingly endless work and evening classes, followed by college education. Young and healthy, the sisters were not afraid of hard work and picked up English fairly quickly, made friends, and came to see themselves as truly Canadian. But despite her self-confidence, linguistic abilities (which enabled her to cross over into "non-survivor" society, as compared to survivors who did not have the time or the capacity to learn the local vernacular), and strong work ethic, Weissenberg Cohen felt wholly unwelcome by many Canadian Jews and communal agencies. It would take the renewed threat of neo-Nazism for the Hungarian Jewish émigrée to carve out her place in Jewish organizational life.[74]

Newcomers to Canada's Pacific Rim faced their own challenges. David S fled his Polish hometown with two older brothers at the first signs of fighting and headed east. When they reached Russian territory, the three young men faced deportation to a Siberian labour camp, followed by three years on a collective farm near the Soviet-Iranian border. At war's end, the brothers returned to Poland and learned of their extended family's demise at the Sobibor death camp. Hoping to leave Europe as quickly as possible, they moved on: his elder brothers married and settled in a DP camp, while David became a self-supporting player on Munich's lucrative black market.

Eager to create a new life in a free country, David applied for entry visas everywhere. While he supported the creation of a Jewish state, illegal immigration to the nascent state of Israel was not on the table. "I knew the minute I got off the boat, they'd put me in a [military] uniform," David recalled decades later. "So I figured I went through all this war without a uniform…. I had enough of war. [Instead] Canada, to me at that time, was the greatest democracy in the world."[75] The country's small population but vast landmass, and especially the moderate west-coast climate, greatly impressed the young man. Even a disappointing meeting with the Canadian Consulate—where the officer rudely vocalized his doubts about the refugee's farming experience—and failure to secure legitimate immigration papers did not deter David's plans. Instead, he assumed the identity, and paperwork, of one survivor's brother, a former acquaintance, who died before his papers came through.[76] Using these falsified papers, David travelled to Vancouver via Halifax in March 1949. Immediately upon arrival, the CJC arranged temporary lodging at an old-age home. Jewish community representatives also secured employment for David, first as an apprentice tailor and later a machine operator. The single man performed poorly at each placement and disliked the work. In addition, Vancouver's moderate climate and attractive scenery failed to make up for its small-town feel and the insensitivity demonstrated by numerous members of the local Jewish community who questioned his knowledge of basic hygiene and frowned upon his limited formal education. These factors, coupled with limited opportunities for professional growth, led David to investigate the possibility of returning to Europe. Instead, David remained in Vancouver, married a Canadian Jew, and later owned and operated several businesses. While memories of the early ostracism he faced in Vancouver never disappeared, David established himself as a community leader and active member of BC Jewish life, supporting the very agencies responsible for his less-than-ideal resettlement process.

---

Holocaust survivors who came to Canada between 1947 and 1950 were the beneficiaries of amendments to the strict and discriminatory immigration policy that had previously restricted the entry of desperate European Jewish refugees seeking asylum in the critical period from 1933 to 1947. This group constituted the first significant movement of Jewish immigration to the country since the 1920s. The newcomers appeared superficially to be a monolithic group. Predominantly young, enthusiastic, and either not married or a member of a small, nascent family unit, the wave closely mirrored the population of survivors in DP camps. This was especially true for survivors included on garment industry and labour schemes; those who arrived via close relatives sponsorship were a slightly more diverse group. Irrespective of country of origin, wartime experiences or family status, all refugees were subjected to stringent Canadian government health, skill, and security screening processes before acquiring entry visas.

Life in postwar Canada represented a period of transition and change. While freed from DP camps and dependence on refugee relief organizations, the survivors' recent experiences of trauma and loss remained fresh and did not disappear on their transatlantic journey. Many hoped that abandoning Europe would help them escape their memories, but this was far from the case. And although emotional currents and despair about the Holocaust, destruction of their homes, and their pre-war lives ran high, such topics typically remained reserved for discussion among survivors. The newcomers believed that Canadian Jews were uninterested in the plight of European Jews or lacked any comprehension as to the magnitude of the tragedy they had so recently endured. Yet, it was these same Canadian Jews who shouldered responsibility for bringing the surviving remnant out of postwar Europe and providing them with housing and maintenance. With minimal comprehension of survivors' scope of suffering, but with good intentions, communal agencies aided refugee resettlement and employment placements. Their efforts met with varying degrees of success.

In addition to their lingering physical ailments and post-traumatic psychological disorders, new Canadians were expected to adapt readily to their environs and fit into the existing Jewish communities. They were required to attain language proficiency, obtain permanent housing, and become financially self-sufficient as quickly as possible. Survivors relied heavily on formal networks like JIAS for English and citizenship classes and job referrals, and on the JVS, as well as the COGC, NES, and informal personal contacts, for job placement. Housing posed a major challenge, and placement arrangements fell to the CJC, JIAS, volunteer organizations, and relatives and friends of the newcomers. Socialization, an equally important factor in survivors' integration processes, took place on several levels. *Landsmanshaftn* helped to establish a sense of belonging among those from similar geographic regions, and filled voids of family and community in the survivors' lives. New World Clubs and like-minded institutions fulfilled similar purposes.

In spite of this movement's homogeneous surface appearance, survivors in fact represented nearly all European nations, educational and professional backgrounds, and degrees of religious observance. The following chapters illuminate some of these diversifying factors, beginning with an analysis of the "war orphans" who arrived in Canada as part of this initial wave of immigration.

CHAPTER THREE

# THE WAR ORPHANS PROJECT

Fifteen-year-old Budapest native Zsuzanna Loeffler arrived in Canada in August 1948 with great expectations. Zsuzanna hoped to continue her education, establish meaningful relationships, and experience arts and culture. Such hopes were seemingly dashed, however, upon her placement in Vegreville, Alberta, a rural farming community. In a diary entry of October 1948, Zsuzanna—now known by the anglicized "Susan"—wrote out her frustrations: "How I hate to be here! How I hate everybody! Did I give up my life at home to come here? I wanted change, adventure and I am here in this awfulness. I want so much to do something, to be somebody, to travel, to see different things, to live a colourful life.... Should I spend my whole life here? I cannot imagine living such a vacant, barren life as most people seem to: live, work, struggle, marry; some may succeed acquiring certain things grinding up their youth doing it. I don't want such a life, I don't."[1]

A participant in the War Orphans Project and a ward of the Canadian Jewish Congress (CJC), Susan had no say in choosing her new home. On the surface, the conditions were relatively good. Unlike many of her contemporaries, she lived in a private home with foster parents who genuinely cared about her well-being. The Kleins, a middle-aged couple with two adult sons no longer living at home, also supported their foster daughter's schooling. Susan tried to settle into her new environs and build a life for herself in what she described as "cow country."[2] But, beneath the surface, the situation was far from idyllic. Only a few Jewish families lived in the town, which was bereft of any other Jewish girls, and there were no Hungarian speakers of any faith. Although the Kleins treated her kindly and with genuine affection, Susan could not envision a future for herself in such a place.

This chapter tells the history of the 1,123 youth who arrived in Canada under the aegis of the CJC-administered and government-of-Canada-approved War Orphans Project. These youngsters typically lacked the guidance of a caring and knowledgeable adult to advocate on their behalf in immediate postwar Europe and, frequently, in new Canadian homes. All had experienced the interruption of their education and the destruction of their pre-war European homes. Children

13. Susan Garfield in Vegreville, Alberta, 1948. Courtesy of Susan Garfield.

witnessed and endured frightening and incomprehensible violence without the
benefit of emotional and physical maturity, or even a basic understanding of
their situations. Some parents, recognizing the magnitude of the situation, had
given up their children to non-Jews in hope of their protection. Other youngsters
were ripped from their parents during round-ups or selections while still other
children took the initiative to escape from incarceration and survived for years
on their wits and good fortune. But irrespective of individual circumstances, all
orphans had lost loved ones and years of their lives to the Holocaust and early
postwar period as they awaited their next move.[3]

Seemingly insurmountable challenges affected the youngsters, aged eighteen
years and under, before even docking on Canadian soil. Few possessed the necessary paperwork, including birth certificates, to immigrate, let alone knew where to
go in order to move forward. Many could not remember identifying details about
their early lives, including the possible existence of relatives living overseas. The
added burden of providing proof of their parents' deaths proved nearly impossible.
And yet, more than 1,000 youth made it to Canada, and started new lives.

The War Orphans Project has been brought to light in two reports prepared
decades apart by two Canadian Jewish social workers, Ben Lappin and Fraidie
Martz. Approaching the subject from different perspectives, both research accounts followed the movement from its inception through to the orphans' eventual rehabilitation.[4] Himself an active caseworker who encountered members of
this survivor cohort in the early postwar years, Lappin's research delved deep into
organizational patterns of resettlement, especially among Toronto youth, while
Martz focused on the orphans' long-term integration. With respect to these
works, this chapter deals with the immediate issues of orphan integration and
adaptation into Canadian Jewish society in the decade following the youths'
arrival. The discussion will address settlement issues through the lens of gender,
geography, and religious observance.

## The Long Road to Freedom

Planning for the War Orphans Project began prior to the Second World War
with the CJC and Jewish communal leaderships' struggles to circumvent stringent Canadian immigration regulations and rescue Jewish children caught under
the snare of Nazi occupation. The impetus for rescue grew exponentially with the
outbreak of war. On 2 October 1942, Director Frederick C. Blair of the Department of Mines and Resources (the predecessor to the Ministry of Citizenship and
Immigration) reluctantly granted permission for 500 Jewish children to enter
Canada via Vichy France via Order-in-Council 1647. Canadian Jewry needed to

provide guarantees for the youngsters' upkeep and locate child-welfare-agency-approved foster homes. Fearful that adult relatives might wish to join their children in Canada after the war, only orphaned children of deportees, between two and fifteen years of age, were eligible for inclusion. If everything ran smoothly, an additional 500 youngsters would be able to immigrate at a later date.[5] But the Allies' invasion of Vichy North Africa in November 1942 halted the mission.[6] None of the children slated for rescue survived.

Nearly five years later, on 29 April 1947, Order-in-Council 1647—the order created five years earlier calling for the rescue of Jewish orphans to Canada—was represented in Parliament and moved by the recently established Ministry of Immigration and Citizenship at the behest of Canadian Jewish leadership.[7] O.I.C. 1647's passing signified Canada's move toward the liberalization of its immigration laws, and the country's first major initiative in helping to relieve the Jewish refugee crisis plaguing postwar Europe.[8] The project's conditions were expanded to include orphans up to age eighteen, and 1,000 visas would be granted at once. The CJC and UNRRA assigned three field workers already involved

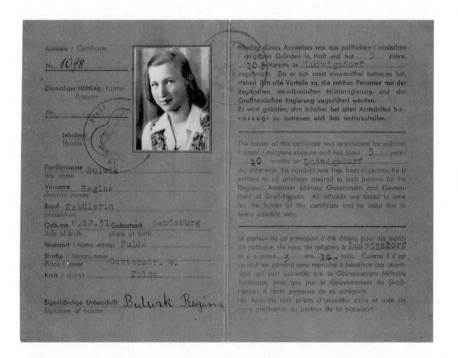

14. Identification card issued to Regina Feldman (née Bulwik) while at Fulda Displaced Persons Camp, 1946. Courtesy of the Vancouver Holocaust Education Centre Archives, Regina Feldman Collection.

with Canadian Jewish communal agencies—Ethel Ostry, Lottie Levinson, and Manfred Saalheimer—the task of seeking out, interviewing, and registering orphaned survivors. Ostry and Levinson, natives of Winnipeg and Vancouver, respectively, received training in social service skills and international development from UNRRA prior to their appointment. Saalheimer, a German Jewish refugee and trained lawyer, had been interned first as a prisoner of war in Britain and later transported to Canada as an "enemy alien," or potential fifth columnist, in 1940. After three years of internment, Saalheimer was released into the custody of Montreal's organized Jewish community. His professional achievements recognized, Saalheimer held various administrative roles in the CJC from 1943 onward. A fourth field worker, Holocaust survivor Greta Fischer, was added to the roster at a later date.[9]

The field workers communicated constantly with their Canadian colleagues and reported on conditions in Europe, the selection centres, and on the Orphans Project applicants.[10] The CJC and UNRRA workers' hopes of finding thousands of young orphans were quickly dashed with news that 1.5 million Jewish children had brutally lost their lives at the hands of Nazi oppressors. Armed with this knowledge and more realistic expectations, Ostry and her colleagues focused on improving the conditions of the few surviving youth by moving them to orphanages and rehabilitation centres in hopes of helping to create stable, secure environs, as well as a return to previously disrupted schooling, as soon as possible.[11] The earlier the youth returned to some sense of normalcy, the better their chance of regaining healthy social tropes and behaviours. One adjustment demanded that the age of inclusion be raised from fifteen to eighteen years in light of the fact that so few "children" survived the Holocaust. Child survivors had to meet several requirements to qualify. Youth needed to prove their status as a "complete orphan" under the age of eighteen. This constituted a daunting task and a seemingly impossible challenge. In the chaos of postwar Europe, international refugee workers helped youngsters try to locate surviving relatives or witnesses who could corroborate their claims of orphanhood and age. A deficit of documentation, such as birth certificates, particularly for youth born in postwar communist countries, made proof of age and orphaned status nearly impossible.[12] Other survivors provided testimony, claiming to have witnessed the murder of X's parents, or have celebrated Y's *bris* (ritual circumcision) fourteen years earlier.

The youth also needed to endure intensive physical examinations and meet with psychiatrists. Stringent health regulations and imperfect examination techniques and equipment caused many problems. Alex (Sruli) Berkowits, a teenager from Sighet, Romania (present-day Sighetu Marmatlei, Romania), a town of

10,000 in a disputed region of Transylvania, learned these lessons the hard way. During the Second World War, Sighet fell under Hungarian administration. In the spring of 1944, Alex and his large family were deported to Auschwitz. One year, two concentration camps, and a death march later, fifteen-year-old Alex was liberated at Buchenwald. After briefly returning to Sighet with three surviving brothers, the four young men evaluated their options. One brother, Joseph, insisted on moving to Palestine. Alex, along with his brothers Meyer and Morris, registered for the War Orphans Project. Having fabricated their documents to alter their names and shave years off their true ages, Meyer and Morris successfully joined an early transport for Canada in late 1947. The young men were among the first war orphans resettled in Winnipeg.

Alex's plans to immigrate with his brothers were thwarted by X-rays that indicated a spot on his lungs. A relatively healthy and strong young man who displayed no outward signs of illness or physical trauma despite a year in concentration camps, Alex fought for his case to be reconsidered. In an attempt to leave Europe at any cost, he applied for a visa to the United States, but citing his "medical condition," his application was denied. Months and multiple tests later, taken only at his insistence, Alex was declared healthy. The authorizing physician admitted that there had been no spot on his lung, but rather a blemish on the screen. Only then, on 23 June 1948, was Alex permitted to join his brothers in Winnipeg.[13] Until his death in 2013, Alex lamented how faulty equipment nearly cost him his freedom. He never received an apology for the error.

Workers charged with identifying, interviewing, and processing the paperwork for project participants needed often to make judgment calls, particularly around the issue of age. Hungarian concentration camp survivor Leslie Spiro was twenty years old when he immigrated to Canada in 1948. Spiro felt that his chances of receiving a quota number as an adult male would be slim and he would do anything to leave Europe. "I just couldn't wait any longer to immigrate," he remembered more than sixty years later. "I had no chance to go to the United States, so when I heard that Canada was letting in war orphans I just made myself three years younger. I had no original papers and dead parents, so they couldn't prove I wasn't eighteen." Many others followed suit. Therefore, although all orphans were, on paper, eighteen years of age or younger, many were in fact substantially older.[14]

A further complication in the recruitment process involved international rescue organizations competing for surviving children. Zionist movements holding the belief that all orphaned youth should make their new homes in Palestine were especially aggressive in the battle for the young souls. Between 1945 and

## FORM TO BE USED IN REFERRING UNACCOMPANIED CHILDREN
## FOR IMMIGRATION TO CANADA

CANADIAN JEWISH CONGRESS
MONTREAL, CANADA

**CHILD**

Family Name  BERKOWITZ                    Name      Sruli

Any other Names    none                   Sex       Male

Date of birth   11 May 1930               Place of birth    Ukliva, Czechoslov.

Nationality  Czech Jew                    Religion  Hebrew

Present Address  Intern.Childr.Center
IRO Team 1069 Prien       Since when    12 Sept. 1946

Last Address in country of origin prior to displacement    Marmaros-Sziget, Hungary

Permanent Address prior to displacement        Marmaros-Sziget, Hungary

Languages spoken by child   Yiddish, German, Hungarian, Roumanian

**MOTHER**

Family Name     does not know        Name    Hanna

Date of birth   1893                 Place of birth   Budust, Roumania

Nationality Roumanian Jewish    Religion   Hebrew      Occupation Housewife

Address prior to displacement  Ukliva,Czech.Date   June 1944

Date and place last heard from    Birkenau, Germany, June 1944

**FATHER**

Family Name   B e r k o w i t z     Name    David

Date of birth       1893            Place of birth   Krösenest, Roumania

Nationality Roumanian Jew       Religion   Hebrew     Occupation   merchant

Address prior to displacement Ukliva, Czech.Date   June 1944

Date and place last heard from    September 1944 in Buna

15. Immigration declaration issued to Alex (Sruli) Berkowits, c. 1946. Courtesy of the Berkowits family.

1953, 29,447 juvenile survivors orphans did immigrate to Israel.[15] But among the teenagers, many chose instead to re-establish lives in a safe and secure Canada, far away from both the European continent and the looming threat of war in then-mandatory Palestine.

The first transport of twenty war orphans (sixteen boys, four girls) docked at Halifax's Pier 21 on 15 September 1947. Ranging in age from eleven to eighteen, these youngsters experienced a warm welcome to Canada, as excited members of the local and national Jewish communities greeted them. Including the final movement of youth on 10 March 1952, an additional 1,103 war orphans would arrive. Polish and Hungarian orphans constituted the majority of the group, comprising approximately two-thirds males and one-third females. Only 106 were under the age of fourteen; most, like Alex Berkowits, were between sixteen and eighteen years of age. The youth came from farms in Sub-Carpathian Rus (an ethnically diverse and contested region in present-day Ukraine), cosmopolitan Vienna, Austria, and Polish shtetls, from both rich and poor pre-war homes. Some had been raised with Hassidic traditions while others professed no knowledge of Judaism. Educational backgrounds varied among the orphans, and were closely correlated with country of origin.[16] They experienced the Holocaust years in different ways, too. Teenagers from Hungary, whose country did not fall to the Germans until 1944, usually had more years of schooling than did Poles, whose opportunities were crushed as early as fall 1939.[17]

Social worker Joseph Lazarus outlined three distinct groups of war orphans:

The first and largest group included those 16.5 years of age and over. Most members of this subgroup turned—and were turned by their hosts—to industry immediately upon arrival with a view to their becoming self-supporting as soon as possible. To encourage their integration and acclimatization into Canadian ways, English and citizenship classes were organized and conducted two evenings a week under the supervision of trained educators and support personnel.

The second group, representing those under the age of 16.5 years, were directed into the public school system. Of these, approximately half received placement in free foster homes.

The third and least populous group, those over 16.5 who, by reason of their exceptional intelligence and educational background, were found to be fit for advanced studies, entered into the upper years of high school and received monetary assistance to remain out of the workforce through to matriculation. Of this cohort, a handful registered at universities with agency support.[18]

Decisions about schooling for orphans older than sixteen years were made by a CJC education committee. Orphans interested in continuing their studies were interviewed to ascertain their academic status (loosely identified as "intelligence"), informal education, and aspirations. Those deemed prime candidates were granted scholarships. All others were referred to the JVS for employment training and work placement. The costs associated with high school and post-secondary education prohibited most orphans from immediately undertaking schooling. But this did not stop them from wishing, and even demanding, that the Jewish community responsible for their upkeep pay greater attention to their educational and skill-training opportunities.[19]

Entirely different issues emerged among the younger, primary-school-aged orphans of the Holocaust who had been brought to Canada, and who were the most sought-after and desirable because they were seen as adoption prospects. In cities large and small, Jewish women's organizations took initiative and worked in cooperation with the CJC and UJRA to meet the needs of the incoming youth by identifying foster homes. The Emergency Homefinding Committee in Montreal stressed the importance of home placements. Comprising women from various local organizations, the committee published a May 1948 memo to the following effect: feelings of belonging and acceptance, and the knowledge that somebody cared for them, would make orphans' day-to-day problems easier to bear—"It is not a roof, a bed, a chest of drawers we want, we want a heart, a warm atmosphere, and small things that make up for a family."[20]

As volunteer home finders, women received explicit instructions on how to proceed with potential home placements. Decrees of the following nature were issued to gain popular support:

> Efforts should be made to elicit interest and response to this project. A woman should discuss with her husband their mutual interest and desire to take a youth into their home. At the point where a positive interest is shown by the prospective family, this family should be notified that they will hear from the agency's home finder.... At the point where the home is approved and a particular youth suggested for placement in it, both the family and the youth will be brought together in a natural, informal way to give each of them the opportunity of making a voluntary decision.[21]

Likewise, the women were encouraged to lead by example, welcoming into their own homes newcomers—both orphans and adult survivors. Few in number, children under the age of ten garnered the most excitement among potential foster families. In these rare instances, placement arrangements often preceded the young refugees' arrival in Canada. Interest in opening the floodgates to teenaged males proved the least popular.

The majority of the youth landed in the large cities of Montreal, Toronto, and Winnipeg, although others were spread across the country. Multiple factors influenced newcomer youths' initial postwar experiences in Canada, the first and most obvious of which was their home placement and the receptiveness of their foster family. Two types of receiving homes existed: "free" homes, where foster parents received minimal or no financial support from social service agencies; and "paid" homes and boarding houses, where primarily older male orphans lived as roomers and maintained little to no relationship with their landlord beyond taking their meals together.

The outcome of the different living conditions varied greatly. Youth placed in free homes, who received more positive welcomes from patient foster parents desirous of helping them rehabilitate, fared better than older youths resettled into highly subsidized homes, who often shared their abodes with other teenaged or adult survivors. Although war orphans routinely defied authority and were emotionally distant and unprepared for familial warmth expressed by foster parents and siblings, these placements in caring home environments nevertheless introduced them to Canadian cultural values and norms, the English language and, often, employment opportunities. Resistance to authority stemmed from their wartime experiences of chaos, violence, and self-reliance. After years of living outside of a family unit, older youth were unaccustomed to social norms and behaviours, including respect for elders and household rules like curfews. Many of the young men (and, to a lesser extent, women), having forged their documents to lower their ages, were in fact adults, and expected to be treated as such.[22]

The process of finding security in expressing healthy emotions and developing trusting, let alone loving, relationships was long and arduous, and tried the patience of both the orphans and their hosts. Home placements routinely collapsed. Despite good intentions, Canadian Jews were wholly unprepared for their house guests, and could not comprehend the trauma these youngsters had experienced during the war, leading to prolonged confusion and a lack of stability in orphans' lives.

A number of factors influenced the ease of the youths' integration into Canadian Jewish society. Aside from the immediate need for food and shelter, education was the single most important factor. Depending on communal settings and available resources, education was available both in terms of full-day schooling and evening classes, as well as through more informal programming by local YM-WHAs and other community agencies. Montreal offered the best system of formal and informal education via the JPL and the YM-YWHA, and thousands of adult and youth survivors took advantage of the waived membership dues for newcomers and wide range of programming in a variety of languages. In this large Jewish metropolis, a small group of survivor youth established a short-lived newsletter, *The New Life*, chronicling their feelings and experiences in postwar Canada and following the newly formed State of Israel.[23] Youth also attended public dances, joined sports leagues, and participated in Zionist activities.[24]

Another element critical to the integration process was work. Employment resources and counselling, the chance to utilize skills acquired in postwar DP camps, and the presence of open-minded employers willing to teach trades to the (primarily male) youth influenced success for the orphans' cohort in the labour market. The ability to preserve preferred life structures (i.e., religious observance), participate in social and cultural activities, and enjoy a supportive peer network also helped determine orphans' comfort and security in their place of settlement. Finally, individual personalities, specifically the openness toward interaction with survivors and, even more important for language and social acculturation, non-survivors (and vice versa), as well as positive attitudes toward their new homes, each played a substantial role in influencing the ultimate success of a youth's placement.

War orphans were not evenly dispersed across the country. The Maritime provinces received few orphans due to the smaller size of the region's Jewish communities. But the limited number of foster homes and employment opportunities did not diminish local groups' efforts to make the youths feel comfortable and secure. Canadian Jewish women took the lead in placing orphans. In Nova Scotia, Hadassah-WIZO and Council of Jewish Women, with the support of local synagogue sisterhoods, campaigned on behalf of education. The small size of the Atlantic Jewish communities did not permit formal JIAS assistance for evening classes. Therefore the groups relied upon local community members to donate supplies and space, and for teachers to provide lessons pro bono. The Nova Scotia school board offered assistance to finance and staff English language classes as well as private tutoring.

The women's groups ran fundraising events to support the orphans' involvement in the arts. Social interaction with Canadian-born youngsters also took priority in the Maritimes. Community leader Ethel Webber wrote to the CJC's Manfred Saalheimer frequently between 1948 and 1950 to report on the orphans' progress. In one letter (dated 7 July 1948) she highlighted the activities of the fifteen orphans settled in Sydney and Glace Bay, Nova Scotia. "To supplement their so-called formal education, we enlisted the help of teen-agers in the district. Each 'new Canadian' was contacted by a young girl and boy who arranged an hour or two each week when they could help them with their English. Our own children know that these contacts are to serve a two-fold purpose—to help in their studies and to provide social contacts. In some cases this is working out very nicely."[25] Mrs. Webber expressed confidence that this approach would render positive results in orphan satisfaction and acculturation into their eastern homesteads.

However welcoming Maritimes Jewry might have been, its efforts to integrate the orphans permanently usually faltered. Most of the youngsters felt stifled by the limited opportunities for growth in the small and geographically isolated communities. Polish survivor Roman (Rubin) Zeigler arrived in Sydney, Nova Scotia in 1948 and was placed with a foster family. The family did not hope to gain a son; rather, they accepted him in order to "save a child and do their duty."[26] Although no strong emotional ties developed between Ziegler and his foster parents, his living and working conditions (in the family's wholesale grocery), as well as private English lessons twice weekly, were conducive to his swift and thorough integration into Canadian society. "I learned the language quickly, and was even offered the chance to go to high school and university from Mrs. Spencer, my teacher and a member of the 'Ladies of the Empire' club," Ziegler recalled. "They offered to send me to school but it was unthinkable where I was coming from [Poland] for a Jewish boy to accept charity from Christians."[27] But Roman Ziegler found Sydney, Nova Scotia, to be too reminiscent of Dabrowa, Poland, his "backward" hometown, and left for Toronto in 1949.

Not one effort at war orphan placement worked out in Sydney. Saalheimer blamed this failure not on organizational efforts or even the youth themselves. Rather, the limiting size of the local Jewish communities, and the lack of appropriate homes in which to facilitate secondary placements when original ones failed to work, accounted (in his opinion) for the failure.[28] Nearly all of the orphans headed west. Montreal and Toronto absorbed approximately 800 of the war orphans (about two-thirds of the 1,123 project total). Owing to their respective sizes, Montreal and Toronto Jewish communities had the most sophisticated communal infrastructures, including religious institutions and social agencies. As such, orphans benefited from a wider range of lifestyle options than did their peers destined for smaller, less central communities.[29]

Young men represented nearly two-thirds of all war orphans to Canada. As noted earlier, many of the male orphans were not boys at all, but rather young men well over the age of eighteen years who, with few opportunities availed to them, falsified their ages and documents to join the project. Hungarian Jewish orphans and friends, Tibor (Ted) Bolgar and Paul Herczeg, fell into this category. Born in 1924 and 1927, respectively, time in labour and concentration camps had taken their toll on the young men's bodies, making them appear far younger than their natural ages. It was this very appearance that scored them spots on the lists for the War Orphans Project. The pair landed in Montreal on 13 January 1948.

Herczeg described the arrival as daunting: "It was with great anticipation that you start a new life," he said. "You have no skill, no language, no trade. I was naïve and shy as they come. But it was my dream to get out [of Europe]."[30] Both young men were placed initially at the reception centre at Montreal's Herzl Dispensary and given a crash course in the English language before being directed to new homes. The Lipes family took in Bolgar, while Herczeg found lodging in an elderly woman's home. In both cases the expenses were covered for a brief time by the CJC. The desire to attain independence, learn English, and integrate into the community as quickly as possible trumped all other ambitions. Higher education did not present a viable option at the time—Herczeg recalled failing an IQ test administered by his social worker since he was unable to answer her questions in either English or Yiddish—and by 1 February 1948, both men were working as unskilled labourers.[31] Herczeg and Bolgar regularly attended events at the New World Club (where Bolgar met his future wife), the Happy Gang Club, and the YMHA in the company of other survivors. As Bolgar described, "We kept our own company. We were simply different."[32] Together, the newcomers shared stories of their pasts, compared present circumstances, and planned for the future.

Bolgar's early months proved far smoother than his close friend's. "They [the Lipes family] were fantastic to me," he recalled. "We always kept up Friday night dinners and they helped me get my first office job. They were more than welcoming to me, and after I got married [in 1954], to my wife. They, and my refugee friends, became my family."[33] Herczeg experienced minimal stability during his first years in Canada. He bounced from job to job, travelling to southern Ontario in a failed attempt to work as a tobacco picker, and to the Laurentian Mountains where he served as a waiter at a hotel. Herczeg returned to Montreal in September 1948, found stable work through a hotel guest he had waited on that summer, and later enrolled at Sir George Williams College. Like Bolgar, he also married a Hungarian Jewish woman who immigrated to Canada after the 1956 Hungarian Revolution.[34]

Herczeg's and Bolgar's experiences were representative of those of older youths who were resettled in Montreal and Toronto. Both lived in paid homes, albeit under different circumstances, and undertook employment soon after arrival. They both attained self-sufficiency within months and required only

16. Joseph Kage, director of Social Services at JIAS, with war orphans at the Herzl Dispensary on Jeanne Mance St., Montreal, 1948. Courtesy of the Canadian Jewish Congress Charities Committee National Archives.

minimal, short-term assistance from JIAS and other organizational supports. As newcomers in a Jewish community teeming with other Holocaust survivors, a plethora of job opportunities, and established social and recreational outlets and networks, the men were able to negotiate their pre-war and postwar identities and rebuild their lives from the ground up, with great success.[34]

War orphans in western Canada experienced the process of resettlement differently than did their cohorts in Montreal and Toronto. Vancouver, home to a young but prosperous Jewish community, received a total of forty-seven war orphans during the project's run, and retained thirty-six of that original number in January 1951. Jean Rose, chairman of the Coordinating Committee on War Orphans, served as newcomer youths' primary point of contact in Vancouver. While not a professional social worker, Rose gained ample experience as a community leader in her capacity as president of Federated Jewish Women, organizing "overseas comfort" packages for British Columbian and Polish Jewish soldiers fighting overseas, providing hospitality for soldiers on leave and over Jewish holidays, and orchestrating national wartime campaigns and a food and clothing drive for survivors of Nazi atrocities.[35] Rose's charitable initiatives continued into the postwar period. She and her committee solicited the community for suitable Jewish foster families, performed home checks, and greeted orphans on arrival. They also administered funds provided by the CJC to cover housing, clothing, and medical expenditures, ranging from $20,000 in 1948 to $10,000 in 1950.[36]

Rose developed especially close and meaningful relationships with several of her charges, and frequently reported on the youths' social integration, first to the CJC's western office, and after 1949, the nascent CJC Pacific region. At the conclusion of the project's third year (31 January 1951), Rose proudly offered a summary of the youths' progress. She boasted of four orphans' weddings and another's established business in Montreal, ten completely self-supporting youth working in technical occupations and trades, and six others receiving only occasional subsidies while they undertook specialized vocational training. The academic achievements of three young men attending the University of British Columbia through scholarships provided by the Council of Jewish Women were noted, in addition to the eight youngsters less than sixteen years of age remaining in free and boarding homes. Alongside these noteworthy success stories, however, there was a dose of cold reality. "A report such as this is not complete without a comment of two on the extreme efforts made by these children in their [sic] struggle to assimilate into their present cultural environment. The often-time painful experiences that seem necessary before their objectives are reached and the desire on their part to win the battle for adjustment has been most revealing to those who work with them," Rose wrote. "It has been a heartbreaking and painstaking task [toward social adjustment] and we are aware of one of two partial failures among them."[37] The fates of these failed troubled youth, and of those who left Vancouver for the more culturally rich environs in the east, do not surface in this report.

The CJC's western division operated out of Winnipeg and officially oversaw and authorized the home placements of approximately 230 orphans resettled west of Toronto.[38] Vancouver's Jewish social service sector and orphans' committee, headed by Jean Rose, received subsidiary support from the western office until 1949, as did Calgary.[39] War orphans placed in small farming communities such as Vegreville (Alberta) and Hoffer (Saskatchewan) also fell under Winnipeg's responsibility. Youth resettled outside of city boundaries rarely communicated with social workers. When necessary, community representatives from nearby cities were dispatched to visit the newcomer orphans' homes, or the foster parents would bring them to the city for a visit.

In spite of organizational limitations, western communities proved particularly resourceful in receiving and attending to the needs of the incoming youth. Many people offered their homes, and local businesses joined together to secure employment for those of working age, usually as unskilled labourers or as trade apprentices. For the first couple of years, youth attended social events, established refugee clubs, and joined sports teams at the YM-WHA; those older than sixteen and not attending regular high school were urged to participate in English language classes. Orphan boys at the Winnipeg YMHA established an award-winning Hakoach soccer team, while their female cohorts began a Hadassah-WIZO branch. Many attended movie nights and dances. In Calgary, weekly gatherings, card-playing nights, and dinners were held in local survivors' homes. And later, marriages among older youth to other refugees or Canadian Jews were celebrated in earnest, with members of the orphan community standing in for deceased relatives. Similar groupings occurred across western Canada.[40] But, far removed from the cultural milieu of their European upbringings, and thrust into small, conservative communities, oftentimes without desirable social, educational, and employment connections, many war orphans struggled to carve out a space in their new environs.

The case histories of fifteen-year-old Susan Garfield in Vegreville, Alberta, and her former Budapest classmate, Anna, aged seventeen, who was placed nearly 400 kilometres away in Calgary, elucidate the host of issues faced by many newcomer youth, particularly those in smaller Jewish communities. Both girls expressed great disappointment in their new homes. Susan wished desperately to move to Toronto. Unlike Vegreville, where there was "no theatre, no opera and no friends," Toronto, according to a male friend, was a wonderful place where Susan could enjoy an active social life, surround herself with arts and culture, and live alongside other Jews.[41] Susan and her foster family held differing opinions about her future. Susan hoped to complete her high school education—for which she had won awards for top grades, meriting newspaper write-ups—and then continue on to university.[42] Her foster parents thought that secretarial schooling would be a more practical option for the precocious young lady, and were determined to see her complete the program and then find employment.

Nothing about Calgary met Anna's expectations. Without close friendships, positive experiences at high school, or promising employment opportunities, Anna's prospects for successful integration into Canadian Jewish society grew increasingly faint. Her poor academic performance proved devastating, and despite her placement in a "free" foster home, Anna was instructed by local community leaders to leave school and go to work. Anna wrote to CJC executive director Saul Hayes begging him for help: "You're the only person in whole Canada to whom I can go, and ask. I don't like it here in Calgary. I can't get used to it and I'm very unhappy here. In Montreal I've friends, and I'm really sure I'll be happy there."[43] A community leader declared, in response to Hayes's request for information, that

> I believe, as do members of our Committee, that Anna does not honestly desire either the move or the education as much as she professes to. She had the opportunity to write some examinations but she chose not to because she felt unprepared. She has made no attempt to study thus far, this summer, in preparation for the Fall session, although this was suggested. We believe that all the disturbance is basically because this is a way of drawing attention to herself. She likely feels the need for this since she has been an only child and craves this type of security.[44]

Without financial support and with the threat of losing her free lodging, Anna dropped out of school and accepted a "hopeless job in a bookstore."[45] Convinced that the longer she remained in Calgary the worse her circumstances would become, she began to contemplate how, and when, she could move eastward, to Montreal.

Neither girl turned to her foster family for help in altering their situations. Within months of arriving in Vegreville, Susan pleaded her case and requested transfer to Toronto. Susan's foster parents arranged for a CJC representative from Winnipeg, Mr. Jabrukow, to visit.[46] Jabrukow's response to the request was

17. Susan Garfield with war orphan friends in Calgary, Alberta, 1949. Courtesy of Susan Garfield.

disappointing for Susan, but not surprising: under no condition could she move to Toronto. If she left Vegreville, she would lose all CJC financial aid and would need to work for her upkeep.

The Kleins tried to alleviate Susan's misery through outings, (unwelcome) surprise birthday party, as well as occasional visits to Calgary and Edmonton to visit with other war orphans, including Anna. On those trips, the girls attempted to behave like normal, carefree teenagers. Susan relates in her diary how "Anna and I often stay up till three, four o'clock in the morning gabbing and reciting poems to each other."[47] The pair attended parties, went on picnics, and even on double dates. Those dates were more than ordinary outings. Susan tried to cheer up Anna by advising her own admirers that she would only join them on a date if a friend could be found for Anna. Other Calgary war orphans recalled Susan's visits to Anna as significant events in the latter's otherwise unhappy life. Oscar Kirshner recalled escorting Anna for New Year's Eve as a favour to a friend who was taking Susan. Afterwards, as Kirshner walked her home, Anna, "a very, very lonesome girl," begged Kirshner to come in and visit. To Anna's chagrin, he declined.[48]

Anna perceived her own host family as distant and apathetic to her condition. In letters addressed to an uncle in Hungary, Anna complained that her basic needs were not met, and that she was starving. Though such claims were later retracted, and admittedly made in what she described as a "state of desperation," Anna insisted that social workers ignored her poor emotional state and lack of opportunities and provided preferential treatment to some war orphans over others. She begged the CJC's Saul Hayes to show compassion and offer her advice as "her great, wise father."[49] A social worker suggested that Anna had misunderstood Congress's role in the absorption and resettlement of survivors. He concluded that "Anna was under the impression that since Congress brought her to Canada that Congress would be interested to see her happy and contented. To this I replied that the primary object of Congress was to save young lives and to bring the boys and girls to a free country."[50] Anna's long-term happiness did not factor into the equation.

Congress took another decision with respect to Susan, agreeing to transfer her to Winnipeg, en route, she hoped, to Toronto. The relocation did not result in newfound happiness, however. Susan quickly learned that Congress had no intention of transferring her case file to Toronto. Moreover, having surrendered the comfort and security of a "free" foster home in Vegreville, she had the misfortune of experiencing exploitation as a nanny, housekeeper, and shopkeeper for an emotionally distant Winnipeg Jewish family, receiving room and board in return. Susan also attended high school, but her heavy work schedule allowed little personal time. The matriarch of the family reminded her to "be grateful" for what she had, and thwarted Susan's participation in social activities and studying. Ironically, relief arrived with the city's great flood of May 1950, when Susan was left "a flood refugee, doubly displaced." As a result of the flood, and her landlady's flight from the city, Susan was relocated to another more pleasant and respectful home in Winnipeg.[51]

By that time, Anna had left Calgary for a fresh start in Montreal, home to more than one-third of all war orphans. Her sense of good fortune, however, dissipated before it even began. She settled into a series of low-paying factory jobs, and experienced difficulties securing housing in a city overcrowded with newcomers by then competing for work and accommodations. Because Anna travelled to Montreal against the wishes of her caseworker, Anna was refused any further financial assistance from Congress. The one and only occasion upon which they relented and lent Anna fifty dollars to purchase a winter coat resulted in what Anna perceived as a direct attack on her person, including degrading letters and calls to her workplace. Frustrated by what she considered to be constant harassment from the Jewish communal bureaucracy over her slow debt repayment, Anna spewed a stream of angry letters to her social workers. She charged that the spiteful social workers were trying to sabotage her career. Nothing in Anna's case file suggests that the outstanding twenty-seven-dollar loan for the winter coat was repaid, or that her resentment toward the organized Canadian Jewish community was mollified.

Both girls experienced great displeasure with their situations. Discouraged by her poor adjustment and depressed mood, Susan contemplated a return to her native Hungary and her relatives. The unstable political situation in communist Europe crushed those plans. Instead, she remained in Winnipeg and put herself through high school, followed by a business course that was subsidized in part by the CJC. She married a Canadian-born Jew in 1954, raised a family, and eventually earned the university degree she so fervently desired from the University of Manitoba.[52] Anna was unable to make similar adjustments to improve upon her situation. Anna's correspondence with CJC employees seeking repayment for her outstanding loan concludes in 1955, when she was still eking out a meagre livelihood in Montreal, unmarried and without any meaningful relationships. She had not tried to return to school. Letters to Susan reiterated her misery and frustrations with her failure to thrive. Beyond this, little is known of Anna's fate. Among the war orphan community in western Canada, rumours circulated that she took her own life, but with scant evidence to substantiate the supposition.

Susan's and Anna's cases illuminate some of the difficulties in the resettlement of war orphans. The girls' respective perceptions of minimal opportunities for personal or academic advancement and socialization, and their feelings of loneliness and injustice, were commonplace among other young Holocaust survivors. They tried to take charge of their situations, actively pursued preferred conditions, and stood up for themselves in interactions with social workers and foster families alike. The girls challenged the parameters established and regulations enforced by local Jewish refugee relief agencies. Other orphans seeking change appeared to either grudgingly accept their lot or took action without fanfare, not wishing to seem ungrateful.[53] Yet despite their proactive behaviour, neither Susan nor Anna enjoyed many benefits from their actions. While Susan did leave Vegreville, she never reached her destination of choice, Toronto. Anna also succeeded in leaving Calgary, yet her ongoing battles to attain and secure employment in Montreal, as well as recurring moves, social anxieties, and loneliness, evidently never dissipated. The real challenge for Anna was to have her mental illness diagnosed and treated, efforts that were never taken. This is where the system truly failed her.

Like Anna, more than one-third of the orphans resettled in western Canada relocated again within a few years of arrival. Of 140 youth originally placed in Winnipeg, fifty-two had left for other cities, mostly Montreal and Toronto, by 1953.[54] Marriage, work, education, and reuniting with surviving relatives all motivated the now-adult orphans to leave their host city.[55] So, too, did religious ideals and values, and access to the services that an observant life required.

## Orthodox Youth

The docking of eighteen-year-old war orphan Bernat's ship at Halifax's Pier 21 signalled the beginning of a new and difficult journey for the Orthodox youth. He was ambitious and determined to preserve his observant way of life. This self-identification was poignantly noted in the closing summary prepared by his JIAS social worker:

> Bernat is a very orthodox boy, who, on his arrival two years ago, was very much the European Yeshivah "bocher." He clung rigidly to his religiosity in the beginning as a way of hiding the real fear he had of moving out and becoming part of the community. He was highly critical of the religious standards at the Reception Centre [for European Youth], starved himself to the point of losing weight, and in this way fought adjusting to the new environment. He had a very odd pathetic appearance, which made him stand out from the others. In his relationship with me Bernat found warmth and acceptance, so that he was able gradually to let go of some of the rigidities to which he had first clung. Bernat became quite Canadianized in his first year here, and began to conform in appearance and conduct to the standard here. He made an excellent job adjustment, and is taking a technical course at night to further himself in that area.[56]

As an Orthodox youth thrust into the custody of a secular communal resettlement agency, Bernat, like his religious peers, stood at a crossroad. Where the social workers sought to provide observant young men (and, infrequently, women) with the basics, and aid them in job searches, their collective focus drifted to yeshiva studies. The values and priorities held by the youth conflicted with the intentions of those who sought to help them become "Canadianized."

Hassidic and other Orthodox youth arrived in Canada primarily via one of three routes. A handful landed in Montreal through the successful 1941 rescue of several Eastern European yeshiva students, alongside their teachers, who had traversed Asia upon their departure from Europe, eventually arriving in Canada from Japan. A sizeable minority made their way to Canada under the auspices of the War Orphans Project beginning in the fall of 1947, embarking on the transatlantic journey from DP camps and children's homes, and with the transplantation of the re-established Mir Yeshiva, out of Italy in 1949 and 1950. Finally, a very small number of Orthodox youth arrived in Canada via relatives' sponsorship.

The challenges facing observant youngsters preceded their disembarkation on Canadian soil. Orthodox orphans, along with their less observant cohorts, travelled on ships from Europe and were led by an appointed UJRA or Congress guide. From the start, the boys made clear their demands: if they arrived on Shabbat or during a holiday, they would refuse to disembark or travel to their permanent destinations by train as planned. In these instances, in order not to cause a commotion or damage the new relationships being established between the youth and the Canadian Jewish constituents, the CJC conceded and rescheduled transport. Religious orphans, like their adult peers, were temporarily housed in local homes and attended synagogue services.[57] This insistence upon religious accommodations continued at reception centers in Montreal and Toronto. In smaller Jewish centres, orphans were typically placed in homes upon arrival. Plans for permanent accommodations, taking into account age, religious needs, personality, and workability, began shortly after. Observant orphans snubbed the food—which, although kosher, did not meet their standards—and refused to eat, argued with their less pious peers over social conduct, and argued with the centres' overseeing committees over a range of matters. The committees approached issues of *kashrut* and Sabbath observance delicately. They usually acquiesced and instituted new provisos for enforcing the observance of Sabbath (no smoking, card playing, or music on site) and more strict supervision to ensure compliance with all regulations of *kashrut*.[58]

Youngsters with connections to pre-war European yeshivas or prominent spiritual leaders typically turned to Canada's three yeshivas in operation before the end of the war: Montreal's Rabbinical College of Canada Tomchei Tmimim (Lubavitch), headed by Rabbi Leib Kramer; Merkaz Hatorah, the *mitnagedim* (non-Hassidic, Lithuanian-style learning), led by Rav (Rabbi)

Pinchas Hirschprung, in Montreal; and Rabbi A.A. Price's traditional Yeshiva Torath Chaim, in Toronto. The First Mesifta of Canada, founded in 1948 by the Klausenberger rebbe, was the first transplanted European yeshiva to arrive in Montreal. The small but active yeshiva evolved quickly under Rosh Yeshiva Shmuel Alexander Unsdorfer, a Holocaust survivor rabbi. The final transplanted yeshiva to Montreal was the Maor Hagolah, which was formed by survivor rabbis and yeshiva students and had flourished in early postwar Italy.[59]

Most observant orphans became official wards of their respective yeshivas, whose leaders provided the affidavits required for their immigration. Until these orphans were self-sufficient, Congress and its affiliated organizations provided the necessary funds to maintain them, both within and outside the yeshiva walls. The students claimed that they had been raised in strictly Orthodox homes, some stemming from long lines of rabbinical dynasties, and declared that they planned to return to the religious fold and become learned men in Canada. Such plans echoed the life paths they had anticipated before the near-destruction of European Jewry.

Rabbis and social workers expressed concern for the boys' futures. The CJC, for its part, was concerned that the yeshiva *bokhers* would one day leave the yeshiva and be thrust out into an unaccommodating world without any transferable trades or skills. It worried that a lack of marketable skills, coupled with the distinctive appearance of Orthodox males, would result in prolonged periods of financial dependency. With the assistance of JIAS workers, JVS counsellors and rabbis tested the yeshiva students' aptitude and intelligence.[60] Boys who demonstrated an especially high aptitude for Torah study, combined with superior intelligence, received financial support from the CJC and its education committees to continue working toward religious ordination.

Members of the War Orphan Education Committee, comprising representatives from JIAS, CJC, UJRA, and volunteer organizations, released public statements about the testing process. One such statement related the following:

On March 2, we had a meeting with reps of several orthodox groups in Montreal (Board of Jewish Ministers, Mizrachi Organization, Jewish Community Council, Council of Orthodox Rabbis, Young Israel, Yeshiva), in regard to the case of 10 orthodox war orphans. Rabbi Price recommended that 2 of them should have the necessary qualifications for study for the Rabbinate in a Yeshiva and 2 should be given courses under the supervision of the Jewish Community Council in Montreal which would give them the experience to become trained at Shochtim.

The balance should be directed to some useful trade. The meeting approved of these recommendations and the JVS and Jewish Child Welfare Bureau.[61]

Those who failed these tests were encouraged to eschew the most obvious markers of religious observance, particularly beards, side curls, and dress, and to learn a marketable trade. The disappointed youth were interviewed and removed from the yeshiva roster and sent to work. Their lack of power, influence, or familial support made their futures uncertain. Some rabbis cared deeply about the boys' well-being, and continued to provide the youngsters with housing and maintenance support even after they ceased their studies.

Most Orthodox war orphans who desired a yeshiva education grudgingly accepted that their dreams were unrealistic. They quietly abandoned their studies and ventured into the workforce, looking for jobs in Jewish businesses and the needle trade, while continuing to learn Torah after work and on Shabbat. Most of the young men preserved their heritage by marrying traditional Jewish women and raising children who then attended yeshiva and girls' schools established by members of the survivor community.[62]

The options for religious schooling were limited outside Montreal and Toronto, though a willingness to leave the security offered by large cities opened up career opportunities. Requests for educators periodically came from small Jewish communities seeking leadership. Unlike established Jewish communities with developed infrastructure, including rabbis, cantors, and ritual slaughterers, small Jewish clusters, often in spread-out farming communities, lacked spiritual guidance. The size of the population did not typically allow for the hiring of religious functionaries, with the exception of Hebrew and religion teachers for the children.

Some young men followed alternative routes to secure entry into religious professions. A Czechoslovakian war orphan in Winnipeg, Bernard K, declared his intentions to the Jewish Family Service social worker assigned to his case: he wished to become a Hebrew teacher. A strict observer of Orthodox Judaism, Bernard hoped to receive a yeshiva education, or at least Jewish teacher's training. However, no such institutions were available in Winnipeg. Fortunately for him, a request from the Jewish community of North Battleford, Saskatchewan, offered a solution, and invited the young man to teach Hebrew, Jewish literature, and history. Like all other potential educators, the case file noted that "the boy's abilities were tested by both A and C of the Bureau of Jewish Education. Both of them were satisfied that the boy could fill the job entrusted to him. The conditions are quite attractive for a boy of his age. He will receive $100 a month plus board and room free of charge. In a community like NB he will find it most difficult to spend $100 per month if board and room are free, unless he develops a yen for playing poker. Besides he has an opportunity to attend High School since his duties as a Jewish and Hebrew teacher will not commence until after school hours and will not take more than between 3 and 4 hours of his time every day."[63]

Although Bernard's move to North Battleford proved far from ideal, accepting the teaching position proved advantageous on several accounts. He completed his high school education, achieved financial independence from the social service agency charged with his care, and most importantly, he earned the opportunity to work as a religious functionary (albeit not at the level he originally desired) and teach Torah to Jewish youth. Bernard served the prairie community for nearly a decade.

The path to receiving a formal Jewish education with the aim of professional certification as a rabbi, cantor, or ritual slaughterer was difficult. Bernard's case was unusual. Even when available, few observant boys took advantage of the opportunities. After surviving the trauma of the Holocaust, followed by the uncertainty and deprivations of postwar Europe, stability and security were precious commodities. Many of the young men had been on their own for years without any relatives or spiritual leaders to turn to for support and guidance. Abandoning their own Jewish community, and risking a lack of access to kosher food or Jewish men for a *minyan* (a quorum of ten men for the purpose of prayer) proved too much. Most turned to unskilled labour or secular education (where available), and remained in their protective communities for the rest of their lives.

---

The War Orphans Project, the CJC-sponsored and Ministry of Immigration-approved rescue mission that brought 1,123 unattached youth ostensibly under the age of eighteen across the Atlantic to rebuild their lives, has been a subject of interest among Canadian Jewish historians and educators. In 1997, the project was used as an education platform by the Vancouver Holocaust Education Centre for its landmark exhibit, *Open Hearts–Closed Doors: The War Orphans Project*, which lives on in an online format. Participants in the project represented a substantial percentage of all CJC-sponsored Jewish refugees from 1947 to 1950,[64] and later many contributed greatly to various aspects of Canadian Jewish and secular life. While these influences are of utmost importance, the value of exploring the orphans' early years in Canada does not relate to their accomplishments. Rather, the orphans' rescue, reception, and resettlement processes shed light on the realities of postwar immigrant life and Canadian Jewish norms and communal values. The vast majority of the youth made adequate adjustments to their new communities and embraced Canadian value systems, although many were confronted with significant challenges along the way, most often with regard to education and employment. Conflicts and differences of opinion between social workers and their "child" clients ranged from benign to malignant, and fill the pages of most case files, while orphans who achieved self-sufficiency or did not make demands for assistance or change of circumstances were quickly dropped from agency rosters to free up the workers' busy caseloads.

Educational plans for younger orphans and work placements for those over sixteen were representative of the times, and closely correlated with norms of working-class Canadians. Orphans did not receive special or preferential treatment over their Canadian-born peers. Older teenagers were sent to work not because they were refugees but because they were of working age. And while the value of education in the integration process cannot be overstated, many orphans recognized that learning did not always need to take place in a regular high school classroom. They attended JIAS evening school classes, participated in public lectures, and joined survivor clubs (like the New World Club) and *landsmanshaftn*. While some orphans, like Anna, sought long-term financial aid, others, especially the young men, desired independence through employment and self-sufficiency, and demanded to be treated like the adults they were. Susan Garfield, for her part, negotiated both work and school to construct her own autonomous future.

Options for Orthodox war orphans' religious education and integration into Canadian Jewish society were limited and depended largely on their site of resettlement, and more specifically, their access to Jewish religious life. Boys placed with yeshivas undertook religious schooling for an indeterminate amount of time, though weak grades and aptitude for Torah learning resulted in removal from yeshiva rosters and the cessation of agency aid. The opportunity to live fully observant lives, however, existed only for young men settled in metropolises with substantial Jewish infrastructure, including kosher food, *shuls*, and women for marriage. A handful accepted the challenge and served as religious educators in smaller, unobservant environments. Yet, despite the inherent challenges to their lifestyles, most Orthodox orphans stood firm by their convictions and found their station in burgeoning postwar religious communities.

While the experiences of the War Orphans Project participants are significant in postwar Holocaust history, these young people were not the only children and youth to immigrate to Canada during the crucial first years of Holocaust survivor immigration. Child survivors who arrived through alternate immigration programs, with or without parents and relatives, did not elicit the same excitement or (intended) goodwill from Canadian Jews as those who came officially as war orphans. In fact, most child survivors were not recognized as survivors at all. Their stories are the subject of the next chapter.

# CHAPTER FOUR

# "I REMAIN ITS RELUCTANT CHILD"

*Never, ever underestimate a child, they are very perceptive. Even if*
*they cannot articulate what they feel.... For me, I was very aware of my*
*surroundings [during the Holocaust], the changes, the moves. I always*
*felt anxiety. Everybody just assumed I would forget.*

—Elly Bollegraaf[1]

Young Mendel Gwiazda arrived in Canada under an entirely different set of circumstances than those of refugees selected for the War Orphans Project. Entrusted by his parents to local Catholic Poles when they learned that their ghetto would soon be liquidated in 1942, the newborn Mendel remained with the Polish family until the end of the war. Then he was left to fend for himself in a blown-out, abandoned warehouse in Warsaw. Discovered by representatives of the surviving Jewish community, he was sick and malnourished. Both of Mendel's parents were murdered in an indeterminate concentration camp. Wolfe Goldberg, a distant relative of Mendel's mother, Elka, in Toronto, learned that Mendel had survived after an elderly lady who cared for the youngster for six months came forward to identify him. Goldberg made it his mission to adopt the boy.[2] Before the Canadian government granted immigration papers, the following report was filed by an AJDC social worker: "Mendel is a rather frail looking child and not having any hair [due to a recent skin infection, trichofita captis, the measles, mumps, and whooping cough] adds to this appearance. He is attractive and has an engaging smile but a rather sad, serious expression. He is normal mentally and very alert. He gets along well with the other children and is very liked by them. He wants to cling to someone and is very devoted to the matron and the others in the Home but they have to be careful not to show him more attention and affection than is given to the other children. He seems so much to want to belong to someone."[3]

Luckily for Mendel, he was wanted. In April 1948, a social worker placed six-year-old Mendel on a ship at Danzig, Poland, requested that two crew members "watch over him" during the fourteen-day crossing, and sent him on his way.[4] When the ship docked at Hudson River Pier, New York City, Wolfe Goldberg stood eagerly awaiting his arrival. "He'll make a good companion for my five-year-old son, Gerald," Goldberg declared, as he glanced down at the joyful face of his new child.[5] Little Mendel accompanied his uncle home to meet his new family in Toronto.

While the experiences of the War Orphans Project participants have garnered considerable attention, little scholarly research exists concerning the resettlement of child survivors who arrived in Canada through other means. These youngsters immigrated primarily through close relatives and labour schemes, or as non-registered orphans sponsored by family members. Although some came with one parent—or, less frequently, both biological parents—many immigrated with step-parents or alone. Relatively few of these children had experienced life inside the concentration camp universe. Most survived the Holocaust in hiding (in convents, monasteries, orphanages, gentile homes, or underground) or deep in the Soviet Union. Many, like Mendel Gwiazda—later known by his adopted name, Melvin Goldberg—were separated from their parents and subsequently orphaned. Others had different experiences. Carmela Finkel (née Shragge) was hidden in the home of a Polish Catholic couple known to her family in the interwar period, with her parents and older sister. The Shragges emerged from hiding as a complete family unit.[6]

Due to their ages at the onset of the Nazi persecution of Jews, many child survivors had no formal education prior to their migration to Canada. Jewish communities and surviving relatives emphasized the importance of providing the youngsters with a Jewish education, especially since many had spent the war years living among, and posing as, non-Jews. Some had learned Christian prayer rituals, taken communion, and adopted anti-Jewish attitudes in order to survive.[7] According to psychiatrist and child survivor Dr. Robert Krell, hidden children persecuted as Jews were safe only when wrapped in the mantle of Christianity. A confusion of identity, a mixed allegiance to their saviour religion—specifically "good Christian" rescuers—and their religion of origin, pursued many into adult life.[8] European and Canadian relatives tried whenever possible to reignite a sense of Jewish identity in the children, many of whom gained knowledge of their origins only after the war's end.[9]

Reintroductions to parents and relatives—from whom numerous youngsters had experienced long-term separations—was often traumatic, and took a considerable period of adjustment. Child survivors also suffered from lingering medical conditions, including years of malnutrition and stunted growth, as well as injuries incurred during the war. The struggle to attain full physical and psychological health persisted for years after arrival in Canada. Many also struggled to connect or find meaning with their Jewish identity. This chapter examines how child survivors embarked upon new lives in postwar Canada. It explores how these youngsters resettled into their new communities as virtually unrecognized survivors, even in the eyes of adult survivors, and the ways in which some challenged the status quo and carved out new identities for themselves.

## Fitting In

Child survivors encountered a slew of challenges during the process of integration into postwar Canadian Jewish society. All faced the debilitating effects of an irreplaceably lost and disrupted childhood defined by fear, loneliness, and exposure to terror, pain, cold, and hunger. Most experienced the interruption of formal (and informal) education, as well as the loss of friends, loved ones, and homes. Few spoke English upon arrival in their new communities, and youngsters experienced severe culture shock as they faced a society with entirely contrary norms and values to those of their formative years. But the experiences of children who came to Canada with parent(s) or other relatives, through labour and close relatives sponsorships, differed greatly from those who arrived as participants on the CJC-sponsored War Orphans Project in respect to familial relations and migration experiences.

Unlike the documented orphans—who were officially recognized as survivors of severe trauma and uprooting, and identified by psychiatrists and social workers as requiring special and intensive care in order to adapt to postwar lives—child survivors who immigrated through other means were not identified as "refugees and trauma survivors" by social service professionals and the Holocaust survivor community itself, but rather as the children, or relatives, of adult survivors. Despite the fact that many non-orphaned youth (as well as a few non-registered orphans who immigrated to relatives in Canada) had similarly experienced years of turbulence in hiding, camps, and in Soviet exile, their histories went unexamined and undefined. Their traumatic histories were, in most cases, elided, as caseworkers, educators, Canadian Jews, and their parents identified them as offspring of adult survivors, unaffected by the traumas of the Holocaust.

Child survivors were far off the radar of social service agencies that bore responsibility for administering services primarily to adult newcomers. These children, although registered as refugees on their parents' passports, did not rank as a priority or as falling within the purview of service providers. Instead, they were considered to be appendages to adult survivors. They remained non-subjects even within family unit case files, meriting attention for only three plausible reasons.

The first such reason revolved around requests for clothing, shoes, or bedding from community donation sites, such as Montreal's JIAS Clothing Centre, or cash to purchase intimate items such as underwear and brassieres.[10] A mother would declare her son's or daughter's lack of weather-appropriate clothing and the need for used winter coats and boots. In such cases, no discussion ever ensued about the school-aged youngsters' other possible needs.

The second plausible reason for survivor children to merit attention involved requests for assistance in practical matters. Questions about enrolling children in school and summer camp, or requisition slips to attend health clinics and obtain doctors' notes in case of illness were commonly noted by caseworkers. Mr. and Mrs. Isador S were among those parents who made such requests on behalf of their son and daughter, ages eight and eleven, respectively. Upon the family's arrival in Toronto in September 1948, Mr. and Mrs. S were eager to enrol their children in school immediately. They sought advice on which schools to visit and what to expect regarding grade placement; they also requested a volunteer attendant to translate. The JIAS social worker assigned to their case agreed: the sooner the children were settled, the sooner both parents could begin their job hunt.[11] Weeks later, Mrs. S reported that both youngsters were having trouble "fitting in" at school and her son was "acting out," problems the worker attributed to their English-language deficiencies. Neither mother nor caseworker seems to have considered that language might have been only one of several issues affecting the children. Born in 1937 and 1940, the children had lived through grave dangers, and if they had not witnessed violence, surely knew about it. And yet there is little mention in the case files of the children's experiences during the Holocaust, which surely was the most important event shaping their formative years. Parents and workers—knowingly or unwittingly—minimized the trauma many of the youngsters endured, not to mention the physical and emotional stinting, that might have contributed to the children's integration difficulties and lack of communication skills. No efforts to investigate were recorded.[12]

The third and final reason to explain why child survivors came to the direct attention of social service providers was in instances where teenagers served as breadwinners for their families, supporting parents and younger siblings. Seventeen-year-old Polish Jew Lucia M resettled in Montreal with her widowed mother, Leah, and eleven-year-old brother, Sam, in July 1949. Leah suffered from various physical and psychosomatic ailments, rendering her unable to find and maintain steady employment. Her married sister and brother-in-law, who preceded the family to Canada and sponsored their admission, were cash-strapped and could not offer financial support. Lucia was instructed by her mother, and encouraged by the caseworker, to undertake factory work. The teenager found a job, foregoing full-time schooling; her hope of attending JIAS English classes was also put off in favour of overtime work to pay for Sam's Jewish day-school tuition.[13] She, like other teenaged child survivors who made the move to Canada with a parent, frequently took on adult caregiver roles. And yet, they were still seemingly perceived and treated by counsellors as ordinary children not requiring special care.

There is scant archival evidence concerning the integration and acculturation experiences of child survivors who immigrated with adult relatives; their lives went largely un-noted in official records and only a faint paper trail of primary evidence relays their early experiences in Canada. Nearly all information about this cohort comes from oral history testimonies, interviews, and memoirs, created decades after the fact and years after most had shed their "refugee skins."[14]

All child survivors faced multiple challenges in adapting to their new, postwar lives. They were forced to reinvent themselves and make sense of their overlapping identities as survivors of trauma, children of distressed and anxious adults, and finally, as "new Canadians." Youngsters' re-encountered freedom—with or without biological parents—and came of age while harbouring dual but parallel lives. The first "life" related to the youths' public persona and outward identity. Child survivors behaved in careful and delicate manners, with perpetual obedience to parents or guardians, and sought to acclimatize as natives to their adopted communities, deliberately avoiding drawing negative attention to themselves. An unwritten rule shared among these youngest survivors was never to speak about the Holocaust and one's wartime experience with anyone, including surviving relatives. The second concealed identity operated under a mantle of secrecy. This parallel existence clung to wartime experiences without relief—out of fear of negative response, discomfort with traumatic encounters, and the inability to confront one's past or reveal one's "true self," the witnesses suffered in silence. Anger and hurt stewed among child survivors for decades as they coped with this self- and societal-imposed closeting of experiences, keeping secret their histories from family members and friends alike.[15]

The first postwar challenge for many of these youthful survivors involved re-establishing relationships with parents or other relatives. The Holocaust abruptly disrupted the development of healthy parent-child bonds, particularly in instances where parents relinquished their children to non-Jewish rescuers or institutions in hopes of sparing their lives. Only a minority of these parents escaped death to find their offspring alive. For these fortunate few, the rebuilding of family relationships had to begin from scratch. Both parties accepted this challenge blindly; neither parent nor child knew each other. Children separated at a young age distrusted their new guardians. Suspicion, paranoia, and anger were rampant, especially among Jewish children removed from the homes of loving rescuers. For their part, adults exposed to ghettos, camps, or hiding returned damaged, at least initially, overcome by traumatic experiences and encounters, and often suffering from physical and psychological ramifications. Many surviving parents found themselves widowed by the war, leading to fervent and sometimes misguided re-marriages. Despite all good intentions, few were ready to adequately parent until they were themselves rehabilitated. Such early struggles made for complicated relationships and placed considerable burdens on "sacred" children to often care for their parents.[16]

Child survivors were overloaded with information, including learning about their Jewish heritage, meeting new siblings and step-parents, hearing about the murder of others, and renewing or beginning their education. These issues interplayed and had an impact on the ways in which child survivors identified with their families, forged relationships, and integrated with Canadian society, culture, and norms. Stunted emotional development during the war years caused them to sacrifice "normal" childhood behaviours such as laughter or roughhous-ing with siblings. A sneeze or cough could expose a hiding place; crying or fighting equalled death. Youngsters, especially those who had experienced the Holocaust in hiding, learned the value of silence at a young age. Unfailing obedience to one's protectors, be they parents or strangers, offered the best chance at survival. These survival skills meant that cultivation of age-appropriate friendships was frequently sacrificed, too, with some youngsters having never experienced the valuable lessons of sharing toys with a playmate or visiting friends' homes.[17] In war (and under the tyranny of Nazi occupation), friendships for children hid-den with Christian rescuers or living under false papers were largely untenable and inconceivable. Socializing with non-Jewish children presented distinct challenges. Even those children with no trace of a Yiddish accent and thorough training in Christian belief and practice could inadvertently expose their true identity with an innocent slip of the tongue, risking their own life and the lives of their protectors.[18] As a consequence, as new immigrants, child survivors entered schools and social encounters without the social maturity and confidence of their Canadian-born peers.

Religious identification posed a problem for some children, especially those who spent the war among practising Christians. For youth whose Jewish identities had already begun to cement prior to the Holocaust, a postwar return to Jewish life and practice was an adjustment, but not particularly problematic. For others, Judaism represented something entirely new and a reversal of long-held practices.

Ellen De Jonge was one child survivor for whom Judaism, and the label Jew, meant death. Born in Amsterdam in April 1936 to assimilated and non-practising German Jewish refugees, Ellen's early years were comfortable. The German invasion on 10 May 1940 turned her world upside down. A foreigner and a resistance fighter, Ellen's father was soon arrested and deported. With the help of Christian friends and, later, aid givers, Ellen's mother had her daughter and herself baptized into the Dutch Reformed Church. "My mother really did not want to be Jewish and didn't want me to go back to Judaism if we survived," Ellen recalled. "I was taught to feel no pride in being Jewish because nobody liked Jews."[19]

Ellen experienced a complete indoctrination into the Dutch Reformed Church faith when she went to live with the Versteegs, a large observant family of twelve, where she posed as the father's illegitimate daughter. There she found complete acceptance and, even upon learning of the murder of her parents, she never felt alone or like an orphan. Such feelings arose only when an aunt and uncle who had immigrated to Canada with her paternal grandmother in the interwar period arrived in the Netherlands in 1950 with the intention of bringing Ellen back with them. As Ellen remembered, "At the time, nobody [in her biological family] wanted me. But they felt an obligation to rescue me from my Christian home. I did not want to leave my family to join their Jewish home and fought to stay with the Versteegs. When they made me go, I refused to speak with them the entire boat ride to Canada."[20]

Ellen's new life on a farm in Trout River, Quebec, a small town unfriendly to foreigners, proved unhappy. Deprived of love and affection at home, Ellen assimilated quickly into the dominant culture and distanced herself from all aspects of Jewish life, which she associated with her relatives. Nobody ever acknowledged Ellen's eight years of life as a Christian, and Ellen knew better than to bring up those years or the trauma she experienced. When Ellen had begun to rebuild her life independently in Montreal as a recent high school graduate, her aunt professed a need to "save my Jewish soul" and, with her encouragement, Ellen began a nursing placement at Montreal's Jewish General Hospital. It was then that she began to acknowledge the huge losses in her life. Her aunt believed that an embrace of Jewish culture and tradition would bring Ellen comfort and a sense of belonging. While Ellen, as an adult, tried to immerse herself in Judaism and "find herself," she felt a void shared by some other child survivors whose religious outlooks were blurred by years spent living under false identities and with persons of different faiths. But neither this realization, nor her marriage to a Canadian Jew with whom she raised four Jewish children, culminated in entry into Jewish communal or religious life beyond a superficial level. Ellen continues to wrestle with her religious identity.[21]

Ellen De Jonge's struggle to connect with her heritage and surviving relatives represents what was a common occurrence among child survivors. Others faced very different challenges, including difficulties adapting to childhood norms, an inability to achieve proficiency in either English or French, a lack of formal education, or embarrassment over differences in appearance, as well as parents' and guardians' foreign accents and socio-economic status.

Born in August 1941 in the ghetto of Vilna, Lithuania (present-day Vilnius, Lithuania), Etti Blitz was the only child of an engineer father, Myer, who was a member of the ghetto's Yiddish literary society and a trained violinist and composer, and a highly skilled linguist mother, Sonia. Etti's first memories were of playing with animals and sleeping on the dirt floor of the Rudnicki Forest. Depending on the conditions, she alternated between hiding in the forest (in warm weather) and with a gentile farming family (in colder months). "In the forest I felt safest, surrounded by my friends, the animals, and trees," Etti recalled more than sixty years later. "And with the [Polish] family, I was well cared for."[22] Her paternal grandparents died of starvation in the forest, but Etti and her parents survived, and eventually made their way to Austria. From there, they moved forward to rebuild their lives. This signalled the true beginning of Etti's childhood.

The Blitzes never planned to immigrate to Canada; they always intended to join Sonia's relatives in the United States, or another cousin in Brazil. Neither plan came to fruition. Myer, a self-proclaimed Zionist, wished to make *aliyah* and restore his family life among survivor friends from pre-war Vienna. Fearful of war in then pre-state Palestine, Sonia declined this option. And so by some means unknown to Etti, the family landed in Toronto in 1948 after over three years in an Austrian DP camp. Etti recalled that her first impressions of her new country were grim: "I hated it. I was an overweight little six-year-old with black braids and red ribbons. I missed my time in the DP camp; it was the happiest time of my childhood. In Austria, I had been 'free as a bird.' But in Toronto, I didn't know the language, I had no friends. Kids beat me up in the schoolyard and I cried everyday. I'd cough every night before going to bed, feigning illness [to not have to go to school in the morning]. On our street, kids would play with me. But I was never invited into their homes beyond their verandas. I felt like we all knew I didn't belong."[23]

The youngster's loneliness was compounded by her parents' poor adjustment. Myer gave up writing music and rarely played his violin. Sonia felt great despair over her perceived rejection by Canadian Jews and her own American cousins who, aside from a handful of visits and a cash loan to get the family on its feet, showed no interest in the Blitzes' well-being. As Etti recalled, they tried desperately to be happy for their daughter's sake. All Etti sought from them was a sibling for companionship. A brother or sister, perhaps, could share in Etti's hopes and fears, and at the very least, fill out their tiny family and provide her with a friend. Such wishes were never granted. Adults never spoke about the Shoah in front of Etti and, sensing their pain, she did not ask. "It was only after many years that I came to terms with the fact that I, too, was a survivor," she recalled. "Just because I was young, I still remembered many things, and still felt the pain of being alone, and so very lonely."[24] Protectiveness over her parents' feelings and circumstances, and a sense of her own inability to take away their sadness, affected Etti's life well into adulthood.

For Sidney (Shie) Zoltak, the urge to protect and care for his parents constituted a similarly major aspect of his postwar existence. Born on 15 July 1931 in Siemiatycze, Poland, and the only child in a traditional, middle-class family, Sidney relished his parents' attention. But with the Nazi occupation and rumours of forthcoming *aktions* in their region, the family fled from the town's ghetto and went underground, protected by a Polish family, the Krynskis, who sheltered father, mother, and son—in addition to four other Jews—on their farm. The trio remained together until liberation, at which time they made their way south to Italy. Although his parents' goal was to immigrate to Canada, home to Mrs. Zoltak's large extended family, Sidney had other ideas. He intended to follow his friends from the children's home where he lived for two years in Italy to *Eretz Israel*, and help to build the Jewish homeland. The death of his father in December 1945 derailed this plan, as familial obligations trumped ideals: "As an only child, I refused to leave my mother. She saved my life."[25] In May 1948, mother and son landed in Montreal.

The pair was enthusiastically greeted at the train station by hordes of aunts, uncles, and cousins. This excitement did not wane, and Sidney Zoltak and his mother were warmly supported for several months in an aunt's apartment on Montreal's iconic Park Avenue. Kindness from the adults aside, Sidney experienced the ignorance of one school-age cousin, who refused to take the teenaged Sidney—who was working full-time and attending night classes at Sir George Williams College—with him to a high school basketball game. Sidney did not discuss the incident with his cousin, or demand an explanation. Instead, the youngster interpreted his cousin's behaviour in the following way: since it was unpopular to be seen with newcomers, the cousin, out of embarrassment, feared that appearing with a European refugee—a *greenie*—would presumably damage his reputation.

Sidney experienced similar coldness from other Canadian Jews, leading him to reach out to fellow European-born youth at Montreal's New World Club and sports leagues. Shared experiences, though not often spoken of, bonded the newcomers, often for life. But, as Sidney recalled, he felt most comfortable playing sports, a social equalizer: "The sports atmosphere was the only place where nobody cared who you were. There [the Hakoach Sports Clubs and Jewish Junior Soccer Club], you were judged on skill and not personality, background. The coaches treated us according to ability and did not care if you were Canadian-born, a newcomers' or *mockey* [another pejorative term for refugees], whatever."[26] Through sports, Sidney found strength and confidence, and this helped him feel like a "real" Canadian. His widowed mother married another Polish survivor.[27]

The same type of strength and determination, and the support of positive social relations and athletic involvement, spearheaded Mark (Shlomo) Nusbaum's process of acculturation and integration. A native of Sandomierz, Poland, Mark, born on 10 October 1935, was the younger of two sons born to Abraham and Regina Nusbaum. In April 1940, Abraham was arrested with other community leaders and imprisoned in a local jail before facing transfer to Buchenwald and then Ravensbruck concentration camps. In June 1940, the Nusbaum family learned of their patriarch's death through an official death notification, which claimed that he "succumbed to his illness." Shortly after this revelation, Regina, Mark, and older brother Aron, along with three other relatives, escaped to Warsaw and found a hiding place on the city's Aryan side through family connections. The six lived on the top floor of an apartment in a 4' by 15' space, protected by nothing but an armoire with a false back, where, as Mark recalled, "[we] hid quietly night and day, fearing that any noise could result in our certain demise."[28]

After the liquidation of the Warsaw Ghetto in spring 1943, Mark's mother left her hiding place and purchased Palestinian certificates, provided by the Palestine Jewish Agency in Istanbul via the Polish Ministry of Foreign Affairs (in exile) and the AJDC. These were the cheapest visas available, and were not expected to be as useful as the more expensive South American and American papers.[29] With the certificates in hand, the family registered at Hotel Polski. When the scheme was revealed, and the family deported to Bergen-Belsen, a "miracle" occurred. "We were part of a protected group of [349] prisoners," Mark recalled. "It was like a little camp within a camp. Our Palestine papers had, unlikely, saved our lives."[30] Mother and sons survived, but bore witness to the illness and suffering affecting all other Jewish prisoners on the other side of the wire. Images of mounds of corpses awaiting cremation remain ingrained in Mark's mind, seventy years later.

18. Portrait of Mark (Shlomo) Nusbaum in Antwerp, Belgium, November 1945. Courtesy of Dr. Mark Nusbaum.

After liberation, Mark's brother Aron migrated from Poland to Palestine with a youth *aliyah* transport to join the Hashomer Hatzair movement. Regina and Mark made their way to Antwerp, Belgium, where the youngster finally began his formal education. There, Regina remarried Chiel Elbaum, another survivor who had been part of the same "doomed" transport. The newly wedded couple and son eschewed Palestine and instead filed papers for Canada, home to Regina's brothers, Pinchas and Sam Landau, who had migrated during the interwar period. On 15 May 1948, the same day Israel was declared a nation state, Regina, Chiel, and Mark arrived at Pier 21 in Halifax. The trio travelled at once to Toronto, where they were met by Regina's two brothers, their wives, and families.

"I remember being very impressed by the huge houses, and abundance of food and goods, nothing like postwar Europe," Mark recalled with an air of nostalgia. "I knew right away that I wanted to be Canadian."[31] The sole refugee at his public school, but one of several at the Brunswick Talmud Torah (Jewish afternoon school), Mark faced constant mocking by classmates due to his foreign dress and accent. One cousin defended him, bragging about Mark's knowledge of languages (he spoke five), intellect, and athletic abilities. These very skills proved crucial to his adjustment. Within one year, Mark spoke perfect English, was performing exceptionally academically, and was eager to partake in recreational sports. Desperate to join the football team, Mark forged his mother's signature on the permission slip. She refused to sign, fearing that it was too dangerous an activity. Eventually, Mark succeeded in joining the school's football and baseball teams, serving as a quarterback and pitcher. "I never spoke about my Holocaust experiences and did not want to be known as a *greener*, so I did everything to meld into society and never stand out. Doing well at sports, and being part of a team, helped me become the person I am today," Mark recalled, sixty years later.[32] Mark continued to flourish as a student of the School of Dentistry at the University of Toronto, and married Edith Juda, a fellow child survivor who immigrated to Canada from Hungary in 1951. With support from parents and extended family, and a devout commitment to Jewish life and tradition, Mark and Edith became community leaders and philanthropists, today speaking openly about their wartime experiences.

Sidney Zoltak and Mark Nusbaum were among the "fortunate" child survivors. Both survived the Holocaust and immigrated with at least one of their biological parents—who remained emotionally available and psychologically stable despite their wartime trauma—and were received warmly by relatives in Canada. They did not suffer materially and had homes to live in, and attended school, albeit through night classes in Sidney's case. But whereas Mark found acceptance and friendship with his school-age cousins, Sidney's cousins were less considerate and turned the newcomer into a social pariah, refusing to accompany him to sports games or social outings. Such early experiences helped shape the boys' outlooks and relationships with Canadian Jews. Mark, for his part, surrounded himself with non-survivor peers at his full-day public schools, and joined non-denominational sports teams. Sidney's first years as a new Canadian were spent primarily with and among other Jewish refugees, at the YMHA, JIAS evening classes, and frequenting the New World Club in Montreal. Both young men developed strong identities as Jews, married fellow newcomers, and in adulthood came to terms with their histories as child survivors of the Holocaust. But Sidney, with his now solid grounding as an active member (c. 2014) in Montreal Jewish leadership, co-president of the Canadian Jewish Holocaust Survivors and Descendants, and board member of the Conference on Jewish Material Claims Against Germany, today appears and participates in public Holocaust educational activities more often than does Mark, a community leader in his own right whose wartime experiences remain a personal, though far from hidden, subject.

---

Child survivors brought to Canada under auspices other than the War Orphans Project, with or without parental accompaniment, have little recognized place in the canon of Canadian Holocaust history. Many of these children were born on the eve of warfare, lived under Nazi occupation and through extreme trauma, and witnessed terror and violence, often before they even learned to read or write. Many experienced their formative years without their parents' love or guiding hand, and reluctantly adapted to inhospitable physical environments. Some spent all or part of the war years residing with non-Jewish rescuers in private homes or Christian religious institutions. Others had been in ghettos and concentration camps. All children faced hardships, and most lost siblings and parents to Nazi murder. And yet despite their suffering, children who immigrated to postwar Canada on their own but outside of the War Orphans Project, or in the company of an adult relative, were not considered refugees in their own right. Considered too young to remember their traumatic past, they were typically seen solely as survivors' offspring. Only rarely did children merit the designation of "survivor," an identifier still used only reluctantly by some members of this community.

Years of this identification by adult survivors, as well as Canadian relatives, drove the youngsters into psychologically diminishing their own suffering, and believing that their Holocaust experiences were inconsequential in comparison to the hardships endured by older victims. They suffered silently and often without complete comprehension of the events that they had lived through, and tried, often in vain, to fill the voids in their parent's (or parents') lives. Many child survivors were plagued by loneliness in postwar Canada, and lacked the ability to express feelings or experiences to others. Some met relatives upon arrival in their new homes, but a distance of both age and world experiences made it difficult to establish deep and meaningful relationships at that time. The youngsters also had difficulty relating to Canadian-born peers, who were oblivious to the experiences of their European Jewish schoolmates. Many lived dual and parallel lives, struggling to create a singular identity that encompassed their host of experiences.

But child survivors were not alone in their feelings of displacement and a desire to fit into their new communities. Hassidic and ultra-Orthodox survivors, too, felt ill at ease in Canadian Jewish society. They faced a slew of issues while helping to revitalize, build infrastructure, and raise awareness of traditional Eastern European Jewish life in postwar Montreal. It is this group to whom we turn next.

# CHAPTER FIVE

# KEEPING THE FAITH

*If my survival as a Jew goes down the drain, then what kind of survival*
*are we talking about? Survival, if you live your life as a good Jew: that is*
*Jewish survival.*

—Miriam Frankel[1]

Holocaust survivors who immigrated in the early postwar period negotiated their religious beliefs and practices within a Canadian Jewish society that did not necessarily endorse their traditions. Each group faced distinct challenges concerning its spiritual beliefs and identities, and its future as "Canadian" Jews. And yet, certain challenges appeared universal. Holocaust survivors, regardless of their personal degree of adherence to Judaism, arrived in Canada with some religious background. During the Holocaust, many survivors had clung to their faith, choosing to focus not on what was lost but on what was saved. Hendel Fasten, daughter of a Polish Bobov Hassidic father and Hungarian Belz Hassidic mother, described the faith of the Hassidic survivors in the following way: "All of their [survivors'] motivation and encouragement to succeed and rebuild their lost communities was directly linked to their faith. G-d never abandoned them during the Holocaust; in fact, He helped them survive. So as long as they had life, they had G-d."[2] For those Jews who were raised in the heartland of Hassidic[3] traditions or within ultra-Orthodox *mitnagedim* communities—the central distinction between the factions being the centrality of the "rebbe," or enlightened spiritual leader in the case of the Hassidim—and whose faith did not waver under the storms of Nazi terror, the drive to re-establish a traditional, *heimish* lifestyle trumped all other goals.[4]

Montreal, the cultural centre of Canada's Jewish community in the 1930s and 1940s, experienced the influx of approximately 16,000 Holocaust survivors and children born in the DP camps of Europe in the immediate postwar period. Several hundred of those individuals were involved in the transplantation, establishment, and development of the city's Hassidic and ultra-Orthodox communities; it is their story that opens this chapter. A discussion of the varied experiences of religious functionaries and workers follows.

## *"Black Hatters" in the City*

Contemporary historiography on Canadian Jewish life minimizes the significance and influence of Orthodox or Hassidic Jewry before the Holocaust. During the first half of the twentieth century, Hassidic movements lacked a significant presence in Canada. At most, there were a few individual practitioners. Hassidic life began to develop and exert influence only with the arrival of those communities during and immediately after the Holocaust. Sociologist Jacques Gutwirth, who conducted foundational research on the history of Montreal's Belz Hassidic movement, concluded that the community developed with the refugees who arrived in the city between 1941 and 1952.[5] In his study of the Lubavitch Hassidic community, also in Montreal, William Shaffir writes, "Before 1941, there were [only] a few Lubavitcher Chassidim and Lubavitch sympathizers in Montreal."[6] One Canadian Jewish observer, writing from the perspective of the 1960s, commented on the growth of the Hassidic presence—and the reaction of the "established" members of the Jewish community—in the following way:

> In recent years Canada has seen the growth in this country of the Hasidic Movement, which flourished in Europe for some two hundred years. This movement is a vital, virile and powerful arm of traditional Orthodox Judaism and is usually centred around a Zaddik (a righteous man) who is the spiritual leader of a community or sect that owes almost blind allegiance to the Zaddik or Rabbi. His followers include not only modern Jews but others who identify themselves as Hasidim by dress, manners and action almost identical to that in vogue when the founder of the movement the Baal Shem Tov (Israel Ben Eliezar, c. 1700–1760) was alive...
>
> To us modern Jews in Canada the Hasidim are a strange and even alien group from the seventeenth century now dwelling in this country. When it comes to religious faith and devotions we are mere neophytes. Who knows maybe their way of life has something?[7]

Sociologist Louis Rosenberg barely acknowledges a Hassidic presence in Canada in the first half of the twentieth century.[8] This assessment was reinforced by the traditional insular predilections perpetuated by scholars of Hassidic leaders themselves. Gutwirth, for instance, argued that during the interwar period,

Hassidic rebbes did not want their congregants to abandon their native communities, and actively discouraged Hassidim from immigrating to the New World.[9] Hassidic scholars echoed this sentiment, declaring that life outside of traditional Hassidic communities would inevitably fail in the spiritual "wastelands"—presumably devoid of religious institutional structures necessary for the maintenance of Jewish traditional life—and adherents would deviate from their religious ideals. This notion is reflected in the behaviour of many religious leaders through the 1930s. Appearing oblivious or, at the very least, ignorant of legislated discrimination and persecution of Jews falling under Nazi reign, many rebbes and rabbis across Europe urged their followers to remain in their traditional homes and communities; rather than encouraging escape, particularly in the early days of the Second World War, before escape routes shut tight, rabbis, as Esther Farbstein has observed, "tried to boost their followers' morale and instil in them faith and trust in Divine assistance, which are attained through prayer, hope, and supplication."[10]

Historians cite the arrival of yeshiva students and educators beginning in 1941 as the first substantive indication of Hassidic life in Canada. Those wartime and immediate postwar Hassidic communities, especially in Montreal, evolved in interesting and important ways unique to Canada's culture and history as well as the history of Canada's Jewish community. Hassidic scholars and their followers challenged the status quo of local Jewish communities and contributed to greater religious observance and standards among rabbinical councils at the organizational level, as well as among ordinary Canadian Jews.

Hassidic and ultra-Orthodox survivors faced multiple challenges in resettlement. They found in Canada a Jewish community bereft of acceptable religious infrastructure, a veritable spiritual wasteland from the Hassidic perspective. Hassidim were doubly identified as "different": the native Jewish community saw them as strange foreigners, with regard to their religious observance, appearance, and status as newcomers. And Hassidim saw no established place for themselves in Canadian Jewish society. Yet remarkably, within two decades of their arrival, various Hassidic communities had blossomed in Montreal. Refugees and their young families had rebuilt strictly religiously observant Orthodox community life, complete with the required infrastructure: yeshivas, *shuls*, and *mikvehs* (ritual baths used according to family purity laws). The Hassidim's fervour sparked a reverence for Torah study unfamiliar to most Canadian Jews, and created a safe, insular space in which traditional Hassidic dynasties were resumed.[11]

## The Shanghai Rabbis

The transplantation of traditional Hassidism to Montreal occurred in several steps and through the intervention of influential individuals. The first significant entry of Hassidism occurred in 1941 in the form of a group of primarily Polish yeshiva students and rabbis who had been diverted on their path to Canada to Shanghai, China. The group entered Canada primarily under the aegis of the Union of Orthodox Rabbis of the United States and Canada (Union) and the United Jewish Refugee and War Relief Agencies (later known as UJRA).

After the invasion of Poland by Nazi Germany and the Soviet Union, an Orthodox Jewish organization founded at the turn of the twentieth century in New York City brought together representatives from organized North American religious Jewry and institutions to establish the Vaad Hatzala, the Committee for Rescue.[12] The primary purpose of the Vaad was to rescue yeshivas disrupted by the war and to transplant religious leaders and students to safe sites for the duration of hostilities. Having successfully removed the remnants of several yeshivas and rabbis from war-torn Europe to Siberia, Shanghai, and Palestine, the Vaad turned its attention to maintaining the refugees until permanent new homes could be found for all of the scholars.[13] The Vaad prevailed upon Canadian and American officials to issue emergency visas to rescue rabbinical teachers.[14] The UJRA, an advocacy and relief organization, "gave the guarantee to the Canadian Government as to the care and the maintenance of the individuals concerned."[15] This group of eighty students and rabbis had (mostly) originated in Otwock, Poland, where they had previously studied at the famous Lubavitch and Mir yeshivas, respectively. With the onset of wartime hostilities, the group moved to then-unoccupied Vilna, which had remained part of Poland until October 1939, at which time the Soviet Union transferred territorial authority to Lithuania. Fleeing Nazi persecution, they traversed Soviet Asia before landing in Shanghai, where they established a yeshiva and resumed their studies.[16]

With the tremendous support of American Jewish leaders—whom he had visited in the 1930s—and with support from his followers and powerful allies in Europe and the United States, the sixth Lubavitcher rebbe, the dynamic Joseph Isaac (Yosef Itzchak) Schneerson, escaped Nazi Europe in March 1940. He travelled out of Warsaw, through Berlin and then-unoccupied Latvia before finally landing in New York City with his daughter and son-in-law. Rebbe Schneerson immediately undertook efforts to rescue his students trapped overseas.[17] Immigration director F.C. Blair resisted the Vaad Hatzala's pleas, outright rejecting the plot as insincere. The rabbis, he argued, could not be trusted; they had sought—and been denied—entry into the United States. Interest in Canada was secondary. Additionally, Blair argued, "The Jewish population of this country is not sufficient to absorb a group of eighty rabbis."[18] Bowing to significant international pressure, the Canadian government eventually conceded. Despite his ardent efforts against it, Blair's office produced eighty emergency entry visas for the refugee rabbis and scholars temporarily stuck in Shanghai. On 23 and 24 October 1941, twenty-nine of the yeshiva students and rabbis landed in Montreal. The rest of the visa-holders, trapped by the spread of war, did not arrive in Canada until July 1946.[19] Nine of the October 1941 refugees were ordained rabbis, and one was the widow of the chief rabbi of Radom. The remaining nineteen stood at various points of their seminary careers.[20] Of this group, nine were former students of the Lubavitcher rebbe Yosef Itzchak Schneerson.

The group's arrival in Montreal evoked excitement and was widely reported in both Yiddish- and English-language newspapers. Leaders of Montreal's Jewish community expressed pride in having supported the rescue of the refugees, and greeted the newcomers eagerly. The excitement radiates from the following public announcement of 30 October 1941, which reads, "The yeshiva scholars of Lubavitch and Mir, now part of the Montreal community, will no doubt constitute an invaluable asset to our communal life. The sacrifices which they have endured since their flight from Poland...are like a beacon of light in these days of darkness and despair. After their wanderings across three continents and an ocean, they now find a resting place in Montreal where they may continue unbroken that noble tradition."[21]

One emissary of the Lubavitcher rebbe Rabbi Schneerson, visiting from New York to greet the refugees, reported that "the interest of the city's Jews was intense: the Talmud Torah [on St. Joseph's Boulevard, the site of a breakfast reception] was packed with rabbis, representatives from synagogues, organizations and just ordinary concerned fellow Jews."[22] Canadian Jews who helped facilitate the entry visas for the religious refugees and planned celebrations in their honour did not themselves observe Orthodox traditions. But, they seemingly (or, reportedly) respected the ultra-Orthodox refugees' reverence for Torah and learning. The students and rabbis, trained in Hassidic and Lithuanian-style yeshivas, signalled a potential for great change in Jewish life—a goal for the refugees if not necessarily Canadian-born Jews, many of whom responded to the newcomers' efforts with ambivalence—and raised hope that their presence might strengthen the status of religious life among Canadian Jews.[23]

Certainly this was the aspiration of the local religious leadership in Montreal. An undated memo from the executive council of the Rabbinical Seminaries of Montreal declared that amidst the destruction of Europe's "great and glorious [rabbinical] institutions," a near-miracle had occurred, and

> a small group of the Yeshiva-students succeeded in escaping from the Nazi hell, and it is a very great privilege for Montreal Jewry, that the centre of the European Torah-learning has been established here. The leaders of Montreal Jewry have not spared any efforts to get the necessary entry permits for these Yeshiva-boys, who were awaiting them in the Far East, in Shanghai. The efforts of Montreal Jewry were crowned with the success 6 months ago, when we had the great honour to welcome the first group of Talmidei Chachamim [esteemed scholars] (29 persons).... The Yeshivos became a very blessing and pride of our Jewish life.[24]

While pleased by the local community leadership's reception, few of the yeshiva students and rabbis planned to remain in Montreal. Most wished to move on as quickly as possible to the United States. The nine former students of the Lubavitcher rebbe in particular hoped to resume learning at his recently established yeshiva, Tomchei Tmimim, in New York. But, when they turned to him for advice, his response shocked them. The rebbe instructed the young men to remain in Montreal and establish a Lubavitch yeshiva immediately. Within two days, the refugees' efforts to bring Lubavitch Hassidism to Montreal through the establishment of the Rabbinical College of Canada (Lubavitch)-Tomchei Tmimim were underway. While the prospect of a respected yeshiva piqued the interest of Canadian Jews, the refugee scholars undertook an enormous task. With very limited resources—including minimal funds from Schneerson and donations from Montreal Jews—and little infrastructure upon which to build, the Orthodox and Hassidic refugees began to build communities from scratch. Religious needs were addressed in Montreal through the organization of the Tomchei Tmimim yeshiva. Initially, the intention was to have the yeshiva function as a joint institution for both the Lubavitch Hassidim and the *mitnagedim* refugee scholars who practised Lithuanian-style, non-Hassidic Orthodox learning. This arrangement existed out of necessity; the limited funds and resources, a select group of educators, and a small pool of potential students did not allow for the establishment of separate institutions.

Among the nine Lubavitch refugee scholars, several had served as rosh yeshivas (principal educators) at the original Lubavitch yeshiva in Otwock, Poland, and shared close relationships with the Lubavitcher rebbe. (The scholars from the non-Hassidic Mir Yeshiva had no comparable leader.) For this reason, Montreal's first yeshiva followed Lubavitch principles. It operated in the basement of Nusach Ari Synagogue, an Orthodox congregation, on Pine Street East.

Although the original yeshiva aimed to provide inclusive education (focusing on Orthodox traditions and observance, not Hassidic thought) for Canadian Jewish children and adults, the Lubavitch Hassidim considered themselves unique from the non-Hassidic Orthodox scholars, particularly with regard to philosophies concerning education and the status of the rebbe in the community. Within the first year of its operation, the yeshiva split into two: the Lubavitch-run Rabbinical College of Canada—Tomchei Tmimim—and Yeshiva Gedola Merkaz Hatorah—the Lithuanian-style *mitnagedim* institute. The nine Lubavitch refugee scholars, including founding Rosh Yeshiva Rabbis Aryeh Leib Kramer, Yitzchak Hendel, and Moses Elias Gerlitzky, wasted no time implementing programming at Tomchei Tmimim, both formal and informal. In everything they did, the religious refugees stressed the relevance and importance of Orthodox Judaism in everyday life. They challenged the organized Jewish community's lack of interest in Orthodox religious practices, as shown by their lax Sabbath, *kashrut*, and family purity observance.

For the first year of its existence, the Lubavitch yeshiva functioned primarily as an after-school auxiliary educational institution, and attracted nearly eighty Canadian-born students during the initial few months of operation.[25] The youth were divided into three groups based on their age and previous instruction in Jewish religious thought, and taught at synagogues throughout the city's immigrant Jewish sector off of Park Avenue. Tuition fees were waived for the first year, so that financial considerations would not deter parents from granting children yeshiva educations. Refugee students never paid tuition.[26] The Orthodox refugees also founded youth organizations and summer camps, both in the city and north of Montreal, in the Laurentian Mountains. The purpose of these institutions was to combine religious instruction, through lectures about Torah and Hassidic stories, and family values, with recreational activities.[27] The Lubavitch strove to make traditional Jewish living attractive to younger generations of less-observant Jews by demonstrating the compatibility of an observant Jewish life in modern Canada.

The founding of Tomchei Tmimim proved to be the first concrete step toward establishing Montreal's diverse Hassidic communities. The yeshiva quickly attained status as the centre of Lubavitch life in all of Canada. It served as a social and religious centre, a place to pray (three times daily for the males), celebrate *simchas* such as weddings and bar mitzvahs, and share social and employment contacts. As the size of the Lubavitch Hassidim grew, the entire community would physically relocate to remain within walking distance of the yeshiva. And grow the community it did, albeit gradually.

The first additions to the community came from among German and Austrian Jews formerly interned by the British as enemy aliens at the Île-aux-Noix, Quebec, camp.[28] After more than eighteen months of internment, many of the men were released into the custody of the Canadian Jewish Congress. Tomchei Tmimim applied to the CJC and provided guarantees for the care and maintenance of any young men released into its custody, while the UJRA put up the financial backing. From this group, fifteen young observant former internees joined Montreal's fledgling Lubavitch yeshiva and strove to complete an education that had been interrupted by the war.[29]

While those fifteen German and Austrian Jewish refugees did not necessarily enter the yeshiva as Hassidim in 1943, more than half exited as confirmed Lubavitchers. They quickly established themselves within Montreal's small Lubavitch community and grew accustomed to Hassidic observance and traditions, which included the adoption of Yiddish as the vernacular.[30] The young men respected the Lubavitch refugees' strength of character and determination to root their brand of Hassidism on Canadian soil, and wished to take part in this transplantation.

The incorporation of the internees increased the Lubavitch community of Montreal's numbers to approximately twenty-five by 1943. Gradually, the male members began to marry. A problem quickly arose—there were no local Hassidic women to wed. No single Hassidic female had been among those rescued by the Union or the CJC, and not one of the German or Austrian former internees was a woman. In Europe, Hassidim married strictly within their own communities. But, in Canada, the Hassidic refugees were compelled to marry Canadian- or American-born women raised in Orthodox, though not Hassidic, homes. The grooms' unstated goal was to marry into families that appeared receptive to Lubavitch ideology and practice, thus increasing the breadth of Lubavitch followers and sympathizers. As we shall see, they achieved their aim.

## Postwar Development

The first substantial postwar influx of Lubavitch refugees to Canada came in 1946 and 1947. This group comprised the remaining handful of yeshiva scholars who were granted Canadian entry visas in 1941, but had been trapped in Shanghai for the war's duration. This group brought years of yeshiva training to the Montreal community.

Lubavitch Hassidim's growing numbers in Montreal were rounded out by the arrival of seventy-eight Lubavitch Holocaust survivors between the years 1947 and 1956. Many of these survivors had narrowly escaped Nazi terror by fleeing German-occupied territory into Soviet Russia early in the Second World War. They waited out the war deep in Soviet Asia, performing forced labour in harsh climates. Yet, despite horrendous living conditions, several arrived in Canada with their families intact, a situation nearly unheard of for Jews who had experienced the Holocaust under Nazi occupation.[31] The presence of "complete" families, with two parents and children, fundamentally transformed the dynamics and structural demands of the Hassidic community, which had heretofore focused on the needs of mainly single, adult males.

Montreal's Lubavitch community grew to include nearly sixty families by the mid-1950s, almost entirely comprising wartime refugees and postwar Holocaust survivors striving to recreate their lives according to the strict customs and traditions of Lubavitch Hassidism.[32] As the community grew, so did the religious and social infrastructure required to serve the population. Tomchei Tmimim began as an institute of higher learning, with the specific intent of continuing the refugee scholars' Torah education and providing the youth in the group with rabbinical ordination. By the 1944–1945 school year, it had added a full-time day-school program and opened a separate girls' school, Beth Rivkah. The latter was especially significant in Canadian Jewish life, since it was the country's first all-girls' Jewish day school.[33] Within less than a decade, the yeshiva offered elementary and high school education and full-time yeshiva study, as well as after-school programs and adult education classes for day labourers. By 1955, members of the Executive Committee on Yeshivoth in Montreal counted twenty-eight students engaged in full-time Torah study; in the 1956–1957 academic year, the number rose to include forty students, thirty-three of whom were postwar refugees.[34]

Between 1955 and 1957, Tomchei Tmimim collected data on its performance and growth over the previous decade to present at the recently established Conference of Jewish Material Claims Against Germany, Inc. (henceforth, "Claims Conference"). Formed in 1951 and consecrated on 10 September 1952, the organization emerged through an agreement between the West German federal government and a body known as the "Claims Conference," consisting of national (American) and international Jewish organizational leaders. The agenda stipulated a program of indemnification of material damages to Jewish victims who survived Nazi persecution, and to the Jewish people at large, through two protocols: direct monetary compensation to survivors through restitution claims, and a provision of 450 million *reichmarks* for the relief, rehabilitation, and resettlement of surviving European Jews.[35] As part of the Conference's focus on aiding needy survivors, the Committee on Yeshivas was established to handle the distribution of funds to transplanted yeshivas in North America, Europe, and Israel. A transplanted yeshiva was defined as an institution that was formed in pre-war, wartime, or postwar Europe, and that, after displacement by Nazi Germany, re-established itself in a new country. In order to qualify for German monetary restitution from the mid-1950s onward, a transplanted yeshiva needed to demonstrate its undertaking of teaching responsibilities for "students who were above the age of 16, engaged in full-time studies on a level of higher learning, and defined as direct victims of Nazi persecution."[36] Based on this criterion, Tomchei Tmimim qualified for—and received—$4,000 from the Claims Conference yeshiva fund in 1957.

Declarations to the CJC and Claims Conference emphasized the support offered to refugee students at Tomchei Tmimim. Rabbi Kramer, the Rosh Yeshiva, reported that students of higher learning received full maintenance and support, including "three meals daily in private restaurants (for six days a week since Saturday meals the students usually have in private homes as guests) at the cost of $11.50 weekly for each student. For boarding, the Yeshiva rented rooms which averaged about $15.00 a month for each student. In addition, the Yeshiva covers occasional expenses for clothing, medical care, etc."[37] S.D. Gameroff, a member of the yeshiva's board of officers, stressed that financial assistance from the Claims Conference was critically important. Fifteen years after its founding, and assuming an ongoing commitment to providing Torah education to survivors of Nazi persecution (and their dependents), the yeshiva was in debt. With six ordained rabbis employed as teachers, and the costs of the yeshiva's physical upkeep, the funding sought and received from the Claims Conference was essential to ensuring Tomchei Tmimim's continuing operations.[38]

The Montreal-based Rabbinical College of Canada granted rabbinical ordination (*smicha*) to eight students, including six Holocaust survivors, in 1955. All eight new rabbis also attended either Sir George Williams College or McGill University on a part-time basis, becoming well-rounded scholars ready and willing to lead congregations throughout Canada, and with the hope of spreading Lubavitch message and tradition. Two years later, Tomchei Tmimim proudly graduated fifty alumni students of its program of higher education (non-elementary or high school levels), including twelve former students holding positions as religious functionaries in various Jewish communities across the country serving as rabbis, teachers or ritual slaughterers.[39] The Lubavitch refugees had successfully transplanted a more observant Jewish life, whether it was Hassidic or *mitnagedim* tradition, to Montreal and transformed the status of Jewish religious life. William Shaffir concludes that although the Jewish community at large bore much of the responsibility for the tenability of Montreal's Lubavitch community, considerable benefits to non-Lubavitch Jews had been great: "The presence of the Lubavitch in Montreal signifies to many, especially non-observant Jews, that orthodox Judaism still flourishes."[40]

Of all observant survivor groups, the Lubavitch Hassidim made the greatest efforts toward outreach and stressed the inclusivity of all Jews, despite the community's own tradition of insularity in pre-war Europe. Lubavitcher Rebbe Schneerson and his successor, Rebbe Menachem Mendel Schneerson, in New York, provided crucial support for the growing community. In addition to educational material, the Lubavitcher rebbe afforded the local Hassidim legitimacy. The refugee scholars and students negotiated places for themselves quickly in all ranks of Montreal Jewish life. They cooperated with, and participated in, community-wide activities alongside non-Hassidic Orthodox rabbis and less observant Canadian Jewish constituents. The implications of such proactive outreach were significant for both the Hassidim and the local Jewish community in general.

Lubavitch (and other Hassidic and ultra-Orthodox) rabbis acquired membership on the Vaad Ha'ir, Montreal's guiding institution on all aspects of Jewish life and law. The refugee rabbis and their congregations thus early on gained a formidable communal voice. Lubavitcher Rabbi Yizchak Hendel and his colleagues helped develop and enforce stricter laws surrounding Montreal's production and distribution of kosher food, and the accreditation of religious functionaries. He served on the Beit Din (the Jewish community's rabbinical court), and through this and other communal functions had vehicles through which to incorporate Hassidic ideology into the daily lives of Montreal Jews.[41] Irwin Cotler, a Canadian Jewish scholar, communal leader, Member of Parliament, and former Cabinet minister, praises these early Hassidic rabbis, and especially Rabbi Kramer, as playing key roles in the ongoing development of Montreal Jewry, and as having served as role models for all Canadian Jews. Lubavitch Rabbi Kramer was, Cotler wrote upon the rabbi's death in 1999, "not only a teacher and *tzaddik*, but also a *meilitz yosher*, a righteous person who was always there for everybody. For me, he was a teacher, a mentor, a confidante, somebody that I could rely on...somebody that played a profound role in my life."[42]

## Mitnagedim

As the Lubavitch community began to plant its roots, another community of religiously ultra-Orthodox non-Hassidic Jews broke ground in Montreal as well. Emerging from among the first wave of refugee students and Torah scholars who arrived via Shanghai in late 1941, Lithuanian-style *mitnagedim* rabbis initially collaborated with the Lubavitch on the establishment of Montreal's Yeshiva Tomchei Tmimim. This arrangement quickly proved mutually incompatible, due largely to significant ideological and pedagogical disputes. By 1942, the *mitnagedim* scholars, led by Rabbi Pinchas Hirschprung (later named the Chief Rabbi of Montreal and a prominent leader on the Vaad Ha'ir) and later, Rabbi Leib Baron, split from Tomchei Tmimim and founded an independent institution, Yeshiva Merkaz Hatorah.[43]

The ranks of Merkaz Hatorah grew significantly in the summer of 1946 with the arrival of the "Shanghai rabbis," the remaining members of the group of approximately sixty refugee rabbis and scholars (and families) of the Lithuanian Mir Yeshiva that had been granted wartime entry visas by Canada but had found themselves stranded in Shanghai until the end of hostilities.[44] The debate concerning these "Shanghai Rabbis," specifically the Canadian Jewish community's obligation to supporting members of the group, raged for years. Individuals granted entry into Canada were expected to settle in the country and contribute to its economic, intellectual, and spiritual development. Nearly all of the religious functionaries, however, viewed Canada as a layover en route to the United States. The Canadian Jewish Congress and United Jewish Relief Agencies adamantly refused to support religious functionaries perceived as attempting to manipulate Canada's humanitarian stance, and refused to provide financial aid or immigration assistance. So in accordance with agreements between the Canadian Jewish Congress and the AJDC, a number of the rabbis grudgingly accepted temporary stays in Canada while they awaited American entry visas.[45] The remainder, however, accepted their lot and quickly integrated with the activities of Merkaz Hatorah. In 1950, it was the first yeshiva to ordain local and refugee rabbis. By the mid-1950s, Holocaust survivors made up only 30 percent of the student body, with the remaining 70 percent of the spaces filled by Canadian-born Jews.[46]

Like the Lubavitch Yeshiva Tomchei Tmimim, Merkaz Hatorah evolved into a highly regarded institute of advanced Jewish learning. School enrolment for survivors' offspring was not necessarily reflective of the families' religious practices. Yeshivas provided survivors with a sense of nostalgia and comfort; rabbis and refugees alike hoped that even without the security of the "old world," a traditional European-style yeshiva education would connect children to their familial and spiritual heritage. Parents not raised in the *mitnagedim* tradition were also impressed by the high standards of both religious and secular education offered by Merkaz Hatorah, and wished to give their children a quality traditional religious education previously unavailable to them.[47] The local *mitnagedim* community's reputation expanded beyond Montreal, and attracted rabbinical students from across Canada. Merkaz Hatorah provided these ambitious young men—refugees and Canadian-born Jews alike—with an alternative to yeshivas in the United States or Israel, and made it possible for Canadian Jews to receive their religious education at home.

Several refugee rabbis from the *mitnagedim* community served on Montreal's Beit Din, but none did more to affect Montreal Jewry's religious standards than Rabbi Pinchas Hirschprung. A refugee rabbi and one of Merkaz Hatorah's original educators, Rabbi Hirschprung first served on numerous councils before accepting the role of chief rabbi of Montreal from 1969 until his death in 1998.[48] Widely respected by his own *mitnagedim* community, Hassidim with whom he cooperated closely, and less observant Jewish groups, the rabbi strove to help incorporate ultra-Orthodox customs and traditions into daily Jewish life in Montreal.[49]

Montreal welcomed two transplanted yeshivas soon after the end of the war. The First Mesifta of Canada yeshiva, founded in 1948 by the Klausenberger rebbe (then residing in New York), began when eight of the Klausenberger rebbe's refugee disciples arrived in Montreal. When the young men discovered that their visas did not permit entry into the United States, the Klausenberger rebbe did the next best thing: he assigned Rabbi Shmuel Alexander Unsdorfer, a Holocaust survivor, to help them establish a branch of the yeshiva in Montreal. The small but active yeshiva evolved quickly.[50]

The other yeshiva transplanted to Montreal was the Maor Hagolah Rabbinical College. Headed by Rabbi Ephraim Oshry, the non-Hassidic yeshiva had been formed by smaller groups of rabbis and yeshiva students inside wartime ghettos and DP camps. Observant survivors travelled from DP camp to DP camp, before a single seminary was established in Austria in late 1945. Soon after, with the aid of a British chaplain, the entire group crossed into Italy, where the yeshiva established itself permanently in Rome. With the assistance of the CJC, and specifically through the inclusion of highly religious youth under eighteen years of age among the War Orphans Project quota, twenty-three of the yeshiva's students and their rabbis entered Canada as refugees on 25 July 1949.[51] With $5,000 in start-up funds donated by South Africa's Jewish community, Rabbi Oshry purchased a house in the overwhelmingly Jewish and immigrant Montreal neighbourhood of the Plateau, from which the yeshiva and surrounding community evolved.[52] Yearly campaign dinners and funding from branches in Israel and New York helped sustain the yeshiva through the 1950s and 1960s.[53]

## Religious Life in Canada, Post-1947

Among the waves of displaced persons to arrive in the country during this period were individual survivors and young families adhering to Hassidic and *mitnagedim* traditions. Although a number of the (male) newcomers had pre-war yeshiva education, including some ordained religious functionaries, most were ordinary persons raised in strictly observant homes.

Orthodox survivors overwhelmingly sought to settle in Montreal, home (in the late 1940s and early 1950s) to the country's largest Jewish community. The trickling in of newcomers gave impetus for the various Hassidic and *mitnagedim* groups and their respective yeshivas to blossom. More than anything, the survivors ached to belong to a community reminiscent of their pre-war lives. With determination and absolute faith in God's presence and support, the ultra-Orthodox survivors helped fill out the communities' ranks, raising funds to build permanent yeshivas and *shuls*, and imparting their religious faith and principles on the non-observant.[54]

At this time, pre-war affiliation with specific Hassidic dynasties and geographical origins carried minimal weight and were of little consequence, except for individuals with long-standing rabbinical lineages.[55] The few surviving Hassidim who had made their way to postwar Montreal, and who had belonged to a specific sect, proved willing to join another Hassidic community. And many of the Hungarian Orthodox survivors not raised as Hassidim happily joined the various Hassidic communities and adopted their principles and distinguishing features, such as dress, within a few years of immigration to Canada.[56]

Montreal's Hassidic and other, non-Hassidic ultra-Orthodox communities continued to develop and flourish, both in terms of influence and numbers, since their establishment in the 1940s. The city's Vaad Ha'ir adopted the religious survivors' high standards with respect to *kashrut*, family purity laws and guidelines for conversion, by the early 1950s. The Hassidim and *mitnagedim* newcomers established schools then attended by Canadian-born Jews, headed Orthodox congregations, produced and dispersed necessary religious items for all Jews (including Torahs, phylacteries or *tefillin*, and prayer shawls or *tallit*), and began to find employment in the secular world. They helped herald in, and preserve, a rejuvenation of Jewish life in Montreal, and attracted previously unaffiliated Jews searching for a sense of belonging. These developments suggest the openness of the postwar community to consider, and sometimes embrace, traditional religious Jewish observance. Hassidic and ultra-Orthodox Judaism offered less observant Canadian Jews what some saw as an opportunity for spiritual growth and awareness, which in turn solidified the influence and significance of the religious community's presence in postwar Montreal.[57]

## Religious Functionaries and Labourers

The approximately 35,000 Holocaust survivors and their dependents who immigrated to Canada in the aftermath of the Second World War faced the challenges associated with all immigrants, including linguistic difficulties and a lack of or unrecognized education or skills. In addition, the Jewish refugees carried the burden of their wartime trauma. Jewish men, whose traditional heritage was all but destroyed during the Holocaust, faced an additional obstacle. For this diverse group, encompassing yeshiva students, rebbes and ordained rabbis, cantors, and ritual slaughterers (*schoichets*), the maintenance of their cultural and religious legacy conflicted with the postwar socially accepted norms, practices, customs, and traditions of Canadian Jewry. Most specifically, the devoutly religious male survivors' values stood at variance with the norms of the secular Jewish social service agencies charged with their care.[58]

Although female Hassidic and highly observant survivors also required aid from service agencies, their voices are noticeably absent from the narrative. In the postwar period, women, particularly within Orthodox survivor communities, were not permitted to train as religious functionaries or hold public positions on religious councils. Very few Hassidic or ultra-Orthodox refugee women possessed formal education beyond elementary school, and usually studied the minimal amount of Hebrew necessary to recite prayers. They arrived in Canada primarily as young wives and mothers, leaving little time or opportunity for employment outside the household during their early years in the country. Although they do not figure largely in the narrative to follow, they played significant roles in their respective communities' developments.[59]

Highly devout survivors received assistance from the same social service agencies as did many other Jewish refugees and immigrants: JIAS caseworkers provided practical settlement supports, and JVS offered employment and aptitude testing, training, and counselling. Regional offices were authorized to expend no more than $100 per immigrant in aid.[60] The Canadian Jewish Congress stance on supporting the religious newcomers was clear—devout survivors brought to Canada under the aegis of the CJC or UJRA should receive the same treatment as their co-religionists. In practice, however, although they sponsored the incoming religious functionaries and scholars, and benefited from the services and wisdom they imparted to the community, the established Jewish community provided only nominal financial support to this particular survivor subgroup in its effort to strengthen religious life across Canada. As an internal memo explained, UJRA funds were "not intended to endow institutions of learning but are solely for the transmission for the relief of starving Jewry overseas and in cases of necessity to enable refugees in Canada to subsist while orientating themselves to Canadian conditions."[61] In the cases of yeshiva students and scholars who opted to learn Torah full-time, and who "had no intention of becoming orientated to the economic life of this country," the memo continued, financial assistance was to be revoked immediately.[62]

JIAS caseworker records indicate that pious survivors required, on average, more intensive support, extending over a longer period of time, than other refugees. A number of factors can help to explain this phenomenon. Hassidic and other ultra-Orthodox men in general possessed certain distinguishing characteristics. For those working in the Jewish social service sector, religious men appeared "pathetic," with their long, unkempt beards and *payes* (side locks).[63] They wore *kippahs* (skull caps) or *streimels* (fur hats worn by married men on the Sabbath and holidays), and the Hassidim sported traditional long coats and dark suits. The social workers reported feeling repulsed by such attire, which frequently evoked discriminatory attitudes from Jewish and non-Jewish employers uneasy with such outward displays of religious affiliation.[64] Social workers acknowledged avoiding taking cases of ultra-Orthodox Jews, whom they perceived as "difficult clients" unable to accept the limitations of organizational support.[65]

Canada was, and remains, a liberal democratic country that tolerates religious diversity. Officially, adult survivors who adhered to strict Orthodox or Hassidic traditions were permitted to live according to their religious standards. But, they faced serious challenges to do so. Ultra-Orthodox and Hassidic survivors found that the greatest obstacles to strict religious observance in their adopted country related to the elements of the existing Jewish communities, and their different understandings of religious observance, as well as social and cultural norms.[66]

Social work professionals and non-Orthodox Canadian Jews acknowledged feeling uneasy not only with the Hassidic and ultra-Orthodox men's outward appearance, but also with the strict family customs and traditions they and their wives practised. In accordance with religious family purity laws, many married couples applied for the provision of two single beds, as opposed to the standard double to be shared between them.[67] In response to this request, one social worker noted (either cynically or out of genuine ignorance) in the case summary, that, "he needed to investigate the need for two beds from a religious standpoint."[68] In another instance, a different caseworker repeatedly reminded the couple in question that granting two beds was an "exception to our rule," for which they should be grateful.[69] Ignorance dictated the social workers' immediate assumption that the very religious survivors were greedy and were likely to take advantage of community assistance.

Uneasiness in the presence of pious survivors was also expressed by other survivors, who viewed their more religious cohorts as an obstacle to—and an unfortunate distraction from—their own integration. Many perceived their observant contemporaries as obsessed with living their lives in outdated and incompatible manners "that should have been left in the old country," and as exceptionally difficult and stubborn people. Frustrated by what they considered to be the eccentricity displayed by their fellow newcomers, less observant survivors tried their best to distinguish themselves through their conduct and manner of life, adopting North American styles of clothing whenever possible.[70]

## The Challenge of Religious Functionaries

Highly observant males, often with professional backgrounds as trained religious functionaries, presented a moral dilemma for Jewish social service workers as well as the Vaad Ha'ir, Montreal's Jewish Community Council. On the one hand, members of the Vaad and some secular Jewish workers respected the background and determination of the survivor rabbis, cantors, and ritual slaughterers. They understood the newcomers' desire to re-establish their former positions as community leaders and preserve their traditional Jewish way of life. On the other hand, practical challenges abounded. In her 1952 master of social work thesis, "The Prevention of Hard Core Cases Among the Immigrant Displaced Persons," JIAS social worker Sylvia Endler discerned that while all newcomers experienced problems, "extreme orthodoxy may affect every area in which the immigrant is attempting to make an adjustment."[71] Her research identified five areas where the incompatible culture patterns of Orthodoxy existed: employer prejudice; problems relating to incompatible culture patterns (i.e., to excuse poor hygiene or ignore agency advice);[72] the inability to take employment under certain working conditions; refusal to accept work other than as a religious functionary; and, the lack of industrial training due to extreme degrees of Orthodoxy.[73] These patterns of incompatibility were compounded by other issues not relating to religiosity, and presented in nearly all cases involving ultra-Orthodox refugees. As noted below, CJC professionals agreed with Endler's assessment:

> The Jewish Vocational Service in Montreal has been encountering considerable difficulties in finding employment for orthodox refugees. At present there are open about 80 cases of new arrivals (mostly under the Close Relatives Scheme) who cannot be placed.... A suggestion

has been advanced at the meeting that special training courses be considered for the orthodox immigrants; it was, however, felt that the problem of providing training courses was a rather complicated one and that immediate steps ought to be taken to cope with the situation and to place the new arrivals as quickly as possible.[74]

Concerns about both Jewish and non-Jewish employer prejudice existed on several levels. In Europe, very religious Jews had traditionally been labelled as weak and unable and unwilling to perform hard manual labour. Such discriminatory attitudes had been transported across the ocean to Canada.[75] Many Jewish employers, mainly in the needle trade or other labour industries, only reluctantly hired Hassidic and *mitnagedim* workers. Moreover, secular or less observant Jewish workers charged with the refugees' care tended to abide by more liberal (and in some cases even radical) ideological views that clashed with those of their more observant co-workers. This, too, led to conflict in the workplace. Refusal to work on the Sabbath and Jewish holidays also proved problematic, leading to a perception on the part of some non-Orthodox workers that the ultra-Orthodox were receiving special privileges or not "pulling their weight."

The alternative for many observant survivors was the route of self-employment. Herschel Perl, a survivor from Romania, faced significant financial challenges upon arrival in Toronto owing to his refusal to work on Shabbat. So, with twenty-four dollars to his name, he opened a small kosher butcher shop in 1954, the first in Ontario to sell meat and chicken already koshered. His company, H. Perl Products, became a major Canadian supplier of kosher deli products and the most successful kosher meat store in Canada. This decision to embrace self-employment enabled Perl to uphold his religious obligations without sacrificing his livelihood.[76] Other survivors were often left lacking the means or drive to establish themselves independently, and so stood at the mercy of primarily non-Orthodox Jewish employers, many of them immigrants from an earlier generation but uncomfortable with visual reminders of their European Jewish heritage, such as *payes* or long beards, in their factories.[77] For such employers, observant survivors represented an outdated, undesirable version of the Jew that they had deliberately left behind when they began their new lives in Canada.

The case of one Rabbi Erlich underlies some of the adaptation issues faced by refugee religious functionaries. A recent arrival to Canada, Rabbi Erlich had frequented the offices of the JVS and undertaken efforts to integrate into Montreal's existing ultra-Orthodox community. Despite such efforts, he was unable to obtain employment as a rabbi or a *mohel* (a person trained to perform ritual circumcisions). During his first six months in Canada, the rabbi and his family received financial support from JIAS but did not, according to their caseworker, make significant strides toward self-sufficiency. Following protocol, Benjamin Goldman, a supervisor at Montreal's Baron de Hirsch Institute, discontinued assistance at the end of the six-month period. Rabbi Herschorn of the Rabbinical Council of Montreal addressed a letter to Mr. Goldman requesting continued assistance for Rabbi Erlich and his family. The following are the crucial paragraphs of that letter:

> I wish to advise you that we know Rabbi Erlich since he came to Canada. He comes to our office frequently, and we discuss with him his personal problem as well as the problem of the other few rabbis who came to Canada in the last two years or so. Rabbi Erlich, as he already advised you, is by profession a "mohel." As time goes on, he may become popular in his vocation and he may also find a Congregation who would take him in as their rabbi.

> It is the opinion of the Council of Rabbis that with this case of new arrivals, organized community must have special consideration and must approach this problem in an entirely different manner. To discontinue assistance will not solve this problem. It will only aggravate the situation.... We should treat these few rabbonim with merited consideration and with the respect due to them as men of Torah.[78]

The Rabbinical Council recognized the difficulties of religious observance in a secular world, and wanted the religious functionaries to return to their former livelihoods. The Council sent out countless letters to Jewish communities in Canada, seeking openings for the refugees. For religious functionaries with recognized *smicha* (rabbinical ordination), like Rabbi Erlich, language barriers did not present a great issue; many pulpits in postwar Canada still operated exclusively in Yiddish and Hebrew.

While some Jewish communities submitted requests to the CJC to sponsor the immigration of specific rabbis, the arrival of scores of qualified scholars among the first wave of Holocaust survivor refugees meant that the supply vastly overwhelmed the demand. There was a virtual free-for-all for a handful of employment opportunities for rabbis, cantors, and other religious functionaries in Canada.

*Shoichets* (ritual slaughterers), in particular, competed for a select few positions. After arriving in Montreal with his wife in August of 1952, fifty-seven-year-old Moses G initiated active contact with JIAS and JVS workers in an effort to secure placement as a *shoichet*. Trained in Hungary, Mr. G's case attracted much attention from social workers and rabbis alike, thanks to his nearly three decades of work experience, including service in postwar DP camps, and impressive professional references. Mr. G's willingness to accept any work, and openness to the possibility of professional re-certification, raised his file's profile. Mrs. Gorby of JIAS's Montreal office composed a letter on Mr. G's behalf to her colleagues at JIAS Toronto, to determine whether opportunities might exist for him in Ontario. D. Drutz, the executive director of JIAS, central region, offered the following reply: "I must advise you that the market for schoichets is loaded in Toronto. There are a million and one shochtom, mashgichim and rabbis in this town all seeking the opportunity of slaughtering a very limited supply of chickens and allied fowl. In fact, there are more people skilled in this art than there are chickens."[79]

Refugee Rabbi Hirschprung of Yeshiva Merkaz Hatorah, by 1952 a standing member of Montreal's Vaad Ha'ir, took an active interest in Mr. G's case. With his assistance, Mr. G began retraining part-time as a *shoichet* according to Canadian standards, under the guidance of the Vaad, and worked part-time at the Sheltered Workshop, an initiative that helped recipients of financial aid earn a nominal income through modified work, thus lessening their dependency on community funds.[80] Nine months after undertaking retraining, JIAS closed Mr. G's case file; still requiring assistance, the case was transferred to Jewish Family and Child Welfare Bureau. Owing to the CJC's immigration sponsorship agreement, whereby the organized Jewish community accepted complete responsibility, financial or otherwise, of Jewish refugees for five years following immigration, service professionals avoided transferring cases beyond Jewish service agencies. Requests for state support could label the refugees as dependents on the state, and jeopardize immigration applications with the threat of deportation. There is no indication in the file that Mr. G's case was transferred beyond Jewish Family and Child Welfare Bureau. Nothing more is known about Mr. G's resettlement experience.

Due to the large influx of ultra-Orthodox refugees, few newcomers (except those receiving maintenance from yeshivas) could afford to consider a career as a religious functionary. Like other survivors, many Orthodox refugees entered into marriages immediately after the Holocaust, and began to rebuild their lost families. The need to earn a living became the first priority. But for some young unmarried men, the option to undertake religious training remained viable, as was the case for Mr. S. Grunfeld, a Hungarian survivor. With a yeshiva education and strong references from Europe, the Vaad Ha'ir in Montreal accepted Grunfeld for training as a religious slaughterer. Believing in his potential, executive director Mordechai Peters pleaded with the city's Family Welfare Department to extend

Grunfeld's subsistence allowance. "Mr. Grunfeld is learning the trade of schechita, to become a shochet of cattle, calves, sheep, lambs and poultry," Peters wrote. "He is a capable young man, very attentive to his studies, and it seems to me that within the next two months he will be able to receive his 'Kabalah,' the rabbinic certificate certifying him to be a fully qualified shochet."[81] With the Rabbinical Council's staunch support and guidance, in addition to extended financial backing, Mr. Grunfeld completed his training and became a successful *shoichet*.

Canadian Jewish institutions and the recently established Hassidic communities in Montreal maintained strict standards regarding *kashrut* and rabbinical training, and often questioned the accreditations of the European-trained functionaries based on the place of their training and rabbinical supervision. Official agency support was based on an imperfect, biased system without mandated selection criteria. Recipients of financial support or subsidies, like Moses G., undertook retraining to upgrade their credentials; without means, religious functionaries could choose either to abandon their preferred profession or find another way to earn their livelihood.

Occasionally, better opportunities for employment came from outside the major city centres. One Avrum Edelstein, a Hassidic *shoichet*, accepted a position with his wife, Helen, at a kosher summer resort in the Laurentian Mountains. There, his butchering experience and high standards of *kashrut* were greatly appreciated and fairly remunerated, since his religiosity strengthened the legitimacy of the resort in the eyes of its wealthy and observant clientele. Edelstein's hard work impressed the visiting Rabbi Herschorn, who then offered him a full-time position under the aegis of the Vaad Ha'ir. Soon after, the couple founded "Edelstein Kosher Catering" and became well-known and respected community figures.[82] Other times, ordained rabbis and cantors accepted pulpits in smaller Jewish communities that Canadian or U.S.-trained functionaries had declined. These positions required the functionaries and their families to live without the stable religious infrastructures available only in established Jewish centres. Nevertheless, for many, the benefits—a steady income and the opportunity to regain their pre-war rabbinical status, albeit in a very different setting—outweighed the sacrifice.[83] In this manner, many former rabbis and cantors were able to resume work in their chosen professions.

Good intentions aside, social workers and vocational counsellors occasionally provided ultra-Orthodox survivors with poor advice. With respect to the placement of teachers, for example, the standards and quality of Jewish education were different in Europe than in Canada, and European-educated yeshiva students' knowledge of Torah and Hebrew did not necessarily indicate skill as an educator. In some instances, prestige and ancestral links to religious family dynasties informed employment decisions, and brought ill-suited functionaries lacking any experience with children into the classroom. Thirty-five-year-old Czech-born ultra-Orthodox survivor Mr. Feiler arrived in Canada with a background in contracting, but no definitive employment skills. Feiler reported that he had studied at yeshiva up until the age of twenty-five, but possessed no teaching experience. A JIAS social worker suggested that even though his self-proclaimed knowledge of Hebrew was "elementary," he might be suited to teach Hebrew. The social worker recorded, "No great knowledge of Hebrew was required in the teaching of local elementary classes."[84] Not surprisingly, Feiler's entry into the teaching profession failed miserably. Other social workers proved equally uninformed regarding education standards and professional capacity, including the emotional and mental skills required to work with children. As a result, workers continued to direct more ultra-Orthodox men into teaching than there were stable, full-time positions available, or who were in fact suitable for such employment.

Community resources from local rabbinical councils and social service agencies eventually ran dry. One last hope remained for ordained refugee rabbis—the Conference Committee for Refugee Rabbis. Founded in 1953 by the nascent Claims Conference, the Committee was mandated to provide financial support to ordained survivor rabbis in North America struggling to secure employment. To qualify, the rabbis needed to meet three requirements: they must have been ordained (have received *smicha*) and have had experience as a rabbi in pre-war Europe; they must have been displaced as a result of the Nazi upheaval; and they had to demonstrate financial need.[85] Only those cases deemed most dire garnered attention. Hungarian Rabbi Wieder was one such case. After arriving in Montreal in 1951 through the close relatives scheme, and the guarantee of employment at a local yeshiva, Rabbi Wieder spent three years eking out a meagre living. With six children born between 1947 and 1953, and no permanent career opportunities in sight, the rabbi learned of the Conference Committee's policy on aiding rabbis. With JIAS' help, Rabbi Wieder successfully applied for assistance, which helped sustain him and his large family until a permanent position arose.[86]

Most ultra-Orthodox and Hassidic survivors never secured careers as religious functionaries. Instead, they grudgingly followed the paths of thousands of other Holocaust survivors and undertook employment in the needle trade, business, and as entrepreneurs. Yet, according to Yitel Nechamah (Kornelia) Bineth, a Belz Hassid and co-founder with her husband of Montreal Kosher Bakery, hard work in the "secular world" served to reinforce the survivors' faith and determination.

With limited resources but a strong will, the Hassidim and *mitnagedim* survivors shaped Jewish religious life in what they saw as a spiritually barren land.[87]

Other subgroups among the first wave of Holocaust survivors to Canada also made significant contributions to postwar religious life through the establishment of synagogues. The following chapter considers the experiences of two Toronto-based congregations.

# CHAPTER SIX

# MOVING FORWARD: SURVIVOR SHULS

The reorganization of postwar Jewish religious life among Holocaust survivors occurred throughout Canada, and in different ways. Montreal served as host to the development of Canada's hub of Hassidic and ultra-Orthodox Jewish life. Elsewhere, groups of survivors joined and established *landsmanshaftn* and over. time initiated the development of spiritual congregations. Membership bases derived primarily from existing mutual benefit societies, and remained limited to individuals (survivors or Canadian Jews) originating in the same European regions. This pattern persisted across much of the country. But in Toronto, two Holocaust refugees survivor groups followed another path. With members originating from diverse parts of Europe, and stemming from different backgrounds and wartime experiences, two distinct "survivor" congregations emerged: Congregation Habonim was a liberal synagogue that operated along the lines of central European traditions, whereas Kehal Machzikei Hadas-Clanton Park Synagogue maintained the religious orientation, customs, and norms of a traditional Orthodox *shul*.[1]

Organizations, free loan societies, and religious communities that emerged in postwar Canada consisted of groups of survivors searching for safe environs and comfort among like-minded persons with similar life experiences. The matter of locale and proximity to affordable living abodes also strongly influenced communal membership and "belonging." Those involved in building Congregations Habonim and Clanton Park were affected by similar forces. But, like the Hassidim in Montreal, the congregations' future founders encountered no place for themselves within Toronto's existing Jewish communities. Numerous factors contributed to this sense of spiritual rootlessness. Inge Spitz, a German Jewish survivor, remembered that her father-in-law helped found Habonim and served as its first president out of a sense of desperation: "We were looking for people from the same backgrounds, and were not accepted by other shuls."[2] Unfamiliar liturgies and melodies, and the sense that their foreign languages, cultures, and religious traditions alienated them from local congregations, prompted the survivors to unite and form their own prayer centres and, subsequently, spiritual, social, and economic communities.

Habonim was one of the first Holocaust refugee/survivor congregations to emerge in Canada.[3] A pair of Czech Jewish refugees, brothers Curt and Willy Fleischer, along with their colleague, Willy Lobel, first conceived of the congregation in 1942 Toronto for the purpose of providing High Holiday services for the small cluster of central and Western European refugees who adhered to a brand of liberal Judaism and attended the social group the New World Club. As was the case with most central European Jewish refugees to enter Canada in the latter part of the 1930s, neither the Fleischer brothers, with Curt's wife, Lola, nor Lobel had any relatives in the country. The Fleischers had escaped from Czechoslovakia to Canada immediately before the onset of hostilities, and soon after came to rural Saskatchewan, posing as Roman Catholic farmers in order to meet Canadian immigration criteria. Curt and Lola moved to Winnipeg in 1941, and joined brother Willy Fleischer in Toronto the following year.[4] There, with Lobel and other wartime refugees and released German and Austrian Jewish internees, the New World Club blossomed.

German (or, as Habonim congregants referred to it, "European") liberal Judaism had been very popular in Western and central Europe and integrated musical accompaniments into traditional, Orthodox liturgy. Liturgical elements and musical accompaniments, and slightly more conservative-leaning services, differentiated such traditions from Reform Judaism.[5]

Standards (levels) of religious observance among the central and Western European refugees ranged. Some briefly attended services at the Reform Holy Blossom Temple, one of Toronto's oldest synagogues. But, despite the congregation's warm welcome, the Reform services lacked key experiential aspects to which the refugees were accustomed. The newcomers chose to conduct separate services in their own fashion.

The demand upon what was then known as the New World Club to provide not only social services but also to act as a religious and spiritual community, intensified as hundreds of liberal Czech, German, and Austrian (as well as a few Polish and Hungarian) Jewish survivors arrived in Toronto in the late 1940s and early 1950s. Gangolf Herman, a co-founder of Congregation Habonim, which literally translates in Hebrew to "the congregation of builders," and one of its most active members for more than half a century, described the growing pressure to establish the congregation in the following manner:

> When you come to a strange country as an immigrant, you feel a
> need for friendly human contact, for some part of your heritage to

be transplanted with you in your new soil. It may be some of the old customs, some music, a language or a belief that was part of your former life and which you can still share in your new surroundings with people of a common background.

When a number of Jews from Central Europe, whom the Nazis had driven out and who had been familiar with Liberal Jewish practice there, came to Toronto, for various reasons, they found it difficult to integrate into existing local Jewish congregations.

Though these difficulties were not substantial, we hoped that a group of like-minded people, embracing some of our traditions and common experiences, would form the cohesive nucleus of a new congregation in which newly arrived refugees would feel at home. Thus, a few of us started to organize Jewish religious and social meetings, and in 1954 Congregation Habonim was founded.[6]

Congregation Habonim was formally consecrated in the fall of 1953. The Fleischers, Willy Lobel, and a handful of other newcomers rented the Borochov Hall from the Council of Jewish Women in preparation for the congregants' first-ever High Holiday services. Advertisements for the three-dollar tickets were placed in *Aufbau*, the German-Jewish communal newspaper. In an impassioned but pragmatic announcement (in German), one of the congregation's founders, Mr. Herbert Faber, reached out to potential members with the following words: "For the first time in Canada, our new home, [our idea is] to establish a new congregation, true to our fathers, worthy and equal to our brothers and sisters in other countries. We want to try to preserve the *European* [liberal] Judaism, forced by the Nazis into foreign lands, here in Toronto, guided by our inherited tradition, and to do our best to furnish our children with this tradition in their lives."[7] And so, with a borrowed Sefer Torah from Holy Blossom Temple, and in a rented space, approximately 150 survivor refugees and their families gathered for Yom Kippur in 1953. Max Adler, a founding member and former opera singer in Europe, performed a memorable Kol Nidre service.[8]

The announcement in *Aufbau* reportedly attracted dozens of newcomers who took a central part in the congregation's development. Among those drawn to Habonim was German Jew Georg Spitz, who had spent the war years as a refugee, first in Cuba and then, with his family, in England. With his wife, Vera, and adult children, Ursula and Erich—all three survivors of the 1939 *St. Louis* affair[9]—along with their respective spouses, in-laws, and young children, the family joined the congregation before its opening service. The elder Spitz, who went on to serve as Habonim's first president, was representative of the congregation's founding members. An older gentleman in his sixties, Spitz came from an upper-middle class European Jewish background and had benefited from post-secondary education and a prosperous pre-war career.[10]

Among the early waves of membership were European-born refugees and Holocaust survivors, with the exception of two Canadian women married to refugees.[11] Congregants were, on average, fifty years old; the youngest, by a generation, was thirty-year-old Gangolf Herman. The entire cohort consisted of educated central and Western Europeans with a wide range of professional backgrounds and wartime experiences. For instance, University of Toronto historian and professor Fritz Heichelheim was a German Jew raised in the liberal tradition who fled to Great Britain in the 1930s, arriving in Toronto in 1951. He joined Congregation Habonim soon after its inception.[12] Opera tenor and Czech Jew Max Adler—who, with his wife, Fritzi, was among the final interwar Jewish refugees to enter Canada as farmers[13]—was a staunch member until his premature death in 1960. Polish survivor and famed visual artist Henry Weingluck served as a Torah reader and secondary singer to Cantor Albert Feldman.[14] A slew of other lawyers, businessmen, engineers, and academics filled the congregation's early membership ranks.

Only one woman's name is listed on the synagogue's charter. Ruth Baumann Linz was born in 1920, in Danzig, to committed liberal Jewish parents who were active members of the Great Synagogue of Danzig and the Jewish community at large. In May 1939, with her parents' support, Linz fled to London, England. Her younger brother Simon followed that August, with the elder Baumanns securing visas for Shanghai. The family was reunited in London in 1947, and thereafter began the exodus to Toronto—Simon immigrated in 1949, his parents in 1950, and Ruth in 1952. Ruth Linz's involvement with Habonim morphed from her initial activity with the New World Club. One year later, Linz's commitment to preserving the liberal Judaism of her childhood was made official when she became the synagogue's only female founding member, and encouraged her brother and parents to join, too. Ruth Linz remained a member in 2011.[15]

The congregation operated out of two temporary facilities in downtown Toronto before following its members to its permanent home at 5 Glen Park Avenue in (what was then) north Toronto, in 1958. Determined to purchase the land on which the rented synagogue sat, the founding families spent the following decade raising funds and entrenching the congregation. While Ruth Linz was denied attendance at the all-male board meetings, the Sisterhood played a crucial role in the congregation's evolution and growth by planning and leading fundraising events, and arranging and catering holiday parties and *mitzvoth*. Women contributed, too, to the promotion of the arts and Jewish culture—specifically, music and the fine arts—within the synagogue.[16]

Women and men worked together to educate their children in the traditions of liberal Judaism. Mrs. C. Schatzky, speaking for the mothers at a congregational meeting in January 1960, stressed the importance of maintaining young people's interest through increased social activities—in addition to religious school—to ensure "the future growth and development of the congregation."[17] One Mr. Herman, a representative of the synagogue's male members, agreed with the mothers: "Since Congregation Habonim is unique in Canada in perpetuating the European Liberal tradition in Judaism," he said, "it was our duty to offer our young people activities giving them this background, which could not be found in any other organization."[18] The group elders sought to develop a cohesive infrastructure that fostered younger congregants' spiritual growth while preserving an inclusive family-friendly environment brimming with culture and social engagement orchestrated largely by the Sisterhood.

Congregation Habonim grew into something far greater than what was initially envisioned by its founders. As the sole Canadian congregation to adhere to the German-Jewish liberal tradition, Habonim's emphasis on egalitarianism and focus on arts and scholarship penetrated deep into the non-survivor Canadian Jewish community.[19] As a veteran member recalled, the congregation took pride in its attitudes toward other newcomer Jews seeking membership in a spiritual community. Hungarian Jewish refugees fleeing the 1956 Revolution received a warm welcome from the congregation, as did Canadian-born members attracted to the congregation's liberal approach toward issues of gender equality and its inclusion of individuals born to non-Jewish mothers or converts to Judaism.[20] As of 2015, Habonim continued to operate as a liberal congregation, although the German liberal traditions have been largely replaced with more universal principles. Founding survivors and their descendants make up a small minority of the current membership.

## Clanton Park

Nearby, the establishment of another survivor congregation, but one following a very different path than that adopted by Habonim, was well underway. Whereas Habonim emerged to address the particular needs of the liberal Jewish refugees who settled in Toronto, the Clanton Park congregation emerged out of a combination of necessity and convenience. Opportunities for religious Jewish life in the northern part of Toronto, well beyond the traditional Spadina corridor of Jewish immigrant and refugee habitation, were scant for even nominally observant survivors. Established Orthodox synagogues Shareei Shomayim and Shaarei Tefillah presented two options for religiously traditional survivors. However, both *shuls* were located more than six kilometres away from the dirt roads leading to the

*Congregation Habonim*
# NEWS
No.4 **BULLETIN** March, 1956

We must
sometimes
laugh -

PURIM 1956

and about
ourselves
too.

Jewish history is loaded with sorrow, persecution and frustration, so much so that, in considering the glory of the Jewish nation, the dark epochs overshadow the bright ones.

There were, however, episodes in which Jewish righteousness triumphed over the adversary, and one of these is the Purim episode. Then, in the face of immediate danger of extinction, the Jewish people of Persia were saved, and their right to live acquired a new significance.

For this reason, Purim is a happy and gay festival, where young and old join in the spirit of carnival-like fun and where present and past worries are for once forgotten. Essentially, there exists in the Jewish inheritance a deep-seated sense of humour, one which is partly hidden and only occasionally rises to the surface. The wealth of humorous stories - with a moral - about the poor and wretched Ghetto Jew, or about the new-rich mid-European Jew, or about the Jeshive-Bocher, is a rich source of an inherently cheerful disposition and an inclination to laugh about ourselves.

It is fit to rejoice again at the delivery of the Persian Jews from the hands of an antisemitic Haman. That this delivery was brought about by the efforts of Mordecai and Esther was due to the fact that fate does not depend entirely on circumstances, but that it is often necessary to strive for recognition of justice among all peoples, as it was done by Mordecai and Esther.

It would be a good thing for the Jew of 1956, to think less of his own individual importance. Only by laughing about ourselves and accepting the other fellow's point of view, instead of laughing about others and recognizing only one's personal viewpoint, can a Jewish community hope to achieve unity in itself and to present a united front to the outside world. Purim should teach us to laugh more and to worry less!

There is the story of the Wonder Rabbi. He was travelling along the road late on a Friday evening. He was beginning to be greatly concerned about what to do because Schabbes was just about

**EVERY MEMBER · BRING A MEMBER**

19. Purim Announcement in the *Congregation Habonim News Bulletin*, No. 4 (March 1956), 1. Courtesy of Lisa-Catherine Cohen, *The Builders: The Fifty-year History of Congregation Habonim* (The Writers Guild of America, 2013).

newly established community later known as Bathurst Manor, and were therefore not within walking distance for the Sabbath and Jewish holidays.

The formation of Clanton Park congregation was premised on the intention to meet the religious interests of a group of "trailblazing" observant Toronto Jews. It grew from a *minyan* of ten male Holocaust survivors and a handful of their Canadian-born Jewish neighbours, and was located in the recently developed Toronto suburb of North York. The earliest members ran small but active Sabbath and holiday services from the home of Sam and Sarah Kideckel. As the number of interested families grew, rented schools and synagogue spaces temporarily sufficed.

"Old timers"—Canadian-born Jews or earlier immigrants from the interwar period—led the development of Clanton Park and determined its direction from the outset. They took the helm in conducting business transactions, selecting structural designs, and hiring rabbis. Better versed in the particularities of local laws and building guidelines, and with greater financial security and language skills, Canadian Jews mustered the authority and necessary community standing to lead the pack. Traditionally observant Holocaust survivors rebuilding their lives in the North York corridor tended to follow suit. However, though it was never intended as a "survivor *shul*," by the time the Kehal Machzikei Hadas-Clanton Park synagogue was consecrated on 15 November 1954, Holocaust survivors accounted for more than half of the twenty-eight founding couples. Within a few years, the original *minyan* had blossomed into a diverse congregation that followed traditional standards of Torah study and *yiddishkeit*.

While the congregation officially followed Orthodox standards, it also accepted its place in modern Canadian—and Canadian Jewish—society, and was best described as "traditional." As one of only a handful of *shuls* north of Eglinton Avenue, Clanton Park attracted to its membership ranks congregants ranging from strictly Orthodox to largely unobservant. For those survivors belonging to the latter subgroup, limited options—and not religious inclinations—dictated synagogue attendance.[21] In the dedication book dated 12 February 1961, the synagogue's first spiritual leader, Rabbi Morris Gorelik, wrote, "Clanton Park Synagogue symbolizes a vibrant traditional community that has not compromised the sacred character of historic Judaism."[22] The founding members of Clanton Park embraced and participated in opportunities for secular education, and staunchly supported the nascent state of Israel.[23]

Survivors featured prominently among the *shul*'s founding couples, including individuals of Hungarian, Czech, German, and Polish origin. Italian-born to Czech parents, Miriam Frankel saw the congregation, like her own marriage to a Polish Jewish Holocaust survivor, as "mixed." The members represented different upbringings, and were raised with varying cultural traditions in a handful of European languages. In tandem with practical considerations and a need for Jewish communal services in then-underdeveloped North York, an insistence on maintaining faith despite immeasurable losses in the Shoah connected the survivors. Though few adhered to strict Orthodox standards of conduct during their first years as Canadians, the survivors unanimously wished to hold on to the customs and traditions of their parents and their childhoods; for most, it was the final connection between their destroyed past and the lived present.

At their *shul*, it was claimed that members were valued for their contribution to the community, rather than their birthplace. Eli Rubinstein, son of synagogue founders Bill (Bela) and Judith Rubinstein, was raised within the congregation and bore witness to its establishment and growth. He noted, "The native-born Canadians in the group enjoyed no privileged status. This did wonders for the newcomers' self-confidence. They began to assume positions of leadership, generally quietly and behind the scenes."[24] In order to combat linguistic issues—for instance, many of the survivors could not speak Yiddish, and few wished to run the congregation in German—the founders decided to lead services in liturgical Hebrew but conduct all other operations and initiatives in English as the only reasonable alternative, as well as the most socially acceptable.[25]

Malka Hahn, a Czech-reared survivor of the Theresienstadt and Auschwitz concentration camps, met her future husband, Benno, a former German Jewish internee released to Rabbi Abraham Price's Toronto-based Yeshiva Torah Chaim, during one of his business trips to New York.[26] The couple married in 1950 and settled in Toronto. Like other young, moderately observant Holocaust survivor families, the Hahns faced difficult challenges and particular needs. Practically speaking, their expanding family necessitated additional space. As Sabbath observers, they required a synagogue within walking distance of their home.[27] Toronto's Spadina corridor (for decades the landing site for thousands of Jewish immigrants to the city) was no longer the core of Jewish habitation, although the area was still home to many Jewish organizational infrastructures, such as the YM-WHA, JIAS, and numerous synagogues. The influx of thousands of Holocaust survivors had tipped the scales in the already densely populated neighbourhood, resulting in slim and expensive housing options for struggling newcomers. Newer housing developments north of Toronto's downtown core offered plenty of space for growth at affordable rates, but few nearby *shuls*. Traditional survivors and their Canadian-born co-religionists stood at what seemed like an existential crossroad. They could readily preserve their traditional lifestyles by accepting cramped conditions in more established Jewish neighbourhoods, or accept the possibility of practical challenges concerning their religious observance and move north into the burgeoning postwar suburbs.[28]

For those adventurous newcomers (and Canadian Jews), the choice was clear: the only direction anyone considered going was north. Social historian Etan Diamond has observed that postwar refugees "had neither sentimental ties to particular neighbourhoods nor any preconceived notions about the community's religious geography."[29] This lack of ties, coupled with relatively inexpensive housing developments, served as pull factors. Other Jews had already begun to make the transition from traditional Jewish neighbourhoods to areas north of Bloor Street by the 1920s and 1930s. But traditional Jews were barely represented in this move, which consisted primarily of middle-class, only mildly observant (or secular) Canadian Jews who did not rely on nearby religious infrastructure, such as a prayer house within walking distance, to live their day-to-day lives.[30] For traditional and Orthodox newcomers, the benefits of breaking religious ground in suburbia, with its endless potential for growth and development, outweighed the short-term costs.

The founders of Clanton Park *shul* were pioneers in the sense of extending Toronto's religious space beyond its limited traditional physical boundaries. And those survivors who remained with the congregation through the 1960s— when less observant survivor members left to join the newly built Conservative synagogues in the area, leaving Clanton Park more homogeneously Orthodox in nature—influenced the development of religious life and Jewish communal infrastructure, including educational institutes, throughout north Toronto. It is the narratives of the latter group that guide public knowledge of Clanton Park, and provide insight into the congregation's defining years.

In spite of all the potential, the move north was not without its challenges. According to Malka Hahn, "Lawrence Avenue was the last civilized spot. The idea of moving all the way to Wilson Avenue [even further north from downtown Toronto, the home of most of the city's Canadian-born and immigrant Jews] was daunting, but there were a number of young couples who were having babies, and we needed a *shul*."[31] Other survivors among the congregation's founding members agreed. Miriam Frankel and her husband, Polish-born Aron, made the move to what was then Toronto's northern periphery, "because it was cheaper to live there."[32] Sam Nussbaum, a German Jewish refugee (who, with Benno Hahn, was interned as an enemy alien and released to Rabbi Price's yeshiva), and his Canadian-born wife, Gilda, married in 1947 and quickly realized that "they had to come up north to get a good price on a house."[33] Following the trail blazed by their friends, the Hahns and Neuburgers, the Nussbaums accepted the poor

makeshift *davening* conditions afforded by the nascent Clanton Park *minyan*. Together, the survivors, alongside their Canadian-born contemporaries, took steps
toward the establishment of their congregation, one steeped in religious tradition
but open to modern ideas about family and social engagement that prevailed in
the postwar period.

Both men and women invested themselves in the development of the *shul*.
Whereas women in Montreal's Hassidic and ultra-Orthodox communities
were compelled to stand on the sidelines of the spiritual renaissance in postwar
Canada, Clanton Park's female congregants played crucial roles in the institutionalization and expansion of their communal hub. Identifying nearly universally as
housewives in the congregation's nascent decade, the founding wives contributed
through the maintenance of an active Sisterhood, much like that of Habonim.
The Sisterhood shouldered the responsibility of running fundraising events.
These included annual teas, fashion shows, and "Monte Carlo" casino nights.
With the financial revenue from such events—combined with $1,000 pledges by
the founding couples—the dream of a social hall on Lowesmoor Avenue (off of
Toronto's iconic Bathurst Street, north of Wilson Avenue) came to fruition in
1956. A permanent sanctuary was completed in 1960, with the dedication the
following February.[34]

Clanton Park's women helped cater at life-cycle events and served alongside
men on educational and social committees (although women were not permitted
to sit on the *shul* executive). The Sisterhood members also formed bible study
groups, drama clubs, and a bowling league.[35] The needs of children and the
creation of a family-friendly environment stood at the forefront of the congregation's activities and developmental goals. It was said that the female congregants
instilled in their children, the first generation of post-Holocaust Jews born in
a free country, a sense of pride in their Jewish identity and afforded them the
educational tools (through religious and secular schooling) to combat anyone
or anything that challenged these beliefs.[36] Possibly as the result of such positive
modelling, many of Clanton Park's youth married within the congregation, and
continued to transmit their parents' traditions to their own children.

The creation of the Clanton Park Synagogue had both practical and
emotional ramifications for its members and the wider Jewish community.
From a practical standpoint, the development of a traditional Orthodox congregation in North York signified the expansion of religious Jewish life beyond
Toronto's downtown core. *Shul* founders played significant roles in the growth
of the city's Jewish religious infrastructure. For instance, the Hofstedter family spearheaded the establishment of Ner Israel Yeshiva, and the Frankels and

Koschitzkys (another survivor family) created the Bnei Akiva schools, Yeshiva Or Chaim, and Ulpanat Orot, and were active participants in the ongoing development of the Orthodox Eitz Chaim, single-sex day schools. With support from a handful of other nascent Orthodox congregations, Clanton Park helped build a traditional community *mikveh* in the heart of North York and provided the impetus and clientele for north-moving kosher butchers, restaurants, and other businesses catering (primarily) to a Jewish clientele. Other services and infrastructure, like the Jewish Home for the Aged, followed soon thereafter. As Malka Hahn suggested, "the moment we did [found the *shul*], people started moving here. They were just waiting for a *shul* to be built."[37]

The founding of the Clanton Park synagogue, as "a place where Torah lives," had an overwhelming impact on its congregants.[38] The *shul* became the focal point of the survivors' socialization within the Orthodox Jewish community in addition to serving as a place of worship. In an interview honouring the congregation's sixtieth anniversary in 2006, Hungarian survivor and founding member Judith Rubinstein explained how the *shul* came to fill the void left by the survivors' murdered relatives: "We created a new family, a Clanton Park family, which is now in its third generation. The *shul* became our second home, and we still *schlep nachas* [derive pride] every time we go to *shul*. We are very grateful to be part of this community. We shared whatever we could and we were always loyal to our values. We always believed that *Shabbos* is *Shabbos*."[39]

The congregants' shared commitment to Jewish faith and Orthodox tradition helped encourage survivors' emotional and psychological healing, and offered many of them a stepping-stone on which to rebuild their physical and spiritual lives. Built upon the religious beliefs and traditions of their ancestors, along with reminders of a world destroyed by the Shoah, the *shul* served as an anchor linking the past and present. Feelings of belonging and friendship, as well as burgeoning kinship ties created through the marriages of the members' offspring to one another, firmly entrenched the Clanton Park Synagogue.

---

The campaigns to establish the liberal Congregation Habonim and modern Orthodox Clanton Park Synagogue arose in response to different stimuli, and involved the participation of different cohorts of Holocaust survivors. And yet the two congregations shared key features that resonate even today. Many among the founding members originated in Europe and entered Canada either immediately before, or after, the Holocaust, although Clanton Park's leaders were substantially younger than Habonim's. The permanent homes of both synagogues were in the northern suburbs of Toronto, away from the traditional areas of Jewish refugee and immigrant settlement and life in the downtown core. Sisterhoods were held in high regard, and women occupied positions of influence on various committees. With few members, the congregations could not afford to take the value of any member's contributions for granted.

Both congregations found their strength in faith, as each defined it, and utilized their collective resources to build their physical and spiritual homes. Through their efforts and commitment, they preserved their respective styles of religious observance, cultures, and tradition in their adoptive country, Canada. Founding members worked together toward the integration of new congregational individual members and member families from whom they garnered support and comfort, which also encouraged a sense of permanence in their new surroundings. New friendships, business ventures, and social (and sometimes even romantic) relationships took root. Even as they have each evolved over the decades, Congregation Habonim and Kehal Machzikei Hadas–Clanton Park Synagogue continue to thrive. The founders' children, and children's children, especially in the case of Clanton Park, remain committed to ensuring that the legacy of their survivor descendants remains strong and active into the twenty-first century. But where these survivors clung to their faith, other new Canadians rejected Judaism and facets of Jewish life. We consider these stories next.

# CHAPTER SEVEN

# ABANDONING TRADITION: ATHEISM AND CONVERTS

Feelings of loneliness and isolation were commonplace among the thousands of survivors who arrived in Canada in the immediate postwar decade. Crises of faith affected many. Fearfulness and deep-rooted anxieties concerning Jewish identity pervaded many Holocaust survivors. Such fears were not completely inappropriate or unexpected. The trauma of the Holocaust remained at the forefront and affected persons across the observance spectrum. Variant theological responses to the Shoah reflected this spectrum of faith and experience. In contemporary literature, Haredi, or right-wing ultra-Orthodoxy, identified the sinning people of Israel as culprits of the Holocaust. The Holocaust represented a pivotal moment whereby the "chosen people" broke their covenant with God and were, in turn, punished. A second approach suggests that responsibility for the Holocaust lies with "wicked" Jews, namely those engaging in modern, secular lifestyles. This school of thought insists that traditional, pious Jews needed to suffer—and atone—for the sins of their brothers. Another theological response proffers that God "hid His face" from Nazism. According to this position, responsibility for the Holocaust lies in the hands of human beings. When God created humankind, He bestowed upon them free will. Rather than interfering and stopping the persecution of His people, God remained passive and inactive. The Holocaust was a human problem requiring a human solution. This leads to a further existential position—that there is no divine will, life plan, or purposefulness. God died alongside six million Jews. Finally, a response reluctantly adopted by countless survivors became one of "I cannot know."[1]

Although existential and intellectual wrestling with faith and spiritual questioning continued among countless survivors for the rest of their lives, most continued to self-identify as Jews. Their deep connections to Jewish faith or culture outweighed their internal struggles to abandon their heritage. For others, however, the wounds and losses caused by the Holocaust precipitated their agnostic, atheist, or anti-Jewish identity.

Few Jewish DPs understood that their experiences of violent anti-Semitism might extend to Canada. Canada's brand of anti-Semitism did not resemble that directed against Jews in Germany and Nazi-occupied Europe. And yet its presence, both real and imagined, proved sufficiently frightening.[2] Given their recent experiences of persecution, more than a few survivors chose to avoid identification as Jews by detaching themselves and their families from active involvement in Jewish life.

Renata Skotnicka Zajdman's experience is typical of many survivors. Helped to escape the Warsaw Ghetto at the age of thirteen, and later disguised as a Polish volunteer labourer in Germany to avoid round-up, Skotnicka Zajdman was left with mixed emotions about her outward Jewish identity after her personal encounters with violent anti-Semitism and racial branding. Her anxieties accompanied her beyond liberation. Skotnicka Zajdman continued to maintain her persona as a non-Jewish Pole throughout her postwar nursing training and service at Bensheim DP camp. Although Canada claimed to need trained nurses, immigration officials denied the diploma Skotnicka Zajdman had earned at Bensheim, deeming it invalid by Canadian standards. As an unattached young woman, however, she could register as a domestic servant, the route that eventually brought her to Canada. Arriving in Montreal in December 1948, the realization that anti-Semitism existed in Canada fed her deep-rooted anxieties. Fearful of discrimination at best, and another genocide at worst, Skotnicka Zajdman distanced herself and her family for many years from Montreal's organized Jewish community. Although she maintained Jewish traditions, observed the holidays, and lived in the mainly Jewish neighbourhood of Côte-St. Luc, her perceived need to keep her Jewish identity private precluded the placement of a *mezuzah* on her door or her children's enrolment in Hebrew schools.[3]

An indeterminate number of survivors arrived in Canada already suffering from a crisis of faith triggered by their traumatic experiences in the Holocaust. Refugees who immigrated with faith intact but worried about possible anti-Semitism resulting from public affiliation with Jewish communal life also steered clear of open observance, but for different reasons. Both sources of anxiety led newcomers to move away from organized Jewish communal life. And yet, notwithstanding—or perhaps, despite—crises of faith and fears of anti-Semitism, only a small proportion of survivors chose to break all ties with Judaism and Jewish life. Instead, like Skotnicka Zajdman, they distanced themselves from organized Jewish religious life while continuing to privately self-identify as Jewish. With time, and gradual physical and psychological rehabilitation, most survivors in Canada returned to some semblance of organized Jewish life, but for diverse reasons.

Not a few male survivors who fell into this category indicated regular synagogue attendance for the social aspect and familiarity of the setting. A case in point was Lithuanian Jew Joseph Riwash, an active member of the Voroshilov partisan brigade, located in the Slutsk region of occupied Belarus. From 1946 through 1949, Riwash devoted his time to hunting war criminals from Munich; he located witnesses and helped bring hundreds of individuals to trial, though few were convicted. Upset by the lack of support for his efforts by the local Jewish refugee community, Riwash left for Canada with his wife, a non-practising Roman Catholic Pole he married postwar. In Montreal, he considered conversion to Roman Catholicism, but never followed through, noting that "Jewish people don't give up on their religion so easily." No longer a believer in God, Riwash still attended synagogue regularly and remained proud of his Jewish heritage.[4]

A host of recorded survivors expressed similar sentiments. In Vancouver, one Hungarian Jew stressed that "[I] went to *shul* not to pray, but to be with other Jews. I felt comforted being there, even if I no longer believed in what I was saying."[5] Some survivors became synagogue members, but sought involvement elsewhere. Thousands found solace and a sense of belonging by joining social and cultural clubs that were not religious in nature, such as the Arbeter Ring (Workmen's Circle), and contributing to charitable organizations that supported Jewish cultural life or Israel. Skotnicka Zajdman, for example, joined Hadassah-WIZO, and served as an advocate for Jewish child survivors and for the recognition of gentile rescuers, including Irena Sendlerova, a Polish Catholic social worker who courageously organized the rescue of approximately 2,500 Jewish children sequestered in the Warsaw Ghetto.[6]

The diminishment of religious observance and faith amongst survivors did not necessarily signify the end of all Jewish practice within their postwar Canadian families. On the contrary; many reported transmitting Jewish culture and tradition to their children and educating them in parochial Jewish day schools.[7] Hebrew day school and Jewish summer camp attendance, as well as the preservation of traditional life-cycle events (including *brit milah*, bar and bat mitzvahs, Jewish wedding ceremonies, and Jewish funerals) suggested that despite their traumatic wartime experiences and internal conflicts with faith and quotidian observance post-Shoah, Jewish tradition still held an important place in the lives of these survivors.

A smaller cohort of Holocaust survivors made the conscious decision to isolate themselves from Judaism and Jewish life entirely. Those disenchanted with religion altogether self-identified as atheists or agnostics; many of these professed socialist political and ideological leanings. A smaller percentage formally convert-ed or adopted another religious identity. This group has been at best overlooked, and more, probably, deliberately ignored by all stripes of the academy, including Canadian Jewish researchers and Holocaust historians alike. This survivor cohort represents an uncomfortable truth about the so-called return to life and the reju-venation of the Jewish nation: not all survivors adhered to the Jewish faith. More still deliberately rejected any affiliation with organized Jewish life.

Agnostics, atheists, and survivors who rejected affiliation with Jewish com-munity membership, along with converts, did not represent a monolith. Rather, these individuals stemmed from various national origins and ranged in age and education background. Among them were survivors who had lived assimilated, non-observant or irreligious lives before the Holocaust. Oral history testimonies collected by the Shoah Foundation suggest that Dutch and Hungarian male sur-vivors constituted a significant proportion of this sub-group.[8] Among them were pre-war or wartime converts, particularly children whose parents deliberately had them baptized in an effort to protect them from persecution. For such youth, conversion was a formality, a means to a positive end, they hoped.[9] Within this group, many chose not to publicly disclose their former Jewish identities.

Survivors who distanced themselves from Jewish observance, traditions, and community integration, and rejected the notion of organized religion en-tirely, rarely sought out an alternative spiritual community to which to adhere or convert. These newcomers remained Jews in name only; a number maintained some degree of involvement in Yiddish or Jewish cultural circles, although not religiously oriented. For so-called Jewish atheists, participation in social groups, and Jewish charitable organizations in particular, increased over time as they gained a sense of security in their environs.

The survivor refugees struggled with challenges surrounding religious practice and identification. Czech and German Jews who immigrated to Canada immediately prior to and during the onset of the Second World War (a movement largely consisting of "enemy aliens" interned on Canadian soil and the Iberian refugees) were the first wave of Jewish newcomers to face these dilemmas. Much of the immediately pre-war group arrived as would-be farmers with sufficient funds to purchase and operate farms, or industrialists who could benefit the Canadian economy. This group comprised primarily self-identifying (if not observant) Jews. Placed in non-Jewish farming communities and unaccustomed to any foreign elements, let alone members of a different religion, most of the refugees hid or minimized their Jewish origins.

The newcomers' shared goal was to blend in as quickly as possible and not draw any anti-immigrant attention to themselves while attempting to secure Canadian entry visas for relatives trapped in occupied Europe. With few options for recreational activity, and often no opportunities for religious instruction, parents typically enrolled their children in Sunday school alongside their Christian peers. Older youth and adults attended church-sponsored outings and events for social interaction and informal English language education. Even with their foreign accents and unfamiliar customs, active participation in the community, which often centred on the local church, proved beneficial to the early refugees' settlement and acclimatization.

Hanna Fischl (later Spencer) and members of her extended family were among the few Jewish immigrants to migrate to Canada as industrial labourers and farmers in the days leading up to the Second World War. A Czech-born native of the German-speaking Sudetenland, Fischl was raised in an assimilated Jewish home and undertook advanced university studies, eventually earning a PhD in German and Slavic languages and literature. In her diary, composed as a one-sided dialogue letter to a former boyfriend in Vienna, Fischl chronicled her daily activities leading up to and following arrival at Halifax's Pier 21. She reflected on her weak Jewish identity, noting, "[W]e did not observe the Sabbath or any dietary laws, and we went to synagogue only once a year, on Yom Kippur, the Day of Atonement. Growing up in a predominantly Christian community, my younger sister and I were more familiar with Catholic than Jewish traditions."[10]

Fischl soon recognized the central role of the church in the small, close-knit farming community of Prescott, Ontario, in which her family first settled. In a diary entry dated 18 June 1939, only two weeks after her arrival, she recalled the following:

> We went to church today, the United Church of Canada. In order to qualify as Canadian immigrants, we had to declare ourselves nondenominational. I had no problem with that. I never did feel particularly Jewish. It was only other people who saw us as different. And since people here seem to assume that one attends a church ("Which church do you go to?" is a common question), Uncle Louis wants us to join this Canadian one. I am told that it's called the United Church of Canada because it was formed through a merger of Methodists and Presbyterians and because it is a strictly Canadian institution.[11]

Fischl's desire to "Canadianize" and gain the acceptance of her peers as quickly as possible, and the fact that her family had officially entered the country as non-Jews, served as two factors in her readiness to jettison her Jewish upbringing. To her delight, Fischl thoroughly enjoyed participating in church life, and found the minister's sermons helpful in relieving the pressure of daily life on the farm. On a more sombre note, Fischl also expressed concern that should her Jewish origins be revealed, the increase in social acceptance by her contemporaries and future rejuvenation of her academic career might come to a swift close. In Fischl's case, the loss of her already weak Jewish identity in exchange for widespread acceptance in social and academic circles represented a reasonable exchange. Neither she, nor any members of her generation (in her extended family) in Canada, revived their association with Jewish religious life.

But, despite Hanna's abandonment of her faith and the absence of strong communal ties, the Fischl family never denied its origins. A case in point is Vera Rosenbluth, daughter of Fischl's younger sister Mimi and German Jewish refugee and former internee Gideon Rosenbluth. In 2010, Vera Rosenbluth—along with former internees and their offspring—helped spearhead the development of the Vancouver Holocaust Education Centre's exhibit, *"Enemy Aliens": The Internment of Jewish Refugees in Canada, 1940–1943*. Rosenbluth played an instrumental role in bringing the previously unexplored subject to light by interviewing a number of surviving gentlemen, including those in her parents' social network, and their children, in addition to exploring personal archives and collections.

Also from the Sudetenland, Edmund and Gretl Waldstein and their young daughter, Helen, faced similar challenges upon arrival in Canada in April 1939, as documented non-Jewish Czech farmers. Raised in an observant Jewish home, Gretl in particular felt unprepared to abandon all connections to her faith. Yet, she and her husband feared that any public recognition of their origins, coupled with their foreign dress and accent, might undermine their efforts at integration. They unintentionally instilled this same anxiety in their young daughter. The Waldsteins enrolled Helen, age five, in the local one-room schoolhouse (close to their farm near Hamilton, Ontario) in order to learn English as quickly as possible. In her account of her family's travails, Helen remembers how religious identification entered into the conversation about her schooling: "Before I was allowed to attend school, my parents made me promise never to say that I was Jewish. If a teacher asked for my religion, I was to answer, 'I am Czech.' There had been several long debates at home about whether people would believe that there was a Czech church. In the end, my parents decided that Canadians knew so little about Czechoslovakia that no statement about the country and its people would sound too far-fetched."[12] At this young age, Helen came to understand the deep roots of secrecy in protecting one's family from potential harm.

Life in rural Ontario proved entirely incompatible with the preservation of Jewish religious observance. Gretl faced great culture shock. Raised in a strictly kosher household, she now ran a farm that required her to care for swine and prepare their slop using the same cooking pots she used to prepare the family's meals.[13] Other traditions, too, slipped away when Helen started Sunday school at the United Church of Canada, "because my parents had wanted me to have some knowledge of religion, because our next-door neighbours were willing to take me to church every Sunday, and because my parents had wanted to protect me from the centuries-old hatred that had destroyed their own lives."[14] After completing their farming contract and relocating to Hamilton, Edmund and Gretl joined a Reform Jewish congregation, which they attended on the High Holidays because of Edmund's desire to maintain some ties with organized Jewry. Helen, by contrast, maintained her affiliation with the United Church's social activities and failed to identify with any religion well into adulthood. While immigration to Canada saved their lives, the fear of a resurgence of anti-Semitism as an effect of Nazism on their psyches proved overwhelming, and stripped the Waldstein family of their confidence to participate fully in Jewish cultural and religious life.

## Proselytization and Evangelization

Amongst the thousands of survivors to immigrate to postwar Canada were those who shed Jewish faith and all identification with Jewish culture and history in response to their wartime trauma. Some formally adopted another religion and lived for decades in denial of their heritage or pre-war identity. Young survivors exposed to alternative faiths as a result of their experiences in surviving the Shoah appeared the most spiritually vulnerable, and on an international scale, Jewish leaders feared for their spiritual future. Jewish communal leadership feared for the souls of Jewish children entrusted by their parents to non-Jewish homes and institutions. The concerns were not unfounded: children indoctrinated into Christian faiths and frequently baptized by their protectors, who themselves often harboured anti-Semitic attitudes, did reject Judaism. The battle to regain these "lost souls" proved long-winded and challenging. To further complicate the situation, while the Canadian Jewish Congress battled with the federal government for the admittance of Jewish refugees, Christian churches increased their own efforts to receive and help resettle Jews and non-Jews from postwar Europe. Christian immigrants were received and aided as fellow believers. In some churches, outreach to Holocaust survivors was shaped by proselytization agendas.

Unlike the CJC (which was motivated, first and foremost, by the need to rescue and resettle as many Jewish survivors of the Shoah as possible), various

Christian groups and their respective churches placed the matter of immigrants' spiritual needs and religious observance at the forefront of their outreach activities. A 12 June 1948 article published in *The Canadian Churchman* (an instrument of the United Church of Canada) suggested that the spiritual health of all new immigrants (including Jewish displaced persons) should rank as a high priority. "Church people have a responsibility," the article asserted, "to make friends with the immigrants and to help them become assimilated in Canadian life; and the Churches possess a great opportunity for rendering service and strengthening their membership and work."[15]

Many churches encouraged their congregants to take a personal interest in newcomers. The stated intent of such actions was to help the displaced persons find "peace in their decision to immigrate, and make the transition from their former lives in Europe to their new lives in Canada."[16] Appearing less concerned with the pragmatic details of adjustment (housing, employment, maintenance) and more concerned with the newcomers' spiritual condition, the churches reached out to survivors struggling with their faith.

Two Toronto-based missionary churches in particular jumped at the chance to further the ongoing process of evangelization of Jewish Holocaust survivors. The Nathanael Institute and the Christian Scott Mission, both institutions run under the direction of "Hebrew Christians," baptized and confirmed former Jews who now accepted the divinity of Jesus Christ. Messianic Reverend Morris Kaminsky directed the daily operations at the Nathanael Institute, a product of the Church of England in Canada. Kaminsky was initially attracted to the Church's outreach ministry in his youth and, with his wife, Ida, managed the "authentic, culturally Jewish community of believers" in the heart of the predominantly Jewish area of Kensington Market (also known as the Spadina corridor) in the 1940s and 1950s.[17] The Institute focused its activities on the evangelization of Jewish immigrants, and specifically Holocaust survivors. Kaminsky and his missionaries hoped, and expected, to attract the attention of survivors who arrived in Canada alone and, presumably, suffering from a crisis of faith. They intended to capitalize on the newcomers' vulnerabilities and sense of unease in their new surroundings by providing a safe and nurturing environment—in Yiddish, no less—conducive to spiritual and emotional rehabilitation.

Able and willing to offer intensive support through their ministry's evangelical volunteers (nurses, teachers, and other trained caregivers attuned to settlement issues), Nathanael Institute missionaries relied on their acts of kindness, and the teachings of Christ, to turn the survivors toward the "true path." "With the steady influx of Displaced Persons from all over Europe we have new and fresh opportunities to minister to these people who realize how fortunate they are to have survived," Kaminsky boasted in 1949. "We thank God for the way they receive the message and for those who have asked for Gospels in Yiddish and declared their interest in the claims of our Lord boldly and unafraid," Kaminsky continued.[18]

Reverend Morris Zeidman, a Hebrew Christian missionary originally from Czestochowa, Poland, oversaw the activities of the Christian Scott Mission. Initially an agency of the Presbyterian Mission but independent from 1945, the Mission took a similar approach as the Nathanael Institute in its work. Zeidman's commitment to proselytizing Holocaust survivors preceded their arrival to Canada. The minister travelled back to Poland in 1946 in search of living relatives who might have survived the destruction, and attempted to help surviving *landsmen* immigrate. He came under fire from the Canadian Jewish leadership, which was suspicious of his missionary activities, but he did not stop. Without revealing his religious identification or professional post with a church, Zeidman shipped goods—including much needed medications and food parcels—to former friends and neighbours in Poland, and drew up sponsorship papers to bring a surviving sister to Canada.[19] In addition, he sponsored the immigration of four of five Polish Jewish families and housed them in the mission's main building. According to his son's biography of his father, "For a number of families their first experiences of the Canadian scene was to live in the shadow of the Scott Mission and to be introduced into the economy and life of the community with the friendly guidance of the Christian Jew."[20] No records remain to indicate how Morris Zeidman's sister and other survivors reacted to the reverend's calling, although the Chenstochover Society decried his efforts and urged its members to steer clear of Zeidman and all other Hebrew Christians.[21]

From a practical and emotional (yet non-spiritual) perspective, survivors seeking membership and belonging within a community might have felt more at ease and welcome in some Christian churches than in the kinds of synagogues they encountered in Canada. Accustomed to small and predominantly informal congregations, known as *shteibels*, numerous in pre-war Europe, Holocaust survivors frequently cited their disappointment with the postwar institutionalization of Jewish life in Canada, which looked inherently different from what they had experienced in pre-war Europe. So, too, did the refugees themselves—distinct styles of dress, language, and customs drew unwanted attention to the newcomers, highlighting not their shared Jewish faith and tradition but rather the differences between refugees and native-born congregants. Unmet expectations around synagogue attendance norms also contributed to refugees' discomforts within postwar Canadian synagogues, which functioned largely on the basis of funds collected through annual membership dues and tickets for High Holiday services, as well as donations.[22] One of the most commonly expressed disappointments among survivors related to their efforts to attend Yom Kippur services.

Hoping to say *yizkor* for their murdered relatives, countless survivors, including those whose own faith remained uncertain, headed to their local synagogues on Erev Yom Kippur (*Kol Nidre*) and requested admission. The overwhelming response was an unequivocal "no"; space was reserved for dues-paying members and ticket-holders only. George Lysy, a Czech survivor, recalled approaching a synagogue in London, Ontario, with his father-in-law, an observant Jew, on Yom Kippur, only days after arriving in the city. Unable to afford the cost of two standing-room-only tickets, Lysy purchased only one for his father-in-law.[23] In Vancouver, one Romanian survivor distinctly recalled anxiously awaiting the High Holiday services at a local synagogue. Like Lysy, this gentleman was shocked to learn that he was welcome to pray, but it would come at a price "no *greener* could afford."[24] He never again returned to that synagogue.

The rationale behind these synagogues' attitudes remains unclear. Survivors perceived that the administration and clergy's refusal to accommodate them with free (or highly subsidized) seats stemmed from ignorance about the survivors' circumstances and spiritual needs. Synagogues, especially those in smaller Jewish communities like London and Vancouver, that received smaller numbers of Holocaust survivors relative to Toronto and Montreal, might have been oblivious to the immigrants' unfamiliarity with the North American practice of purchasing seats. Even if a congregant had been kind enough to familiarize the immigrants about this practice, the issue remained the same: survivors' inability to pay for the seats, coupled with the unwillingness of most synagogues to offer subsidized rates, left bad tastes in survivors' mouths. Perhaps the situation would have played out differently had rabbis been contacted directly by CJC and other community leadership and prevailed upon to make concessions—and seats available—for the newcomers, or had the rabbis on their own reflected upon the needs of new Canadian Jews. These experiences, and the ramifications on survivor absorption and integration, did not go unnoticed. Congregations, including those established by survivor refugees, welcomed late-arriving newcomers and post-1956 Hungarian refugees into services free of charge, determined not to impart their own negative experiences on others seeking new lives in Canada.[25]

In direct contrast to the icy reception and social isolation experienced by survivors at synagogues that welcomed their membership, but at a price, the missionary churches embraced the newcomers.[26] Services offered by the churches, which included religious services in Yiddish, English classes, Christian holiday dinners, and summer camps for children, were all offered free of charge. Although there is no evidence to suggest that the same survivors who were turned away from High Holiday services moved toward the Christian church, it stands to reason that individuals already struggling with their faith and an urge for community belonging might have turned to the missionaries. Rev. Kaminsky of the Nathanael Institute boasted that his mission offered staff visits to survivors' homes to provide counselling and childcare for refugee mothers, services not easily accessible or available through Jewish agencies. Despite Jewish immigrant organizations' offering of similar services, the Institute's English and citizenship classes consisted nearly entirely of Jewish DPs, and stood at capacity in the early 1950s from the steady influx of newcomers.[27] Rev. Zeidman, for his part, tried to direct surviving *landsleit* to his mission under the guise of it serving as a Jewish centre. Through his linguistic skills, and Polish Jewish upbringing and culture, Zeidman hoped to sway the survivors from Jewish living and embrace what he proclaimed to be a richer, redemptive faith.[28]

The arrival of thousands of postwar Holocaust survivors presented crucial opportunities for Christian missionaries to spread their messages of faith, good will, and the love of Jesus Christ. In its reports to the Anglican Synod, the Nathanael Institute consistently drew attention to its influence on the impressionable newcomers. Older survivors and single newcomers without familial supports and experiencing crises of faith made the ideal targets for the missionaries' proslyetization and evangelization efforts. Pre-schools served a two-fold purpose, according to Kaminsky, who believed that "a little child shall lead them," that is, that through the children, parents and other adults in the family would feel "God's great love."[29] But, owing to their disproportionate representation among survivors of the Shoah and refugees offered resettlement in Canada, young survivors, some of whom had lost all connections to Judaism during the war, accounted for most of the recorded cases of baptized and confirmed Hebrew Christians. Among the 1951 baptisms was the infant daughter of a Hungarian Jewish refugee who had recently been baptized as a Hebrew Christian. The Institute expressed pride in having influenced this second generation of Jews and helping them find their true way.[30]

Older and elderly survivors, such as one Mr. Fromovitz, also found themselves drawn into the mission's fold. Kaminsky's report described Fromovitz as a widower survivor raised as an observant Jew. Fromovitz and his cohorts represented a small but significant fraction of the survivor population and received few community services or supports to help promote their adjustment and integration into Canadian Jewish life. Some of these individuals, struggling to acclimatize to their new surroundings, found solace in the missions' empathetic and culturally sensitive programs (which operated in Yiddish). With nothing and no one grounding them in Canadian Jewish society, these survivors found that Christian missions that highlighted the importance of "Hebrews" while listening to their tragic experiences empathetically served as an acceptable alternative to less receptive synagogues. Reflecting upon the annual Christmas dinner for Hebrew Christians, Kaminsky recalled how Fromovitz, an aged concentration camp survivor, "declare[d] the whole counsel of God in Yiddish. He reminded us over and over again of God's goodness in having spared him and many others from death; he challenged us also with the great responsibility which is ours in helping to bring our people to Christ. To hear this man so praise the Lord Jesus Christ, and to witness the light of God's countenance upon his face in spite of the fact that he lost all his family in gas chambers in Poland, was indeed a rebuke to us."[31] This conversion signalled true success for the Hebrew Christian missionary.

There is little evidence to suggest that organized Canadian Jewish communities expended significant time or energy trying to stop survivors from moving away from Judaism. War orphans, rescued from postwar Europe and brought to Canada as wards of the CJC, were the sole notable exception to this rule. Congress feared that some of the youth, many of whom having spent the war years under the protection of non-Jews and educated in Christian doctrine, might not reacquire and resume ownership over their Jewish identity in their new home. This proved particularly applicable with regard to youth placed in smaller Jewish communities, where fewer options for placement presented themselves. "We are quite anxious to avoid any possible danger that young people whom we saved from Europe should be exposed to conversionist influences in non-Jewish environments," the CJC's Manfred Saalheimer advised Hamilton-based social worker Dorothy Shekter.[32] Whenever possible, it was advised that the war orphans should be resettled in Jewish homes and their religious lives—synagogue attendance, Sunday school—nurtured. Yet, despite CJC efforts, some of the youth fell through the cracks. In a 14 September 1948 inter-office notice entitled "Orphan Boy Placed in Calgary Induced to Changing Religion," the CJC reported on one such case. The report reads, in part, as follows:

> The report of Mr. M. Wolochow, Chairman of the Calgary Branch of Congress, stated that "a 17-year-old Hungarian born orphan was placed in one of the finest homes we have here; we were under the happy impression that this young man was adjusting himself very nicely, was working, was learning English fast and we did not anticipate any

trouble with him whatsoever"; afterwards the war orphans committee had a psychiatrist examine him who found that he was not well.
In July he advised his foster parents that he was quitting his job to
work on a farm. He was then seen going to the home of a Hungarian
Minister who is pastor of a Calgary Church. The Congress Committee contacted the Minister who, however, refused to receive them and
only after a few days advised them that the boy was baptized by him.[33]

In this case, the CJC took legal action due to the boy's status as a minor, and
instructions were issued for the Calgary Child Welfare Officer and the Royal Canadian Mounted Police to return him to the care of Calgary's CJC office. Future
bulletins do not provide a follow-up on this case, nor address any others like it. A
handful of other instances in which war orphans deviated from Jewish lifestyles
made their way into social service records, but none were featured in Congress
bulletins.[34] One instance featuring similar issues, but meriting no "bureaucratic
address," involved a thirteen-year-old orphan in Vancouver. The girl (who was not
a ward of the CJC but had immigrated to Canada through private sponsorship
and not the War Orphans project) had been moved from a Jewish home into a
practising Christian one at the behest of her sponsors. A member of Vancouver's
Jewish community showed concern for the child's spiritual well-being and wrote a
letter to the CJC to apprise them of the situation. Since the girl did not fall under
Congress' domain of responsibility, an unidentified person put the issue to rest,
scribbling at the bottom of the file, "Leave it alone. This is not our problem."[35]

As noted above, the Canadian Jewish Congress's primary concern was the
rescue and resettlement in Canada of as many survivors of the Shoah as possible.
The religious identification of the survivor, including the war orphans, did not
top the agenda for the CJC, JIAS, or most secular social service agencies interact-
ing with the survivors. A number of the war orphans, like some of their adult
survivors, turned to Christianity. Yet those survivors who formally abandoned
the Jewish community are usually overlooked by scholars, or, more frequently,
treated as an atypical sidebar or exception to the norm. Including their history
challenges the stereotypical notion of Holocaust survivors as religiously observant and invested in Jewish communal life. It widens the scope of complexity and
richness of Holocaust and Canadian Jewish studies. Exploring their experiences
also sheds light on how and why some newcomers traded religious affiliation, or
abandoned religion altogether, after liberation.

One child survivor of the Budapest Ghetto, Thomas Kramer, docked in
Canada on 25 December 1945, with his mother and stepfather, and joined his

stepbrother in Montreal. Raised in a non-observant Jewish household, Kramer himself knew very little about Judaism. His bar mitzvah, celebrated in a DP camp in Austria, took place only to please his stepfather. In Montreal, Kramer's parents enrolled him in the local high school, the Park Extension School. With no comprehension of English or French, and as the only Jewish student, immigrant or Canadian-born, in his class, Kramer "stood out like a sore thumb." Still, Kramer recalls, he performed well at school and quickly established friendships with his classmates. At the behest of his new friends, Kramer accompanied them in attending services at the Anglican Church and participating in its social activities. "I had no faith; I was totally areligious—I joined for community participation," Kramer recalled.[36] So at age fourteen, Kramer joined the church.

Kramer's family viewed this development with mixed emotions. His mother, never a religious person, had lost her own faith in God entirely "after all that happened during the war." As for her son's membership in the Anglican Church of Canada, she did not care for the religious aspect but, according to Kramer, "she was just happy that I had friends, and that I found a place for myself in a new community." His more traditional stepfather was less supportive of Kramer's decision, but eventually made his peace with it. Although Kramer severed all connections to the Jewish community, and in later years joined the Centenarian Church with his Canadian-born wife, Kramer never officially converted to Christianity.[37]

Shedding his Jewish identity did not arise from a personal crisis of faith. His youth, peer circle, and desire to belong to a community navigated Thomas Kramer toward the Anglican Church. Unlike some adult survivors with greater awareness of and experience with anti-Semitism  and fearful of its Canadian manifestations, Kramer did not leave the Jewish community in trepidation, and never felt pressure to deny his heritage. For him, it was a move toward, not away from, a religious community. As such, Kramer's transition from life as a non-practising Jew to a believing (albeit never baptized) Christian occurred smoothly and signified positive change in his life as a free Canadian.

Other survivors did not experience such an easy transition, nor did they receive acceptance by their families. For these survivors, wartime traumas had a profound impact on their postwar religious lives, which proved wrought with pain, fearfulness, and surreptitious behaviour. Rotterdam native Bob Gosschalk grew up in a non-practising Jewish family and received no religious education. When the Germans invaded the Netherlands in May 1940, Gosschalk's beloved maternal grandfather, the only observant member of the family, jumped to his death. This suicide prompted his mother to push her family, including Gosschalk, his younger brother, and her husband, into hiding. "In many ways," Gosschalk recalled, "I lived the life of Anne Frank, but alone with no family."[38] For nearly four years, Gosschalk hid his true identity and passed as a Christian. He and his younger brother received Catholic indoctrination and served as altar boys during the war, and his brother became a life-long devout Roman Catholic. Liberation failed to fully release Gosschalk from his personal persecution. "Nauseated with the idea of being a Jew," and horrified by the legacy of Jewish history, Gosschalk vowed never again to reveal his origins.

The young man's painful history accompanied him to Woodstock, Ontario, when he immigrated as a farmhand in the summer of 1948. Neither his employers on the farm, nor his friends in nearby Hamilton, where he settled months after arriving, knew anything about his Holocaust experiences or true identity. He married Elizabeth, a Canadian-born woman of Dutch ancestry, and raised two children in the Anglican Church, in which he taught Sunday school and for which he edited the church magazine. His secret past persisted until a visit to the Netherlands in the mid-1990s, when Gosschalk's brother revealed the brothers' history, to the shock and dismay of Gosschalk's wife and daughter. At first, Elizabeth refused to believe that Gosschalk was not only a Jew but also a Holocaust survivor. In his seventies, Gosschalk began to publicly accept his Jewish heritage and discuss his Holocaust experiences with family and friends with Elizabeth's encouragement.[39]

For Thomas Kramer and Bob Gosschalk, the move away from Judaism proved permanent, though Kramer's parents continued to lead Jewish lives. For other young survivors, like Slovak Jew Vera Gold (née Szusz), a return to the Jewish faith coincided with the rebuilding of their lives in postwar Canada. Gold was raised in Czechoslovakia in a home deeply steeped in the neology traditions of central Europe. Neology was a dominant Jewish movement among Hungarian and Slovak Jewish communities in the second half of the nineteenth century up until the Second World War. Ideologically it was situated to the left of Orthodoxy, but less extreme than German Reformism.[40] Vera's parents had their two young daughters baptized as Lutherans following the rise of the National Socialist Party in neighbouring Germany, hoping that genuine baptismal records would save the girls' lives. Unlike those many of their friends, the Szusz family's conversion protected them from early persecution and delayed their entry into hiding, and later concentration camps, until 1944. At war's end, Gold, her older sister, father, and paternal grandmother—in addition to several aunts, uncles, and cousins—emerged, alive. In November 1948, through the sponsorship of two uncles already residing in Canada and the financial assistance of the Joint Distribution Committee and JIAS, Gold—with her father (now known by the last name Marten), stepmother, sister, stepsister, and paternal grandmother, a survivor of Theresienstadt—arrived in Toronto, ready to begin their lives anew.[41]

Once in Toronto, the Marten family worked hard to integrate into the non-Jewish Czech and Slovak immigrant communities. Living as non-Jews, albeit while maintaining relationships with observant Jewish relatives (some of whom were among the early members of Clanton Park Synagogue), the family's patriarch proved keen to move his brood away from the predominantly Jewish community surrounding Kensington Market. Soon after their arrival, Vera's father purchased a house in the city's east end, far from any Jewish communal infrastructure or institutions. Religion, like the Holocaust, was not a subject of conversation in their household. Yet Vera, to her father's initial dismay—as well as the disdain of her Jewish fiancé's observant family, who nonetheless referred to her as a *shiksa*—"returned to Judaism" through conversion in order to raise her family in the Jewish community.[42]

Gold's conversion did not serve to reignite a flame inside of her. Though she kept a kosher home, belonged to a conservative synagogue, and sent her children to Hebrew school, she did so more for the sake of her loved ones than out of any sense of personal spiritual fulfilment. Among her nuclear family, Vera Gold was the only one to reclaim a Jewish identity and live as part of the Jewish community. Kornel Marten and his wife lived happily as Lutherans, and Gold's sisters raised their children as Christians, with no connection whatsoever to Judaism. But whereas the elder Martens never denied their wartime suffering and Jewish heritage, Gold's sisters refused to discuss their experiences prior to immigrating to Canada or reveal the details of their Jewish past to their offspring.[43] While their denial of their shared histories and Jewish origins upset Gold, she accepted their positions in time. Rather than creating intra-family rifts and denying her own children the opportunity for family engagement, Gold upheld the sisters' explanations that Gold converted to Judaism from Christianity for marriage, and respected their wish to keep their secrets safe.

---

Holocaust survivors who abandoned Judaism and Jewish organizational life do not occupy a central voice in the broader narrative. Challenging the stereotypical image of all survivors as traditional, insular Jews, the inclusion of atheists and converts confronts an unspoken taboo about whose history is worthy of inclusion and analysis. Drilling down on their postwar experiences elucidates how religious identification or affiliation influenced survivors' integration and absorption into diverse Jewish communities across Canada. It also illuminates the contributing factors in newcomers' decisions to wilfully abandon Jewish communal life, sometimes reaching an outstretched arm to other faith groups.

It is impossible to ascertain with any certainty the number of Holocaust survivors who ceased to identify as Jewish or converted to another religion in postwar Canada; there is no scientific data on this. Evidence suggests that such actions were driven by self-protectionist behaviours and out of fear of perceived or anticipated anti-Semitism—based on previous encounters with persecutory violence due to their Jewishness—as well as the result of a loss of faith due to wartime trauma. The abandonment of, and later revelations about, Jewish heritage carried the potential threat of creating divisions and disconnects within extended family units. In Thomas Kramer's case, his parents, while not ecstatic about his membership in the Anglican Church, supported his choice of social and religious community. Conversely, Vera Gold's sisters' refusal to acknowledge their past lives as Jews and Holocaust survivors resulted in intra-family tensions, and prohibited other Orthodox Jewish relatives from revealing their own wartime experiences, so as not to "out" the women. For others still, the formal transfer of allegiance away from Judaism had little outward impact whatsoever. Hanna Spencer, for example, and her family seemed unperturbed about concealing their religious roots, and readily integrated into the folds of the United Church of Canada, although Hanna herself never formally converted.

Survivor converts or apostates merit inclusion in the broader narrative of postwar Holocaust history. But, they represent only one of the groups whose experiences have been marginalized in postwar Holocaust and Canadian social histories. Israeli transmigrants and late-arriving survivors, those who immigrated to Canada in the early to mid-1950s following previous attempts at resettlement elsewhere, are rarely discussed as a distinct group with defining features that separate them demographically and ideologically from the first wave of survivors to immigrate by 1950.

# CHAPTER EIGHT

# THE FINAL MOVEMENT: ISRAELI TRANSMIGRANTS AND OTHER "LATE ARRIVALS"

Before the Holocaust, Morris Faintuch never gave much thought to Palestine. A Polish Jew, Faintuch spent the war years masquerading as an Aryan before capture landed him in Auschwitz-Birkenau. With liberation, the orphaned seventeen-year-old Faintuch faced a difficult choice. As he had aunts, uncles, and a brother in Canada, he was eligible for sponsorship under the close relative scheme, a move that could take years to materialize. Or, he could leave for Palestine with other orphaned child survivors. Impatient to escape from Europe, Faintuch followed the latter path, joined a youth *aliyah* movement, and immigrated to Palestine in October 1945. He attended school and worked on a *moshav* (cooperative farm) with other orphaned youth before joining the nascent state of Israel's national army, Haganah, and fought in the country's War of Independence, for which he received numerous medals for bravery. But a few years later, Faintuch faced a serious decision: he had contracted a debilitating case of malaria during his army service and his doctor advised him that a change in climate would offer the best chance of recovery. Faintuch reluctantly accepted his brother's offer of sponsorship and in 1952 he immigrated to Canada as an Israeli citizen.[1]

By the time of Faintuch's arrival, the first major wave of postwar Jewish Holocaust survivor immigration to Canada had concluded. This chapter considers the "second wave," focusing on individuals who arrived as refugees or immigrants from late 1950 until 1955. The discussion stops before the arrival of refugees (including some 7,000 Jews—among them many Holocaust survivors) from the aborted Hungarian Revolution of 1956. It explores how this second movement of Holocaust survivors to Canada, differed from the initial wave, both with regard to demographic composition and the circumstances under which migration occurred.

From the start, the experiences of Holocaust survivors landing in Canada after 1950 diverged from those of the earlier arrivals. Few in the initial wave (i.e., pre-1950) of survivors had attempted permanent resettlement elsewhere prior to arriving in Canada. This group of survivors emerged at war's end from hiding, concentration or forced-labour camps, the forests, or the Soviet Union, and returned briefly to their pre-war homes. By late 1946, the vast majority had made their way, legally or illegally, out of the Soviet-controlled countries and into DP camps in zones under Western Allies occupation. At this time, opportunities for Jewish DPs to enter Canada remained limited to close relative and labour schemes sponsorship, or the War Orphans Project. Immigration proved impossible for those without a personal guarantee from a relative or potential employer. With few exceptions, nearly the entire first wave of survivors came as bona fide refugees.

Those survivors migrating to Canada after 1950 arrived primarily through one of two avenues, and under one of two statuses. One group consisted of trans-migrants from the nascent State of Israel. Citizens and Israeli passport holders, these survivors entered Canada as immigrants. Unable to travel directly from Israel due to a lack (at that time)[2] of official Canadian representation in Israel, members of this cohort travelled first back to Europe, and then spent anywhere from several weeks to a few years awaiting clearance to immigrate.

The remainder of the post-1950 group came directly from their countries of residence in Europe and, to a lesser extent, as survivors leaving their wartime countries of asylum, or earlier postwar sites of resettlement, including Asia (specifically Shanghai), South America, and Africa. This included refugees, many from major European city centres and dwindling DP camps, those who had undertaken efforts to resettle elsewhere in Europe without success, and the remainder who, for various reasons, had chosen to continue on their journeys toward permanent homesteads. Some members of this group had spent a considerable amount of time since liberation in DP camps, and frequently served in coordinating or leadership capacities in the local DP camp infrastructure or Jewish refugee enclaves that emerged in civilian areas, often adjacent to sites of rehabilitation. This cohort included individuals employed by occupying Allied armies as translators and administrators, and those serving in official capacities as employees of the United Nations Relief and Rehabilitation Administration (UNRRA) or the International Refugee Organization (IRO, post-1947). Among the cohort of refugees engaged by international organizations and militaries were rabbis who had spent years providing spiritual leadership and guidance for the thousands of survivors waiting in DP camps. These men, along with their families, refused to abandon their posts until the remainder of their constituents had moved on to other, more permanent sites of resettlement.[3] The second-wave survivors fell into two categories: displaced persons of primarily Eastern and central European origins; and citizens of Western European states, and Israel, who entered Canada as immigrants.

20. Canadian Jewish Congress overseas relief, c. 1950s. Courtesy of the Canadian Jewish Congress Charities Committee National Archives.

## Waves of Change

Much had happened to the refugees during the years between liberation and immigration, and Canadian immigration policy had changed significantly during that period as well. The first wave of Holocaust survivors originated mostly in Poland or Hungary; there were few Czechoslovak, German, or French Jews amongst their ranks.[4] Most were young, with men vastly outnumbering women. Aside from the war orphans and rare surviving youngsters accompanying their parents, few child survivors were included within the first wave of refugees. Similarly, very few "elderly" survivors—individuals over the age of fifty—gained entry at this time. The explanation for the absence of this latter subgroup is twofold. In the first instance, relatively few aged Jews survived the Holocaust. Second, the conditions pertaining to early postwar immigration schemes largely negated survivors deemed unable to contribute to Canada's growing economy. The stigma of advanced age deemed most senior survivors automatically ineligible for inclusion in the labour schemes.

The 29 June 1950 promulgation (and 1 July 1950 implementation) by the government of Prime Minster Louis St. Laurent of Order-in-Council P.C. 2856 signalled great change in the national stance on immigration and refugee issues. More liberalized in approach, P.C. 2856 significantly lowered barriers that had formerly identified thousands of Jewish survivors as ineligible for immigration through the Occupational Settlement Scheme (OS8).[5] The broadening of the criteria occurred in response to the declining number of refugee labourers arriving in Canada through the labour schemes and the country's need for workers in general. As Canadian social historian Valerie Knowles has explained, "When the available supply of manpower could no longer keep up with the insatiable demands of the Canadian labour market, the government was forced to the conclusion that further action was required: measures that would allow more people into Canada and at the same time ensure the right kind of immigrants."[6]

While maintaining the country's historical preference for northern European and English-speaking immigrants, the 1950 regulations revived hope among advocates for European Jewish refugee immigration that Canada would finally widen its gates. Other would-be immigrants previously lumped into ineligible categories due to age or ethnicity, or who had been considered unsuitable and unassimilable to the Canadian way of life due to their national origins, gained entrée into the country. This included, but was not limited to, persons from southern Europe, and immigrants from the Arab world. Italians and Germans previously declined entry owing to their respective nations' fascist pasts, made up the two largest immigrant populations in the 1950s.[7] The new measures expanded the admissible classes of immigrants to include any healthy individual of good character with skills. Applicants also needed to demonstrate their ability to integrate easily into Canadian society. The revised guidelines permitted Canadian residents and citizens to sponsor relatives of any degree; it also enabled sponsorship of survivors through other routes, like the labour schemes.[8]

The reins of Canada's new immigration policy control continued to loosen throughout the 1950s. Authority over immigration and refugee determination admissibility was transferred from the Ministry of Mines and Resources into the newly established Ministry of Citizenship and Immigration. A myriad of reasons, including the Western world's commitment to the democratization and "civilization" of foreign nations to prevent the ascent of future fascist dictatorships and to create a unified front in the morally astute West against communism, influenced the parliamentary restructuring. Cold War fears topped political agendas, and served to inadvertently accelerate previously downplayed questions of immigrant eligibility and integration. In 1952, a new and much anticipated Immigration Act was passed. The first new immigration act since 1931, this bill granted the Minister of Immigration nearly absolute discretion over which applicants received admittance or rejection to Canada.[9] While such discretionary authority ensured that only legitimate and law-abiding immigrants, in terms of political, cultural, and climatic compatibility, were granted entry to Canada, it also widened the variety and parameters (including the age and ability of persons falling under close relatives sponsorships) of approved immigrant sponsorship programs.

From the perspective of the Canadian Jewish community, none of the new proposals proved more beneficial than the "Approved Church Program: OS8–Sponsorship by Voluntary Agency." An amendment to, and updating of, the extant OS8 Settlement Scheme, the new plan permitted greater numbers of Holocaust survivor immigrants (among others) to enter Canada as a myriad of professionals. A field letter from Louis D. Horwitz, the director of the American Jewish Joint Distribution Committee (AJDC) in Paris, confirmed that "consideration will be given to a stated number of immigrants qualified in any of the trades, skills and occupations currently in demand in Canada to be brought forward under the guarantee of the Canadian Jewish Congress."[10] Horwitz attached lists of 154 approved trades, skills, and occupations.[11]

To ensure the inclusion of Jewish immigrants in the program, communal leadership (representing the interests of the wider Jewish community) reluctantly agreed to accept fiduciary responsibility for all applicants granted entry into Canada. Confirming the terms of the agreement, the director of the Department of Citizenship and Immigration, C.E.S. Smith, noted, "The Canadian Jewish Congress and the Jewish Immigrant Aid Society jointly undertake to accept full responsibility for reception, accommodation and employment on arrival of all unsponsored Jewish immigrant workers brought forward under the 'Approved Church Programme,' and to provide for the reception and accommodation of their dependents."[12]

In light of these developments, the composition of the second wave of Holocaust survivors to Canada looked very different from the first. Alongside youth and young couples stood a substantial minority of so-called hard-core cases, including those unable to readily achieve self-sufficiency due to age, ability, and poor health. Joseph Kage, the director of Social Services for JIAS's Montreal office, reported that the types of immigrants to arrive in Canada in 1951 and utilize JIAS services, were markedly more diverse than their predecessors. "The kind of immigrant that we are receiving now," Kage wrote, "is definitely different from that which we received two years ago. They are older, more physically disabled, less skilled, more children per family, more people who are difficult to adjust either because of religious beliefs, former occupations."[13]

The national origins of the survivors changed, too. More French, Romanian, and Czechoslovakian Jews arrived, greatly increasing the number of French-speaking Holocaust survivors in Canada. Considerably more women with young children arrived as well, although they remained outnumbered by men. And hundreds of Hassidim and *mitnagedim* survivor families gained permission to enter the country under the new conditions, many arriving via Antwerp, Belgium.[14]

In the years before they immigrated to Canada, many amongst the second group of survivors had made efforts to reconstruct their lives elsewhere. They laid new, if temporary, roots in their host communities, learned new trades and languages, and married and bore children. These experiences lent themselves to the survivors' decisions to immigrate to Canada, and their eventual integration—or lack thereof—with Canadian Jewish society.

Holocaust survivors who immigrated to Canada from Israel in the 1950s gave the decision to leave much thought. In most cases, pragmatic and ideological considerations contributed to what many viewed as a significant sacrifice—abandoning the nascent Jewish state many of the survivors had recently helped establish.

The day-to-day realities of life in Israel prompted many survivors to leave their self-described homeland. Climate emerged as a key problem. The hot temperatures and extreme dryness led, in some case, to the aggravation of medical conditions contracted during or resulting from the Holocaust, including heart conditions and permanent nerve damage.

For some, like Shlomo Friedman, the extreme climate proved too much to bear. Friedman suffered heart strains from his years of imprisonment in several Nazi slave labour and concentration camps. Within months of his arriving in Israel, a doctor informed him that the unforgiving climate, completely unfamiliar to Europeans, could contribute to a premature death. Thus, at the age of forty-nine, Friedman packed up his wife and two young daughters and set off for Canada.[15] Many others in similar predicaments followed suit.

The climate was one reason to leave Israel. The low standard of living and severe economic hardships in the nascent state (in comparison to postwar Canada and the United States) was another serious contributing factor. Almost immediately upon disembarking in Palestine, nearly all survivors were moved to socialist *kibbutzim* and *moshavim* (cooperative settlements similar to *kibbutzim*, consisting of small farms) and put to work. Young, able-bodied male and female newcomers were quickly drafted into the burgeoning army, handed a weapon, and sent off to fight for the Jewish people's freedom, trading one battlefield for another.[16] With little in the way of resources or expertise, survivors assisted the *sabras* (Jews born or raised in pre-state Palestine) in cultivating the land, building infrastructure, and protecting against Arab hostilities. Some, mainly youthful newcomers, enjoyed this arrangement and actively helped develop the Jewish homeland. For them, this proved especially meaningful after experiencing the Holocaust. But, for others, particularly older survivors unaccustomed to agricultural labour or communal living, or refugees not in line with the dominant nationalist ideology, the conditions proved unbearable. The appeal of Zionism could not always triumph over the realities of life in late-1940s to early-1950s Israel, which offered little in the way of an upward economic trajectory, material goods and products, or opportunities for former professionals.

Israel's Zionist ideology, with its emphasis on a new type of Jew,[17] in stark contrast with the stereotype of the weak European Jew, propelled some Holocaust survivors to transmigrate to Canada. The "new Jew" was strong and tanned, healthy and fit for manual labour, and religiously non-observant; the new Jew stood against everything that the Zionists found wrong with traditional Judaism, as exemplified in the *shtetls* of Russia and Eastern Europe. The Zionist ideal denigrated European Jewry, and criticized Holocaust survivors for "going like sheep to the slaughter" and failing to fight back against their Nazi oppressors. The Yishuv (the native, pre-war Jewish community) glorified and romanticized wartime resistance and partisan movements, and silenced personal suffering. Such attitudes disturbed individual Holocaust survivors, and divided survivor communities. By refusing to minimize their own suffering, or publicly criticize their murdered relatives for their inability to "fight back," some survivors, particularly those of advanced age, seemed unable to adapt to the new Israeli Jewish culture.[18]

While ideology undoubtedly exerted an influence, cultural incompatibility was, in many cases, the determining "push" factor leading survivors to emigrate from Israel. Some survivors found the Hebrew language difficult to learn. Rarely used in pre-war Europe, except for prayer and among Zionist organizations, modern Hebrew proved exceedingly difficult to learn, particularly for those older survivors whose last encounters with education took place decades earlier. With the official adoption of modern Hebrew as the lingua franca of the new Jewish state, some survivors simply could not adapt to Israeli cultural norms or feel settled. A certain number of these survivors searched to join a more *heimish* (i.e., traditional, warm, and welcoming) Jewish community, which they found, to varying degrees, in large Canadian centres.[19]

To be sure, many survivors willingly adopted and adapted to Zionist norms and values. Others, however, struggled with the country's strong nationalist tone. To them, Israeli society's cultivation of Zionist ideology appeared disturbingly reminiscent of National Socialism in pre-war and wartime Germany. Elsa Engler, an Austrian Jew who survived the war with her husband and son in Shanghai, likened the social polarization she experienced in Israel, including discrimination on the basis of political affiliation with regard to employment and education, to the pariah status of Jews in the early years of Nazi dictatorship. As moderate Zionists with an upper-class upbringing, Engler recalled that, in Israel, she and her family faced ostracism and unfair treatment as compared to their actively Zionistic contemporaries.[20] The nascent country's zealousness and nationalist propaganda, coupled with survivors' own suspicions of political movements, prompted some survivors, including Engler, to seek permanent residence in Canada, a country they did not associate with extreme ideologies.[21]

In some cases the decision to transmigrate to Canada appeared inevitable. Although Zionism flourished in Europe's DP camps, not all Holocaust survivors adhered to its principles.[22] Many survivors, while perhaps sympathetic to Zionism in general, viewed immigration to mandatory Palestine (later Israel) from a more practical standpoint. Morris Faintuch originally travelled to then-Palestine because the opportunity to immigrate there arose before an affidavit for Canada materialized. More concerned with rebuilding their own lives and families than contributing to the development of the Jewish state, these survivors immigrated to Palestine/Israel out of desperation; their destination proved of lesser importance than emigration from Europe, particularly for those who feared becoming trapped in postwar communist regimes.

One example of this reluctant *aliyah* surfaces in the case of Romanian Holocaust survivor Lazer (Lou) Hoffer, who manipulated strict Canadian immigration laws and secured a place on the War Orphans Project with his younger brother. Shortly after, in the late 1940s, the boys' parents applied unsuccessfully to join their sons. After his parents' plan to join their sons failed to materialize, the elder Hoffers became fearful of remaining in Romania and becoming trapped behind the Iron Curtain. With few options, they applied instead to immigrate to Israel. Within a few years, Hoffer and his brother saved enough money to sponsor their parents to transmigrate to Canada as close relatives.[23]

For others, a visit to Canada led to unplanned permanent immigration. Betty Warshawsky represents one such case. Born into a traditional Jewish family in pre-war Poland, Warshawsky was raised in a home with strong Zionist beliefs and received Hebrew language instruction alongside secular schooling. These factors, as well as her youth and determination to help build a Jewish homeland, made Warshawsky an ideal candidate for the new Israeli culture. While life was not easy, practical difficulties did not prompt Warshawsky to leave Israel; she simply missed having a large family close by. When her family in Winnipeg applied for a three-month visitor's visa for Betty and her young daughter, nobody anticipated what would happen. Overwhelmed by the warm reception and love showered upon her by her aunts, uncles, brother, and sister-in-law, Warshawsky called for her husband to join her. Although she loved Israel and remained an ardent Zionist, family trumped nationalism for her.[24]

Existential fear fuelled some survivors' decision to leave Israel. Well aware of the dangers and losses that accompany war, thousands of Holocaust survivors arrived in Palestine and, within three years of liberation from the Nazi camps in Europe, embarked on another battle, this time to fight for, and achieve, Israeli statehood.[25] Survivors often made the connection between their motivation to emigrate and their experiences during the Second World War and its aftermath. Polish Jews Frieda H and her husband survived a series of concentration camps and endured a year of internment on Cyprus before finally gaining permission from the British to enter mandatory Palestine. Straight from the dock, Frieda's husband was conscripted into the Haganah to fight in Israel's 1948 to 1949 War of Independence. A few years later, however, the couple left Israel, citing fear of future conflicts and war with neighbouring Arab populations.[26] Others who made *aliyah* both before and after the War of Independence shared Frieda's fears. Magda Hilf, a survivor from the small town of Maly Kovesd, Czechoslovakia, was twenty-eight years old when she, her husband, and her two-year-old daughter immigrated to Israel in 1949. Four years later, the family left for Canada. "After so much suffering, we wanted to move away from the fighting.... We wanted our children to grow up somewhere safe,"[27] she explained. JIAS case files reveal numerous cases of transmigrants, like Frieda H. and Hilf, who sought to escape Israel's unstable security environment. Scarred by war, they could not bear the prospect of living through any further conflict.[28]

Making the decision to leave Israel was half of the challenge of migrating to Canada. The other half lay in the method of movement. As noted, no Canadian representation or embassy existed in Israel to process applications or provide medical clearances for survivors wishing to immigrate to Canada. Without on-the-ground official Canadian government clearance, approval for immigration visas and successful sponsorship applications could not be processed directly. Prospective immigrants needed to travel to a country with a Canadian presence, such as Italy, France, or Germany, in order to apply for immigration. Physically returning to the very European continent that represented so many painful and horrific memories, and that they had fought to leave, represented phase one in Israeli transmigrants' travels. This began a process that could take from a few weeks to several years.[29]

Once back in Europe, this time as Israeli passport holders, survivors faced their first of many major obstacles on the path toward immigrating to Canada. As the following policy statement reflects, the AJDC, the single largest advocate for Holocaust refugees in the world at that time, opposed Holocaust survivors emigrating from Israel:

> The JDC policy regarding Israeli transmigrants has been clear since the beginning of this unpredictable movement. We have offered no financial assistance of any kind to this group of people, and at the most all we have done is to extend minimal technical support. We have never asked any cooperating committee to do anything special for these people, nor will we do so in the foreseeable future. We have always taken a hands-off policy...we should not be held in any way responsible for the movement of Israeli transmigrants.[30]

Simply put, the AJDC refused to provide any special intervention on behalf of the Israeli survivors wishing to migrate to Canada (or elsewhere). From the agency's perspective, Israeli transmigrants, as citizens of Israel, were not refugees, and therefore did not merit the provisions and assistance bequeathed to bona fide refugees. Faced with this significant obstacle, the prospective immigrants were thus forced to turn for assistance to local Hebrew Immigrant Aid Service (HIAS) offices as Israeli returnees (i.e., those who had abandoned their site of resettlement).

Additional issues complicated the survivors' second (or perhaps third or fourth) chance at immigration. Formal anti-Semitic overtures continued to plague individual survivors while they waited for their Canadian entry papers. A 1952 letter from a World Jewish Congress representative asserts that Jewish potential immigrants faced discrimination at the Canadian consular office in Rome. The consul, the sole agent with executive powers over immigration at the office, it was reported, "has an extremely unfriendly attitude toward the Jewish candidates who are received only after all other visitors have been seen." Cold War ideology and fears played a role as well. According to the same report, "Mr. Klein [HIAS director at Rome] had reason to believe that [the] rejections are made because of political reasons as most of the group of applicants have spent some period during the war in the USSR."[31]

Long, drawn-out delays became the norm. Without means or permission to undertake employment legally, Israeli transmigrants and their families were compelled to live leanly during their stint in European stopover countries. While many managed to maintain themselves with funds brought out of Israel, others, especially those stuck with long wait times, required financial assistance from the poorly funded local HIAS offices, since the AJDC remained intransigent.[32]

The pathway to immigration progressed, bumpy and full of obstacles. Holocaust survivors granted Israeli citizenship lost the chance to enter Canada as refugees (due to their status as citizens of another country), but could still potentially resettle in the country as sponsored immigrants. Wherever possible, individuals tried to procure such sponsorship through a friend or relative already residing in Canada. For several years, the Immigration Department approved only personal sponsorship applications from close relatives. The CJC, fearful of any additional financial obligations, officially supported this practice.[33] In a letter to one concerned Mr. J. Klinger of Lethbridge, Alberta, CJC executive director Saul Hayes reiterated, "I can assure you that the Department [of Immigration] is not making any exceptions and in particular does not accept 'sponsored cases' involving residents of Israel except for people who are 'close relatives' in the sense of the law, which restricts this category to husband or wife; son or daughter, brother or sister, together with husband or wife and unmarried children; father or mother; grandparents; orphan nephew or niece under 21 years of age; fiancé(e)s."[34] Hayes and his office had no intention of challenging the status quo at that time. Instead, Israeli citizens were encouraged to apply for inclusion on the Canadian government's Occupational Settlement Scheme (OS8), which (as noted) supplied immigration visas to individuals of good health and character, and in possession of some specific skill or area of expertise.

While Israeli transmigrants accounted for a significant portion of Holocaust survivors to arrive in Canada in the 1950s, there was another cohort of survivors who travelled directly from Europe; an even smaller group emigrated from alternate states of resettlement, including Asia, Africa, and South America. European-based survivors acquired visas to Canada through one of two mechanisms. The first mechanism involved those identified under international humanitarian law as "stateless refugees" transferring from DP camps, while the second involved moving to Canada both refugees and immigrants who held citizenship from primarily Western European states. The methods of transportation and sponsorship did not differ greatly from those affecting the Israeli transmigrants. The survivors entered Canada either through the close relatives scheme, the OS8, or as immigrants with passports from another country with sufficient means to resettle independently. Stateless Jewish refugees arriving directly from DP camps, or following temporary stays in a host country, still required sponsors' affidavits guaranteeing that they would not require financial or material assistance from the government.

This group of 1950s Holocaust survivors cited various reasons for their decision to immigrate to Canada. Similar to many of the Israeli transmigrants, most sought better economic and political conditions than what they were currently experiencing in early postwar Europe. The acquisition of legal, stable work proved particularly difficult for stateless survivors lacking permanent residence status in their country of resettlement. Walter and Erika Absil, Viennese survivors who spent the war in hiding in Belgium, were compelled to emigrate from their country of refuge due to financial hardships. The Belgians treated the couple very well, and little anti-Semitism existed in their community. But, as Mr. Absil recalled, "Without a work permit, it was very hard to make a living. We survived day to day."[35] Unable to obtain Belgian citizenship, the Absils felt they had little option but to migrate to a more welcoming country, like Canada, where they could legally undertake work opportunities.

In other instances, economic considerations fell secondary to kinship ties in drawing otherwise content survivors to leave Europe. The Rubenfeld family represented one such case. Natives of Belfort, France, the Rubenfelds—David Hersh and Cyla, and children Georges, Rachelle, and Regine—survived the Holocaust in hiding throughout France. Musical prodigies, the children had performed in concerts and in fundraising benefits for French prisoners of war before they were forced to go underground. Following liberation, the family vowed to remain together. Decades later, the daughters explained how they lost everything in the war, including their home and all their worldly possessions. But the Rubenfelds started over, and returned to work, school, and most importantly, their music. By the early 1950s, the family had succeeded in re-establishing themselves financially.[36] Georges' visit to cousins in Winnipeg during his university holidays changed everything when he met a woman he wished to marry. The family was faced with a dilemma—should they remain in France, or move to Canada, a country they did not know? "While we had no intention to come, and did not have to come, we wanted to be together," Regine recalled more than fifty-five years later.[37] In 1953, the entire Rubenfeld family arrived in Winnipeg as immigrants.

As was the case for some Israeli transmigrants, the threat of ensuing conflict and war drove a number of Holocaust survivors to reconsider their future on the European continent. One survivor of Soviet labour camps, Michael Bienstock, immigrated to Norway in 1947 in response to calls for skilled tailors. Living among what he described as "some of the finest people in the whole world," Bienstock enjoyed a good life for over four years before the outbreak of the Korean War in 1950.[38] He feared that the Cold War tensions might spread to northern Europe and that he and his family might become trapped in a warzone for the

21. Studio portrait of the Rubenfeld family before Georges' departure from France to Winnipeg, Manitoba, 1950. Left to right: David Hersh, Rachelle, Georges, Regine and Cyla. Collection of the author.

second time. Unwilling to take such a risk, Bienstock followed the lead of others in the community and filed applications to emigrate to Canada.

Hundreds of Hassidic and ultra-Orthodox survivors faced their own concerns about remaining in post–Second World War Europe. According to the Montreal Belzer commemorative book, "The worry of the Korean War, which threatened to engulf Europe in another war, was too much for these survivors of the Holocaust to take. Escape!! Where to?? Eretz Yisrael was out of the question because of war and great poverty. The USA had closed its doors to most immigrants and the waiting list grew longer and longer day by day."[39] With the approval of the Belzer rebbe, congregants identified Canada as a suitable option for resettlement.

Some survivors who had previously been identified as ineligible for immigration because of a lack of transferable skills or dormant medical conditions were now, as a result of the liberalized immigration regulations, deemed acceptable candidates for Canadian visas. Many of them had resided in DP camps since shortly after liberation. Canada represented their first opportunity to live lives independent of institutional control and finally lay down roots. At least, that was their intention.

European Jews who arrived after 1950 entered into a very different Canada and Canadian Jewish society than that experienced by the first wave that had arrived, with few exceptions, as refugees. The changes in Canada's immigration policies and practices offered this latter wave of survivors an opportunity to re-establish, they hoped for the last time. Developments in Canadian Jewish social service agencies, especially JIAS, improved the quality and breadth of services available to them. The growing professionalization of social work training and practice, accompanied by a greater understanding of survivors' trauma issues, was extremely beneficial for many of the latest newcomers. Although the core institutional objectives remained the same—housing, employment, and sustenance—time and experience had helped the social workers and employment counsellors prepare to better address the survivors' particular needs. David Weiss, a social worker and the executive director of Montreal's Baron de Hirsch Institute and Jewish Child Welfare Bureau, described social workers as holding "statesmen's roles in making Canadian Jewish life more meaningful here and now." No longer ad hoc care providers, "trained, professional social workers are employed by the agencies," Weiss continued. "They are experienced and understand the social and psychological problems of people who are in pain and in need of assistance."[40]

The increased professionalization of agencies servicing the needs of the second-wave survivors cut both ways. While more robust and sophisticated operations certainly benefited some survivors, most faced increasingly intense screening to determine eligibility for JIAS services. JIAS served as a first point of contact for refugees and immigrants alike. But, over time, societal and organizational attitudes led to changes that proved detrimental for some segments of the survivor community. The organization initially determined eligibility based on several criteria, including the financial status of survivors' sponsors, medical incapacity, and clients' efforts to secure work.[41] Notwithstanding such strict guidelines, those who demonstrated a genuine need for rent and maintenance support typically received some degree of funding.

These strict eligibility conditions rendered some newcomers ineligible for financial assistance. Israeli transmigrants did not qualify for JIAS maintenance because Israel was viewed as a country of resettlement, not transition. Therefore, those survivor/Israeli citizens were deemed as having left for Canada willingly as citizenship holders and bona fide immigrants, and without threat of persecution, stripping them of potential "special treatment" allocated officially only to Holocaust survivor refugees.

In reality, however, many cases of Israeli transmigrants ended up on agency blotters when the newcomers threatened to become burdens on the Canadian welfare system, thus increasing their risk of potential deportation. Conversely, all close relative and OS8 sponsorship cases fell under JIAS responsibility, and thus automatically gained access to services and financial support denied to others. The sheer number of cases, many of which required prolonged attention, it was reported, caused the transmigrants to become more of "a burden on the community for a much longer period of time" than their predecessors.[42]

Institutional improvements benefited the latecomers. Social workers increasingly accepted "psychiatric cases," that is, survivors considered to be suffering from the psychological effects of their wartime traumas. Just a few years earlier, lacking training and wholly unprepared for the enormity of the tragedy that had befallen their clients, caseworkers referred such survivors to in-patient psychiatric institutions. By the early 1950s, however, some social workers felt prepared to provide psychiatric support to survivors. Twenty-one-year-old Hungarian survivor Mr. W, who presented himself at Montreal's JIAS office in May 1952, was one such case. Mr. W complained of physical and psychological deterioration, and professed his inability to cope in his new surroundings. Upon learning of an unreasonably long wait for institutionalized care, Mr. W's JIAS caseworker offered him intense counselling. The pair met three to four times weekly for several months. Mr. W soon undertook his first job, working one hour per day, gradually overcoming his emotional problems and gaining confidence in his abilities. Mr. W severed ties with the agency and accepted full-time employment shortly thereafter. Closure of this case was deemed an organizational victory.[43]

Changes in reception policies and practices were closely related to other societal advances and opportunities. In the brief interval since the first survivors had arrived, Canadian Jews had experienced a number of important changes, including the fast and furious development of Hassidic and *mitnagedim* communities; the successful resettlement of the initial wave of Holocaust survivors and their dependents; a downward trend in the economy (effecting the demand for labour); a national housing crisis; the emergence of a professional Jewish social service sector; and Israel's independent statehood. These changes greatly influenced the second wave of survivors' experiences of reception and integration, for better and for worse.

Canadian Jews had welcomed the initial wave of Holocaust survivors who had arrived beginning in the late 1940s. Communities came together to receive refugees and materially supported them in obtaining suitable employment, housing, and necessary goods. The project of rescuing the remnants of European Jewry was considered noble, and while their efforts did not always suffice, Canadian Jews behaved relatively empathetically, at least in the early stages. But this enthusiasm and generosity quickly dissipated with the recognition that most survivors seemed young, strong, and physically sound—nothing like the images of emaciated concentration camp survivors portrayed in the media—and presented as industrious and hardworking. With the emerging lack of contact and communication between the two groups, and disconnect between expectations and reality, some Canadian Jews made the false assumption that the survivors must be unappreciative and insatiable *greeners*.

Perhaps as a follow-up to this earlier experience, the local Jewish population seemed largely uninterested in the second wave of survivors that arrived in the early 1950s. Having already expended limited communal resources greeting one group of penniless Holocaust survivors, the second group was initially regarded with ambivalence. There are a number of reasons for this apathetic response. For one—although the term had not yet been created nor intended for use in this context—by the early 1950s, many JIAS and other social service caseworkers were suffering from a version of "Holocaust fatigue." Exhausted from attending to the needs of, and hearing about the trauma experienced by, their Holocaust survivor clientele, some professionals removed themselves emotionally from yet another group of trauma survivors. Then, too, professional social workers felt building frustration over the fact that the influx of Holocaust survivors and their dependents entering Canada appeared unending. The professionals feared that their work would never come to closure; they could seemingly never do enough or serve a sufficient number of clients. Their sense of powerlessness or insufficiency undermined their efficiency and engagement. High staff turnover rates suggest that the burden of servicing survivors proved greater than anticipated.

Organizational rivalries also played a part in diminishing the efficiency and effectiveness of services offered to the 1950s arrivals. The CJC resented the AJDC and its affiliates for constantly pushing Canadian Jewry to advocate for, and support, the integration and resettlement of new groups of Holocaust survivors. In a letter to Saul Hayes, executive director of the CJC, AJDC director Henry L. Levy placed not-so-subtle pressure on the CJC and Canadian Jewish community to continue its immigration resettlement efforts, stating: "It is unthinkable that Canada should not represent for us an open door where the Jewish migrants can go to for firm resettlement."[44] At the bottom of the letter, an unnamed author scribbled the following message that echoed the sentiment of Canadian Jewish officials: "Saul, Colonial Canada will always remain the dumping place."[45]

And yet, in spite of the frustration exhibited by social service agencies and professional caseworkers in handling the influx of new arrivals, and in spite of CJC complaints about Canada as a perceived "dumping place" for the world's Holocaust refugees, advocacy continued for potential Jewish immigrants who wished to leave Europe. In an article entitled "Emigrants Stranded in Rome," published in the *Canadian Jewish Chronicle* on 2 November 1952, an anonymous author wrote, "The Canadian Jewish Congress has made strong representations to the Canadian Government on behalf of the refugees in Italy. It is pointed out that the refugees, by emigrating from Israel, lost their Statehood inadvertently, and should be treated by the Canadians as refugees. The Congress has urged the re-examination of each case. The Federal Government has instituted an investigation in Italy, and the Congress has extended guarantees that the emigrants will be found employment and accommodations on their arrival."[46] It appeared that resettlement organizations felt prepared to greet the latest group of newcomers.

Still, even the most empathetic of social workers grew weary as they dealt with the second wave of survivors to arrive in Canada. Citing the temporal distance between the end of the Second World War and the newcomers' departure for Canada, social workers, like most Canadian Jews, inaccurately assumed that the post-1950 survivors would require less institutional support and be less "needy" or "deserving" than the earlier arrivals.

Emotions ran high, and reflected organized Canadian Jewry's own ambivalences and insecurities when the subject of Zionism and Israel was discussed. Unfortunately, for the Israeli transmigrants, they were the unwitting targets of many of these insecurities. In the eyes of the majority of Canadian Jews, the state of Israel marked the culmination of the Zionist vision of the creation of an independent Jewish homeland in which threatened or homeless Jews could find safe haven. Certainly, this included Holocaust survivors. From a Canadian Jewish perspective, it was incomprehensible that survivors made stateless by the results of the war but still residing in DP camps (or wandering between European capitals in search of lost relatives) would not take the first opportunity to migrate to the nascent Israeli state (where they would be offered immediate citizenship under the Law of Return). And it was absolutely unconscionable, a violation of fundamental Zionist values and an abandonment of fellow nation-builders, for those Holocaust survivors who had already 'ascended' to Israel by making *aliyah* to even consider leaving the country permanently.[47]

Members of the Canadian Jewish community at large were seemingly unaware of the challenges faced by survivors who remained in postwar Europe beyond the early 1950s. While some who had regained their health by that point were engaged in rebuilding their lives, many other survivors experienced ongoing physical and emotional suffering. For refugee survivors denied asylum in a free country, and thus forced to remain in limbo in DP camps long after liberation and the war's end, personal and professional rehabilitation had not yet taken place. These differing degrees of rehabilitation affected the process of integration and adaptation in 1950s Canada, and the survivors' experience with the established Jewish community.

Armed with substantial knowledge of Canada's geographic, social, and religious landscape, many second-wave survivors independently selected a site of resettlement. Several influences determined the survivors' selection process in deciding where to lay roots, and typically depended upon the presence of relatives and friends. Devoutly observant survivors sought to relocate directly to large Jewish centres with Hassidic and ultra-Orthodox religious infrastructure. Those hoping to distance themselves from organized Jewish life, conversely, often headed to western Canada, or they resettled in Montreal or Toronto in specifically "non-Jewish" areas. In Montreal, this usually meant living in French-speaking neighbourhoods, where few other Jews resided; in Toronto, it entailed moving away from the central downtown core, or settling outside the city limits.[48]

Housing in major Canadian metropolises in the 1950s stood at a premium, with affordable and suitable homes few and far between. Landlords routinely refused to rent rooms to families with children, and when housing was acquired—often only after an outrageous sum in the form of "key money" was delivered—conditions rarely met the most basic living standards. As a rule, JIAS did not rent houses for the second-wave survivors; it rented individual rooms on an as-needed basis. Household goods, including beds, a table with chairs, and bedding, came from the community charity chests and second-hand collections.[49]

A number of the second-wave refugees were welcomed by already established—or in the process of becoming establishing—relatives and *landsleit* who helped to ease the house-hunting process. Since many of the first movement were themselves still in settlement mode and without access to substantial financial resources, they provided other forms of aid. Friends' and relatives' experiences of resettlement, English (or, less frequently, French) language acquisition, navigating the housing market, and business connections alleviated some of the anxieties surrounding the new immigrants' first days. Most survivors sponsored by relatives, including the Rubenfelds and Warshawskys, moved in with their families, albeit temporarily.

A brief downturn in the Canadian economy in the 1950s compounded the survivors' resettlement pressures. Jewish and non-Jewish displaced persons who arrived in the late 1940s had been recruited specifically to meet Canada's growing market and agricultural demands. With their expertise and competencies, skilled newcomers among this first wave typically found employment reasonably quickly. Indeed, workers were in such great demand that unskilled labourers found employment quite soon, too. By 1952, after the enormous boom, labourers suffered from a decrease in opportunities. Workers in the country's needle trade, including Holocaust survivors who received technical training in their fields before immigrating, were hit especially hard.[50]

Jewish communal service providers' policies focused largely on the immediate placement of newcomers in work positions. Employment counsellors provided referrals based on clients' credentials and skill sets, as well as the current labour conditions and job opportunities. In rare instances, loans and subsidies to undertake professional upgrading were granted to survivors with foreign professional accreditations that might benefit Canadian society.[51] Work placement proved critically important on several levels. Working entailed earning an income, which left survivors less vulnerable to poverty and more inclined to take proactive stances in rebuilding their lives. It eased financial pressures on community funds, even when maintenance funds were remitted to cover all necessary expenses (particularly when children and large families were involved). And, work placement and employment aided in the development of peer groups, provided insight on social norms and customs, and helped encourage integration into new environments.

Survivors routinely accepted employment contracts where their education, training, and work experiences received no appreciation, in the hope that their lot would improve over time. And in some cases, this eventually did occur. For others, however, unable to find permanent and sustainable work, situations proved far more complicated. Labour leaders in the immediate postwar period had rallied alongside Jewish and non-Jewish community leaders to demand the admission of Holocaust survivors into Canada and readily submitted guarantees on their behalf. Five years later, empathetic employers—or those needing survivor labour—had largely gone by the wayside. Many of the same employers and union representatives who had extended a supportive hand to the first wave of survivors turned away from members of the second seeking employment. As a result, new-comers frequently ended up self-employed, running small businesses, often out of their cramped homes. In western Canada, approximately a dozen ran motels and bars in seedy and unsafe areas, frequented mostly by Native Canadians.[52] This specific subgroup of survivors remained more socially isolated from the Jewish community, struggled to acclimatize, and took longer to learn English or French.[53]

Other circumstances applied further stressors. Families among the second movement of survivors were often large, and included several children. The presence of young children placed considerable strain on both the survivors and social service workers, and increased the already substantial demand for assistance to young mothers (many of whom had no experienced relative to guide and help them) and nursery care.[54]

Older survivors also immigrated to Canada in the early 1950s. Most members of this subgroup were admitted through the sponsorship of their adult children, often Holocaust survivors themselves, who had entered Canada as labourers during the first wave of immigration. The remainder arrived as part of a family constellation—for instance, a fifty-year-old woman piggy-backing on her daughter's work contract as a domestic labourer. The immediate postwar im-migration regulations barred entry of any persons unable to undertake work and not in optimal health; the post-1950 amendments widened the scope of eligible immigrants, leading to an influx of less "desirable" and less adaptable newcomers, which included older survivors.

All sponsorship cases required the demonstration of financial security on the part of the sponsors along with guarantees that their relatives would not become dependent on the country's welfare system. This condition was strictly upheld with regard to newcomers over the age of forty-five. According to JIAS social worker Sylvia Endler, Holocaust survivors who immigrated at the age of forty-five and above "were considered old because they cannot sell their skills in the employment market, and because forty-five years is too old to become an apprentice in a new trade."[55] A willingness and ability to embark on a new career did not suffice in helping the newcomers. Age intensified other compounding problems among survivors, including non-transferable skills, a depreciated sense of self-worth and independence, loss of kinship or community ties, and physical ailments, often related to wartime trauma. The decreased capacity to support family proved particularly painful for older males accustomed to being the primary family breadwinner.

Endler identified older survivors of the second wave of immigration as the "displaced of the displaced," requiring longer and more intensive support, and facing greater difficulties in securing work or becoming self-supporting than did their younger cohorts. Employer prejudice loomed large. Older survivors, who frequently lacked transferable skills or the language needed for professional employment, faced discrimination by their potential employers who associated old age with diminished learning and performance capacity. In 1949, approximately 90 percent of breadwinners among Holocaust survivor immigrant families were under the age of thirty. Three years later, most were just shy of forty years, and nearly all heads of households were between thirty and fifty years old.[56]

Sheltered workshops provided an alternative for some older newcomers not suited, or physically unable, to secure gainful employment. In November 1950, in response to an increase in the number of marginal and "hard core" cases among the immigrant population, the Federation of Jewish Philanthropies, Jewish Vocational Services (JVS), and the Family Welfare Department of the Baron de Hirsch Institute opened such a workshop in Montreal. It served as a protective environment in which aged or impaired survivors (in addition to a handful of Canadian citizens) worked full-time. The program employed persons receiving long-term financial support who were, according to JVS director Alfred Feintuch, "anxious to work, both to contribute to their own support and that of their families and to feel that they are worthwhile contributing members of society."[57] A cooperative venture, the workshop employed one administrator alongside JVS counsellors who closely monitored their clients' progress.

The goal of the project was twofold. JVS and its affiliates strove to transfer older newcomers into the competitive economic market, or at least help the workers become partially self-supporting. Employees earned wages based on piecework projects commissioned to the workshop by manufacturers; the Family Welfare Department (responsible for ongoing support of survivors in the country longer than six months) covered the difference between the workers' earnings and maintenance. Thus, this work alleviated some financial strains on community agencies, families, and friends of older survivors unable to penetrate the outside workforce.[58] The second goal related to restoring the downtrodden and frustrated newcomers' frame of mind by boosting their morale and confidence through work. The acquisition of employment and income meant that despite receiving some institutional assistance, survivors could perceive themselves as contributing and useful members of society, and not relief cases unable to support their families.

Employment at sheltered workshops, however, was not an option for most senior newcomers. Much about these survivors' experiences remains obscure. Few lived long enough to witness the advent of Holocaust awareness and testimony collection. Relatively few in number, they were largely ignored in the 1950s and 1960s, and relegated to their private spaces. Most information about this cohort and their lives in postwar Canada comes through anecdotal evidence (and in some cases, memoirs) offered by their children. Rachelle Fink recalled how unhappy her parents were in their adopted country. "They couldn't do anything," she said. "Our father couldn't be a businessman [his former profession] here, even though he was young. The weather [in Winnipeg] was the worst. They never made peace with being here. My mother learned English at night school, but my father did not want to learn. He was depressed and wanted to go back home."[59] Feelings aside, the family remained in Calgary and gradually accepted their lot.

Esther Friedman recalled similar traits in her father. A fifty-year-old Israeli transmigrant, Shlomo Friedman arrived in Canada with his much younger wife and two daughters, the product of a second, post-Holocaust marriage. He expressed his disdain for his new surroundings (Calgary) and occupation (shopkeeper) through self-imposed social isolation. Friedman's feelings of helplessness and isolating behaviour affected his entire family negatively—his wife in particular, who abandoned her own desires for community participation and socializing in order to support her husband. The senior Friedman's unhappiness remained with him until his death.[60]

The second wave of Holocaust survivors, like the first, included Hassidim and ultra-Orthodox Jews. But unlike the first wave, the second group of religious survivors arrived when the postwar Jewish spiritual rejuvenation started by earlier groups of refugee rabbis and their disciples had already begun to yield results.[61] By the early 1950s, highly observant survivors were directed to immigrate to Canada, and Montreal specifically, by rabbinical leaders in Europe, Israel, and the United States. Of this group, some survivors had opted initially to settle wherever they could gain entry. Although the United States was the preferred location for resettlement, Canada was considered the second-best option over Israel—where both pragmatically as well as spiritually, conditions remained poor—and other parts of the world, like Australia—where religious infrastructure was weak. Yitel Nechamah Bineth, a devout Hungarian survivor, recreated her family first in Melbourne, Australia. The later decision to immigrate to Canada stemmed from fears for her children's spiritual lives, and echoed the sentiment of other highly observant survivors:

> When we celebrated the occasion of the *bris* of our third child—our first son—the Pupa Rav [Rabbi Yankev Yitzchak Neuman] accompanied the *mohel*, Mr. Rosenbaum, to examine the baby. At that time, our oldest daughter was three years old. At the sight of the *rav*, she started crying in fear. The *rav* noticed this, and he told us in his beautiful and quiet manner that if a child fears the sight of a man with a beard and *payos* because she is not accustomed to it, then it is time to leave the country. He went on to tell us that he himself had decided to leave his position and move to Montreal, Canada. This thought penetrated our minds deeply.... As beautiful as this country was and as happy as we were here, we knew we had to be *moser nefesh* for *Yiddishkeit*, in order to secure the future of our children.

With this knowledge, Yitel Nechamah Bineth and her young family travelled to Montreal as landed immigrants, as did a number of her contemporaries.[62]

By late 1950, Canada hosted five yeshivas and numerous Jewish day schools representing several Hassidic and ultra-Orthodox streams. Although the institutions welcomed enrolment of all Canadian Jews, in their first years of operation the schools found their greatest number of students from among young Holocaust survivors and survivors' children. Second-wave newcomers also had immediate access to other crucial infrastructure for observant Jewish life, such as the *mikvehs*, and reaped the benefits of the improved standards of *kashrut*. The arrival of several hundred religiously observant Holocaust survivors to Canada in the 1950s helped to solidify the importance, and justify the efforts, of the small, postwar Hassidic and ultra-Orthodox factions, and provided impetus for their further growth.

Questions of identity and belonging ran rampant among the post-1950 wave of Holocaust survivors to Canada. Temporally, only a few years separated them from members of the first survivor immigrant wave. And yet, many newcomers found no clear-cut place in the survivor communities or among Canadian Jews at large. Hassidic and ultra-Orthodox newcomers deliberately sought out the religious communities they planned to affiliate themselves with and self-identified as members of a particular faction, largely because of kinship and social ties already in existence from the pre-war period. But, relatively few post-1950 secular survivors enjoyed a ready welcome. For most, the path toward integration and community belonging did not occur with the same ease or immediacy as it did for religious survivors. These newcomers struggled to carve out spaces for themselves within Canadian Jewry.

Late-coming Holocaust survivors who emigrated directly from DP camps as refugees appeared to find greater acceptance and understanding from other survivors already settled (or in the process of resettling) in Canada than did their cohorts from Israel or elsewhere in Europe. Second-wave survivors who came directly from established European cities ripe with culture often took longer to establish a sense of permanency and comfort in their new environs. To a greater extent than those from DP camps or Israel, some members of this subgroup avoided association with Canadian Jewry's developing survivor enclaves, preferring to fraternize with cultural societies related to their country of origin. Concerns about segregation and anti-Semitism, largely in response to the voluntary ghettoization of Canadian Jews and survivors in particular locales, fuelled the European arrivals to—at least in the public sphere—create distance from other Jews, and thus prolong their experience of integrating into any specific communities.[63] Some new Canadians, hoping to disassociate from the Jewish community, deliberately moved into non-Jewish enclaves, be it among other immigrant nationals or native-born Canadians (for those arriving with some accumulated funds).

Survivors were received unevenly across Canada. Neither of the groups, including the early and late arriving survivors or the local Jewish communities, knew what to make of each other. Smaller Jewish communities in the west, such as in Winnipeg and Calgary, showed greater receptiveness toward the second wave of survivors than did their co-religionists elsewhere. Unlike in Montreal and Toronto, Jewish groups in some prairie communities attempted (with significant success) to integrate the late-incoming survivors as quickly as possible. The influx of fewer persons (as compared to the initial wave of postwar refugees) meant less competition for jobs, even during the 1950s economic downturn. Local employers and community leaders appeared willing to sponsor survivor immigrants, and followed through on their promises of employment. Winnipeg, for its part, committed to receiving as many refugees as for whom employment contracts could be furnished.[64] New Jewish constituents served to strengthen these smaller, organized Jewish communities of the west, and participated in various aspects of cultural and religious life. Many of the survivors' children enrolled in Hebrew day or auxiliary schools, which frequently hired Holocaust survivors as educators.

The influence of these survivor educators was meaningful, and had long-lasting implications.[65] Perhaps best known for his contributions to Jewish education, Polish survivor Aron Eichler attended Montreal's United Jewish Teachers Seminary (on full scholarship) and Sir George Williams College. Eichler was recruited to Calgary in 1952, accepting a position as a teacher and then principal at the I.L. Peretz School, where he overhauled the curriculum and prioritized modern Hebrew language, Yiddish, and contemporary Jewish education, which included teaching about the recent devastation of European Jewry by Nazi Germany. Eichler simultaneously served as the co-director, with his wife, Ida, of both the Alberta Young Judea and B'nai Brith summer camps.[66]

In Winnipeg, home to an established and Zionistic Jewish community, the Peretz Folk Shul benefited from the arrival of survivor educators. A staunch Zionist from Poland, Betty Warshawsky taught Hebrew and Yiddish for more than thirty years, while Henny Paritzky, a native of The Hague, served as a long-standing French and Hebrew teacher. Lithuanian survivor Gita Kron enrolled at Montreal's Jewish Teachers' Seminary and, following a move with her family to Vancouver, secured a permanent teaching post at Vancouver Talmud Torah (VTT), the only Jewish day school operating in British Columbia in the 1950s. She remained at VTT for more than two decades, earning the love and respect of students as well as parents from "over there."[67] And in a small Jewish community in Saskatchewan, Hungarian survivor Chaim Kornfeld took the helm of the local Hebrew school. An attractive offer—the guarantee that a successful applicant could attend university and teach after-school classes—brought the former yeshiva student and observant newcomer from Toronto to Saskatoon, Saskatchewan, in August 1954. Within one year of his arrival, Kornfeld was promoted to the position of school principal, and registered at the University of Saskatchewan, completing a Bachelor of Arts and Commerce, in addition to a law degree, while working full-time. Even after establishing a legal career, Kornfeld did not stray from the school, continuing to offer Hebrew and bar mitzvah lessons until his 1973 departure for Vancouver.[68] Through this steadfast commitment to Judaism and Jewish education, these and other survivor educators helped to fortify western communities and infused their Jewish school systems with Hebrew-language instruction, Zionist values, and a love of Judaism.

Other newcomers faced a far more rocky transition. Israeli transmigrants faced unique and unprecedented challenges as the first post-independence "Israelis" to immigrate to Canada. Two such transmigrants, Esther Ratz and Betty Warshawsky, recalled that "Israelis"—referring to European Jewish Holocaust survivors who settled temporarily in Israel after the war—"stuck together" in Canada. "We were more comfortable around each other," Warshawsky recalled, "we just understood each other better."[69] Such statements lead to difficult questions. Did the Israelis feel ill at ease among the Holocaust survivors who preceded them to Canada only a few years earlier, or with Canadian Jewry at large? And, how did the already resettled survivors respond to the Israelis' presence? If a disconnect existed between the Israeli transmigrants, first-wave Holocaust survivors, and Canadian Jews, what contributed to it?

Social service case files and interviews shed minimal light on the dynamics of this situation. With the exception of Hassidic and ultra-Orthodox cases, Holocaust survivor Israeli transmigrants did not readily integrate into the greater Canadian Jewish populations. The early presence of the "Israelis" made the local Jewish community uneasy.[70] Some Canadian Jews might have felt betrayed and confused by the Israeli transmigrants, whom they perceived as *yordim*, a Hebrew pejorative used to describe those who have "descended" from the challenge of fulfilling the Zionist vision of nation-building by emigrating from Israel. How, as one Canadian Jewish man wondered, could survivors abandon Israel, the country Jews worldwide "had fought so hard to give them?"[71] Caseworkers similarly treated the transmigrants with some animosity, and applied more stringent rules concerning services rendered. The Israelis therefore tried to avoid confrontation with the agencies, and were loath to turn to them for support.[72]

Much of this separateness from the Canadian Jewish mainstream seemed at the time to be deliberate on the part of the Israelis. The survivors' experiences in Israel, however brief, profoundly shaped their identity and world views. In spite of their short time in Israel, the country, language, and experience of nation building had a transforming effect and influence on the survivors. The shared experiences of living in collective *moshavs* and *kibbutzim* (collective living compounds) and even learning to speak Hebrew in a uniquely Hebrew-speaking culture separated the Israelis from other Canadian Jews whose knowledge of the Hebrew language was typically limited to prayer. Israeli transmigrants' experiences of the Holocaust, and then Israel's War of Independence in which many had fought, shaped their personalities and self-identification, and granted them membership in an exclusive club inaccessible to other survivors or Canadian Jews.[73]

While most first- and second-wave survivors eventually created a place for themselves among Canadians, Jewish and otherwise, others remained on the periphery. For these persons, full integration into Canadian society and a sense of comfort in their surroundings took many years. For some, wartime trauma and losses proved too devastating to overcome. Many spent years enduring emotional and psychological distress, often forcing them into psychiatric treatment centres. Other survivors, unable to adapt to life in Canada, migrated once again, in the hope that they would experience greater happiness elsewhere.

Two latecomers' experiences elucidate how difficult it was for some to acculturate into Canadian and Canadian Jewish society. Born on 26 November 1926 in Warsaw and raised in a religiously-observant home, Sam Weizenbluth (Sewek Wajcenblit) survived the Warsaw Ghetto Uprising and was one of "the Boys" of Buchenwald concentration camp.[74] In 1945 with other child survivors liberated at Theresienstadt he traveled to Britain to rehabilitate after years of physical and psychological trauma. He studied for one year at a Hassidic-style yeshiva before moving to London to train as a pastry chef in a Jewish bakery. There he met a French Canadian chef who espoused the glories of life in Canada, presenting it as a wonderful, free, and open space. Restless and without any ties to the British Jewish community or to Britain, Weizenbluth entered Toronto as a landed immigrant in 1952 with big dreams. He recalled his first impressions as discouraging. "When I got to Toronto, I had no money and no place to go. So I went to the immigrant centre [JIAS]. They handed me $10 and said, 'You're on your own.' They wouldn't give me a loan because I was a single male. But I couldn't find work because there were no jobs. I was too proud and didn't want to ask for handouts, but the Jewish community never helped me at all."[75]

Weizenbluth went on to hold a handful of jobs before finding his niche as a self-employed collections agent. His first marriage, to a Russian-born Jew who had immigrated to Canada before the Second World War, produced four children, all of whom were raised in the Jewish faith. His second marriage, this time to a Roman Catholic Polish woman, produced three children. They were raised with a mixed-bag of religious traditions. Weizenbluth possessed a life-long ambivalence and discomfort toward organized Canadian Jewry that he passed on to some of his children. Although he attended services at an Orthodox synagogue and stayed active within the '45 Aid Society until his passing in 2013,[76] Weizenbluth found himself living perpetually on the periphery of organized Canadian Jewish society.

Morris Faintuch also faced daunting challenges in acclimatizing to life in Canada and feeling at ease in his new community. On some levels, he and Weizenbluth were quite similar. Faintuch also arrived in Canada after spending years rebuilding his life elsewhere. Both were Polish Jewish child survivors, and neither transmigrated with a family. Yet, a crucial difference distinguished the two cases: whereas Weizenbluth immigrated to Canada on his own and without the support of any relatives or friends, Faintuch's elder brother and uncle sponsored his entry. Faintuch did not choose Canada because of his political ideology or employment prospects. He agreed to join his family in Winnipeg only after his physical ailments failed to improve in Israel.[77] Faintuch's early years in Winnipeg were miserable:

Well, I liked Israel better than Canada. You know there, I had a good [work] position, I had lots of friends, lots of girlfriends, I had a car. You know, in 1950 having a car was a very big thing, there weren't many in Israel. Then, I come here, and I start to work and it was hard, they laid you off a lot. I was laid off a lot. So in the summertime I told my uncle, "Let me go back." He said, "Are you crazy?" Then after a while, he saw that I was not happy and he offered to lend me the money, and I told him, "No, I don't want to go."[78]

His brother, Dr. Henry Faintuch (a survivor of a Soviet forced-labour camp), by then the director of Winnipeg's Jewish Old Folks Home of Western Canada (today the Sharon Home), and sister-in-law, Sonja, tried their best to help Faintuch become established. Their efforts came to naught. "When I come, my brother was responsible for me. If I didn't have a job, he had to feed me. But the more connections my brother used, the worse it got," Faintuch recalled. "Let's put it this way: the Jewish community didn't help me; I had to help myself," he continued.[79] Persevering during poor economic times as an upholsterer and, later, owner of a successful grocery store, Morris Faintuch married a Canadian Jewish woman in 1956, and together they raised three children. He eventually shed his aversion toward Canada, and while maintaining close ties to Israel, became a proud Canadian citizen.

---

The second wave of Holocaust survivor resettlement in Canada that occurred in the first half of the 1950s differed from the earlier wave of survivors in terms of demographics, path of immigration, and quality of reception. Survivors in the first movement immigrated primarily as refugee labourers or through close relatives programs, plucked from DP camps to fill the demand in Canada's booming economy. The cohort consisted mostly of young, able-bodied men and women, few large families, and even fewer survivors of advanced age. By contrast, survivors who immigrated after 1950 represented a wider range of ages and experiences, and many were children, adults over the age of thirty, or elderly. In contrast to the first wave (who arrived mainly as refugees), many in the second wave entered Canada as immigrants and had experienced at least one previous attempt at resettlement elsewhere. Most were admitted through close relatives sponsorship or via the Occupational Settlement Scheme (OS8), with smaller numbers arriving directly from DP camps as refugees. They demonstrated personal agency in determining their place of resettlement, typically joining relatives and sponsors.

Second-wave survivors were received with ambivalence by many Canadian Jews and earlier survivors, and did not garner the same degree of resettlement support and after-care treatment as their predecessors. They entered Canada during a period of economic downturn and severe housing shortage. Their arrival also coincided with the landing of thousands of other non-Jewish European immigrants, who also needed work and housing. Social service agencies and workers at the secular Jewish agencies, though more professionalized and experienced than they were a few years earlier when dealing with the first wave of survivor refugees, were exhausted by the seemingly endless influx of needy survivors. And more stringent eligibility regulations instituted by JIAS and its affiliated social service agencies resulted in the early denial of support to some groups.

Older survivors in particular faced immense challenges in re-establishing themselves and becoming self-sufficient. Montreal's sheltered workshop offered work and an opportunity for older newcomers to restore a sense of dignity and independence, but it accommodated only a limited number. Older survivors who lived in smaller Jewish communities were often dependent on their families and service agencies for long-term support. Many were subjected to scorn either for having abandoned Israel, their first place of postwar refuge, or for having remained in postwar Europe until so late a date. Others were not perceived as "survivors" of the Shoah deserving of, or requiring, support, but rather as ordinary Jewish immigrants.

And yet, the first group of newcomers blazed the trail for their co-religionists in many ways. Whereas much of the first wave immigrated through labour sponsorships, post-1950 survivors came largely at the behest of relatives. Even when survivor relatives were themselves barely making ends meet financially, their presence proved especially helpful in light of the poor economic conditions and housing shortages. The first wave's language acquisition, experience navigating the housing market, and business and social connections helped the later wave of survivors acclimatize more readily than did their predecessors. Religious survivors particularly benefited from the first wave's efforts. They settled predominantly in Montreal's growing Hassidic and ultra-Orthodox communities and utilized the religious infrastructure founded by their co-religionists.

Other factors played into the second-wave survivors' experience of resettlement and integration. In western Canada, the situation was slightly different due to two factors: the smaller size of the existing Jewish communities, and the relatively small number of incoming survivors. Although limited monetary resources were available to aid the survivors, their value was more obvious and they made swift and substantial contributions to Jewish life and education in these smaller centres.

Israeli transmigrants established their own insular communities, in response to ostracism from Canadian Jews as well as a perceived need to preserve and foster Israeli culture, Zionism, and the Hebrew language. This group served as Canadian Jewry's first up-close-and-personal brush with Israeli personalities, politics, and traditions that, prior to their arrival, had been viewed solely through the lens of journalists, photographers, and visitors. Later-arriving survivor immigrants who came directly via Europe also turned inward, reaching out to individuals and groups from their country of origin. Many accepted and embraced their status as non-survivor immigrants, and separated from Canadian Jewry entirely. The second wave challenged the local Jewish community's notion of what constituted a "survivor," and contributed to the country's cultural landscape through the introduction of Israeli culture, enrichment of Jewish day school programs, and the ongoing development of Hassidic and ultra-Orthodox communities.

The Israeli transmigrants and other post-1950 arrivals represented the final wave of Holocaust survivors to immigrate to Canada before the promulgation of the country's first refugee policy, born largely in response to Hungarian refugees seeking asylum from the 1956 Revolution. Approximately 39,000 Hungarians—7,000 of them Jewish—entered Canada through these emergency measures.[80]

# CHAPTER NINE

# MOTHERS AND MISTERS: PARENTING, WORK, AND GENDER

The postwar road to rehabilitation was long and arduous. Liberated from camps, hiding, or resistance groups, survivors sought to locate long-lost loved ones, re-connect with friends and neighbours, and regain control of their lives. For many, that journey brought despair; many found themselves alone, without relations or homes, and utterly lonely. Determined to re-establish themselves and rebuild their lives, marriage and childbirth rates among survivors soared in DP camps. Young men and women whose childhoods were cut short by Nazi terror entered into quick, fervent unions. Marriages between European Jews bereft of their first families and hoping to soften the ragged edges of their loss took place as well. Whether as the result of loving partnerships between individuals, or of loveless marriages, children frequently followed shortly thereafter, and became the focus of those relationships.[1]

Youthful survivors' formative childhood and adolescence had been shorn by the war and the Holocaust. They missed crucial chances to observe adult relation-ships or receive substantial education, formal and informal. Lacking mothers to turn to for support or advice, unfamiliar with child-rearing practices, and often out of touch with their sexuality, female survivors faced additional challenges as parents. Immigration to Canada, a foreign and frequently unfriendly country, exacerbated these challenges. The women strove to accommodate the demands of their growing families with minimal assistance (financial, emotional, or practi-cal), and usually before they had the time (or means) to achieve adequate language skills and establish a peer support group. Much of this was true for young men as well, but the gender roles of the day assigned mothers more responsibility in the areas of child rearing and parenting.

Men, for their part, struggled to uphold traditional patriarchal values relat-ing to work and waged earnings owing to linguistic and cultural barriers, stunted educational or skills training, and the lingering psychological and physiological effects of wartime traumas. The social structures and job markets of postwar anglophone and, to a lesser extent, francophone Canada, did not resemble Jewish refugees' pre-war communities. Nor, too, did the opportunities offered by these geopolitically, chronologically, or culturally variant worlds. As we will see later in this chapter, male survivors' challenging experiences with employability road-blocks greatly affected Jewish family structures and gender expectations.

In the aftermath of the Second World War, the idea of procreation occupied survivors' thoughts. Social and communal pressures encouraged quick marriages among the mostly youthful survivors, and the forthcoming pregnancies and live births to occur in DP camps were applauded. Although statistics differ slightly, Jewish DP camps boasted extraordinary birth rates; in 1947 alone, the birth rate in DP camps in the American-occupied zones in Germany rose to 50.2 per thou-sand, one of the highest in the world.[2] These births did much to contribute to the triumphant ideology of Jewish survival in the face of Nazi tyranny.

For many young female survivors, pregnancy and motherhood emerged as joyous, but anxiety-ridden, experiences. On the one hand, bearing children served as proof that they, and perhaps the Jewish people as a nation, had survived, and were rebuilding families. Babies, often named for recently murdered relatives, symbolized hope for the future and gave purpose to post-Holocaust existence. They offered women the chance to reaffirm positive agency over their bodies that had, for years, been subjected to inhumane treatment. On the other side of the coin, there were few family members with whom to share the joy of renewal. Young mothers birthed children into high-stress and cash-strapped environments that pushed traditional North American middle-class values around gender and relationship norms.[3] These circumstances, coupled with the realization that the women possessed minimal understanding of child-rearing techniques and had no mothers to assist them in raising healthy and productive offspring, presented a far from idyllic situation for motherhood among the survivors.

The myth that all survivors were eager to recreate families persists in Holo-caust literature and historiography, and masks the complexity of postwar family life. The experiences and voices of these women (and sometimes men) who chose not to participate in the postwar reproduction frenzy are largely absent from the grand narrative. Multiple factors influenced women's decisions about family planning. For women whose bodies had been permanently scarred by physical trauma at the hands of the Nazis, the option of whether or not to bear children was not their own.[4] For women able to conceive and birth healthy offspring, the imperatives to do so—to prove triumphant over oppression, reaffirm physical capabilities, replace murdered family members—competed with the reasons not to do so. Some, citing a lack of maternal instincts unrelated to their wartime experiences, harboured no inclination to bear children. Others had been victims of sexual violence during the war years that deterred them from entering healthy and loving relationships postwar.[5] Most often, however, those who chose not to raise families postwar did so as a result of the wholesale violence inflicted on Jews during the Holocaust. Survivors had witnessed acts of terrible cruelty, including the brutal murder of their own and others' children. After living under such conditions, and seeing first-hand the inhumane treatment one group meted out to another, some survivors refused to bring another generation into the world.

The risk of subjecting potential offspring to future genocides frightened many survivor refugees to Canada. Mila (Amalia) B represented one such case. Born in 1923 Poland, Mila was imprisoned with her parents and two sisters in the Kolomyia Ghetto after the region fell under German occupation on 1 August 1941. En route to the Belzec death camp, the three young women escaped from a train and made their way to German-occupied Lwów (present-day Lviv, Ukraine). There, Mila lived out the war using false papers that declared her a Catholic Pole. After a brief sojourn in Paraguay with one sister and her new family, Mila received sponsorship papers from an uncle who had immigrated to Canada during the interwar period and she arrived in Montreal in 1949. Four years later, she married a fellow survivor. Mila revealed that although her marriage was happy, and she and her husband financially secure, they agreed to remain childless: "I was afraid of bringing children into the world," she recalled. "I did not want my own children to be endangered and have to live with the fear of persecution that [I] had experienced in [my] life."[6] While Mila was certainly not alone in her thinking, the prevailing triumphalist narrative persisted, intentionally or unintentionally silencing non-conformist voices, thus leaving a gaping hole in historical records.

At the same time, the triumphant narrative did reflect some facts on the ground. Couples with young children accounted for a substantial minority of cases attended to by JIAS workers. In January 1952, for instance, JIAS Montreal reported 769 active cases (family units) comprising 1,925 individuals. Of these, 540 were children under the age of seventeen. Out of a total of 536 ongoing cases, 290 were families with at least one child. The August 1952 caseload report documented fewer cases involving families, but with comparable findings. It recorded 336 cases comprising 874 persons; 230 children were aged seventeen or under. Of the 275 ongoing cases, 157 were families with children.[7]

The larger the family, the more likely the need for agency supports. Social workers often served as young mothers' first point of contact in Canada and with the services available to them through the Canadian Jewish community. Perhaps out of compassion or sympathy for the newcomers, or because of social workers' discomfort or ignorance about the years of physical assault the female survivors had endured, the subject of mothering—specifically, women's pre-war families and postwar desires for re-establishing families—remains a blank spot in casework literature. But while Jewish social workers seem to have remained silent about survivors' decisions to establish families, they had a great deal to say about the women's mothering practices. Lacking a comprehensive understanding of pre-war social and gender norms, as well as minimal information relating to the enormity of the Holocaust, the workers relied on their own cultural norms and gendered expectations to evaluate the women survivors and their familial situations. These workers openly doubted the immigrant women's (and potential mothers') capacity to parent effectively. According to an article published in the November 1948 edition of the *JIAS Record*, "the immigrant mother knew nothing about shopping and prices in this country nor how to enrol her child in school."[8] The workers were correct in their assumption: many of the women were indeed in need of help enrolling their children in school and learning the local pricing systems. As Canadian social historian Franca Iacovetta explains, it was up to each ethnic community's social and resettlement workers, employment counsellors, and educators to help shape mothers and create a "healthy body politic," producing healthy and successful young Canadians.[9] Newcomer women needed substantial assistance to ensure that they, and their offspring, stayed on the right track.

Social workers expressed particular concern about what they perceived as coddling of young children by their survivor mothers. Social workers and nurses were convinced that this would damage the children irreparably, and destroy their potential to become independent young women and men. Ilona G, a widowed mother who immigrated with her daughter, Judith, age ten, in 1952 through close relatives sponsorship, was the subject of such criticism. Joseph Lazarus, a social worker at the JIAS Montreal office, reported that Mrs. G was experiencing difficulties with Judith: "She said that the child was rude, did not obey, and was generally a case of great anxiety to her."[10] Mrs. G blamed their difficulties on a troubled relationship with her sister, their sponsor. Lazarus had a different reading of the situation. He blamed Mrs. G's "considerable disturbance over her child" on the mother's poor attitude and destructive behaviours, including her possessiveness and refusal to allow Judith to play with other children in the neighbourhood. Lazarus advised the mother to relax and encourage her daughter to integrate, but offered no guidance as to how this might be accomplished. The case closed before any advances in the mother-daughter relationship were reported.[11]

Workers like Joseph Lazarus could not comprehend the origins of the survivor mothers' fears and anxieties, which exceeded apparently normal parent concerns, nor their seemingly unreasonable demands for goods and services to benefit their children.[12] They assumed the neuroses and unremitting demands were "based on deep rooted insecurities as women and mothers." Social workers simply did not possess the insight or imagination, or practical training, to understand that the survivors' concerns and fears related to the loss of previous families and the imperative many newcomers felt to protect their new families at all costs and to repopulate the nearly destroyed Jewish people. They failed to grasp that, despite shared Jewish values, survivor families differed greatly in composition, experience, and ideas from the stereotypical North American nuclear family.

While the social workers may not have comprehended the survivor mothers' anxieties, they were correct in their opinions that motherhood constituted a daunting task for many of the women. As a teenager, Helen Schwartz spent two years in the Bialystok Ghetto before surviving Treblinka, Auschwitz, and Bergen-Belsen concentration camps by herself. After liberation, Schwartz married Eric, a man fourteen years her senior whom she had met in camp, and together they moved to Canada in 1948. Though they arrived to her husband's sister and some extended family on his side, presence of these kin did nothing to alleviate their poor circumstances. Having lost two children in postwar Germany while awaiting immigration papers, Schwartz was desperate to birth a healthy baby. Her wish was granted with the birth of her son four months after landing in Canada. "For him," Schwartz remembered, "I was okay. He was a good baby, so I didn't need a lot of help. Which was good, because there was no one to give it."[13] Things became far more challenging with the birth of her second child, a daughter born a few years later. With her, mothering was especially difficult. "My daughter was very bad as a child, very challenging," Schwartz recalled. "She was the worst! And I didn't know how to respond to her, how to make her better." Between sighs, she continued, "I was too young and had nobody to help me. Maybe if I would have had a mother, or a sister, it would have been better for all of us."[14]

Schwartz was not alone. Judy Weissenberg Cohen, a Hungarian concentration camp survivor who immigrated to Canada in her early twenties with her sister as industrial workers, recalls having similar feelings of despair. Happily married to a Canadian Jew, Cohen had two children, a biological daughter and an adopted son. Yet, even with "good kids," a supportive husband, and stable household income, she recalled motherhood as an isolating and scary experience. "Parenting was a very lonely task," she said. "We [young female survivors] lacked skills as parents; we never learned how to take care of children, keep a house."[15]

Esther Birnbaum, who arrived in Toronto in 1950 with her husband, Richard, and four-year-old son, Arthur, also experienced social isolation for her first years of residence in Canada. Much later, Arthur recalled that she "had no money to go out, a child at home, and no daycare services or time off. Her only 'alone time' was when she attended English classes with Father."[16] In addition, Arthur remembered how Esther bemoaned the poor treatment she experienced at the hands of the Canadian Jewish community, specifically the snobbishness of wives and mothers who refused to invite the young immigrant mother into their homes or events. "Because they would have nothing to do with her, her only network of friends and acquaintances [in the early years] were other survivor women," Arthur recalled.[17] Such feelings of rejection and segregation plagued Esther Birnbaum for years.

Health problems and treatments caused additional mothering hurdles. Chronic medical problems and even joyous occasions like childbirth requiring short- or long-term hospitalizations created obstacles to parenting. Survivor women experienced bouts of legitimate physiological and mental, as well as psychosomatic, health problems, necessitating referrals to public health clinics and Jewish hospitals for examination and care. Not a few suffered from medical conditions relating directly to their wartime traumas, and many required ongoing monitoring and frequent in-patient treatments in hospitals and sanitaria.

Hospitalizations often necessitated the placement of young children in foster care. So, too, did instances of chronic illness, such as the case of a young mother suffering from the symptoms of "post-encephalitic Parkinson's disease," typified by uncontrollable tremors rendering her unable to safely or confidently care for her infant son.[18] The alternative was for families to hire housekeepers for a steep fee. Fathers were not expected to perform household duties, including child rearing, and in any case, could not risk losing employment security by taking time off to care for the children in the mother's absence. Few women had relatives or a close network of friends to help them through such rough patches. And fiercely protective of their families, the women did not trust strangers who, they worried, might compromise the healthy and safety of their offspring and spouse. They did not know where, or to whom, to turn for assistance. The women's closest allies were usually other survivors, struggling to make ends meet themselves.

The challenges associated with such situations were exacerbated for unmarried mothers. Without a partner to rely on, these women feared that their illnesses, and subsequent inability to earn an income or keep house, might deem them unfit mothers in the eyes of overseeing community and social service workers. Their greatest fear was having children removed from their home, a move that rarely occurred unless physical abuse or neglect was reported.[19] But not all widowed mothers experienced unsettling encounters with social service workers; some never turned to the organized community at all. The Galician-born and Vienna-raised survivor Bronia Schwebel Sonnenschein arrived in Vancouver in June 1950 with

22. Bronia Sonnenschein and Emily Schwebel in Vancouver, British Columbia, 1956. Courtesy of Dan Sonnenschein.

her husband Kurt, son Daniel, and a lifetime of experiences. In the early months of the Second World War, the Schwebel family, including parents Emily and Abraham, and sister Paula, were interned in the Litzmannstadt Ghetto (present-day Lodz, Poland), where then-25-year-old Bronia served as secretary to the Head of the Judenrat (Jewish Council), Ghetto Elder Chaim Rumkowski. The young woman's position staved off her and her immediate family's deportation until the ghetto liquidation in August 1944; at that time, the Schwebels and Bronia's first husband were deported to Auschwitz. Bronia, along with her mother Emily, and her sister, Paula, experienced—and survived—a series of degradations and life-threatening challenges. These included a brief internment at Auschwitz, imprisonment at Stutthof concentration camp and a munitions factory in Dresden, Germany, and a death march to Theresienstadt.[20]

Liberation presented the opportunity for the three women to rebuild their lives. Paula reunited with her husband, Stan Lenga, at the Bergen-Belsen DP camp. Bronia and her mother travelled to Prague, Czechoslovakia, in search of their respective husbands. Only there did they learn of the men's demise at Stutthof. With her knowledge of English, French, German, and Polish, Bronia found work with the American Jewish Joint Distribution Committee (AJDC); she also found her second husband, Dr. Kurt Sonnenschein. The two married in December 1948 and made *aliyah* to Haifa, Israel, in May of the following year. Son Daniel was born in December 1949. Life in Israel proved less than ideal for this young family. "I loved and will always love Israel for its courage and determination," recalled Bronia in retrospect, "but I could not face again the prospect to struggle, especially not when having a baby."[21] Fortunately, opportunity struck quickly. Kurt's younger brother Eric and his wife had recently arrived in Canada through connections to the Koerners, an extended Jewish refugee family who escaped Europe and established themselves in the lumber business. With financial support from distant relatives and contacts, Eric sponsored the Sonnenscheins' entry into Canada. Emily Schwebel, and Paula and Stan Lenga, followed shortly after.[22] The families resided together for several years.

Kurt, a doctor of law, immediately secured manual labour work on "green chain," where he pulled lumber off a conveyor belt for hours on end. After Kurt failed to perform in this role, Eric intervened and had his brother transferred to an office job at the Jewish-owned lumber company Alaska Pine. The family enjoyed relative stability and happiness; they took solace in Vancouver's beautiful, if sleepy, demeanour, and welcomed daughter Vivian in June 1951. This peace was short-lived. As Bronia remembered, "On September 1, 1952 we were taken on a ride, by car, to some of Vancouver's surroundings, we never completed that ride.

The car we were in was involved in a head-on collision and my husband got killed. My son and I survived; the baby, our little girl, was at home with my mother."[23] Bronia was summoned to once again pick up the pieces. Emily Schwebel, described as a source of great physical and moral strength during the war, provided childcare so her eldest daughter could take an office job with Alaska Pine. Bronia scrounged up a sizeable down payment from Kurt's life insurance policy for a house in central Vancouver; Emily, Paula, and Stan moved in, too.

Bronia's life after trauma revolved around her family, friendships with other European refugees, and her work. What made her case extraordinary, however, was the wealth of support already at her fingertips. Most young survivor mothers in Canada arrived bereft of familial support, experienced difficulty securing stable employment, and struggled to attain English (or less frequently, French) language skills. The Sonnenscheins' immigration to Canada was arranged through a close relatives sponsorship; Eric Sonner provided short-term housing for the family and arranged work for Kurt. Bronia and Kurt spoke sufficient English. And upon Kurt's untimely death, an insurance policy provided temporary relief. But it was the presence of Emily, a woman in her fifties who defied all odds to survive, that perhaps contributed most significantly to Bronia's personal and professional achievements. Because of Emily, as well as Paula and Stan Lenga, Bronia never required organizational support for subsidized and safe childcare (which was gravely lacking in Vancouver) or rent money. The family's closeness provided Bronia the strength to trudge past her losses, reassert herself as a strong and independent woman, and raise two healthy and socially integrated children.[24]

Bronia's close-knit family support network and language skills set her apart from other immigrant mothers. Aside from daycare, Jewish settlement organizations promoted little in the way of mother-infant services, leaving mothers with few opportunities for leisure, English-language training, and socializing. For most, summertime offered no respite from their daily hardships in large, isolating cities and poor living conditions. Day and overnight summer camps (with highly subsidized fees) proved a viable option for some school-age children. But childcare, when available at all, was offered solely to working mothers. Some social workers recommended that mothers congregate in each other's homes to chat and commiserate. Little else was offered in the way of support for survivor mothers.

Canadian Jewish leaders had reason to worry about the lack of opportunities for leisure and parenting support, not to mention respite from city living, offered to immigrant mothers. They worried, too, that impressionable newcomers feeling unfulfilled or cared for by Jewish agencies, might run into the warm and inviting arms of Christian missionaries.[25] In her bellwether report on the effectiveness and efficiency of Canadian Jewry's integration and resettlement efforts, the New York Association for New Americans' Mary Palevsky voiced concerns about survivor mothers' lack of community involvement. She worried that empty wallets, and lack of social and familial supports (which prevented mothers from attending important programs such as English language and citizenship classes) could adversely affect their ability to become healthy, productive citizens. Palevsky suggested one possible solution: "Afternoon courses for mothers, whose children of preschool-age could be taken care of on the same premises by a nursery school-teacher, would take the mothers out of their cramped houses, help them master the language and give them a much needed lift."[26] This recommendation, and others like it, was quashed by Congress before any plans got under way, which attributed its decisions to a lack of interest and funds.[27]

One community-based service made available for new Canadian mothers in Toronto was the Mothers' and Babes' Summer Rest Home. A respite for Jewish mothers, the camp at Hollendale, Ontario, on the shores of Lake Simcoe, was jointly operated by the Mothers' and Babes' Rest Home Association and Jewish Family and Child Services (JF&CS) and financed through fundraising events and Toronto's Jewish Community Chest. The camp began operations in 1919 in Bronte, Ontario, under the auspice of the Hebrew Maternity Aid Society, and functioned at that site until 1941. That year, the respite camp was moved from Bronte to Tollendale, Ontario, where a larger, permanent home was built to

23. Women in a chorus line at the Mothers' and Babes' Summer Rest Home, c. 1948. Ontario Jewish Archives, fonds 52, series 1-7, file 5, item 3.

accommodate the growing demand for respite. The camp served new Canadians almost exclusively from 1948 to 1956. For example, in the 1949 summer season, the Home accommodated a total of 370 persons. Of that number, 238 were Holocaust survivors and their dependents, having arrived within the previous twelve months. By the summer of 1952, more than three-quarters of applicants, and nearly 100 percent of attendees, were survivors and their children.[28]

Established as a rest and recreational facility for mothers and infants, the camp provided survivor mothers with highly subsidized childcare and a few weeks away from the pressures of city life. Mothers enjoyed clean, fresh country air, socialized with other newcomer and Canadian mothers, and received insight on how to live the "Canadian life." In 1950, the cost to attend a ten-day session was $14 per mother and $6 per child, with recent immigrant mothers paying at a geared-to-income rate. Subsidies came from several sources, including a JF&CS grant of $5,060, along with the proceeds of a fundraising tea totalling $1,000, and a $670 grant from the Toronto Star Fresh Fund (to send low-income city children to summer camp). Combined, these sources offset that year's operating costs of $12,461.03 by more than half.[29] The Mothers' and Babes' camp was described as offering an "essential health service" in the form of practical and emotional support to help "young, inexperienced mothers meet their physical and emotional needs."[30] Recreation, while important, was secondary to rehabilitation.

According to JF&CS president E.I. Shapiro, the camp was intended to service the "neediest sector of the Jewish community."[31] Referrals came from social workers and settlement agents, with nominal registration costs reimbursed by the UJRA and the Community Chest. Application numbers soared with the influx of Holocaust survivors from the late 1940s onward, forcing the sessions to be shortened and average stays reduced from three to two weeks, in order to accommodate as many women and children as possible.[32] The camp's goal was twofold. First, as noted, it provided a respite for tired and stressed mothers. In addition to scheduled recreational activities, women received "time off" when nurses stepped in to watch after youngsters.

The second goal of the program, of benefit to the immigrant mothers and the Canadian Jewish community, was to provide a crucial opportunity for social workers, teachers, and medical professionals to indoctrinate and educate women/clients on a variety of subjects, including parenting techniques (especially pertinent since few of the women had living mothers to turn to for advice), nutrition, and English language and citizenship training in a secure and nurturing environment. The informal setting put the women at ease, and increased their receptiveness and participation in the mothering and language programs. English was the lingua franca of the camp, and mothers were encouraged to speak to one another, and their children, in their adopted tongue.[33] Above all else, however, survivor mothers could share their Holocaust experiences, uncertainties about their adopted country, and hopes for the future with one another in a safe and secure environment. The therapeutic benefits, and the support networks that emerged, became the happy legacy of the Mothers' and Babes' Summer Rest Home.

---

While survivor mothers faced the greatest obstacles with regard to effective and caring parenting, fathers also experienced significant challenges. Such challenges, however, are rarely part of the Holocaust narrative. Single fathers, made widowers by the Holocaust rather than divorced, sought mightily to provide their children with suitable, if motherless, homes. Wholly unschooled in child rearing, these men took the reins of single parenthood. They were forced to learn quickly (and in a foreign language, and unfamiliar and often harsh culture and workforce) how to negotiate the conflicting roles of wage-earning patriarch and caring homemaker. In all respects, they were fish out of water. Few of the men possessed any knowledge of household arts, including cooking and cleaning, activities traditionally left to women. Rarely helped by mothers, sisters, or other adult female relatives, single fathers were highly reliant on family service agencies for assistance and practical support in all aspects of their new roles.

Anxieties and insecurities ran high. Some, like Sari G's father, took out their frustrations and unhappiness on their children. A soldier in the Polish army and former labour camp inmate, Mr. G spent the war years away from his wife, who perished in Soviet Asia, and his children. Unable to handle the stressors of his postwar life, he was physically violent with his children, driving his working teenage son from the home—and, in large part, his life. He diminished his daughter's self-worth and commitment to her education through ridicule and taunts about women's rights and abilities. Sari never graduated high school, married, or raised a family.[34] Others, like Kopel Schmeltzmann, whose Canadian-born wife died within a decade of their marriage, leaving him to raise four young daughters, handled their lots in a healthier way. He credited his wife's family, especially his mother-in-law, with helping him rear healthy, happy children.[35]

Single fathers shared the fear that their precious children might be removed by child protective services because of their lack of experience in child rearing, not to mention maintaining a suitable home environment, or because the injuries they sustained during the war, both physical and emotional, might make them unsuitable fathers. The men need not have worried. Single fathers tended to evoke great sympathy and compassion among family service workers, who strove to help preserve the often-weakened family units.

Rabbi Berl M, a fifty-year-old Polish survivor, and his son David, just shy of thirteen, were one such case. Sponsored for immigration to Canada by a second cousin in Montreal in May 1950, the rabbi and his son were sole survivors of a large family. For the first time in his life, the rabbi (who had served pulpits in postwar France before coming to Canada) found himself looking for full-time employment as either a ritual slaughterer or Hebrew teacher while simultaneously single-parenting. Extended family members proved unable or unwilling to support them, so father and son turned to local social service agencies for help. They received assistance from JIAS for their first six months in Canada and financial aid from the Jewish Family Welfare Bureau (JFWB) for an additional half-year. In fact, JFWB continued to support Rabbi M with parenting advice, employment counselling, and clothing donations for three years after he ceased to receive direct financial support. Over the course of four years, Rabbi M developed a close, dependent relationship with his social workers. Together, they enrolled David at the Lubavitch Yeshiva School and arranged for the boy to take two meals a day at a religious woman's house for a small fee.

Social workers seemingly approached the rabbi and his case with a sensitivity not exhibited toward single mothers. Herb Weinstein, a social worker with JFWB, composed a letter (dated 3 November 1954) on the rabbi's behalf to the Conference Committee for Refugee Rabbis. Weinstein described Rabbi M as a broken, lonely man. "His family life was destroyed as a result of the war, and it is his great desire to be able to recreate a home for his son," Weinstein wrote. He went on to attest to the man's desire to remarry and establish a new home and life in his adopted country. Weinstein stressed that, like others in his situation, Rabbi M feared that his lack of financial stability could prove detrimental to his plans.[36] JIAS social worker Sylvia Endler, who also worked with the rabbi, depicted him as deeply invested in his son's welfare: "Rabbi M continually stressed the fact that he wished to, 'train [him] right.' He felt that the boy had had a confused upbringing because of the war.... Mr. M. was very suspicious and fearful that the boy might be taken from him and placed because there was no mother at home. He was reassured that resources for placement were available for his use but that he need not fear interferences, particularly since the boy seemed to be cared for."[37] It took a great deal of discussion to persuade the rabbi that David would not be taken away.

Though Rabbi M lacked parenting experience and faced financial struggles, social workers connected to his case appeared confident that he had the competency to raise his son in a safe and secure environment. Parenting young daughters, on the other hand, presented additional, unforeseen anxieties for single fathers. Time apart during the Holocaust, coupled with a lack of knowledge of "women's issues," made for particularly apprehensive fathers.

Latvian-born survivor Leon Ginsberg (an immigrant to France during the interwar period) was the widower father of one daughter, Jocelyne, born in 1939 in France at the outbreak of the Second World War. Ginsberg and his wife had entrusted Jocelyne to a French Catholic family when she was an infant. Mr. Ginsberg survived a series of concentration camps; his wife did not. Upon his return to France, Ginsberg had no idea how to parent any child, let alone a young girl. So, he placed her with a Jewish family and worked to put his life back together. The foster family wished to adopt Jocelyne after the war, but Ginsberg adamantly refused to abandon his only surviving relative, despite his personal hesitation about raising his child as a single parent.[38] By the time they reunited permanently, the two were complete strangers. With little to lose and much to gain, the pair packed up and immigrated to Canada in 1952, settling in Toronto, the same city as her former foster family, who had immigrated one year earlier through a close relatives sponsorship. The choice of destination was largely influenced by the presence of the foster family and their promise of parenting advice and support.

The move did little to alleviate Leon Ginsberg's insecurities regarding parenting as a single man. He boarded Jocelyne for several months with another refugee family, but this time took charge of her schooling and summer camp arrangements. Though battling anxiety and loneliness, Ginsberg gradually built a home deemed "suitable for a young girl." The two grew into a rhythm, and established a close relationship; Ginsberg, a professionally trained engineer, took great pride in putting his only child through university. Like Rabbi M, Ginsberg never remarried. In his case, however, his decision to remain single revolved around Jocelyne, who sharply critiqued all potential spouses. No woman met her high standards, and none, in her eyes, demonstrated sensitivity toward the unique father-daughter bond the pair shared.[39] Jocelyne truly was the centre of Ginsberg's universe. In this regard, Ginsberg's case resembles that of other widower survivor fathers. Even when remarriage was desired, the question of finances, emotional security for their motherless offspring, and difficulties establishing romantic relationships stopped most men from remarrying, at least until their children reached adulthood.

Exploring gender and parenting in the framework of postwar Holocaust history presents several challenges. The first concerns the issue of gender itself, which many Holocaust historians treat superficially. Researchers often attach the term "gender" to discussions relating solely to women. Yet, as discussed, gender roles were significant for men, women, and family formation. Furthermore, focusing on women and men also sheds light on how Holocaust survivors and social and resettlement workers constructed family values, and the interpretation of seemingly appropriate and inappropriate gender roles. Single fathers who evinced a lack of experience in child-rearing and housekeeping skills were pitied and fawned over by caseworkers who regarded these men with respect and admiration, and did everything in their power to provide them with the necessary supports to rear their offspring successfully in motherless homes. Single and married mothers tended not to be received with the same sensitivity and compassion as single fathers. Young survivor women faced particular challenges with regard to parenting. Having had their formal schooling and informal education in household and child-rearing matters cut short, few female survivors were prepared for motherhood. Without supportive and trusted female role models to turn to for advice or practical assistance, motherhood emerged as a lonely period for these young women and relegated them to their own segregated private spheres. Citing a lack of safe and affordable childcare services, or relatives to babysit, mothers were less likely to be able to attend English and citizenship classes or social events, thus preventing them from learning the local vernacular in a timely manner, and lengthening their integration process. Social workers routinely criticized the survivor mothers' parenting skills, labelling them as overbearing or overprotective, and ignorant about suitable homemaking and nutritional standards. Yet, for all of the criticism, the workers were unlikely to intervene in survivor homes and offered little in the way of actual support.

Social workers' judgments about survivor women (and, to a lesser extent, men) extended into other arenas of the newcomers' lives. Many refugee women, in addition to mothering responsibilities, were required to enter the Canadian workforce in order to fulfil immigration sponsorship contracts and supplement the income of cash-strapped households.

New Canadian women of all races, creeds, and nationalities occupied a marginal space in popular narrative in the early postwar period. Immigrating in lesser numbers than men, women were under-represented in the workforce and, in the case of women with specialized pre-war occupations, they enjoyed fewer opportunities for professional advancement.[40] Female Holocaust survivors were no exception. From their first encounters with Canadian Jewish representatives in Europe, certain facts were made clear: young, single, able-bodied men with no dependents represented the "ideal" immigrant to Canada. Married men with demonstrable skills as tailors or furriers came next on the list of preferred immigrants among Holocaust survivors. Single female survivors were considered acceptable candidates for positions as domestics, milliners, or dressmakers.

The presence of young children placed women, married or otherwise, hoping to gain admittance into Canada through sponsored labour schemes, into a less desirable category. Labour industry sponsors, Jewish community leaders, and immigrant advocates agreed that single mothers with nursery-aged children should be rejected from inclusion on DP immigration schemes. The rationale, as offered in communication between the AJDC in France and the CJC headquarters in Montreal, worked as follows: the mothers would be unable to become self-supporting and productive citizens because Canadian Jewish communities had no daycare facilities in which to place the children during working hours.[41]

Traditional Canadian social norms and refugees shared particular gender values that typically placed men in the workforce and women in the home. According to the 1931 Canada census, only 16 percent of women aged eighteen to fifty years were engaged in paid employment, as compared to 70 percent of men, and women headed only 10.2 percent of households.[42] But poverty trumped gender roles and led many female Holocaust survivors (mothers included) to undertake paid employment while their children attended school. Most joined the ranks of Jewish workers in the country's booming needle trade as sewers, assemblers, and milliners.[43] The gender role reversal—whereby women took on the role of breadwinner—had an impact on all aspects of their lives, including marriage. Among survivor females with pre-war professional training, few garnered the necessary support to undertake retraining or certification programs to re-enter their fields of expertise; if assistance went to anyone, it was to their husbands. A handful successfully circumvented serious obstacles and entered (or in some instances, re-entered) professional careers outside of the family home.

## Female Occupations

Female Holocaust survivors arrived to a Canada in the throes of transition and transformation. The end of the Second World War signalled the exodus of women—who had contributed greatly to the war effort by stepping into the labour market en masse to fill in for men serving overseas—from the workforce back into the home.[44] Traditional gender roles, which had shifted by necessity of war, had returned. Women's lives were once again revolving around the home. It was no longer they, but their husbands, whose stories merited telling. Case studies of Holocaust survivors reflect these attitudes, and offer crucial insight into the ways in which women were received, and perceived, by social service and settlement professionals. Incoming client families' "personal histories," recorded at the point of contact with social workers, refer almost entirely to the patriarch's education, skill sets, and wartime experiences. Within a family unit, women's wartime experiences are almost always overlooked, though employment history is included. The intake file of the G family provides a clear example of this gender-based imbalance: "The immigrant, Mr. G., related the following: He was born in Czechoslovakia, where he had 12 years of schooling and after 3 years apprenticed as an optician, he obtained his diploma in 1943. He worked for 1 year and from 1944 to 1945 was in a forced labour camp. After the liberation in 1945, he left for Paris, where he worked at a variety of jobs, such as packer and presser. He was married in 1948. His wife has experience as [a] cosmetician and operator on men's shirts."[45] Such a description of a survivor couple illuminates little about their pre-war family life or relationships. It sheds even less light on Mrs. G's Holocaust travails, let alone her nationality or professional employment opportunities.

Summaries of contact between "new Canadians" and social and settlement workers offer more insight into women's experiences and personalities, but in a very different way than that of their husbands or other men. Female survivor clients were judged, and subsequently evaluated, in accordance with their physical appearance and personality. Unlike men, whose appearance was noted secondarily to their wartime experiences and professional attributes, women—irrespective of their age, education, or skills—were assessed by the (mainly) female social service workers on their looks. Appearance mattered greatly for immigrant women of all nationalities. Women described as attractive, specifically of a "healthy figure" with "shiny hair and clear skin," and "sunny, positive outlooks" but "not overbearing or aggressive," tended to receive more empathetic and preferential treatment, and warmer receptions than did their unattractive and more ill-at-ease contemporaries.[46] These seemingly benign descriptions were in fact loaded and carried significant weight. Intake reports and summaries of services rendered travelled with the newcomers throughout the Jewish community's social service system, and were read by social workers and vocational service counsellors, and presented to prospective employers and loan committees.

Where women arrived as part of a family unit (rather than as individuals), such biased reporting was particularly explicit. The B family, part of the Iberian refugee group to reach Canada in April 1944, stands as an illustrative example. Mr. B, an engineer and concert violinist, and Mrs. B, a PhD political economist, reported to Toronto's UJRA office immediately upon arrival for processing. Their social worker prepared a summary highlighting not only the couple's professional prospects but also Mrs. B's unfortunate physical state: "Mrs. B. is a short slight person with unattractive features, an unfriendly, almost hostile expression, and the manner of the intellectual woman snob of Berlin. Her hair, which she wears in a peculiar bob, is bleached, with poor effect; she uses very cheap nail polish, applied in several coatings." In comparison to her assertive, yet soft-spoken husband of "medium height and good looks," Mrs. B "is less sensitive and obviously more rigid than [he] is," the report continues.[47] Such judgments delivered a clear and decisive message to women as to their place in their adopted society. Attractive, polite, and cheerful girls, seemingly unscathed by their experiences, garnered greater empathy than ugly, "difficult" women. Appearance was routinely highlighted as an indicator of successful integration into the workforce, and social workers and vocational counsellors were more likely to provide intense assistance to attractive clients over others.

Regardless of their appearances and attitudes, or the avenues through which they immigrated, all female survivors faced particular challenges immediately upon arrival. Single women who entered Canada either under labour contracts, specifically as domestics, dressmakers, and milliners, or with relatives, were vulnerable to poverty and exploitation. Teenage daughters regularly served as the sole providers for their families, including middle-aged parents and younger, school-aged siblings. Recipients of lower wages and more likely than their male counterparts to accept poor working conditions, young unmarried women proved better suited to finding work in the needle trade than did older parents or single mothers.

Racial and gender expectations shaped newcomers' experiences at work. Denoted as racially inferior and discriminated against in the open marker, "second tier" immigrants were largely directed to segregated ethnic labour markets with limited access to fair wages or job security. Gender expectations and values further intensified the stratification of marginalized female immigrants, who occupied the lowest rungs of the disadvantaged occupational and pay ladders.[48] Assumed to be strong candidates for domestic and needle trade labour schemes, these women filled gaps in service occupations deemed "undesirable" by Canadians.[49]

In the case of the M family, who immigrated to Toronto in 1949, seventeen-year-old daughter Leah acted as breadwinner for her single mother and eleven-year-old brother. Leah abandoned her plans to attend high school when her mother, plagued by deteriorating health triggered by what is today recognized as post-traumatic stress disorder, failed to hold down a job.[50] In Montreal, seventeen- and eighteen-year-old child survivors Anna and Goldie F, who immigrated to Canada under the family patriarch's tailoring contract and independently as a DP dressmaker, respectively, also worked to support their family of five. Excited to explore their new city, learn English, and spend their income frivolously with the friends they met at evening language classes, Anna and Goldie instead delivered their salaries to their unemployed parents. Rather than celebrating their new-found freedom, they paid rent and financed their brother's Talmud Torah education.[51]

Single women who immigrated independently of surviving relatives (if any) also faced impoverishment and limited opportunities for professional advancement. With their education interrupted by war, and postwar skill training and certification from organizations like the Organization for Rehabilitation through Training (ORT) unrecognized in Canada, the women had little hope for financial security short of marrying. Judy Weissenberg Cohen immigrated to Canada with an older sister under a contract arranged through the needle trade. Although she planned to uphold the conditions of her contract and provide one year of labour in the industry, she also hoped to utilize her ORT-issued dental technician cer-tification. But she learned that her skills would be of no use in Canada, where strict training laws, coupled by a lack of employment opportunities, made her certification of no value.[52] As one of 150 female survivors permitted to immigrate to Canada as domestics in the postwar period under the Domestic Displaced Persons Project of the Dominion of Labour, Hungarian survivor Valerie Blau Good faced her own trials in securing meaningful work as a refugee. Sponsored through the National Employment Service (NES), the eighteen-year-old was recruited by labour representatives determined to entice European Jews to fill their allotted quota of fifteen—out of 3,000—for single Jewish ladies. The Second World War had cut short Good's formative teenage years, and left her with little experience in housekeeping and cooking, key elements of domestic work. Good was informed that some Ottawa Jewish families had promised to take on domestics "just to get them out [of postwar Europe]," and that she would be released from her contract immediately upon arrival.[53] Along with five other girls, she reluctantly registered as a domestic.

The terms of her immigration contract dictated that Valerie Blau Good work as a domestic for a minimum of eleven months. Her first job, in the home of a wealthy, religious, but childless family, began without a hitch. "At first," Blau recalled, "the lady of the house was nice to me, and sympathetic. But that changed. I had to wear a uniform, [was] treated like a servant, and exploited, working more hours than I was supposed to for less money. I earned $35 a month and lived with the girls I came over with."[54] Later, the NES placed Blau in other homes, where she worked primarily with children and under more reasonable conditions. Blau completed her contract, and then married Polish survivor Mendel Good.

Like all Jewish domestics, Valerie Blau Good's work placements fell under the authority of the NES. Jewish immigration officers were to intervene only in matters of social adjustment or acculturation, including referrals to English classes and social outings. As an outgoing and confident teenager, Valerie Blau Good attended Jewish community events on her own initiative. Less sociable or self-assured Jewish domestics found life in Canada isolating and depressing. Unlike other survivors who typically boarded in rooms among other immigrants, domestics usually lived in their employers' homes and worked long hours. As a result, some had little interaction with other recent arrivals and few opportunities to develop friendships and romantic relationships.

Among those who encountered adjustment difficulties was Czech Jewish survivor-turned-domestic Sonja W. Ms. W was twenty-three years old when she left her elderly father in Prague and immigrated to Montreal in 1949 as a domestic worker. An educated, pleasant, and engaging young woman, Ms. W fell into a downward emotional spiral within months of her arrival and began exhibiting troubling behaviours. She refused to attend work, dropped out of English night classes (which was her only form of social activity and interaction with other Jewish newcomers), locked herself in her bedroom in a rooming house, and followed a starvation diet. JIAS social workers learned of her conduct from a concerned neighbour and went to investigate. According to a report prepared for her case file, Ms. W was discovered in poor straits, unable to speak lucidly and communicating only through "bizarre thoughts and frantic speech." She was "disturbed, out of contact with reality," wrote the unnamed social worker, whom Ms. W threatened with a knife.[55] Later, Ms. W apologized for her actions, claiming that she had no intention of injuring the worker, but felt overwhelmed and under attack. She relayed feeling lonely, without friends or loved ones, and wished only to return to her father in Prague. The social worker felt that Ms. W was psychologically deranged as a result of her social isolation, and referred her for a psychiatric consultation. Nothing more is known about the case.

For Valerie Blau Good and Sonja W, the commitment to undertake employment was an integral part of their immigration contracts. But for married women, the situation was more complicated. Community agencies refused to grant financial assistance to homes without working adults. Only women with children too young to attend full-day school were exempt from this stipulation. Such blanket terms resulted in the emergence of two types of newcomer women: those who willingly sought out jobs despite medical and emotional conditions that prevented them from performing certain tasks, and women who attempted to circumvent the rules and avoid accepting any employment at all. Most female survivors fell into the former category and undertook work to help support themselves and their families (in instances where childcare was available for youngsters not yet of school age), and turned to organizations like JIAS when their income proved insufficient to cover their costs. Those falling into the latter group caused serious problems for social and settlement workers, who failed to recognize the deeply imbedded issues contributing to some of the women's resistance toward work, including traditional gender norms and a lack of skills or education.

Most female survivor-immigrants lacked formal education or skills, let alone experience as waged employees. For many young women, their sole work experiences occurred in Nazi slave labour and concentration camps, where they performed back-breaking unskilled tasks. And, they were unable to communicate in the local vernacular and depended on interpreters and informal peer networks of fellow survivors to help navigate the workforce. It is thus not surprising that many experienced crippling anxiety in their work searches. Such anxieties inevitably followed into their places of employment, and persisted for months, if not years. Then too, for some women, the notion of accepting employment out of the household presented as an undesirable and foreign concept that threatened their traditional way of life.

A more prevalent predicament, however, arose among women with lasting disabilities and poor health on account of the Holocaust. Regina G, who arrived in Montreal in November 1949 with her husband, Rabbi Jacob G, represented one such case. As a married couple with no children in Canada (the rabbi had two adult children from a previous marriage residing in Belgium), both husband and wife were expected to accept employment in order to qualify for social service assistance. At first, Mrs. G indicated her interest in finding work and recognized the need for her to support her family financially. But, according to her JIAS caseworker's notes, "she did not feel she could consider this at the moment as she was suffering from a gynaecological condition and was experiencing haemoraging [sic]."[56] Appointments for check-ups were scheduled for Mrs. G with the clinic, but she failed to show on a number of occasions. When she finally attended, Mrs. G was given a clean bill of health. The social worker assigned to the G family's case grew increasingly frustrated with Mrs. G's perceived attitude and inaction, and threatened to cut her maintenance checks. Mrs. G, the social worker reported, "denied that she was unwilling to accept employment, stating that she had been refused work by the firm[s] in question on the basis of age and orthodoxy."[57] Her resistance to work continued, and maintenance checks ceased. Only then did the rabbi reveal what he felt to be the underlying reason for his wife's unwillingness to work. As recorded by the caseworker, "Rabbi G. expressed his bewilderment concerning this policy [of providing assistance only to newcomers willing to work]. He stated that we failed to understand that physical hardships experienced during the war had markedly affected the health of many European Jews. From a humanitarian point of view, he added, how could we compel his wife to work?"[58]

Rabbi G attempted to explain how years of slave labour and malnutrition had scarred his wife permanently and rendered her frail, downtrodden, and physically unable to work. The caseworker, demonstrating her ignorance of the recent plight of European Jews, interpreted things differently. She incorrectly attributed Mrs. G's refusal to work or accept the agency's stipulations on the couple's Orthodoxy and the traditional place of *rebbetzin* (a rabbi's wife) in religious communities. No amount of documented suffering—including Mrs. G's multiple hospital visits and doctors' reports declaring her unsuited for most types of work—convinced the worker that Mrs. G's resistance came from anything but stubbornness and laziness. Unable to convince JIAS that Mrs. G's physical hardships were real, the G family stood fast in their decision to challenge the agency's work policy and had their case closed. They received no further assistance from Jewish social service agencies.[59]

While single and childless married female survivors like Mrs. G were automatically expected to take employment, the situation was less transparent for mothers with children not yet school-aged. Most survivor families required two incomes to stay afloat and not rely on community funds or personal loans from relatives or *landsmanshaftn*. But the lack of suitable childcare, or the absence of helpful relatives or peer networks, made this close to impossible. Plans for foster daycare and nursery schools for survivors' young children evoked debates among the Jewish resettlement and social service agencies, which shouldered responsibility for the newcomers' resettlement and survivors' primary contact for employment opportunities and childcare provisions. By September 1949, Canadian Jewry had welcomed seventy-five Jewish milliner families, with an additional twenty-five expected imminently. Amongst the group, thirty families were receiving monetary assistance from JIAS; of this number, female heads of households—that is, women DPs under whose names Canadian immigration papers had been procured—represented more than half of the cases. Approximately thirty mothers had been forced to forego employment in order to provide childcare for their young preschool-aged children. JIAS, as the first stop for newcomers, expressed the concern that unless the Jewish community developed and instituted a daycare program at once, these families (as well as over fifty married women sponsored by the labour groups as dressmakers) could face the threat of deportation.

As the official representation of Canadian Jewry, and the responsible stewards of the DP labour schemes, the community leaders moved forward with their plans for accessible and affordable childcare.[60] Demands for change, beginning with representatives of Jewish service agencies, grew loudest in Montreal and Toronto, home to more than two-thirds of the Holocaust survivors and their young families to settle in Canada.[61] While both Montreal and Toronto survivor communities struggled to find acceptable solutions to support families in their search for childcare to permit parents to undertake employment, their efforts were uneven and produced varied results.

Representatives from Montreal's Jewish organizations participated in a series of meetings between 1948 and 1949 intended to address the lack of suitable—and affordable and accessible—daycare programs for the children of survivors. The CJC reported on this issue frequently. In response to ongoing struggles to implement programs due to inter-agency conflicts, a CJC Inter-Office Information Summary from 27 July 1949 concluded that

> The Millinery Industry work project differs from the other group movements in that the selectees are women. A problem arises where such selections are mothers with children. Congress asked the Federation of Montreal to convene meetings to discuss the possibility of some daycare arrangements for such children and three meetings have been held. We also contacted the Millinery Industry reps to find out if the industry could arrange that these mothers be exempt from their contracts. Since this latter possibility is deemed not feasible, we will have to continue arrangements for some kind of foster care during the day so that the mothers can work.[62]

The participants in these meetings consisted of both lay leaders and professional staff, including Mr. Diamond, head of the Canadian Overseas Garment Commission (COGC), Miriam Weiner of JIAS, Mr. Schrier of the Neighbourhood House, and David Weiss and Jean Henshaw of Jewish Family Child Welfare (JFCW). Other prominent community leaders, including Saul Hayes of the CJC, and M.A. Solkin of JIAS, also offered their views via written correspondence. The issue of childcare arose in part as a response to continuous requests by Holocaust survivor mothers (and, less frequently, fathers) brought to Canada through DP settlement programs. More significant, however, was the agencies' concern that the women, sponsored by the COGC as part of the milliners and dressmakers schemes, would prove unable to fulfil the terms of their contractual obligations with the Canadian government if solutions were not found to their childcare dilemmas. If the women were found in violation of their contracts and threatened with deportation, the COGC could be held responsible and forced to advocate on behalf of the newcomers. In addition, it would have a potentially detrimental effect on future labour schemes and refugee aid programs.

Opinions relating to Montreal's proposed community-run daycare services for Holocaust survivors' offspring were mixed. Director of JFCW David Weiss believed that the proposed project, initially recommended by Diamond, leading selection representative from the COGC, was a desirable and necessary service. "I would naturally say that a day nursery for children is an indispensable tool in the adjustment of both the family and the youngsters who may require its services," Diamond reported.[63] Mary Palevsky, a deputy director from the New York Association for New Americans (NYANA) seconded to evaluate Canada's reception and integration of Jewish DPs, also weighed in on the benefits of full-day, subsidized nursery care, stressing how married mothers needed such services in order to supplement their husbands' often meagre incomes.[64]

National Executive Director of JIAS M.A. Solkin's response to the initiative was markedly less enthusiastic. For him, negative elements of the plan outweighed the positives. As Solkin wrote to Saul Hayes, "My immediate personal opinion is that the project is not likely to prove feasible. It seems to involve planning for a new institution, fully equipped to handle infants and children of pre-kindergarten age, receive them early in the morning and discharge them quite late in the evening."[65] Hayes, for his part, argued that the program should fall under the responsibility of the JFCW, since it represented a potential solution to a "social problem" necessitating facilities, staff expertise, and experience acquired only through social service agencies.[66] Others, including David Weiss, agreed with this assessment, but refused to accept complete financial responsibility for the program's establishment and maintenance. Since most of the women searching for day nursery care came to Canada through sponsorship by the COGC, Jewish leadership posited that the program should receive funding through the Commission's pocketbook, at least in the case of Montreal.[67]

After much deliberation, the plan was proposed. JFCW would shoulder the responsibility for staffing and overseeing the daycare, which would operate six days a week (excluding Saturdays) between the hours of 7:30 a.m. and 6:00 p.m. The estimated cost for users stood at approximately thirty dollars a month per child, not including additional fees for overtime hours. Rather than pay upfront for services, fees would be collected directly by JFCW from the parents' employers through income deductions. This proposal was met with intense opposition.

Citing low wages and high rents, few newcomer families believed they could manage the weekly cost of using the daycare services. Even if the program would permit contracted mothers to uphold the conditions of their agreements, most of the refugees' paycheques would never reach them.[68] In the end, Montreal's Jewish Federation opted not to institute community-run daycare services. Its position was summarized in the following manner: "An attempt was made to initiate a program using the millinery project as an experiment. The latter was well designed for such an experiment since the mothers had contractual obligations vis a vis the Government and, therefore, it was of legal importance for them to avail themselves of services enabling them to fulfil their contracts. After a thorough study and many meetings the project was abandoned in favour of the usual nursery care, whereby the client pays a fee to the foster mother."[69]

While community leadership failed to negotiate nursery care plans in Montreal, survivor families elsewhere in Canada found greater support for their pleas for affordable and safe childcare. By the summer of 1948, extraordinarily high birth rates among "new Canadians" were being reported by the CJC and its affiliated organizations. This growth was especially rapid in Toronto. Various groups took the opportunity to assist the survivor population and proactively engaged in the establishment of helpful services for new mothers and infants. The UJRA made arrangements to assist expectant mothers and newborn babies through prenatal care in health clinics, public health nurses visits, and hospitalization at Mount Sinai Hospital for the delivery. The Council of Jewish Women supplied volunteers for home visits, while synagogue sisterhoods and sewing clubs committed to providing diapers, cribs, blankets, and other knitted items for the newborns. Interpreters were also supplied to help new mothers best utilize the services of the Child Health Clinic run out of St. Christopher's House, a downtown non-Jewish settlement agency.[70] This newfound interest in refugee welfare spearheaded community engagement and advocacy, and brought the newcomer women's particular needs and concerns to centre stage.

In addition to these volunteer initiatives, a committee composed of professional representatives from CJC's central region, the UJRA, and JIAS met in Toronto to determine how to most efficiently and cost-effectively tackle the dilemmas facing the growing number of would-be working mothers within the survivor community. Unlike their Montreal counterparts, the Toronto leadership seemingly recognized the value and importance of establishing nursery school services for the children of working survivor mothers. The committee launched a survey of Jewish schools, synagogues, and social service providers to locate an appropriate venue for the program. Within a matter of weeks, it was concluded that existing facilities and schools were overcrowded and could not easily or safely integrate any more children into their classes.[71] The D'Arcy Street Talmud Torah could, however, set aside one classroom to accommodate a nursery school. On 19 April 1949, Congress committed to "bear the cost of equipping the school, and operating costs (food, teachers salaries, maintenance) will be met totally through fees to be charged for each child." The fees were geared-to-income, and arranged privately between the UJRA and parents.[72]

The Toronto committee rose to the occasion and acted quickly. Within weeks, a nursery school had been established for working mothers in the survivor community with young children. By 9 May 1949, the program had already reached its physical capacity of twenty-five children.[73] Even though it was bursting at the seams, Talmud Torah administrators shared in the leadership's commitment to ensuring care for all eligible youngsters, as illustrated by the case of one Toronto refugee family with three children, aged ten, eight, and five. Unable to sustain her family with her husband's earnings, and desperate to become independent from social service assistance, Mrs. X turned to Jewish Family and Child Services for help in securing employment for herself as a dressmaker. But, before she could do anything, she needed to find an available daycare space for her five-year-old son. Mrs. X refused to accept placement in non-Jewish homes, and wanted her children educated in a Jewish environment. Hearing of her case, Mr. Goldwasser, the principal of the Talmud Torah, showed compassion for the new Canadian family. With some careful rearranging, Mr. Goldwasser created vacancies for all three of the X family children in the school, the older two in primary classes and the youngest in the nursery room. Acknowledging their financial situation, the school agreed to temporarily waive all tuition charges, thus permitting the children to receive a Jewish education while simultaneously allowing Mrs. X to take much-needed employment.[74]

Females with post-secondary education or professional certifications faced a harsh reality in their adopted country. On the one hand, their accreditations, like those of most newcomers educated outside of North America or Britain, were not recognized by Canadian professional organizations representing the interests of members in their fields. Return to their previous work required months, if not years, of retraining, and affected everyone from hairdressers to physicians. Discriminatory rules and regulations prohibited many immigrants from entering certain fields, citing improper training and educational standards as well as citizenship and language requirements. For example, in postwar Quebec all practising (and thus certified) doctors were required to hold Canadian citizenship, which necessitated a minimum of five years of residence in the country. The monetary costs and lengthy processes associated with recertification deterred many talented DPs from rejoining their respective ranks. Female professionals faced an additional obstacle: the imbedded sexism and biases of communal service agencies and loan associations. Such groups more readily supported male survivors with professional backgrounds, and considered them more suitable candidates for education upgrading subsidies and loans than women with similar credentials.

Employment counsellors and settlement workers assigned to assist these men and women frequently recognized their clients' potential contributions to Canada and Canadian Jewish society. Many of these survivors even spoke fluent English or French (or both), having studied overseas. Such was the case with Drs. David and Maria S, Hungarian survivors who immigrated to Canada in October 1949 on a millinery contract. A medical doctor and dentist, respectively, the couple arrived with proof of their credentials and letters of reference from JDC officials attesting to their service in postwar DP camps. They turned to JIAS for maintenance and rental support while David—who one social worker described as "impressively well-groomed and highly educated"—applied for internships in Montreal and beyond. Funding to cover his travel to Saskatchewan (where he had been accepted as an intern at Regina General Hospital), and to defray his daily costs and cover his accommodations, were granted.

By contrast, Maria S's requests for release from her millinery contract in order to protect her "fragile hands, only used for dentistry and playing the piano," were routinely denied, and described by the same social worker as "aggressive" and "demanding."[75] Workers recommended she put her suturing skills to use designing hats. Desperate to gain community support, and eager for at least one partner to succeed professionally, Maria S accepted these stipulations and rescinded her own requests for support. The family's case was closed two years later when David S completed his medical residency. At this point, Maria S indicated no intention of trying to return to her pre-war profession as a dentist.[76]

Like Dr. Maria S, most female Holocaust survivors were denied the community support they needed to return to their pre-war careers. Drs. Stefan (a radiologist) and Mina W (a chemist) faced similar obstacles in their mutual efforts to return to their pre-war professions. As the "head of the household," Stefan received $150 each month to subsidize his family's rent and living costs while he volunteered at a local Montreal hospital.[77] This support continued through his medical internship and licensing examinations, during which time Mina raised their two children and acted as a landlady, renting out rooms in their apartment. Mina's file includes early reminiscences about her previous life, including a doctorate and ten years of teaching experience, and her expressed desire to return to academia, but there is nothing in the couple's record to suggest that her life in Canada lived up to her expectations.

A clear pattern emerges in case files: educated survivor women grudgingly accepted their positions as homemakers for their breadwinner husbands and waited years, if ever, to have the financial means to undertake retraining and resume their professional careers. There were some notable exceptions. The histories of Dr. Mina Deutsch, a physician, and Chava Rosenfarb, a Yiddish writer, and the challenges they encountered as career women—while caring for and raising children—illuminate their lasting contributions to the Canadian medical field and Yiddish life and literature in Canada, respectively, and suggest how much was lost by the lack of support offered their cohorts.

To Dr. Mina Deutsch, medicine was more than a profession. Her and her husband Leon's medical training as psychiatrists in pre-war Czechoslovakia helped secure their and their young daughter Eva's survival in wartime Poland.[78] During the Holocaust years, the couple, under Nazi guard, treated Polish, Russian, and German patients. At one point they managed to go into hiding, and traded safe spaces in exchange for medical services. Mina's employment opportunities in postwar communist Poland were optimal: she and her husband were assigned a pharmacy, and permitted to return to their medical practices at once. But uncomfortable living, working, and raising Eva behind the Iron Curtain, the Deutsches fled to Germany in 1946 and spent two years running the medical facilities at DP Camp Riedenburg and in nearby communities. Their plan was to join relatives in either the United States or Canada.

Canadian immigration papers came first, and the doctors and their child arrived in Halifax on 11 February 1948. Following an emotional reunion in Montreal with members of extended family from Canada and the United States, they travelled with Mina's brother Willy to his home in Perth, Ontario, and began the long and trying process of professional reaccreditation. Already thirty-seven years old, Mina was determined to revive her career—and thus reclaim financial independence and security—as quickly as possible, which meant beginning by learning English. With a small loan from an American cousin, and free lodging with her brother, the Deutsches enrolled Eva in school and they spent every waking moment studying in preparation for medical licensing exams. There were no guarantees. As Mina recalled in her memoir, opportunities for advancement in Montreal, the closest major city to Perth, were nil: "As soon as our English improved, Leon went to Montreal to look for work. He discovered that we would have to begin with a year of internship, but that in Quebec one had to be a citizen to get the Enabling Certificate to take the Dominion Council Examinations.

Since that meant a five-year wait, we decided to go to Toronto, instead, where we both got internships."[79]

The decision to move to Toronto came at a price. Medical interns were required to live on-site at the city's Mount Sinai Hospital. Although married, the doctors were forced to live in cramped, gender-segregated dormitories. And there was no place for their daughter, Eva, let alone time to care for her. These conditions, coupled with low wages, required the family to separate for the first time since the war. Their school-aged daughter—not permitted to live with her mother in residence—remained in Perth with her uncle's family. Within six months, the Deutsches transferred to Grey Nuns Hospital in Saskatchewan, where they were conferred licensing and medical certification after a year of internship. Eva joined her parents, but the family was once again prohibited from living together; instead, Eva was boarded at several homes in Regina.[80] This pattern of instability, including numerous school transfers and home placements, persisted for several years, before both husband and wife found secure work as physicians in New Brunswick. Years would pass before Dr. Mina Deutsch managed to return to her original field, psychiatry, which she ultimately practised at Montreal's Douglas Hospital for more than two decades. She had achieved her goal but the obstacles she had faced took a toll on her personal and family life. The hospital residency regulations had forced her to live apart from her husband and daughter for nearly two years after immigrating to Canada, and she struggled to retain strong bonds, both spousal and parental.[81]

One of the "grande dames of Yiddish literature," Chava Rosenfarb followed another route to establishing a career in Canada.[82] Born in 1923 in Lodz, Poland, into a Socialist Bundist family, Rosenfarb's life-long love affair with Yiddish-language poetry and literature was awakened during her four years in the Nazi-imposed Litzmannstadt Ghetto. There, she "found [herself] within a doomed community of distinguished Yiddish-speaking writers, poets, painters and intellectuals who accepted her as their youngest member and became her mentors."[83] Membership in the Lodz writers' group spurred her creativity, and Rosenfarb produced hundreds of poems in the ghetto. Surviving incarceration in a series of concentration camps, Rosenfarb and her then-husband, Dr. Henry Morgentaler, lived in postwar Belgium, where he undertook medical studies. With little opportunity to complete her own formal education, no familial support, and in need of an income, Rosenfarb did what she knew best: she wrote poems, stories, and essays, which she sent to Yiddish-language publications in the United Kingdom, Canada, and the United States. These early works attracted the attention of Montreal-based Yiddish poet and publisher Melech Ravitch, who subsequently sponsored the couple's immigration to Canada.

Rosenfarb's arrival was cause for celebration. Ravitch informed Yiddishists throughout North America, and dozens of literary personalities flocked to greet the couple at Montreal's Windsor Station in February 1950.[84] Montreal, once home to a flourishing Jewish community steeped in *Yiddishkeit*, had changed dramatically in a matter of decades. But as decline was settling in, the influx of Hassidic and ultra-Orthodox survivors, as well as their secular Yiddish-speaking cohorts, rejuvenated the city's traditional Yiddish culture. Rosenfarb's official indoctrination into Yiddish society was held on 22 April 1950. Hirsch (Harry) Hershman, a leader in Montreal's Yiddish community and Rosenfarb's publisher, helped organize the event with the Arbeter Ring, and mailed invitations to community members. The invitation read as follows:

Dear friend,

I have recorded that you were one of the first to obtain Chava Rosenfarb's book: the ballads from yesterday's forest and other songs— which I published a time ago. I think it would be interesting for you to discover that the poet finds herself already in our circle and that Montreal is now her permanent home.

Chava Rosenfarb will hold her first opening performance Friday 22 April, at 8:30 in the evening at the Arbeter Ring forum in the auditorium of the Arbeter Ring, 4348 St. Lawrence Boulevard. The poet will perform Y. Y. Sigal, Rokhl H. Korn, and Melech Ravitch. Chava Rosenfarb will read one of her newest creations, a biblical poem.... I think that after you are already familiar with Chava Rosenfarb's poems, it will be even more interesting for you to meet her in person. Chava is not only an excellent poet but also a magnificent speaker.[85]

Rosenfarb found herself surrounded by, and became a prominent member of, an elite group of Montreal-based Yiddish writers, including fellow Holocaust survivor Rokhl Korn.[86] With this group of professionals, or "postwar vagabonds," Rosenfarb garnered the strength not only to preserve Yiddish—also a victim of war—but also to eat, sleep, breathe, and work in it.[87] While raising two children (Goldie, born in 1950, and Abraham, born five years later) and without any formal education, Rosenfarb carved out a career for herself producing Yiddish literature for a readership that had mostly "perished with the smoke of the crematoria," and a small group of committed Yiddishists.[88] Her writings were exclusively in Yiddish, the language of her home, her childhood and community, and her thoughts. Rosenfarb's work dealt nearly entirely with themes relating to the Holocaust, its survivors and victims, and frequently evoked a Canadian backdrop. An anomaly among young female survivors, Rosenfarb balanced her work and home lives, while simultaneously helping to rejuvenate the declining Yiddish culture of postwar Montreal. Rosenfarb's success can be attributed in large part to two factors: community support and money. As a talented writer with a demonstrated commitment to preserving Yiddish, she derived support and interest from Yiddishists who sponsored her immigration and actively promoted her work. And, owing to Morgentaler's recognized medical degree, the family did not necessitate financial aid on par with other newcomers. This vastly differentiates her experience from those of refugee women attempting entrance into professions who required agency support to secure accreditation, for instance Mina Deutsch's foray into Canadian medicine.[89]

Rosenfarb's anomalous experience of complete integration and acceptance into postwar society by Canadian Jews (as well as those born in Europe who had immigrated in the interwar period) is, in and of itself, significant. That she did so as a female in the male-dominated Yiddish writers' community is significant, as well. Her story is most significant, however, because it sheds light on the state of the Jews of Montreal, who bestirred themselves for *Yiddishkeit*, a tradition largely depleted by the end of the interwar period due to a lack of interest on the part of younger generations of Canadian-born or Canadian-raised Jews. As a person who would contribute greatly to the cultural and linguistic preservation of Yiddish life, Rosenfarb received preferential treatment in Montreal (and later, other Canadian Jewish communities), including support for her writing career. Female survivors with alternate professional or personal aspirations of lesser interest to Canadian Jews were not granted equal assistance or attention.

### Dethroned Breadwinners: Men at Home

While their wives engaged with the labour market, some survivor fathers struggled to adapt to a new role, that of stay-at-home parents. These husbands were forced to forego their position as breadwinner and depend on their wives for financial upkeep, which was seen as both emasculating and shameful—and in contradiction to the traditional standards of homemaking and family values promoted by Jewish and non-Jewish settlement groups, which the men shared. Husbands and social workers alike abhorred these arrangements. For husbands accustomed to providing for and protecting their loved ones, this loss of authority took a devastating toll on their self-esteem. Depending on community agencies for rent and daily expenses was humbling enough; relying on one's wife to keep a roof over their heads defied tradition and threatened the balance of power in the home.

Men feared that their dependency and involvement in household chores cast them as weak or effeminate, and that their current (and, they hoped, temporary) condition would influence their community status negatively. Survivor-wives and social workers also shared concern over the gender role reversals. While working mothers might have felt pride in their ability to earn an income and support their loved ones, their pride was mixed with a sense of unease with their spouse's discomfort and the possible impact on their children. According to Franca Iacovetta, concern was expressed that swapped male-female roles, and children's witnessing of it, would be interpreted as normal by impressionable first-generation Canadians. "Spineless stay-at-home father" or "aggressive, manly working mother" figures would damage the body politic and destroy traditional family values, critical elements for developing healthy and productive Canadian citizens.[90] As a result, the majority of employed immigrant women performed their job and acted as breadwinner only until their husband could undertake work, at which time most ceased working outside the home or took on subsidiary roles.

24. Rebeka (Rena), Slomo (Sioma), and Frankie Bialystok celebrating Frankie's fourth birthday, 22 June 1950. Courtesy of Frank Bialystok.

Some families handled their newfound situation relatively well. Hungarian survivors Joseph and Martha G arrived in Montreal in June 1951 thanks to the support of a nephew who had immigrated earlier under the War Orphans Project. With them came a three-year-old daughter. Mr. G, a "well-spoken man" in his mid-thirties, had worked in pre- and post-occupation Hungary in the family business dealing in medicinal herbs. He hoped to return to his former career and turned to JIAS for advice on applying for a business loan. Refused the capital needed to start a company, Mr. G was advised to find work in another area, and referred to JVS for employment assistance. But, because of the broader economic downturn in the early 1950s, nothing turned up.

With no work opportunities for Mr. G, the caseworker's attention turned toward his wife. Social workers recommended Mrs. G find work as a hairdresser, for which she had been trained in postwar Europe. Interpreters accompanied Mrs. G to meetings with potential employers, and provided financial assistance while she prepared for—and passed—tests in hygiene and practical exams. Mrs. G found a full-time position immediately, leaving her husband in charge of childcare. Neither party was pleased with this arrangement, and requested referral to a daycare so that Mr. G could continue his job search. The response was bleak: with no available programs, Mr. G could either stay home with his daughter until she began school or find other "new Canadians" to watch her in their homes. Refusing the latter option, Mr. G settled reluctantly into the role of "house-husband."[91]

The Gs had good reason to distrust in-home, unmonitored daycare services for their daughter. Polish survivors Sioma and Rebeka Bialystok arrived in Toronto in 1948 with their two-year-old son, Franklin, on a farmer's work contract. After more than one year of trials and health scares, including a near-fatal spinal injury, Sioma finally secured stable employment with a real estate office as a junior salesman; on the side, he worked for a Polish Catholic photographer. Despite both of these jobs, Sioma's meagre income could not sustain the family of three. With a diploma from the Soviet Union, Rebeka began the search for work as a nurse or a bookkeeper, quickly realizing that without Canadian experience, these goals were beyond reach. Eventually, a sympathetic factory owner's son hired her as a finisher Monday to Friday, 9:00 a.m. to 3:00 p.m. The couple enrolled three-year-old Franklin in a home-based daycare. Rebeka later recalled that the entire experience lasted only three weeks: "Every morning I would take him there. That was before my husband started to work. My son was three and a half years old and he would cry from the moment I left him until the time I came to pick him up. Every time I left him, I was leaving with a broken heart. Later I found out, that one of the two women, who was there, was Ukrainian. She was mistreating him. One time, I saw that she was punching him."[92] As soon as she learned of this abuse, Franklin was pulled from the daycare. For a slightly higher fee but peace of mind, Rebeka enrolled her son in the nursery at the Borochov Centre, a Yiddishist, leftist Zionist organization to which Sioma belonged.

These experiences made refugee families like the Gs understandably apprehensive and desirous of more suitable daycare solutions. Although far from pleased with the circumstances, Mr. G accepted his new role graciously. Others faced with similar circumstances responded to the upheaval of patriarchal power with anger and violence. In his past life as a butcher, Czech survivor Josef K embodied the prototypical breadwinner male. But upon arrival in Canada with his wife Berta and her son from her first marriage, ten-year-old Sam, physical ailments—the result of wartime abuse—forced the family to reconfigure itself. Chronic pain and partial paralysis in his legs rendered Mr. K indeterminately unsuitable for employment. Mrs. K "picked up the slack," earning praise from the family's settlement worker for pulling herself together "to support her family when her husband could not do so."[93]

The effects of the situation on the family were dramatic and led to discord in the home. Though the social worker attested that Mr. K "attended to the household duties and appeared outwardly to accept this situation," cracks in the familial relationship developed, and the already tumultuous relationship between Mr. K and his stepson Sam escalated into violent episodes.[94] When it emerged that his violence toward Sam stemmed from his feelings of helplessness and frustration, the worker's proposed solution was for JVS to step up its efforts to find Mr. K appropriate, sedentary work, thus permitting him to contribute to his family's upkeep. Seemingly, neither Mr. K's injuries nor Holocaust-related trauma were considered important elements in the equation. Mr. K was determined to exit his role as "stay-at-home father" and re-embrace the life of breadwinner. So far as JVS and the family's social workers were concerned, this was an ideal end to a less-than-ideal set of circumstances. Without any notation on the family's records as to whether or not JVS was able to place Mr. K, the case was closed.

---

The study of working women, gendered and social norms about appropriate male-female roles, and the broader implications of undesirable gender role reversals on survivor family units evokes many questions and provides few answers. Providing a balanced perspective on how male and female survivors experienced the process of resettlement, integration, and acculturation relies upon rich sources of information. Female survivors who immigrated with a husband, or young women who arrived with a family unit, were given scant attention by social workers. Consequently, less is known about their pre-war lives, education, or wartime experiences in comparison with their male relatives. The written narrative is about the latter, not the former. This imbalance in primary sources offers more insight into the agendas and biases of the social workers than the newcomers' hopes and fears. Instead of relaying details that might have helped social workers and employment counsellors best meet the female newcomers' needs, case studies tended to focus on superficial physical attributes, such as appearance, weight, and personality. Judgments toward women's abilities as workers and mothers—based largely on emotional and physical health—trumped logic or reason in case files. Poor emotional health or psychosomatic symptoms stemming from wartime trauma and postwar depression and isolation evoked little sympathy from Canadian Jewish "gatekeepers," who appeared more concerned with moulding the newcomers (female survivors in particular) into healthy, conforming citizens than providing counselling and treatment for those adapting more slowly.

A shortage of safe and affordable nursery daycares affected all newcomer families and placed stress on their daily lives and relationships, threatening their hopes of becoming successful Canadians. Mothers felt the lack of spaces acutely. The family values promoted in postwar Canada—and shared by Holocaust survivor communities—espoused the preservation of traditional male-female roles. Men were expected to participate in the workforce and act as the primary breadwinner. Women were expected to embrace their status as mothers and raise healthy new Canadians. For survivors, the maintenance of such stereotypical family roles conflicted with the realities of their postwar lives. Some men (whose voices and experiences rarely enter the historical narrative) could not fulfil their prescribed duties as wage earners. In these cases, they relied on their wives to undertake employment to subsidize their low incomes. Others, suffering from health conditions or a lack of transferable skills, found themselves unable to hold a job at all and depended on wives and daughters to keep the family afloat. These men became silent actors in the postwar survivor saga, and were elided from history. They expressed embarrassment and frustration with their situation of gender role reversal and some took out their distress on their children.

Some women, albeit few in number, could not, or would not, accept the dominant gender norms espoused by Canadian Jewish society and community workers. For some, that meant choosing to remain single or not bear children for a variety of personal reasons. But most documented instances of survivors challenging mainstream family values related to professional women who embraced careers.

Women like Dr. Mina Deutsch and Chava Rosenfarb stood out as anomalies to the typical "female survivor experience." Unlike single and married women pushed into employment out of necessity, Deutsch and Rosenfarb acted on their own initiative and entered (or, in the case of Deutsch, struggled to re-enter) their respective careers notwithstanding, or independent of, their husbands' ability to act as providers. Financial aid from Jewish communal agencies and familial support contributed to Dr. Deutsch and her husband's eventual medical relicensing. Rosenfarb's drive and literary achievements emerged from a different kind of unofficial aid: the rich community of Yiddishists who appreciated the Polish Jewish refugee's authoritative and authentic prose, and shared in Rosenfarb's commitment to preserving a final vestige of pre-war Jewish life and culture.

The cases explored in this chapter offer a lens into the distinct host of challenges that plagued displaced persons who settled, and attempted to earn a living, in postwar Canadian society. Earning one's keep and attaining independence from social service structures and relatives trumped all other endeavours, no matter the sacrifice. A lack of recognized degrees and marketable skills, combined with linguistic shortfalls and emotional and physical ailments relating to Holocaust tribulations, limited countless newcomers from securing meaningful or profitable employment in the first years after immigration. For the minority of survivors to arrive in Canada with designations or a recognizable talent or skill set, discriminatory systems regulating entry or reaccreditation into fields diminished the likelihood of professional fulfilment in their chosen areas. Owing to a rigid value system steeped in patriarchal gender norms and religious division, females in particular faced paralyzing prohibitions in the pursuit of higher education and professional success.

# CONCLUSION

During the Nazi era, Canada exhibited the poorest humanitarian record in the Western world with regard to the granting of asylum to European Jews fleeing persecution. Between 1933 and 1947, only 4,000 to 5,000 Jewish refugees entered Canada at the behest of W.L. Mackenzie King's Liberal government. Canadian Jewish efforts to effect political will and secure asylum for refugees were foiled by xenophobic and racist ideology. A growing popular animosity toward immigrants and immigration in general, coupled with strong anti-Jewish sentiment among French Canadian voters, as well as voters elsewhere in Canada, influenced the political agenda to uphold tightly sealed immigration laws. Canadian parliamentarians, led by Prime Minister Mackenzie King and Director of Immigration Frederick C. Blair, rejected any and all refugee pleas: "We must...seek to keep this part of the Continent free from unrest and from too great an intermixture of foreign strains of blood." Permitting Jewish refugee entrance into Canada beyond the prescribed quotas could create internal conflict and denigrate national unity; Jews were not Canada's problems. Humanitarianism occupied no place in Canadian immigration law.[1]

The gradual liberalization of Canada's position on immigration, beginning with P.C. 2071 on 28 May 1946 and culminating with the formal promulgation of the country's amended immigration policy on 1 May 1947, as well as the Canadian Citizenship Act (enacted on 27 June 1946 and effected 1 January 1947), signalled a veritable sea change in Canada's law and popular attitude toward immigrants and refugees. The changes in immigration policy were especially meaningful for Canadian Jews. They permitted the near-uncapped sponsorship of Canadian citizens' surviving *landsleit*, at the time lingering in DP camps and other inhospitable European environments rife with traumatic memories and persistent anti-Jewish violence, through close relatives and labour schemes. Between 1947 and 1955, the 170,000-strong Canadian Jewish community sponsored and absorbed approximately 35,000 Holocaust survivors plus their dependents.

The newcomers, representing diverse European national, cultural, and religious traditions, as well as wartime experiences, greatly influenced Canadian Jewish life. Although the organized community had been utterly unprepared to receive the earliest arrivals—an unprecedented refugee movement—and did not have sufficient expertise or always demonstrate sensitivity to attend to the newcomers' physical or emotional needs, the Canadian Jewish Congress (CJC), Jewish Immigration Aid Services (JIAS), and *landsmanshaftn* ultimately joined together to develop a comprehensive immigrant reception system. The CJC was lauded at the time by national (secular) newspapers as one of the most active, engaged, and helpful national ethnic organizations in the process of immigrant rehabilitation in Canada.[2]

The path to integration and acculturation was rarely smooth and, as we have seen, Holocaust survivors navigated it with varying degrees of success (often measured as personal satisfaction). Still, survivors participated in the labour market, provided professional expertise in academic institutions and business ventures, and introduced diverse national cultures and languages to postwar communities. Their contributions to Jewish communal life were immeasurable. Hassidim and *mitnagedim* survivors led a rejuvenation of reverence for Torah study and East European religious traditions in Montreal and, to a lesser degree, Toronto. They developed Jewish religious infrastructure, including comprehensive networks of religious day schools and yeshivas, synagogues, and *mikvehs*. Devout survivors' high standards with respect to *kashrut*, family purity laws, and guidelines for conversions were generally adopted by local rabbinical councils. The presence of European refugee rabbis in official community leadership influenced observant and less-observant Canadian Jews alike, too. At the same time, the arrival of thousands of Yiddish-speakers catalyzed a revival of long-forgotten or neglected traditional aspects of Jewish culture and social interaction—in a word, *Yiddishkeit*—in many established communities. Survivors of all backgrounds joined and formed mutual aid societies, social groups, and spiritual congregations. Many of these organizations remain in existence to this day, servicing second- and third-generation survivors.

Survivors are all too often seen and discussed as a monolithic group. This approach neglects the particular experiences of women, children, converts, and other individuals who do not conform to the accepted narrative. This study has broadened the analytical lens to include the experiences of these diverse communities, as well as the smaller number of refugees who had earlier found their way to late-interwar and wartime Canada.

The experiences of the few thousand late-interwar and wartime refugees who successfully penetrated Canada's tightly sealed borders remains relatively unknown. Among this cohort were central European Jews who severed their formal connections to Jewish communal life and observance in order to gain entry to Canada. Some converted after spending time in the country while others rejected all forms of organized religion and religious practice. A number of survivors who immigrated in the postwar period followed a similar path of self-imposed estrangement. Conversely, other survivors raised in secular European homes or those who felt abandoned by God sought out spirituality and organized religion as an avenue through which to explore their traumatic wartime experiences, and to establish community ties and identities in their new Canadian Jewish enclaves.

Religious identity influenced survivors' integration and helped many among them carve out new lives and places of belonging in their new surroundings. Positioning converts and apostates among survivors traces why, and how, some survivors abandoned connections to Judaism entirely while others recovered from the temporary loss of faith resulting from Holocaust experiences. Discussion of converts and apostates elucidates how wartime experiences, postwar encounters with regional and international relief organizations, and the rehabilitation process affected survivors in remarkably different ways. Drilling down on this subgroup's postwar experience not only challenges the stereotypical image of the observant, insular survivor, but also confronts the taboo subject of conversion from, and the rejection of Judaism within the Jewish community while elaborating this under-explored interdisciplinary history.

Survivors who maintained highly traditional religious principles and lifestyles also established new lives and, sometimes, distinct communities for themselves both within and outside of the confines of existing Canadian Jewish life. Traditional Eastern European Hassidic and non-Hassidic *mitnagedim* rabbis and yeshiva students, representing centuries-old dynasties, began to trickle into Canada as refugees as early as 1941 (through Shanghai). Realizing that European-style ultra-Orthodox religious infrastructures with which they were familiar did not exist in Canada, the rabbis and their students went about establishing their own network, encompassing all elements of traditional Jewish life, and extended their warm embrace of *Yiddishkeit* to the broader Jewish community. The Hassidim and *mitnagedim* survivors successfully recreated their old-world traditions in Montreal, and the community blossomed.

Where the Hassidim and *mitnagedim* ultra-Orthodox survivors chose to preserve and strengthen their traditional lifestyles by drawing other Jews into the fold, and converts and apostates withdrew from the community entirely, the overwhelming majority of survivors sought to rebuild their lives and preserve their religious traditions while attempting to integrate into the larger Jewish community. Spiritual congregations often developed out of practical considerations to accommodate the needs of particular demographics. In Toronto, two very different synagogues emerged: Clanton Park Synagogue-Kahal Machzikei Hadas, a traditional Orthodox congregation founded by survivors from across Europe, and Congregation Habonim, a liberal synagogue established by Czech, German, and Austrian Jews. These congregations helped to cement new social contacts, community and business enterprises, and familial relationships. Most importantly, they allowed survivors to preserve traditions amongst *landsleit* and others with similar national or linguistic backgrounds, and shared historical experiences.

If religious survivors tried to live amongst each other, some newcomers had little say in choosing their place of resettlement. Youngsters immigrated through the War Orphans Project, as well as through relatives' sponsorships, and with parents via labour schemes. Despite accounting for only a small number of all survivors, children and youth represented a substantial minority of early postwar Jewish refugees to Canada. Yet only War Orphan participants were treated as wartime refugees. The remaining youth were considered as merely attached to their relatives' passports, and were expected to pursue new lives as the children (or nieces and nephews) of survivors, or simply as immigrants. Social service professionals, adult survivors, and most Canadian Jews tended to pay scant attention to this youthful subgroup, presuming that they were too young to have been affected by wartime trauma. The evidence demonstrates that this perception was inaccurate, that irrespective of how they arrived in Canada, the young refugees had been affected by traumatic wartime experiences during their formative years and, as such, were bona fide Holocaust "survivors" in their own right. They experienced their own tribulations adapting to a post-Holocaust universe and integrating—or, as was frequently the case, not integrating—into seemingly inhospitable or unaccommodating Jewish enclaves across Canada. Their stories of resettlement, fostering, educational aspirations, and familial relationships illuminate the prescribed place of children in the postwar period. It also exemplifies how settlement successes positively correlated to circumstances, location, and personality; no one factor existed in isolation.

The history of Israeli transmigrants and late arrivals in the first half of the 1950s is new to the academic dialogue concerning Holocaust survivor resettlement in Canada. Members of this cohort were no strangers to the resettlement process. All had laid down roots at least once already since the end of the war, the transmigrants having done so in Israel, and other survivors in DP camps and across Europe, and in sites of wartime asylum including Shanghai and South America. Except for Western and Central Europeans who had made the conscious decision to return to their native countries as citizens, and not refugees, all had studied new languages, adapted to different cultures, and acclimatized to unfamiliar geographical environments. The groups' demographics, their process of emigration, and their life experiences stood at variance with the mostly young, able-bodied workers of the first postwar wave of survivors.

Although they represented a relatively sizable movement of approximately 10,000, these late arrivals are not recognized as distinct subgroups within the larger survivor community.[3] There are two explanations for this omission. The first relates to a lack of awareness of these groups' differentiating characteristics. Some individuals blended into the established (and establishing) survivor communities and joined friends and relatives. Others, especially Western European nationals, who entered Canada as immigrants rather than refugees, eschewed the largely Eastern European survivor enclaves and instead settled in non-Jewish neighbourhoods. Their differing postwar experiences, specifically the survivors' cohorts' return to their pre-war homes and careers, and opportunities for further education, further distinguished them from the first, earlier wave of Holocaust survivors that arrived in Canada, and thus resulted in intentional and unintentional surface divides. Moreover, some among the later arrivals did not wish to be associated with the "survivor" label, and presented themselves as non-denominational European nationals, rather than as victims of the Holocaust. In these instances, historians' oversight of this subgroup is understandable, if unfortunate.

The second explanation for Canadian Jewry's apathy toward the Israeli transmigrants related to its reluctance to come to terms with what the new immigrants represented: the failure of the nascent state of Israel to fulfil the Zionist vision of becoming the idyllic homeland for all elements of the Jewish Diaspora.

Women constitute another subgroup largely overlooked in Canadian Holocaust and immigration studies, but are highly representative among case studies and significant in their contributions to their adopted communities and country. Gender-based research reveals much about survivors' resettlement and adaptation processes, including the effects of the Holocaust on family planning and work, and social norms and values. Holocaust research usually relegates women to the private sphere as mothers, with an emphasis on family creation and re-creation as demonstrations of triumph over Nazi policy and persecution. Such discussions are not without merit: procreation and child rearing occupied an enormous place in female survivors' lives and did help shape their postwar existence. Yet, employing an analytical model based on the narrow postulation of motherhood as the females' sole identifier undermines her multiple responsibilities as wife, labourer, professional, and mother. Just as men's and women's experiences under Nazism differed, from the earliest iterations of racist legislation to physical hardships within the concentration camp system, so too did the postwar experiences of rebuilding their lives.

Female survivor immigrants to Canada engaged in all aspects of communal life. They participated in the workforce and ran burgeoning households to the best of their ability. Many did so without the guidance or support of older women such as sisters or mothers, and most lacked education or experience in child rearing or marital relations. Community professional social service workers were quick to criticize the women's occasional errors, but slow to recognize the innate challenges of balancing their new lives and growing responsibilities. Studying gendered differences in adaptation, skills, personal and professional aspirations, and family re-creation adds a new perspective to the narrative on life beyond liberation.

More than six decades after the initial flood of postwar immigration (1947–50), Holocaust survivors have left their mark on all aspects of Canadian Jewish communal life and on broader secular society, as well. The lasting legacy and accomplishments of this defined community, however, cannot be measured solely in terms of dollars, degrees, or social and religious infrastructure. Rather, from a Canadian historical perspective, the influx and absorption of approximately 35,000 Holocaust survivors, plus their dependents, in the decade immediately following the Second World War laid the groundwork for fundamental changes to Canadian immigration and refugee policy and public opinion.

Canada's discriminatory immigration policy and Canadian nativist popular attitudes in particular, had created near impenetrable walls confronting Jews seeking asylum from Nazi Germany. Nearly all of the European Jewish refugees who entered Canada between 1933 and 1947 did so either surreptitiously, disguising themselves as socially acceptable Christian agriculturalists, or through temporary war measures acts, including the internment of 2,300 German and Austrian Jewish refugees in 1940, and the Iberian Refugees movement in 1944.

Liberation and the acknowledgment of 6 million murdered Jews failed to cause a correction in national immigration policy. It would take two years, significant international pressure, and the retirement of one prime minister, Mackenzie King, and the ascension of a new one, Louis St. Laurent, before the Canadian government addressed the country's serious policy shortcomings and gradually permitted the immigration of a trickle of Holocaust survivor refugees, mostly into skilled-labour posts. And still the residual effects of anti-Jewish policy and public sentiment remained, reflected most poignantly in housing and social challenges to those who created new lives on Canadian soil.

A more humanitarian approach to international refugee relief was reflected in Canada's granting of political asylum to Hungarians fleeing their country's violent revolution only a few years after the post–Second World War Jewish refugee crisis. Beginning in December 1956 and extending through much of 1957, more than 39,000 Hungarian refugees received a historically unrivalled welcome to Canada, by way of Austria.[4] Though the estimates vary, Jews accounted for upwards of 7,000 of these Hungarian refugees; many among this group had been survivors of the Holocaust, thereby doubly displaced. Hungarian refugees were spared questions concerning their religious or ethnic affiliation and strictly enforced quotas; in fact, immigration officers at the Canadian embassy in Vienna, Austria, were forbidden to request personal information from applicants beyond their health and membership in the Communist Party. For the first time, identification as a Jew no longer indicated separate and discriminatory treatment in Canadian immigration regulations. While Jewish communities across Canada actively raised funds to resettle and help facilitate the refugees' swift integration, bureaucrats and citizens alike applauded the Canadian government's proactive response to the refugee crisis.[5] And this positive change in immigration and refugee policy proved only the beginning.

In 1960, Canada launched the Year of the Refugee and formally relaxed immigration laws alongside much of the Western world. Since then, Canada has welcomed significant migrations of French-speaking North African Jewish refugees in the 1960s and 1970s, supported the Soviet Jewish exodus in the 1970s and 1990s, and provided asylum for hundreds of thousands of refugees of all religions, backgrounds, and creeds fleeing Asia, Africa, and Latin America, primarily. Although the country's immigration and refugee policies remain imperfect, the developments witnessed since the first wave of Holocaust survivors entered Canada in the late 1940s are significant—in fact, extraordinary. Is there a direct, causal correlation between the pronounced liberalization of Canada's immigration and refugee policy—and popular support for this transformation—over the past half-century, and Canada's response to the European Jewish refugee experience during the Holocaust? No. That being said, during a particularly intense debate about whether or not Canada should admit refugees among the 1979 Vietnamese "boat people," an unnamed Canadian government minister was overheard telling his colleagues that he was not prepared to be part of "another *St. Louis.*" Such is the lasting legacy of Canada's complex relationship with the victims and survivors of the Holocaust.

# ACKNOWLEDGMENTS

Many people were involved in bringing this project to fruition, but nobody deserves more thanks than my Doktormutter, Debórah Dwork: role model, mentor, and teacher extraordinaire. She was a tireless cheerleader during my time as a doctoral student at the Strassler Center for Holocaust and Genocide Studies at Clark University, and I would not have wanted to complete this journey under anyone else's guiding light.

Frank Bialystok and Richard Menkis offered guidance and a critical eye, informing me of untapped sources and serving as community liaisons in Toronto and Vancouver, respectively. Their advice helped guide my focus and contributed immeasurably to the final product.

Margaret Hillard, Thomas Kuehne, and Mary Jane Rein stood behind my project from the beginning. Robert Melson first suggested I undertake this project, while Beth Cohen's groundbreaking research on postwar social history inspired my original research model. I offer my gratitude to my colleagues at Clark for their friendship, support, and scholarly insight during this lengthy process: Cristina Andriani, Betsy Anthony, Mikal Brotnov, Emily Dabney, Michael Geheran, Steven Heise, Alexis Herr, Stefan Ionescu, Jeffrey Koerber, Natalya Lazar, Jody Manning, Ilana Offenberger, Raz Segal, Joanna Sliwa.

In Toronto, I thank Mark and Gail Appel, Michael Brown, and Mark Webber, and my Teaching for the Future family for introducing me to the field of Holocaust and anti-racism education. Thanks, too, goes to the staff at the Vancouver Holocaust Education Centre, who offered access to important sources, critical insight, and friendship during this process.

My research took place in archives and through community agencies across Canada. A special thanks goes out to those who went above and beyond the call of duty—and their job descriptions—to help me out: Janice Rosen and Hélène Vallée at the CJCCC National Archives, Shelley Faintuch and Judy Shapiro of the Jewish Federations of Winnipeg and Calgary, respectively, and Cassidy Bankson and Jennifer Henevor at the Canadian Museum of Immigration at Pier 21.

Friends, family, and strangers warmly welcomed me into their homes. The Silvers, the Tarases, Fran Goldberg, Elissa Tepperman, and Christy Logeman made the research experience more enjoyable.

I thank David Carr at the University of Manitoba Press, for his early interest in and enthusiasm for my project. My editor Glenn Bergen provided guidance throughout the publication process, while David Larsen showed great care and thoughtfulness in marketing the final product.

My family provided me with constant love and support during this process. Shirley and Sol Goldberg's commitment to volunteerism and dedication to family and Jewish life has inspired my research and career path from day one. I know this book would have made them proud. And Jacqueline and the late Mike Rotblott believed in this project every step of the way. Thank you for your love and encouragement, Bubbie. My parents, David and Sheri Goldberg, shared ideas, sourced documents, and helped identify Holocaust survivors across the country whose stories of resettlement enliven this book. Thanks to their keen interest and determination, these narratives will not be soon forgotten. Thanks to Rebecca Moscuzza, Miranda Veltheer, and Michael and Rose Penhale for asking all the right questions. Daniel Weizenbluth pushed me to persevere and get the job done, for which I will always be grateful. Shayna Goldberg generously gave her time, critical eye, and friendship from the start. And Kevin Veltheer graciously served as a research assistant, transcriber, dog walker, housekeeper, and unwavering supporter from the beginning. Thank you for helping to make this happen.

Finally, I am grateful to the survivors who generously entrusted their stories to me. It is their voices that give meaning to these pages.

# ABBREVIATIONS

AJDC: American Jewish Joint Distribution Committee

CJC: Canadian Jewish Congress

CJCCC: Canadian Jewish Congress Charities Committee

CNCR: Canadian National Committee on Refugees and Victims of Persecution

COGC: Canadian Overseas Garment Commission

CPR: Canadian Pacific Railway

DP: Displaced person

HIAS: Hebrew Immigrant Aid Society

IRO: International Refugee Organization

JF&CS: Jewish Family and Child Services

JFCW: Jewish Family Child Welfare

JFWB: Jewish Family Welfare Bureau

JIAS: Jewish Immigrant Aid Society

JPL: Jewish Public Library

JVS: Jewish Vocational Services

LAC: Library Archives Canada

NCJW: National Council of Jewish Women

NES: National Employment Service

NYANA: New York Association for New Americans

OJA: Ontario Jewish Archives

ORT: Organization for Rehabilitation through Training

OS8: Occupational Settlement Scheme

UJRA: United Jewish Relief Agencies

UNRRA: United Nations Relief and Rehabilitation Administration

YM-WHA: Young Men-Women's Hebrew Association

# NOTES

## Introduction

1 Mary Palevsky, "Report on Survey of Jewish Refugee Settlement in Canada for the Canadian Jewish Congress," October 1949, file 2, "War Efforts, 1933–1950," CJC Papers, Canadian Jewish Congress Charities Committee National Archives (CJCCC), Montreal.

2 Ibid.

3 JIAS meeting of Board of Directors, 17 October 1948, file 23, Series 1, Fonds 9, The Joseph Kage Collection I0037, SQ, Ontario Jewish Archives (OJA), Toronto.

4 JIAS Social Services Report, 1953, J604, JIAS Fonds, CJCCC, Montreal.

5 Franklin Bialystok, *Delayed Impact: The Holocaust and the Canadian Jewish Community* (Montreal: McGill-Queen's University Press, 2000), 65.

6 Susan Garfield, interviewed by the author, 26 June and 28 October 2009, Winnipeg, MB.

7 Melvin Goldberg, interviewed by the author, 31 December 2010, Toronto, ON.

8 Canadian institutions have undertaken efforts to preserve and make public Holocaust survivor narratives. These include the Azrieli Foundation's "Azrieli Series of Holocaust Survivor Memories" (Toronto), the "CURA Project: Life Stories of Montrealers Displaced by War, Genocide, and other Human Rights Violations" (Montreal), and the Montreal Institute for Genocide and Human Rights Studies' (MIGS) "Holocaust Memoirs Project" at Concordia University (Montreal).

9 Irving Abella and Harold Troper, *None Is Too Many: Canada and the Jews of Europe 1933–1948* (Toronto: Lester & Orpen Dennys, 1983); Bialystok, *Delayed Impact*; Paula Draper, "Accidental Immigrants: Canada and the Interned Refugees" (PhD dissertation, University of Toronto, 1983); Paula Draper and Richard Menkis, eds. "New Perspectives on Canada, The Holocaust and Survivors," in *Canadian Jewish Studies*, Special Issue, vol. 4–5 (Montreal: Association for Canadian Jewish Studies, 1997); Jean Gerber, "Opening the Door: Immigration and Integration of Holocaust Survivors in Vancouver, 1947–1970" (MA thesis, University of British Columbia, 1989); Myra Giberovitch, "The Contributions of Montreal Holocaust Survivor Organizations to Jewish Communal Life" (MSW thesis, McGill University, 1998); Joseph Kage, *With Faith and Thanksgiving: The Story of Two Hundred Years of Jewish Immigration and Immigrant Aid Effort in Canada, 1790–1960* (Montreal: Eagle Publishing, 1962); Ben Lappin, *The Redeemed Children: The Story of the Rescue of War Orphans by the Jewish Community of Canada* (Toronto: University of Toronto Press, 1963); Jack Lipinsky, *Imposing Their Will: An Organizational History of Jewish Toronto, 1933–1948* (Montreal: McGill-Queen's University Press, 2011); Fraidie Martz, *Open Your Hearts: The Story of the Jewish War Orphans in Canada* (Don Mills, ON: Véhicule Press, 1996).

10 Judith E. Berman, *Holocaust Remembrance in Australian Jewish Communities, 1945-2000* (Crawley, W.A.: University of Western Australia Press, 2001); Michael Blakeney, *Australia and the Jewish Refugees, 1933-1948* (Sydney, NSW: Croom Helm Australia, 1985); Beth Cohen,

*Case Closed: Holocaust Survivors in Postwar America* (New Brunswick, NJ: Rutgers University Press, 2007); Hasia R. Diner, *We Remember with Reverence and Love: American Jews and the Myth of Silence after the Holocaust, 1945–1962* (New York, NY: New York University Press, 2009); Leonard Dinnerstein, *America and the Survivors of the Holocaust* (New York, NY: Columbia University Press, 1982); William Helmreich, *Against All Odds: Holocaust Survivors and the Successful Lives they Made in America* (New York, NY: Simon & Schuster, 1992); and Dorothy Rabinowitz, *New Lives: Survivors of the Holocaust Living in America* (New York, NY: Avon Books, 1977).

11    Judith Tydor Baumel-Schwartz, *Kibbutz Buchenwald: Survivors and Pioneers* (New Brunswick, NJ: Rutgers University Press, 1997); Sharon Kangisser Cohen, *Child Survivors of the Holocaust in Israel: "Finding Their Voice": Social Dynamics and Post-War Experiences* (Brighton, UK: Sussex Academic Press, 2005); Dina Porat, *Israeli Society, the Holocaust and Its Survivors* (Portland, OR: Vallentine Mitchell, 2008); Abram Leon Sachar, *The Redemption of the Unwanted: From the Liberation of the Death Camps to the Founding of Israel* (New York: St. Martin's Press, 1983); Hanna Yablonka, *Survivors of the Holocaust: Israel After the War* (New York: New York University Press, 1999); Idith Zertal, *From Catastrophe to Power: Holocaust Survivors and the Emergence of Israel* (Berkeley: University of California Press, 1998).

12    Simon Belkin, *Through Narrow Gates: A Review of Jewish Immigration, Colonization and Immigration Aid Work in Canada, 1840–1940* (Montreal: Canadian Jewish Congress/Jewish Colonization Association, 1966); Sonia Cancian, *Families, Lovers, and Their Letters: Italian Postwar Migration to Canada* (Winnipeg: University of Manitoba Press, 2010); Gerald E. Dirks, *Canada's Refugee Policy: Indifference or Opportunism?* (Montreal: McGill-Queen's University Press, 1977); Franca Iacovetta, Roberto Perin, and Angelo Principe, eds., *Enemies Within: Italian and Other Internees in Canada and Abroad* (Toronto: University of Toronto Press, 2000); Franca Iacovetta, *Gatekeepers: Reshaping Immigrant Lives in Cold War Canada* (Toronto: Between the Lines, 2006); Franca Iacovetta, *Such Hardworking People: Italian Immigrants in Postwar Toronto* (Montreal: Institute for Research on Public Policy, 1993); Ninette Kelley and Michael J. Trebilcock, *The Making of the Mosaic: A History of Canadian Immigration Policy* (Toronto: University of Toronto Press, 1998); Valerie Knowles, *Strangers at Our Gates: Canadian Immigration and Immigration Policy, 1540–2006* (Toronto: Dundurn Press, 2007); Hans Werner, *Imagined Homes: Soviet German Immigrants in Two Cities* (Winnipeg: University of Manitoba Press, 2007).

## Chapter One: A Door, Slightly Ajar

1    Marion A. Kaplan, *Dominican Haven: The Jewish Refugee Settlement in Sosua, 1940–1945* (New York: Museum of Jewish Heritage, 2008).

2    Michael Aronson, *Troubled Waters: The Origins of the 1881 Anti-Jewish Pogroms in Russia* (Pittsburgh: University of Pittsburgh Press, 1990), 49–58. For more on Jewish conscription into the Russian army, see Yohanan Petrovsky-Shtern, "Jews in the Russian Army, 1827–1914" (PhD dissertation, Brandeis University, 2001).

3    Robert Harney and Harold Troper, *Immigrants: A Portrait of the Urban Experience* (Toronto: Van Nostrand Reinhold, 1975); Kage, *With Faith and Thanksgiving.*

4    Gerald Tulchinsky, *Taking Root: The Origins of the Canadian Jewish Community* (Toronto: Stoddart Publishing, 1992), 249–51.

5    Irving Abella and Harold Troper, "'The Line Must Be Drawn Somewhere': Canada and Jewish Refugees, 1933–39," in *The Canadian Jewish Mosaic,* eds. William Shaffir, M. Weinfeld, and Irwin Colter (Toronto: John Wiley & Sons, 1981), 51.

6    Louis Rosenberg, *Canada's Jews: A Social and Economic Study of the Jews in Canada in the 1930s*, ed. Morton Weinfeld (Montreal: McGill-Queen's University Press, 1993), 10, 31, 33. It is noteworthy that an additional 9,273 Jews lived in the Greater Montreal Area. See Rosenberg, *Canada's Jews*, 31, and Allan Levine, *Coming of Age: A History of the Jewish People of Manitoba* (Winnipeg: Heartland Associates, 2009), 75–99.

7    A similar trend was concurrently taking place in the United States. See Daniel J. Elazar, *Community and Polity: The Organizational Dynamics of American Jewry* (Philadelphia: The Jewish Publication Society of America, 1980).

8    "Introduction" to Franklin Bialystok, *Delayed Impact: The Holocaust and the Canadian Jewish Community* (Montreal: McGill-Queen's University Press, 2000); Israel Medres, *Between the Wars: Canadian Jews in Transition*, 2nd ed., trans. Vivian Felsen (Montreal: Véhicule Press, 2003), 31–3.

9    Ira Robinson, *Rabbis and Their Community: Studies in the Eastern European Orthodox Rabbinate in Montreal, 1896–1930* (Calgary: University of Calgary Press, 2007), 12–13.

10   Gerald Tulchinsky, *Canada's Jews: A People's Journey* (Toronto: University of Toronto Press, 2008), 199–241.

11   Bialystok, *Delayed Impact*, 19.

12   Rabbi Harry Joshua Stern of Montreal's Temple Emanu-el described anti-Semitism , and the fight against it, as a timeless preoccupation among not only Jews, but also society as a whole. See Harry Joshua Stern, "Jewish Congress Goals," in *Judaism in the War of Ideas: A Collection of Addresses* (New York: Bloch Publishing, 1937), 73, as cited in Pierre Anctil, *Le rendez-vous manqué: Les juifs de Montréal face au Québec de l'entre-deux-guerres* (Montreal: Institut Québécois de Recherche sur la Culture, 1988), 282.

13   Abella and Troper, *None Is Too Many*, 5.

14   Michael Brown, *Jew or Juif? Jews, French Canadians, and Anglo-Canadians, 1759–1914* (Philadelphia: Jewish Publication Society, 1986). In Quebec, most Jews preferred to conduct business transactions and political affairs in English, not French. This said, many Québécois Jews did speak French; however, because of their political alignment with the Liberal Party, which was largely English-speaking, French nationalists labelled the Jews as anglophones and, consequently, anti-French. See Morton Weinfeld, "Quebec Anti-Semitism and Anti-Semitism in Quebec," *Post-Holocaust and Anti-Semitism* 64 (January 2008).

15   Groulx's anti-Semitism  has elicited debate among Canadian historians, and has been the subject of at least two theses: see Esther Delisle, *The Traitor and the Jew: Anti-Semitism and the Delirium of Extremist Right-Wing Nationalism in French Canada from 1929–1939* (Montreal: Robert Davies Publishing, 1993); and Ross Gordon, "The Historiographical Debate on the Charges of Anti-Semitism Made Against Lionel Groulx" (MA thesis, University of Ottawa, 1996).

16   Tulchinsky, *Canada's Jews*, 312–7. For a history of Lionel Groulx, see Esther Delisle, *Myths, Memory & Lies: Quebec's Intelligentsia and the Fascist Temptation, 1939–1960*, trans. Madeleine Hébert (Westmount, QC: Robert Davies Multimedia Publishing, 1998), 43–5, 212–25.

17   Adrien Arcand Collection, Canadian Jewish Congress Charities Committee National Archives (CJCCC), Montreal; Richard Menkis, "Anti-Semitism  in the Evolving Nation: From New France to 1950," in *From Immigration to Integration: The Canadian Jewish Experience: A Millennium Edition*, eds. Ruth Klein and Frank Dimant (Toronto: Malcolm Lester, 2001), 44.

18   Medres, *Between the Wars*, 325–8.

19    For discussion about postwar Quebec, see Elliot J. Feldman and Neil Nevitte, *The Future of North America: Canada, the United States, and Quebec Nationalism* (Lanham, MD: University Press of America, 1984); Robert Rutherdale, *Creating Postwar Canada: Community, Diversity, and Dissent, 1945–75* (Vancouver: University of British Columbia Press, 2008); and Garth Stevenson, *Community Besieged: The Anglophone Minority and the Politics of Quebec* (Montreal: McGill-Queen's University Press, 1999).

20    Janet Martin-Nielsen, "An Engineer's View of an Ideal Society: The Economic Reforms of C.H. Douglas, 1916–1920," *Spontaneous Generations* 1, no. 1 (2007), 95–109.

21    Janine Stingel, *Social Discredit: Anti-Semitism, Social Credit and the Jewish Response*, vol. 6. (Montreal: McGill-Queen's University Press, 2000), 9–31.

22    Ibid., 17–19.

23    Menkis, "Anti-Semitism in the Evolving Nation," 45–7. University quotas and anti-Jewish enrolment tactics, in addition to segregated primary school education systems, were also present in French Canada. See Pierre Anctil, "Interlude of Hostility: Judeo-Christian Relations in Quebec in the Interwar Period, 1919–1939," in *Anti-Semitism in Canada: History and Interpretation*, ed. Alan Davies (Waterloo, ON: Wilfrid Laurier University Press, 1992), 135–53.

24    For a breakdown of Jewish professions and an occupational analysis, see Rosenberg, *Canada's Jews*, 169–243.

25    Stephen Speisman, "Anti-Semitism in Ontario: The Twentieth Century," in *Anti-Semitism in Canada*, ed. Davies, 120–1.

26    Tulchinsky, *Canada's Jews*, 318–27.

27    Lita-Rose Betcherman, *The Swastika and the Maple Leaf: Fascist Movements in Canada in the Thirties* (Toronto: Fitzhenry &Whiteside, 1975); Cyril H. Levitt and William Shaffir, *The Riot at Christie Pits* (Toronto: Lester & Orpen Denys, 1987).

28    Irving Abella, *A Coat of Many Colours: Two Centuries of Jewish Life in Canada* (Toronto: Key Porter Books, 2002), 179–81.

29    Thirty-two societies were established in Winnipeg alone between 1906 and 1925; see Levine, *Coming of Age*, 109.

30    The Zionist Federation of Canada eventually came to represent the interests of Canadian Jewish Zionists, and played a significant role in lobbying for the declaration of an autonomous Jewish state in Palestine after the Balfour Declaration of 2 November 1917.

31    Gerald Tulchinsky, *Branching Out: The Transformation of the Canadian Jewish Community* (Santa Rosa, CA: Stoddart, 1998), 87–116.

32    Winnipeg and Manitoba Jews were especially ardent Zionists, leading the Canadian fundraising efforts per capita for the Jewish National Fund. For an excellent analysis of Zionism education and fundraising in Winnipeg, see Levine, *Coming of Age*, 179–91. The Balfour Declaration stated the commitment of the British government toward the establishment of a Jewish homeland in Palestine. See Zachariah Kay, *Canada and Palestine: The Politics of Non-Commitment* (Jerusalem: Israel Universities Press, 1978).

33    On Canadian Jewry's inability to move policy, see Kage, *With Faith and Thanksgiving*, 93–112.

34    Simon Belkin, *Through Narrow Gates: A Review of Jewish Immigration, Colonization and Immigration Aid Work in Canada, 1840–1940* (Montreal: Canadian Jewish Congress/Jewish Colonization Association, 1966); Kage, *With Faith and Thanksgiving*.

35    For discourse by Jewish Members of Parliament, see Abella and Troper, *None Is Too Many*, 19–26.

36    Canadian Jewry successfully secured asylum for only one group of Jewish refugees during the interwar period. This movement was spearheaded by Lillian Freiman, a major player in Canadian Jewish history, and involved the rescue of 150 Ukrainian Jewish children following the pogroms in post–First World War Soviet Union. Operating independently and not under the capacity of any central organization, Freiman and her husband, Archie, rallied legislative bodies and used their influence and close relations with government officials to bring these children to Canada in 1919 and 1920. Although this was an isolated incident, Freiman's efforts and eventual success offered hope that others might try to elicit change to rigid immigration laws. This hope became especially important with the tightening of the gates of entry in the mid-1920s, an action that would not be seriously challenged until 1947. See Bernard Figler, *Lillian and Archie Freiman* (Montreal: Northern Printing and Lithography, 1962). Postwar changes to Canada's immigration policy are the subject of Chapter 2.

37    On the Evian Conference, see Debórah Dwork and Robert Jan van Pelt, *Holocaust: A History* (New York: W.W. Norton & Company, 2002), 124–5; Martin Gilbert, *The Holocaust: A History of the Jews of Europe During the Second World War* (New York: Henry Holt & Co., 1985), 64–5; Saul S. Friedman, *A History of the Holocaust* (Middlesex, UK: Valentine Mitchell, 2004), 81–2.

38    Diary entry, 29 March 1938, MG26-J13, The Diaries of William Lyon Mackenzie King Fonds, LAC, Ottawa.

39    Abella and Troper, *None Is Too Many*, 20–2.

40    Paul R. Bartrop, "The Dominions and the Evian Conference, 1938: A Lost Chance or a Golden Opportunity?" in *False Havens: the British Empire and the Holocaust*, ed. Paul R. Bartrop (Lanham, MD: University Press of America, 1995), 54–78.

41    Kaplan, *Dominican Haven*.

42    Letter from M.A. Solkin, director of JIAS, 27 February 1939, Toronto, ON, as cited in Abella and Troper, *None Is Too Many*, 61.

43    Kenneth Craft, "Canada's Righteous: A History of the Canadian National Committee on Refugees and Victims of Political Persecution" (MA thesis, Carleton University, 1987); George M. Wrong et al. to King, 7 June 1939, 238579, William Lyon Mackenzie King Papers, LAC, Ottawa. See also communication between Jewish Liberal MP A.A. Heaps and Mackenzie King, 9 September 1938, as cited in Abella and Troper, *None Is Too Many*, 35–6.

44    Diary entry, 8 June 1939, MG26-J13, The Diaries of William Lyon Mackenzie King Fonds, LAC, Ottawa.

45    Abella and Troper, *None Is Too Many*, 8–19.

46    Lita-Rose Betcherman, *Ernest Lapointe, Mackenzie King's Great Quebec Lieutenant* (Toronto: University of Toronto Press, 2002).

47    Joe King, *From The Ghetto to The Main: The Story of the Jews of Montreal* (Montreal: Jewish Publication Society, 2000), 212.

48    Abella and Troper, "'The Line Must Be Drawn Somewhere,'" 179.

49    Sarah A. Ogilvie and Scott Miller, *Refuge Denied: The St. Louis Passengers and the Holocaust* (Madison: University of Wisconsin Press, 2006), 174–5.

50    Obituary of Walter and Jeanny Bick, *The Toronto Star*, 19 October 2011, GT7.

51    Sheri Shefra, "Pickle King Was Committed to Jewish Causes," *Canadian Jewish News*, 3 November 2011, 30.

52    Blair instructed railway colonization agents to deter the applications of prospective Jewish agriculturalists at any cost. Despite his official denial of all Jewish farmers, several hundred slipped through the cracks. See Abella and Troper, *None Is Too Many*, 16.

53   Marianne Ferguson, "Tales from My Hometown of Danzig," 2003, Ferguson Collection, Research Department, Canadian Museum of Immigration at Pier 21, Halifax, NS.

54   Marianne Echt Ferguson, interviewed by the author, 20 January 2011, Halifax, NS.

55   Ferguson, "Tales from My Hometown of Danzig."

56   Helen Waldstein Wilkes, *Letters from the Lost: A Memoir of Discovery* (Edmonton: Athabasca University Press, 2010), 51.

57   Ibid., 52.

58   Ibid., 40.

59   Ibid., 231–2.

60   Karl and Elsa Abeles' daughter, Wilma, chronicled her family's story in a joint memoir with her husband, Georg Iggers, a fellow Czech Jewish refugee. See Wilma and George Iggers, *Two Lives in Uncertain Times: Facing the Challenges of the 20th Century as Scholars and Citizens* (New York: Berghahn Books, 2006), 1–22.

61   For a full history of this movement, see Paula Jean Draper, "The Accidental Immigrants: Canada and the Interned Refugees" (PhD dissertation, University of Toronto, 1983).

62   For details on the establishment and functions of the CNCR, see Report MG28-V43, R3386-0-7-E, Canadian National Committee on Refugees Collection, 1934–1948, LAC, Ottawa, and Valerie Knowles, *Strangers at Our Gates: Canadian Immigration and Immigration Policy, 1540–2006* (Toronto: Dundurn Press, 2007), 147–8, 159–60.

63   Paula Jean Draper, "The Accidental Immigrants: Canada and the Interned Refugees: Part II," *The Canadian Jewish Historical Society Journal* 2, no. 2 (Fall 1978): 82–4.

64   Erwin Schild, *The Very Narrow Bridge: A Memoir of an Uncertain Passage* (Toronto: Adath Israel Congregation/Malcolm Lester, 2001), 233.

65   Michael Guggenheim, interview no. 34573, 1997, Visual History Archive, University of Southern California Shoah Foundation Institute (SFI), http://sfi.usc.edu/; Erwin Schild, interviewed by the author, 1 October 2009, Toronto, ON. For more on the internees' plight, visit the Vancouver Holocaust Education Centre's acclaimed online exhibition, *"Enemy Aliens": The Internment of Jewish Refugees in Canada, 1940–1943*, at http://www.enemy-aliens.ca.

66   Draper, "The Accidental Immigrants: Part II," 94–9; Schild, *The Very Narrow Bridge*, 231–7.

67   Paula Draper, conversation with the author, 29 May 2011, Fredericton, NB.

68   Draper, "The Accidental Immigrants: Part II," 98–101.

69   Interview with Michael Guggenheim, 1997, SFI.

70   Julius Pfeiffer, "From Amsterdam to Montreal for $1.25," *Jewish Life* (Montreal), July 1973, 47.

71   Ibid., 49.

72   Erwin Schild, interviewed by the author, 1 October 2009, Toronto, ON.

73   Schild, *The Very Narrow Bridge*, 249.

74   Vancouver Holocaust Education Centre, *"Enemy Aliens."*

75   Eugen Banauch, "'Home' as a Thought Between Quotation Marks: The Fluid Exile of Jewish Third Reich Refugee Writers in Canada 1940–2006" (PhD dissertation, Universität Wien, 2007); Draper, "Accidental Immigrants: Part II": Internee and Post-Internment Papers, P0224, Alfred Haiblen Fonds, CJCCC, Montreal; Eric Koch, *Deemed Suspect: A Wartime Blunder* (Halifax, NS: Goodread Biographies, 1985); and Schild, *The Very Narrow Bridge*.

76    Thomas O. Hecht, as told to Joe King, *Czech Mate: A Life in Progress* (Jerusalem: Yad Vashem, 2007), 104.

77    Ibid., 108–10.

78    The Hecht family benefited from the Czech consul's intervention on their behalf in Lisbon. In cooperation with the Land Settlement Department of Canada, the Czech government-in-exile paid for the refugees' transportation across the Atlantic, and acted as guarantors that the newcomers would not become a strain on the Canadian social welfare system. See letter from Louis Rosenberg, executive director of the CJC western division, to H.M. Caiserman, general secretary of the CJC, 24 October 1941, Winnipeg, MB, file 102, box 10, CJC ZA 1941, Sudeten German Jewish Refugees, CJCCC, Montreal.

79    Hecht, *Czech Mate*, 134.

80    Ibid., 137.

81    Ibid., 184.

82    Patrick Reed, "A Foothold in the Whirlpool: Canada's Iberian Refugee Movement" (MA thesis, Concordia University, 1996).

83    Abella and Troper, *None Is Too Many*, 170–1.

84    Gerald E. Dirks, *Canada's Refugee Policy: Indifference or Opportunism?* (Montreal: McGill-Queen's University Press, 1977), 93–8.

85    Jewish Immigrant Aid Society of Canada Report of Activities, January–October 1944, Toronto, file 19, series 1, Fonds 9, OJA, Toronto.

86    Ethel Vineberg, Survey of the Refugees by the Refugee Committee of the National Council of Jewish Women, Montreal Section, 1 November 1945, J526-Refugee Cases, CJCCC, Montreal.

87    Ibid., 2.

88    Ibid.

89    R.J.B. Bosworth, *Mussolini's Italy: Life Under the Fascist Dictatorship* (London: Penguin Books, 2007); Renzo De Felice, *The Jews in Fascist Italy: A History* (New York: Enigma Books, 2001); Aaron Gillette, *Racial Theories in Fascist Italy* (Florence, KY: Taylor & Francis, 2007); Susan Zuccotti, *The Italians and the Holocaust: Persecution, Rescue and Survival* (Lincoln, NE: University of Nebraska Press, 1996).

90    Magda Kohn Klein, interviewed by the author, 9 November 2011, Toronto, ON.

91    Ibid.

92    Ibid.

93    "B, Steven and Edith," case file, 5, RG 292, file 53, box 1, OJA, Toronto.

94    Ibid., 7.

95    Ibid., 3.

## Chapter Two: "Ordinary Survivors"

1    Anna (Szczercowska) Holtzman, interviewed by the author, 12 November 2009, Toronto, ON.

2    Ibid.

3    Bella Singer sponsored Sidney and dozens of other survivors of the Holocaust. Today, her descendants and those of her relatives represent the largest Jewish extended family in Calgary.

See *Land of Promise: The Jewish Experience in Southern Alberta* (Calgary: Jewish Historical Society of Southern Alberta, 2006), 266; and Dr. Eli Gottesman, *Who's Who in Canadian Jewry* (Montreal: The Canadian Jewish Literary Foundation for the Jewish Institute of Higher Research of the Central Rabbinical Seminary of Canada, 1965), 473. Bronia and Sidney Cyngiser, interviewed by the author, 26 October 2009, Calgary, AB.

4    Sidney Cyngiser, interview no. 6008, 1995, Visual History Archive, University of Southern California Shoah Foundation Institute (SFI), http://sfi.usc.edu/; Bronia Cyngiser, interview no. 6007, 1995, SFI.

5    Ethnic organizations, such as the Polish labour society in Toronto and the Ukrainian cultural group in Winnipeg, were charged with providing welfare and social services.

6    The War Orphans Project is discussed in Chapter 3.

7    Knowles, *Strangers at Our Gates*, 161.

8    Official Report of Debates, House of Commons, Third Session 1 May 1947, 2644-6, LAC, Ottawa.

9    For more about the politics of the schemes, see Abella and Troper, *None Is Too Many*, 190–237.

10    Untitled document, 7 March 1947, CA Series Tailors Project 1947, CJC Central Files, CJCCC, Montreal.

11    Pregnancy or the presence of young children was grounds for rejection, since the children would require care that a working mother could not provide. This did not pose as great a concern if children were of school age, or if a highly skilled father was present. For more on motherhood and work, see Chapters 8 and 9.

12    UNRRA transferred authority for the daily operations of DP camps to the temporary Allied occupying forces shortly after establishment in postwar Europe. On Canada's involvement in UNRRA, see Susan E. Armstrong-Reid, *Armies of Peace: Canada and the UNRRA Years* (Toronto: University of Toronto Press, 2008).

13    Non-negotiable qualifiers resulted in the rejection of many survivors. See Louise W. Holborn, *The International Refugee Organization: A Specialized Agency of the United Nations, Its History and Work, 1946–1952* (London: Oxford University Press, 1956).

14    Letter from Saul Hayes, executive director of the CJC, to Norman Genser, COGC, 22 February 1949, Montreal, QC, file 300T, box 31, Garment Workers Project 1947–1950, CJC Central Files, CJCCC, Montreal.

15    "Sponsorship of Immigrant Movements to Canada," CJC I.O.I. Bulletin V, 1 June 1948. CJC Fonds, CJCCC, Montreal..

16    Jews who emigrated from the United States were also included in these statistics.

17    Joseph Kage, "The Jewish Immigrant Aid Services of Canada (JIAS)," in *Canadian Jewish Reference Book and Directory*, ed. Eli Gottesman (Ottawa: Mortimer Limited, 1963), 249.

18    Marianne Ferguson, "Tales From My Hometown of Danzig," 2003, Ferguson Collection, Research Department, Canadian Museum of Immigration at Pier 21, Halifax, NS.

19    Carrie-Ann Smith, "The Reunion," undated, Research Department, Canadian Museum of Immigration at Pier 21, Halifax, NS.

20    For a history of North American social work, see John Ehrenreich, *The Altruistic Imagination: A History of Social Work and Social Policy in the United States* (Ithaca, NY: Cornell University Press, 1985); Therese Jennisen, *One Hundred Years of Social Work: A History of the Profession in English Canada, 1900–2000* (Waterloo, ON: Wilfrid Laurier University Press, 2011); and

Stanley Wenocur, *From Charity to Enterprise: The Development of American Social Work in a Market Economy* (Urbana: University of Illinois Press, 1989).

21  Jennisen, *One Hundred Years of Social Work*, 212–15.

22  Service Standards, undated, file 16, vol. 22, MG 28, I 441, LAC, Ottawa (cited in Jennisen, *One Hundred Years of Social Work*, 33).

23  Joseph Kage, "24 Casework Principles in Short Term Contact," undated, J608 Social Welfare Needs of Immigrants, CJCCC, Montreal; Meeting of JURA staff, 29 June 1949, Toronto, ON, file 4, box 1, RG 286 Ontario Jewish Archives (OJA), Toronto.

24  Jean Tweed, "Security, Not Paternalism, Behind Aid to Immigrant," *Saturday Night* (Toronto), 13 March 1948), 6. The community organizations expressed concern for the newcomers' feelings. At a meeting of JIAS executives, it was noted that "all future reference to new arrivals [should] be referred to as 'New Canadians' rather than DPs, which the immigrants feel as slightly slanderous"; JIAS Canada meeting of Board of Directors, 7 December 1948, file 23, Series 1, Fonds 9, OJA, Toronto.

25  Benjamin Schlesinger, interview no. 37516,1996, SFI.

26  Molly (Harrendorf) Bainerman, interviewed by the author, 26 October 2011, Thornhill, ON.

27  Minutes of Housing Committee meeting, 13 May 1949, Toronto, ON, file 9, box 1, RG 286, UJRA Central Executive Minutes, OJA, Toronto.

28  The War Orphans Project is the subject of the following chapter.

29  "G, Moritz and Irene," JIAS Immigration Case File Series CA, CJCCC, Montreal.

30  Letter from Joseph Shapiro, partner at Robinson and Shapiro Advocates, to Saul Hayes, director of the CJC, 13 November 1947, CJCCC, Montreal.

31  Mary Palevsky, "Report on Survey of Jewish Refugee Settlement in Canada for the Canadian Jewish Congress," 28, October 1949, file 2, "War Efforts, 1933–1950," CJC Papers, Canadian Jewish Congress Charities Committee National Archives (CJCCC), Montreal.

32  CJC I.O.I. Bulletin VII, 14 January 1949. CJC Fonds, CJCCC, Montreal.

33  Ibid.; Sarah Miller, "Immigration: Dinah Lily Caplan Social Service Group," *JIAS Record* (Montreal) 1, no. 2, October, 1948, 12.

34  Letter from H. Frank, executive director of the western branch of the CJC, to W. Friedman, COGC, 27 October 1948, file 27, box 31, Needle Trade 1948, CJC Central Files, CJCCC, Montreal.

35  Letter from Charles Walfish, chairman of the CJC B.C. branch, to CJC national executive-director Saul Hayes, 23 January 1948, file 21, box 31, Needle Trade 1948, CJC Central Files, CJCCC, Montreal.

36  Joseph Kage, "A Helping Hand to the Newcomers," *JIAS Record* (Montreal) 1, no. 2, October 1948, 6–7.

37  Former Jewish Vocational Service worker, interviewed by the author, 14 March 2010, Montreal, QC; Letter from Dr. M. Wolochow to Saul Hayes, 14 February 1950, Calgary, AB, file "Anna CB," Series CB, UJRA Collection—War Orphans, CJCCC, Montreal.

38  "Aron H." case file, 1, RG 292, file 309, box 3, OJA, Toronto.

39  Ibid.

40  This protocol of non-interference applied to all labour sponsorship schemes, but was most often brought up in cases of farmers and other manual labourers. See letter to Edna Keller from Manfred Saalheimer, CJC memorandum, 9 January 1950, Montreal, QC, file 555, box 1, RG 292, OJA, Toronto.

41 Rebeka Bialystok Zloto, testimony no. 27, 1990, The Testimony Project, The Holocaust Centre of Toronto.

42 Ibid.

43 Joseph Kage, "The JIAS Evening School," *JIAS Record* (Montreal) I, no. 6, February 1946, 2.

44 Palevsky, "Report on Survey of Jewish Refugee Settlement in Canada for the Canadian Jewish Congress," 26–31.

45 Tweed, "Security, Not Paternalism," 7.

46 Palevsky, "Report on Survey of Jewish Refugee Settlement in Canada for the Canadian Jewish Congress," 5.

47 Ibid, 7.

48 Paula J. Draper, "Canadian Holocaust Survivors: From Liberation to Rebirth," in Paula J. Draper and Richard Menkis, eds., *New Perspectives on Canada, The Holocaust and Survivors*, Canadian Jewish Studies Special Issue Volumes 4-5 (Montreal: Association for Canadian Jewish Studies, 1996-1997): 50; Faye Schulman, interview conducted by author, 25 July 2008, Toronto, ON.

49 Howard Chandler, a Holocaust survivor and member of the Wierzbniker Friendly Mutual Benefit Society, interviewed by the author, 20 October 2010, Toronto, ON.

50 Bainerman, interview.

51 Lola Olmer, interviewed by the author, June 2007, Thornhill, ON.

52 Ibid.

53 Bainerman, interview.

54 Minutes of the meeting of the Executive Committee of the Societies Division, 15 February 1949, Toronto, ON, file 1, box 1, RG 265, OJA, Toronto.

55 Abe and Margot Zukerman, "Margot & Abe Zuckerman," accessed 13 September 2011 at the *Jewish Foundation of Greater Toronto: Book of Life*, http://www.feduja.org/bookoflife/story_Zukerman-Margot&Abe.php.

56 Ibid.

57 Obituary for Abram (Abe) Zukerman, 2009, Steeles Memorial Chapel (Toronto, ON), accessed 31 October 2011, http://www.steelesmemorialchapel.com/condolence_prt.html?fid=2454871.4294213.

58 Minutes of the meeting..., 15 February 1949, OJA.

59 Minutes of the meeting of the Executive Committee of the Societies Division, Toronto, ON, 2 January 1949, file 1, box 1, RG 265, OJA, Toronto.

60 "B'nai B'rith: Final Phase of Membership Drive," *The Jewish Western Bulletin* (Vancouver), 20 May 1948, 7.

61 Henry Weingluck Fonds, OJA, Toronto.

62 "Toronto News," *The Canadian Jewish Review* (Montreal), 26 November 1948, 15.

63 Candice Lichtman, "At 70, Artist Shows no Sign of Slowing Down," *The Canadian Jewish News* (Toronto), 15 September 1972, 5; Eli Rubenstein, telephone conversation with the author, 15 November 2011, Toronto, ON.

64 *JIAS record* (Montreal), April 1949, collection of the author.

65 Joseph Riesenbach, interviewed by the author, 28 June 2009, Winnipeg, MB.

66 Belle Millo, ed., *Voices of Winnipeg Holocaust Survivors* (Winnipeg: Jewish Heritage Centre of Western Canada, 2010), 290.

67    Riesenbach, interview.

68    Ibid.

69    Draper, "Canadian Holocaust Survivors," 55.

70    Pola C, interview, 21 March 2003, Research Department, Canadian Museum of Immigration at Pier 21, Halifax, NS.

71    Ibid.

72    Judy Weissenberg Cohen, interviewed by the author, 6 March 2006, Toronto, ON.

73    Judy Weissenberg Cohen, interviewed by the author, 13 December 2005, Toronto, ON.

74    Weissenberg Cohen, interview, 6 March 2006.

75    David S, interview no. 82, 1987, Oral History Testimony Project, Vancouver Holocaust Education Centre, Vancouver, BC.

76    Anita Shafran, interviewed by the author, 1 March 2013, Vancouver, BC.

## Chapter Three: The War Orphans Project

1    Diary of Zsuzanna Loeffler (Susan Garfield), September 1948. Private diary.

2    Ibid., 2.

3    Child survivors who immigrated to Canada under other auspices shared in these emotional and physical upheavals. Their experiences are the subject of Chapter 4.

4    The history of the War Orphans Project has received attention in two landmark studies by social workers Ben Lappin and Fraidie Martz; Lappin, in *The Redeemed Children: The Story of the Rescue of War Orphans by the Jewish Community of Canada* (Toronto: University of Toronto Press, 1963), which was commissioned by the CJC as a follow-up to measure the project's success. Lappin based his findings on questionnaires distributed amongst orphans resettled in Toronto, now adults with families of their own, as well as through community social service reports. His results illuminated the newcomers' high degree of self-sufficiency and integration. The study looked at the group as a whole; it placed little emphasis on the individuals themselves. Martz's *Open Your Hearts: The Story of the Jewish War Orphans in Canada* (Don Mills, ON: Véhicule Press, 1996), undertaken nearly forty years later, included an in-depth discussion of the background of the project, social service reports, clippings from newspapers, and interviews with the survivors.

5    Abella and Troper, *None Is Too Many*, 111–17.

6    The Allied invasion of Vichy-held French North Africa, known as Operation Torch, began on 8 November 1942. See Orr Kelly, *Meeting the Fox: The Allied Invasion of Africa, from Operation Torch to Kasserine Pass to Victory in Tunisia* (Hoboken, NJ: Wiley, 2002).

7    Order-in-Council, P.C. 1647, Ottawa, 29 April 1947, Ca Children's Movement. CJCCC, Montreal.

8    Lappin, *The Redeemed Children*, 10–14.

9    Fischer later immigrated to Canada and undertook studies in social work; see Martz, *Open Your Hearts*, 76–107. Fischer's UNRRA contributions are well documented in Anna Andlauer, *The Rage to Live: The International D.P. Children's Center Kloster Indersdorf 1945–1946* (CreateSpace Independent Publishing Platform, 2012).

10    Lappin, *The Redeemed Children*, 12–21.

11    Fewer visas were reserved for youth residing in western and northern Europe. The one exception was France, since high numbers of Eastern European–born child survivors were sent there

for rehabilitation. Orphans resettled in the West were in relatively comfortable situations, and removed from the communist activities threatening Jews further east. The less stable the orphans' situations, the better their chances of being included in the immigration project. See the communication files from the Jewish Refugee Committee, based in London, with the UJRA/CJC reps in Canada, concerning immigrant resettlement, case file "Lottie Levinson, AJDC emigration officer, 1948," box 26, UJRA Collection–War Orphans Project, CJCCC, Montreal. See also Jewish Family and Child Welfare Bureau Reports, 1948–1949, ZA 1948-7-84. CJC Fonds, CJCCC, Montreal. For more about the younger war orphans discovered in Belgium more than two years after liberation, see "Cases from Belgium, 1947–1948," box 25, UJRA Collection–War Orphans Project, CJCCC, Montreal.

12   Martz, *Open Your Hearts*, 91–6.

13   Alex (Sruli) Berkowits, interviewed by the author, 29 June 2009, Winnipeg, MB; letter from Ethel Ostry-Genkind to Dr. M. Saalheimer re: Israel (Sruli) Berkovitch [sic], Canadian Immigration for European Children–Poiro Area Team 7, Germany, 27 January 1948, box 25, CA Administrative Structure, establishment of 1947–1948, UJRA Collection–War Orphans Project, CJCCC, Montreal.

14   Leslie Spiro, interviewed by the author, 22 June 2009, Vancouver, BC.

15   Sharon Kangisser Cohen, *Child Survivors of the Holocaust in Israel: "Finding Their Voice:" Social Dynamics and Post-War Experiences* (Brighton, UK: Sussex Academic Press, 2005), 6.

16   Lappin, *The Reedemed Children*, 10–21.

17   Nazi proclamations did not stop youth from learning. Ghetto schools taught by renowned scholars, religious and Zionist studies, and skill training for life in Palestine frequently operated illegally. For more examples of education in ghettos and camps, see, inter alia, Hannelore Brenner, *The Girls of Room 28: Friendship, Hope, and Survival in Theresienstadt* (New York: Schocken Books, 2009); Debórah Dwork, *Children With A Star: Jewish Youth in Nazi Europe* (New Haven, CT: Yale University Press, 1991); and S.L. Schneiderman, ed., *The Diary of Mary Berg: Growing up in the Warsaw Ghetto*, 2nd ed. (Oxford: Oneworld Publications, 2006).

18   Joseph Lazarus, untitled report on orphans progress, undated, box 25, Administration, UJRA Collection–War Orphans Project, 1948-1950, CJCCC, Montreal.

19   "Report: Special meeting convened to clarify the function of the Education Committee of the Youth Refugee Project," 3 November 1947, box 25, Education Committee–Youth Refugees Project 1947–1948, UJRA Collection–War Orphans Project, CJCCC, Montreal; Various memos from Jean Henshaw, JFCW, to Minda Posen, July 1949, box 25, Education 1948–1950, UJRA Collection–War Orphans Project, CJCCC, Montreal.

20   Subject files, 1948, box 26, Emergency Homefinding Committee, UJRA Collection–War Orphans Project, CJCCC, Montreal.

21   Ibid.; Martz, *Open Your Hearts*, 67–75.

22   Paul Herczeg, interviewed by the author, 19 August 2009, Montreal, QC.

23   A few copies of the paper can be found in box 1, ZC YM-YWHA, Jewish Public Library, Montreal, QC. See also Lappin, *The Redeemed Children*, 129–31.

24   Anna Sheftel and Stacey Zembrzycki, "'We Started Over Again, We Were Young': Postwar Social Worlds of Holocaust Survivors in Montreal," *Urban History Review/Revue d'histoire urbaine* 39, no. 1 (2010): 23–4.

25   Letter from Mrs. Ethel Webber to Manfred Saalheimer interpreting the adjustment of "new Canadians" in Nova Scotia, 7 July 1948, box 26, Maritimes 1947–1948, UJRA Collection–War Orphans Project, CJCCC, Montreal.

26    Case file on Roman (Rubin) Ziegler, box 26, Maritimes 1947-1948, UJRA Collection—War Orphans Project, CJCCC, Montreal.

27    Roman Ziegler, interviewed by the author, 4 March 2006, Toronto, ON.

28    Letter from Manfred Saalheimer to Ethel Webber, 23 August 1948, box 26, Maritimes 1947–1948, UJRA Collection–War Orphans Project, CJCCC, Montreal. A few cases succeeded elsewhere in the Maritimes, including Blanca and Celie (Blanche Jacobs and Cecilia Halzel) Lakner, Romanian-born sisters adopted by Noa and Sarah Heinish, leaders in the Halifax Jewish community. See interview with Blanca Jacobs and Celie Halzel, 15 July 1998, Research Department, Canadian Museum of Immigration at Pier 21, Halifax, NS. See also the biographical sketch of Noa Heinish in National Executive of the Canadian Jewish Congress notes, Montreal, QC, 6 December 1962, and the letter from Noa Heinish to Benjamin Robinson, 13 February 1948, Montreal, QC, both found in MG 20 Vol. 1603, Noa Heinish Collection, Nova Scotia Archives and Records Management, Halifax, NS.

29    Opportunities for religious youth are discussed later in the chapter.

30    Herczeg, interview.

31    Ibid.

32    Tibor (Ted) Bolgar, interviewed by the author, 18 August 2009, Montreal, QC.

33    Ibid.

34    Herczeg, interview.

35    Report of Federated Jewish Women, October 1939 to March 1946 by Mrs. Jean Rose, president of Federated Jewish Women, to undetermined recipient undated, Jean Rose Fonds, Vancouver Holocaust Education Centre (VHEC), Vancouver.

36    Report from Mrs. Jean Rose, chairman of the Coordinating Committee on War Orphans, to undetermined recipient, on the progress of orphans in Vancouver, BC, 31 January 1951, Jean Rose Fonds, VHEC, Vancouver.

37    Ibid.

38    A total of 798 war orphans were originally resettled in Toronto and Montreal. The remainder was dispersed among Jewish communities in the Maritimes and in the west, with the bulk of approximately 230 landing in Winnipeg and its surrounding regions. Interview with (former) JIAS social worker, conducted by the author, 23 October 2009, Winnipeg, MB. List of war orphans to western division, undated, JIAS Winnipeg files, accessed 23 October 2009, Jewish Child and Family Services, Winnipeg, MB.

39    The Pacific region of the CJC was established in Vancouver in 1949.

40    "D.P.'s Find New Life at Y," *Y.M.H.A. Review,* Anniversary Edition (Winnipeg) 12, no. 6 (March 1948): 1–4; "Letter to the Editor," *Y.M.H.A. Review* (Winnipeg) 13, no. 1 (January 1949); Alex (Sruli) Berkowits, interviewed by the author, 23 June 2009, Winnipeg, MB; Aron Eichler, interviewed by the author, 27 October 2009, Calgary, AB; Barbara Goszer, interviewed by the author, 22 October 2009, Winnipeg, MB; Robbie Waisman, interviewed by the author, 31 January 2013, Vancouver, BC; Elliot and Minnie Zuckier, interviewed by the author, 27 October 2009, Calgary, AB.

41    Loeffler (Garfield) diary, 27–30.

42    Susan Garfield, telephone conversation with the author, 5 November 2010, Toronto, ON.

43    Letter from Anna to Saul Hayes, executive director of the CJC, 15 January 1950, Calgary, AB, file "Anna B.," UJRA Series CB, CJCCC, Montreal.

44    Letter from Esther Goresh, Calgary War Orphans Committee member, to H. Frank, executive director of the CJC, western division, 7 July 1949, file "Anna B.," UJRA Series CB, CJCCC, Montreal.

45    Letter from Dr. Dezso (Anna's uncle) to the CJC, 17 June 1949, Budapest, Hungary, file "Anna B.," UJRA Series CB, CJCCC, Montreal.

46    Susan surmised that the Kleins' genuine fondness and protectiveness for her, and the fear of embarrassment if the placement failed, motivated their actions to retain her.

47    Loeffler (Garfield) diary, 10.

48    Susan revealed later that those dates were more than ordinary outings. Oscar Kirshner, interviewed by the author, 26 October 2009, Calgary, AB.

49    Letter from Anna to Saul Hayes, 15 January 1950, file "Anna B.," UJRA Series CB, CJCCC, Montreal.

50    Letter from Dr. M. Wolochow to Saul Hayes, 14 February 1950, Calgary, AB, file "Anna B.," UJRA Series CB, CJCCC, Montreal.

51    Susan Garfield, interviewed by the author, 26 June 2009, Winnipeg, MB.

52    Ibid.

53    Jack Kuper, *After the Smoke Cleared* (Toronto: Stoddart Publishing, 1994); Anita Weiner, *Expanding Historical Consciousness: The Development of the Holocaust Educational Foundation* (Skokie, IL: Holocaust Educational Foundation, 2002), 4–10. The latter includes the story of Zev Theodore Weiss, a war orphan originally resettled in Montreal, who immigrated to the United States in the 1950s and later spearheaded the Holocaust Educational Foundation.

54    The breakdown of the fifty-two war orphans to leave Winnipeg is as follows: 16 to Montreal; 14 to Toronto; 3 to Hamilton; 12 to other parts of western Canada, primarily Vancouver and Calgary; 3 to the United States; 2 to Israel; 1 returned to Europe; and 1 to an unknown destination. See the list of war orphans to western division, undated, JIAS office, Winnipeg, MB, and the list of URO cases, 3 March 2003, JIAS office, Winnipeg, MB.

55    A handful of the orphans who left Winnipeg later returned. Alex Berkowits, for instance, travelled to Saskatchewan for employment and remained there for several years. After marrying his Canadian-born wife, Sandra, the couple relocated to Winnipeg and raised four children.

56    Progress Report, undated, file "Bernat M.," 1. UJRA Series CB, CJCCC, Montreal.

57    Lappin, *The Redeemed Children,* 57–60. The CJC's Noa Heinish arranged for all transports arriving on the eve of major holidays to remain in Halifax for the duration. As the official greeter for JIAS at Pier 21, Meta Echt helped orchestrate the (mainly) boys' stays; Marianne Ferguson, interviewed by the author, 20 January 2011, Halifax, N.S, and Marianne Ferguson, "Tales From my Hometown of Danzig," 2003, Research Department, Canadian Museum of Immigration at Pier 21, Halifax, NS. See also the Noa Heinish Collection, MG 20 Vol. 1609, Nova Scotia Archives and Records Management, Halifax, NS.

58    CJC I.O.I. Bulletin Vol, 26 July 1948. CJC Fonds, CJCCC, Montreal.

59    A CJC I.O.I. summary dated 26 June 1949 describes the arrival of the group in Montreal: "We provided temporary accommodation at our War Orphans Reception Centre in Montreal for 15 Yeshiva students from Rome, Italy, who arrived July 25th. The group (Maor Hagolah) will have permanent quarters at a newly purchased house which was provided by its leadership. Another 7 students are to come at a later date; the group also includes three rabbinical families which arrived jointly with the 15 students. Upon termination of our using the Reception Cen-

tre for war orphans, the Federation of Jewish Philanthropies which owns the premises, agreed to our directing immigrants to the Centre for temporary accommodations as the needs may arise and in accordance with these arrangements, we placed the Yeshiva group at the Centre." CJC Fonds, CJCCC, Montreal.

60   All orphans seeking financial support from the service agencies were subjected to similar subjective tests.

61   CJC I.O.I. Bulletin, Vol. 586, 3 March 1949. CJC Fonds, CJCCC, Montreal.

62   Yitel Nechamah Bineth, interviewed by the author, 22 August 2010, Montreal, QC.

63   Letter from H. Frank to M. Saalheimer, October 1948, Winnipeg, MB, file "Bernard K.," UJRA Series CB, CJCCC, Montreal.

64   List of war orphans to western division, undated, JIAS office, Winnipeg, MB.

## Chapter Four: *"I Remain Its Reluctant Child"*

* Chapter title is taken from Ruth Kluger, *Still Alive: A Holocaust Girlhood Remembered* (New York: The Feminist Press at the City University of New York, 2001), 60.

1   Elly Bollegraaf, interview no. 16821, 1996, Visual History Archive, University of Southern California Shoah Foundation Institute (SFI), http://sfi.usc.edu/.

2   Ernie Paine, "Kept Hidden in Box, Boy Finds Home Here," *Toronto Daily Star*, 17 April 1948, News Section, 2.

3   Case report by AJDC worker, Case No. 2283E, in response to request for information on Mendel Gwiazda by the Canadian Jewish Congress Children's Home, 9 August 1947, Otwock, Poland, 1.

4   Melvin Goldberg (Mendel Gwiadza), interviewed by the author, 31 December 2010, Toronto, ON; "Mendele's New Home," *JIAS Record* (Montreal) I, no. 5, January 1949, 5.

5   Paine, "Kept Hidden in Box, Boy Finds Home Here," 2.

6   Carmela Finkel, interviewed by the author, 18 October 2009, Winnipeg, MB; Leon Shragge, interview no. 12457, 1995, SFI.

7   The challenging re-education of Jewish children who survived the Holocaust in Christian homes and institutions is the subject of Nachum Bogner, *At the Mercy of Strangers: The Rescue of Hidden Jewish Children in Poland* (Jerusalem: Yad Vashem Publications, 2009).

8   Robert Krell, interviewed by the author, 2 May 2013, Vancouver, BC.

9   Bogner, *At the Mercy of Strangers*; Emunah Nachmany Gafny, *Dividing Hearts: The Removal of Jewish Children from Gentile Families in Poland in the Immediate Post Holocaust Years* (Jerusalem: Yad Vashem, 2009); Alex Grobman, *Battling for Souls: The Vaad Hatzala Rescue Committee in Post-Holocaust Europe* (Jersey City, NJ: KTAV Publishing House, 2004).

10   The JIAS Clothing Centre of Montreal Clothing Room was run nearly entirely by local women's organizations, including the Council of Jewish Women, the sisterhoods of Temple Emanuel and Shaare Hashomayim congregations, and the Junior Welfare League. These women ran the centre's daily activities, helped collect and sort clothes, and serve the newcomer clientele. See *JIAS Record* (Montreal) 1, no. 8, April 1949, 4.

11   "Isador S.," 3, file 701, box 6, RG292, JIAS Immigration Case Files Series CA, OJA, Toronto.

12   Ibid., 4.

13   "Leah M.," 2, box 5, JIAS Immigration Case Files Series CA, OJA, Toronto.

14   Anonymous child survivor, interviewed by the author by telephone, 9 February 2009.

15    Robert Krell, "Hiding During and After the War," in *Childhood Survivors: Memories and Reflections,* ed. Robert Krell (Victoria, BC: Trafford Publishing, 2007), 33–9.

16    Marion Cassirer, Yom Hashoah keynote address, Vancouver Holocaust Education Centre, 8 April 2013, Vancouver, BC.

17    Haim Dasberg, "Children of the Holocaust: Now and Then," in Krell, ed., *Childhood Survivors,* 55–60.

18    Lillian Boraks Nemetz and Rachel Bernardo, interviewed by the author, 13 February 2013, Vancouver, BC.

19    Ellen (De Jonge) Tissenbaum, interview no. 25034, 1996, SFI.

20    Ibid. "Home Study of Little Holland," from M. Jean Henshaw, supervisory at the Family Welfare Department and Jewish Child Welfare Bureau of the Baron de Hirsch Institute, to Dr. Manfred Saalheimer, CJC, 15 June 1949, box 30, Special Case Files CB 02, 1949-1950, UJRA Collection–War Orphans Project, CJCCC, Montreal.

21    Ibid.

22    Etti Blitz Miller, interviewed by the author, 7 January 2011, Toronto, ON.

23    Ibid.

24    Etti Blitz Miller, email correspondence with the author, 29 July 2008.

25    Sidney Zoltak, interviewed by the author, 4 May 2010, Montreal, QC. Sidney's mother remarried a Polish survivor in Montreal.

26    Ibid.

27    Sidney Zoltak recounts his experiences holistically in his newly released memoir, *My Silent Pledge: A Journey of Struggle, Survival and Remembrance* (Toronto: MiroLand, 2013).

28    Mark and Edith Nusbaum, correspondence with author, 12 March 2013.

29    International passports and guarantees for Central and South American countries were sold by Jewish collaborators at Hotel Polski and came from Switzerland. The Gestapo most likely profited from these transactions. Palestinian certificates came from the Palestine Agency in Istanbul at the behest of AJDC leader David Guzik. Palestinian certificates were free or sold for a pittance; Agnieszka Haska, email correspondence with the author, 15–6 November 2011. See also: Collections file 6001–Hotel Polski, Beit Lohamei Haghetaot—Ghetto Fighters House Archives; Agnieszka Haska, "Adam Żurawin, a Hero of a Thousand Faces," *Holocaust. Studies and Materials,* no. 1 (Warsaw: Association Polish Center for Holocaust Research & IFiS PAN Publishing House, 2008), 123–146; Abraham Shulman, *Case of Hotel Polski: An Account of One of the Most Enigmatic Episodes of World War II* (New York: Holocaust Library, 1982); Yitzhak Zuckerman and Barbara Harshav, *A Surplus of Memory: Chronicle of the Warsaw Ghetto Uprising* (Berkeley: University of California Press, 1993), 441–445.

30    Mark Nusbaum, interviewed by the author, 9 November 2009, Toronto, ON. Mark, his mother, and brother are listed on the so-called Weiss list, a list of 349 Polish Jews held in protective custody at Bergen-Belsen in 1944; see Izaak Lewin, "Przez pryzmat historii" (Warsaw: Jewish Historical Institute, 1994), 4.

31    Mark Nusbaum, telephone conversation with the author, 28 November 2009, Toronto, ON.

32    Mark Nusbaum, interviewed by the author, 9 November 2009, Toronto, ON.

## Chapter Five: Keeping the Faith

1    Miriam Frankel, interviewed by the author, 6 October 2010, Toronto, ON.

2    Hendel Fasten, interviewed by the author, 20 August 2010, Montreal, QC.

3   This study borrows contemporary historian Steven Lapidus's definition of Hassidism: "The term Hasid or Hasidic refers specifically and uniquely to the formal Hasidic movement—the religious revival movement that began in eighteenth century Ukraine with Israel Bal Shem Tov and that is characterized by deference to charismatic leadership, the belief in daily union with the Divine, and a distinct liturgy, all of which set Hasidim apart from other traditionalist or Orthodox Jews." Steven Lapidus, "The Forgotten Hasidim: Rabbis and Rebbes in Pre-war Canada," *Canadian Jewish Studies* 12 (2004), 22. See also William Shaffir, *Life in a Religious Community: The Lubavitcher Chassidim in Montreal* (Montreal: Holt, Rhinehart and Winston of Canada, 1974), 57.

4   Fasten, interview; Yitel Nechamah Bineth, interviewed by the author, 22 August 2010, Montreal, QC. It is important to recognize that Hungarian and Polish Jews were not universally familiar with Jewish traditions, nor raised in observant Jewish households. Even traditional Jews were substantially acculturated or exposed to secular norms.

5   Gutwirth's research, while monumental, remains controversial among Jewish Studies scholars largely due to his arguments about the dispersion and practice of Hassidism prior to the Second World War. In particular, Gutwirth posits that Canada, and Montreal in particular, was entirely bereft of Hassidim before the Second World War, a claim proven false by Ira Robinson and Steven Lapidus, who have presented evidence of a small, yet active, Hassidic population in the interwar period. Jacques Gutwirth, "Hassidim et Judaicité à Montréal," *Recherches Sociographiques* 14 (1973), 291.

6   Shaffir, *Life in a Religious Community*, 12.

7   Max Bookman, "Orthodox, Conservative and Reform Congregations," in *Canadian Jewish Reference Book and Directory,* ed. Eli Gottesman (Ottawa: Mortimer Limited, 1963), 228, 230.

8   See Rosenberg, *Canada's Jews.*

9   Jacques Gutwirth, "Hassidism and Urban Life," *Jewish Journal of Sociology* 38 (1996), 107.

10  Esther Farbstein, *Hidden in Thunder: Perspectives on Faith, Halachah and Leadership during the Holocaust,* vol. 1 (Jerusalem: Old City Press, 2007), 54.

11  In an interview years after his arrival, Rabbi Pinchas Hirschprung, one of the yeshiva refugees and later the Chief Rabbi of Montreal, stressed the impact of the Hassidim, particularly the Lubavitchers, on Jewish life in Montreal: "It later turned out that it was precisely the young, bearded Lubavitchers who disseminated Judaism in the city, and helped build its Jewish character, and helped create harmony among the Jews of the city.... As it turns out, all the [Judaism] in Montreal today is the result of the selfless work of Lubavitch, which built up the city's Torah infrastructure"; see Reb Shalom Ber Wolpo, "The Gaon: Rabbi Pinchas Hirschprung Z"L," accessed 21 August 2010 at *Chabad Info,* http://www.chabad.info. Rabbi Leib Baron wrote that "the Canadian Jewish community also witnessed a Torah rejuvenation when a group of Yeshiva students set foot on Canadian soil in 1942 [sic: 1941]"; see Leib Baron, "Origin of Yeshivas in Canada" in *Canadian Jewish Reference Book and Directory,* 243.

12  Vaad Hatzala (Committee for Rescue): Major Jewish Orthodox organization for rescue, relief & religious rehabilitation among war-torn Jewry, 1946, CJC box 23, Vaad Hatzala Committee for Rescue, 1943–1948 Collection, CJCCC, Montreal.

13  Memorandum on Vaad Hatzala from the Council of Jewish Federations and Welfare Funds, National Office (165 West 46 Street, New York); CJC box 23, Vaad Hatzala Committee for Rescue, 1943–1948, 1, 4, CJCCC, Montreal.

14  Vaad Hatzala (Committee for Rescue), 3–4, CJCCC, Montreal.

15  Untitled public announcement by the UJRA, 15 July 1942, CJC box 23, Yeshiva Students Maintenance 1941–1946, CJCCC, Montreal.

16    Untitled documents, Rabbinical College of Canada Tomche Tmimim Collection, Yeshivoth Conference on Jewish Material Claims Against Germany Collection, 1953–1958, box 63–64, CJCCC, Montreal. For details on the re-establishment of the Mirrer Yeshiva, see Chaim U. Lipschitz, with Sonia Winter, Hallie Cantor, and Judy Bendet, eds., *The Shanghai Connection* (New York: Maznaim Publishing, 1988).

17    Most Hassidic rebbes were murdered alongside their followers during the Holocaust. In the Warsaw ghetto, for instance, only one rabbi survived; see Judah Lifschitz, *The Klausenberger Rebbe: Rebuilding* (Southfield, MI: Targum Press, 2007), and Farbstein, *Hidden in Thunder*, vol. 1, 67–145.

18    Letter from F.C. Blair to Victor Podoski, Polish ambassador to Canada, 8 July 1941, Ottawa, ON, UJRA Files, as cited in Irving Abella and Harold Troper, *None Is Too Many: Canada and the Jews of Europe 1933–1948* (Toronto: Lester & Orpen Dennys, 1982), 90.

19    For further descriptions of the refugees' arrival, see Shaffir, *Life in a Religious Community*.

20    Untitled public announcement by the UJRA, 15 July 1952, CJC box 23, Yeshiva Students Maintenance 1941–1946, CJCCC, Montreal.

21    "An Academy of Learning," 30 October 1941, Rabbinical College of Canada Tomche Tmimim Collection, CJCCC, Montreal.

22    *Di Yiddishe Heim* (translated from Yiddish) 10, no. 3: 4–5, as cited in Shaffir, *Life in a Religious Community*, 13.

23    Erwin Schild, interviewed by author, 1 October 2009, Toronto, ON; and Louis Rosenberg, "Two Centuries of Jewish Life in Canada" in *Canadian Jewish Reference Book and Directory*, 188, 190.

24    "The Yeshivos, Rabbinical Seminaries–The Pride of Montreal Jewry!," undated, CJC box 23, Yeshiva Students Maintenance 1941–1946, CJCCC, Montreal. For a history of the refugee scholars of the Mirrer Yeshiva who remained in Shanghai through the end of the war, see Lipschitz, *The Shanghai Connection*.

25    Shaffir, *Life in a Religious Community*, 17.

26    Ibid. Tuition fees were introduced when the yeshiva moved into its new and permanent location on Park Avenue in 1943.

27    Ibid.; Lubavitch community member, interviewed by the author, 17 June 2010, Montreal, QC.

28    Refer to Chapter 1 for a broader consideration on the "enemy aliens."

29    See untitled files from the UJRA, 22 July 1942, and "The Yeshivos, Rabbinical Seminaries...," CJCCC, Montreal.

30    German and Austrian Jews were overwhelmingly German speakers, and saw Yiddish as a bastardized German used by Eastern European Jews. See author's interview with Erwin Schild, 1 October 2009, and Inge Spitz, interviewed by the author, 24 October 2007, Toronto, ON.

31    For Winnipeg Holocaust survivors' experiences in Soviet Asia, see Millo, *Voices of Winnipeg Holocaust Survivors*.

32    Shaffir, *Life in a Religious Community*, 22; see also institutional records from the Rabbinical College of Canada Tomche Tmimim Collection, CJCCC, Montreal.

33    Shaffir, *Life in a Religious Community*, 21; Lubavitch community member, interviewed by the author, 20 August 2010, Montreal, QC.

34    Memorandum from Samuel Levine to Saul Hayes, 31 May 1955, and other untitled documents, Rabbinical College of Canada Tomche Tmimim Collection, CJCCC, Montreal; letter from Saul Hayes to Judah J. Shapiro, 3 June 1955, Yeshivoth Conference on Jewish Material Claims Against Germany Collection, 1953–1958, CJCCC, Montreal.

35   Marilyn Henry, *Confronting the Perpetrators: A History of the Claims Conference* (London: Vallentine Mitchell, 2007); Ronald W. Zweig, *German Reparations and the Jewish World: A History of the Claims Conference* (London: Routledge, 1987).

36   Letter from Judah J. Shapiro, director of the Department of Cultural & Educational Reconstruction for the Conference on Jewish Material Claims Against Germany, to Saul Hayes, national executive director of the CJC, 24 May 1955, 2, CJC box 63, no. 598, Yeshivoth Conference on Jewish Material Claims Against Germany Collection, 1953–1958, CJCCC, Montreal.

37   Report on visit by Solomon Tarshansky to the Yeshivoth Committee, 12 March 1957, 2, Yeshivoth Conference on Jewish Material Claims Against Germany Collection, 1953–1958, CJCCC, Montreal.

38   Letter from S.D. Gameroff, president of Tomchei Tmimim, to Saul Hayes, 19 November 1956, CJC box 63,Yeshivoth Conference on Jewish Material Claims Against Germany Collection, 1953–1958, CJCCC, Montreal.

39   Israel Medres, "Rabbinical College of Canada," *The Canadian Jewish Chronicle*, 1 April 1955, 1; unauthored announcement, "Rabbinical College of Canada Tomche Tmimim Lubavitch," *The Canadian Jewish Chronicle*, 2 December 1955, 9.

40   Shaffir, *Life in a Religious Community*, 147.

41   Community member, interviewed by the author, 16 August 2010, Montreal, QC; "Montreal Community Marks First Yahrtzeit of Rabbi Yitzchak HaCohen Hendel, the Former Head of the Montreal Beth Din," *Jewish Community Council of Montreal*, accessed 16 August 2010http://mk.ca/rabbihendel.html.

42   Janice Arnold, "Rabbi Leib Kramer to be Commemorated," *Canadian Jewish News*, 9 December 2010. Rosh Yeshiva of Tomchei Tmimim Rabbi Kramer acquired a considerable following that has attempted to preserve his legacy posthumously on the website, *Rabbi Kramer's Legacy: A Project Dedicated to the Memory of Rabbi Leib Kramer*, accessed 18 September 2010, http://www.rabbikramerslegacy.com.

43   Letter to Judah J. Shapiro, director of the Department of Cultural & Educational Reconstruction for the Conference on Jewish Material Claims Against Germany, from Saul Hayes, national executive director of the CJC, 7 May 1954, 1–2, CJC box 63, no. 598, Yeshivah Merkaz Hatorah, Yeshivoth Conference on Jewish Material Claims Against Germany Collection, 1953–1958, CJCCC, Montreal.

44   "Fin d'un voyage de 7 ans," *La Patrie* (Montreal), 8 August 1946, 6; "Polish Jews Arrive Soon," *Halifax Herald* (Halifax), 12 July 1946.

45   Correspondence between Saul Hayes, national executive director of the Canadian Jewish Congress, and Henrietta K. Buchman, Joint Distribution Committee, 4 February 1942, CJC box 23, 200A, Yeshiva Students, Rabonim Guarantees, 1941–1942, CJCCC, Montreal; Letter to Saul Hayes from the rabbis of the Mir Yeshiva, 2 August 1946; Memo from Edna Keller of the CJC to Saul Hayes, 31 January 1947, CJC Box 23, 203A, Shanghai Rabbinical Students, 1946–1947, CJCCC, Montreal.

46   Letter from Rabbi Leib Baron, principal, Yeshivah Merkaz Hatorah, to Mr. Judah J. Shapiro, director of Cultural and Educational Reconstruction, Claims Conference, 6 January 1955, CJC box 63, no. 70, Yeshivah Merkaz Hatorah, Yeshivoth Conference on Jewish Material Claims Against Germany Collection, 1953–1958, CJCCC, Montreal.

47   Former Merkaz Hatorah teacher, interviewed by the author, 18 August 2010, Montreal, QC.

48   1965 and 1968 Yearbooks, CJC box 63, Yeshivah Merkaz Hatorah, Yeshivoth Conference on Jewish Material Claims Against Germany Collection, 1953–1958, CJCCC, Montreal; anonymous community member, interviewed by the author, 15 May 2010, Montreal, QC.

49  Tibor Juda, a survivor from Hungary, married Rabbi Hirschprung's daughter, Leah. He is an urologist and Talmudic scholar in Toronto. His sister, Edith, also a survivor, married Mark Nusbaum (see Chapter 4).

50  Still in operation today, the yeshiva has ordained dozens of rabbis and educated thousands of Jewish children who now participate in, and lead, Jewish communities across the country. Lifschitz's *The Klausenberger Rebbe,* 86–91, provides an accounting of the Klausenberger rebbe's efforts to provide his *bokhurim* in Montreal with a yeshiva when they were unable to attain visas to enter the United States.

51  A CJC Inter-Office Information (I.O.I.) dated 26 June 1949 describes the arrival of the group in Montreal: "We provided temporary accommodation at our War Orphans Reception Centre in Montreal for 15 Yeshiva students from Rome, Italy, who arrived July 25th. The group (Me'or Hagolah) will have permanent quarters at a newly purchased house which was provided by its leadership. Another 7 students are to come at a later date; the group also includes three rabbinical families which arrived jointly with the 15 students. Upon termination of our using the Reception Centre for war orphans, the Federation of Jewish Philanthropies which owns the premises, agreed to our directing immigrants to the Centre for temporary accommodations as the needs may arise and in accordance with these arrangements, we placed the Yeshiva group at the Centre." By 1948, Montreal also housed two elementary schools for Orthodox girls' education.

52  Letter from Saul Hayes to Mr. Judah J. Shapiro, director of Cultural and Educational Reconstruction, Claims Conference, 7 May 1954, 15, box 64, Maor Hagolah Rabbinical College, Yeshiva Conference on Jewish Material Claims Against Germany Collection, 1953-1958, CJCCC, Montreal.

53  The yeshiva's yearly campaign dinners were well-publicized events: "All friends of the Maor Hagolah yeshiva and all Jews for whom Torah and Jewish ideals are rich, who want to see a generation brought up in the spirit of our old Jewish traditions, are invited to the yearly yeshiva dinner, which will be held next Sunday in the evening, 8 February, in the chevra kedisha auditorium. The campaign's opening dinner must be a strong success and a great manifestation of Torah, and we must make an effort to strengthen and stabilize the difficult financial situation of our yeshiva in order so that the high level of studies and also the upkeep/welfare of the students with hardship will not, God forbid, discontinue their studies. The dinner will strive to transform into an impressionable evening with a rich program, which will be led by the favourite cantor Shlomo Giser of Shaarei Tsion synagogue, with the help of his brother M. Giser, on the piano. The brilliant speaker Rabbi Mordkhe Zelig Hirsh of New York is the guest speaker. And many other guests from the Jewish religious intelligentsia. You will all certainly have a Jewish good time"; S. Mazel, "A word on the yearly dinner of the Yeshivat Maor Hagolah of Satmar, Sunday evening, February 8," (translated from the original Yiddish), undated, Maor Hagolah Rabbinical College Collection, CJCCC, Montreal.

54  Yitel Nechamah Bineth, interview.

55  Steven Lapidus, interviewed by the author, 15 June 2010, Montreal, QC; Ira Robinson, *Rabbis and Their Community: Studies in the Eastern European Orthodox Rabbinate in Montreal, 1896–1930* (Calgary: University of Calgary Press, 2007).

56  Steven Lapidus, conversation with the author, 17 June 2010, Montreal, QC. Hassidim also founded other smaller yeshivas and communities from the early 1950s onward, including the Vishnitz and Satmar Hassidim. These communities are not included in this study. In the case of the Vishnitzers, a lack of access to community leaders and documentation hampered my ability to reconstruct the community development. The Satmar Hassidim, composed primarily of Hungarian survivors and the most devout and isolated of Montreal's Hassidim, developed slightly later than this book's parameters, and moved its yeshiva to Ste. Agathe, Quebec, to maintain its separateness. See Israel Rubin, *Satmar: An Island in the City* (Chicago: Quadrangle Books, 1972).

57 The religious groups spearheaded by a handful of determined Holocaust survivors constitute the fastest-growing Jewish communities in Canada today. Based on the findings of a
1997 demographic study, approximately 6,400 Hassidic and ultra-Orthodox Jews resided in
Montreal, with an additional 1,400 in nearby Boisbriand. These figures suggest that 22 percent
of Montreal Jews identified as Orthodox, as compared with 14 percent in the rest of Canada,
and 6 percent in the United States. Although the communities on the whole have become
increasingly insular, the impact and influence of Hassidic and *mitnagedim* traditions remain
entrenched in the spiritual and daily lives of Montreal Jewry. Randal F. Schnoor, "Tradition
and Innovation in an Ultra-Orthodox Community: The Hasidim of Outremont," *Canadian
Jewish Studies* 10 (2002), 55–56. To read the study in its entirety, see Charles Shahar, Morton
Weinfeld, and Randal F. Schnoor, eds., *Survey of the Hassidic and Ultra-Orthodox Communities
in Outremont and Surrounding Areas* (Montreal: Coalition of Outremont Hassidic Organizations, 1997).

58 The experiences of observant orphans are considered in Chapter 3.

59 For more on women, see Chapters 8 and 9.

60 JIAS meeting of Board of Directors, 17 October 1948, and Minutes of the Executive Board
and Board of Directors of JIAS, 27 July 1948, file 21, Series 1, Fonds 9, Ontario Jewish Archives (OJA), Toronto.

61 Memorandum from the United Jewish Refugee and War Relief Agencies, 13 July 1942, 2,
CJC box 63, Yeshivoth Conference on Jewish Material Claims Against Germany, 1953–1958,
CJCCC, Montreal.

62 Ibid.

63 Ibid.

64 Sylvia Endler, "The Prevention of Hard Core Cases Among the Immigrant Displaced Persons:
A Study of 77 Immigrant DP Families Served at the Jewish Immigrant Aid Society, July 1,
1951 to February 29, 1952 Who Required Further Service After a Six Months' Period" (MSW
thesis, McGill University, 1953).

65 Significant issues arise concerning the definition of "ultra-Orthodox." The term is traditionally applied by non-Orthodox Jews to describe their co-religionists whose dress, manner, and
behaviours appear extreme, specifically beyond the realm of modern comprehension, to Jewish
practice. Individuals who adhere to Orthodox Jewish practice, which includes strict family
purity laws and rules surrounding modesty and prayer, are no less observant than Hassidim.
Rather, behaviours and ideology differentiate the groups. See Max A. Lipschitz, *The Faith of a
Hassid* (New York: Jonathan David Publishing, 2003).

66 Jacqueline Rotblott, a Canadian-born Jew, recalls the odd appearances and skittish behaviour
of the Hassidic newcomers who settled in her Montreal neighborhood after the war, and how
"the men would always cross the street when they saw me or my girlfriends walking. It was like
they were afraid of us"; Jacqueline Rotblott, interviewed by the author, 7 September 2008,
Toronto, ON.

67 Endler, "The Prevention of Hard Core Cases."

68 "A. Feiler," 4, JIAS Immigration Case Files Series CA, CJCCC, Montreal.

69 "J. Goldberger," 3, JIAS Immigration Case Files Series CA, CJCCC, Montreal.

70 As survivors grew more confident and settled into Canadian Jewish society, the differentia-
tion between the groups dissolved slightly, and they came together to support mutual causes,
such as Israel; ten anonymous cases, 1951, JIAS Immigration Case Files Series CA, CJCCC,
Montreal.

71 Endler, "The Prevention of Hard Core Cases," 102.

72 This research has found little evidence to support this particular claim.

73 Endler, "The Prevention of Hard Core Cases," 103–15.

74 CJC I.O.I. Summary III, 3 February 1950, 4.

75 Endler, "The Prevention of Hard Core Cases," 107–12.

76 "Canadian Society for Yad Vashem Honouree Biographies," *Canadian Jewish News*, 29 April 2010; "Competitor assists kosher deli destroyed by fire," *The National Post*, 13 November 2006.

77 Fasten, interview.

78 Letter from Rabbi S. Herschorn to Benjamin W. Goldman, 17 June 1952, Montreal, QC, 1, box 4, Vaad Ha'ir Assistance Files, 1948-1981, Jewish Public Library Collection, CJCCC, Montreal.

79 Letter from D. Drutz to Mrs. C. Gorby, JIAS, 18 December 1952, Toronto, ON, "M. Grosz," JIAS Immigration Case Files Series CA, CJCCC, Montreal.

80 Mrs. C. Gorby, Case Summary, 4, 18 December 1953, JIAS Immigration Case Files Series CA, CJCCC, Montreal.

81 Letter from the Jewish Community Council of Montreal to David Weiss, executive director of the Family Welfare Department, Baron de Hirsch Institute, 15 May 1952, Montreal, QC, file "S Grunfeld," box B, Vaad Ha'ir Assistance Files, 1948–1981, Jewish Public Library Collection, CJCCC, Montreal.

82 Helena Edelstein, interview no. 39805, 1996, Visual History Archive, University of Southern California Shoah Foundation Institute (SFI), http://sfi.usc.edu/.

83 Many ordained rabbis and cantors initiated their Canadian careers by undertaking employment in smaller Jewish communities. Rabbis Aivadia Rosenberg and Chaim Dov Ber Ginsberg led congregations in Glace Bay, Nova Scotia, and Vancouver, British Columbia, respectively, and Cantor Nathan Liberman served as a cantor and Hebrew teacher at the Welland Hebrew Congregation in Welland, Ontario. For further examples, see Gottesman, *Who's Who in Canadian Jewry*.

84 "A. Feiler," 3, JIAS Immigration Case Files Series CA, CJCCC, Montreal.

85 "B. Wichnin," Conference Committee for Refugee Rabbis application, 20 September 1954, 1–2, Yeshivoth Conference on Jewish Material Claims Against Germany, 1953–1958, JIAS Immigration Case Files Series CA, CJCCC, Montreal.

86 "M. Wieder," JIAS Immigration Case Files Series CA, CJCCC, Montreal.

87 Yitel Nechamah Bineth, interview.

## Chapter Six: Moving Forward: Survivor Shuls

1 Referred to henceforth as Habonim and Clanton Park, respectively.

2 Inge Spitz, interviewed by the author, 5 November 2005, Toronto, ON.

3 Refugee rabbis established congregations at the same time in Montreal. See Chapter 5.

4 Eli Rubenstein, "Curt Fleischer Eulogy," Congregation Habonim (Toronto, 8 May 2002), 3; "Lola Fleischer Eulogy," Congregation Habonim (Toronto, 7 June 2001), 3–4.

5 Spiritual director of Congregation Habonim Eli Rubenstein, interviewed by the author, 24 November 2011, Toronto, ON.

6 "Excerpts from the Eulogy by Eli Rubenstein for Gangolf Herman," *Congregation Habonim Bulletin* 48, no. 8 (June 2004–Sivan-Tamuz 5764), n.p..

7    Herbert Faber, "Introductory Speech to Potential Joiners of Habonim," translated from German by Gangolf Herman, 12 December 1954, Toronto, ON, cited in Lisa-Catherine Cohen, *The Builders: The Fifty-year History of Congregation Habonim* (The Writers Guild of America), 15–16.

8    Curt Fleischer, "The Beginnings of Congregation Habonim," *Congregation Habonim Bulletin* (December 1983), as cited in Cohen, *The Builders*, xvi.

9    See Irwin F. Gellman, "The St. Louis Tragedy," in Jeffrey S. Gurock, ed., *American Jewish History: America, American Jews, and the Holocaust Edition*, vol. 7 (New York: Routledge, 1998); Barry J. Konovitch, "The Fiftieth Anniversary of the *St. Louis*: What Really Happened?" *American Jewish History,* 79, no. 2 (1989/90); Sarah A. Ogilvie and Scott Miller, *Refuge Denied: The* St. Louis *Passengers and the Holocaust* (Madison: University of Wisconsin Press, 2010); and Gordon Thomas and Max Morgan Witts, *Voyage of the Damned* (New York: Konecky & Konecky, 2006).

10   Rubenstein, interview; Spitz, interview.

11   Cohen, *The Builders*, 8.

12   Werner Eugen Mosse, *Second Chance: Two Centuries of German-speaking Jews in the United Kingdom* (Tübingen, Germany: J.C.B. Mohr, 1991), 161–2.

13   The Adlers and the Fleischers are listed among the Sudeten Jewish refugees receiving financial assistance from the Canadian Jewish Congress in 1941. At the time, the families were both described as active farmers serving out their labour contracts in Alberta and Saskatchewan, respectively. Memorandum, 20 March 1941, 3, file 102, box 10, CJC ZA 1941–Sudeten Germany Jewish Refugees, Canadian Jewish Congress Charities Committee National Archive (CJCCC), Montreal.

14   Henry Weingluck's history is discussed in Chapter 2.

15   Eli Rubenstein, "Simon Baumann Eulogy," Pardes Shalom Cemetery (Toronto, 3 July 2001), n.p..

16   Spitz, interview.

17   "Community Events," *The Canadian Jewish News* (12 February 1960), 2, *Multicultural Canada,* accessed 5 February 2011, http://www.multiculturalcanada.ca.

18   Ibid.

19   Canada was home to several Reform synagogues by the 1950s, the most prominent being Holy Blossom Temple in Toronto.

20   Anonymous community member, interviewed by the author, 16 March 2011, Toronto, ON.

21   With the development and prosperity of Orthodoxy that emerged in North America from the 1960s, Clanton Park became increasingly observant. This transition pushed some early members to seek out alternative and less observant spiritual communities—specifically, Conservative congregations such as Beth David, Adath Israel, and Beth Emeth in the now-robust North York Jewish community. The Beth Am, another Conservative *shul*, arose just west of Bathurst Manor around the same time. It served the relatively robust Jewish community that resided in that area in the early 1960s onwards.

22   "Message from the Rabbi," in *Dedication of the Machzikai Hadath Clanton Park Synagogue*, 12 February 1961, North York, ON, file 73, Series 6, Fonds 4, Ontario Jewish Archives (OJA), Toronto.

23   For more on the congregants' commitment to Israel, see Robert Eli Rubinstein, *An Italian Renaissance: Choosing Life in Canada* (Jerusalem: Urim Publications, 2010), and Miriam Frankel, interviewed by the author, 6 October 2010, Toronto, ON.

24   Rubinstein, *An Italian Renaissance*, 83.

25   It seems likely that most of the congregants functioned sufficiently in English by 1955, the first year the *Clanton Park Synagogue Bulletin* was published. All volumes, presumably read by the members, were written in English, with survivors' contributing pieces in their original form. See *Clanton Park Synagogue Bulletins* 1955–1962, file 72, Series 6, Fonds 4, OJA, Toronto.

26   See Chapters 1 and 5 for the internment of German and Austrian Jewish refugees in Canada.

27   Featured interview with Malka Hahn, *The Clanton Park Herald*, 2, Issue 7 (Adar Beis, 5765), n.p.

28   Etan Diamond, *And I Will Dwell in Their Midst: Orthodox Jews in Suburbia* (Chapel Hill: University of North Carolina Press, 2000), 51–3.

29   Ibid., 39.

30   Ibid., 29–30.

31   Featured interview with Malka Hahn, *The Clanton Park Herald*.

32   Miriam Frankel, interviewed by the author, 6 October 2010, Toronto, ON.

33   Featured interview with Sam and Gilda Nussbaum, *The Clanton Park Herald* 2, Issue 5 (Shevat, 5765).

34   Featured interview with Aron and Miriam Frankel, *The Clanton Park Herald* 2, iss. 4 (Teves 5765), n.p.

35   "Our Sisterhood," in *Dedication of the Machzikai Hadath Clanton Park Synagogue*, 12 February 1961, North York, ON, file 73, Series 6, Fonds 4, OJA, Toronto.

36   Robert Eli Rubinstein, lecture and book launch, Shaarei Shomayim Synagogue, 7 November 2010, Toronto, ON; Frankel, interview.

37   Featured interview with Malka Hahn, *The Clanton Park Herald*.

38   Diamond, *And I Will Dwell in Their Midst*, 90.

39   Featured interview with Bill and Judith Rubinstein, *The Clanton Park Herald* 2, Issue 8 (Nisan 5765), n.p. Italics in original.

## Chapter Seven: Abandoning Tradition: Converts and Apostates

1   For a selection of reflections on Jewish theological responses to the Holocaust, see Eliezer Berkovits, *Faith After the Holocaust* (Jersey City, NJ: KTAV Publishing House, 1973); Martin Buber, *Eclipse of God* (Amherst, NY: Humanity Books, 1988); Emil Fackenheim, *To Mend the World: Foundations of Post-Holocaust Jewish Thought* (Bloomington: Indiana University Press, 1994); Viktor Frankl, *Man's Search for Meaning* (Boston, MA: Beacon Press, 2006); Nehemia Polen, *The Holy Fire: The Teachings of Rabbi Kalonymus Kalman Shapira, the Rebbe of the Warsaw Ghetto* (New York: Jason Aronson, 1994); Richard L. Rubenstein, *After Auschwitz: History, Theology, and Contemporary Judaism* (Baltimore, MD: Johns Hopkins University Press, 1992); and Elie Wiesel, *Night* (New York: Bantam Books, 1982).

2   An important element of Canadian Jewish and postwar history, the role of anti-Semitism in Canadian society is discussed in Chapter 1. See Betcherman, *The Swastika and the Maple Leaf*; Cyril Levitt and William Shaffir, *The Riot at Christie Pits* (Toronto: Lester & Orpen Denys,1987); Howard Palmer, *Patterns of Prejudice: A History of Nativism in Alberta* (Toronto: McClelland and Stewart, 1982); and Janine Stingel, *Social Discredit: Anti-Semitism, Social Credit and the Jewish Response* (Montreal: McGill-Queen's University Press, 2000).

3   Renata Skotnicka Zajdman, interviewed by the author, 22 October 2009, Montreal, QC.

4    Riwash, Joseph, interview no. 46406, 1998, Visual History Archive, University of Southern California Shoah Foundation Institute (SFI), http://sfi.usc.edu/.

5    Hungarian Jewish Holocaust survivor, interviewed by the author, 15 June 2009, Vancouver, BC.

6    Zajdman, interview. ; Anonymous community member, interviewed by the author, 24 October 2009, Montreal, QC; Jack Mayer, *Life in a Jar: The Irena Sendler Project* (Middlebury, VT: Long Trail Press, 2011).

7    For more about Toronto's Jewish day school system and its role in the greater Jewish community, see Diamond, *And I Will Dwell in Their Midst*; and Randal F. Schnoor and Alex Pomson, *Back to School: Jewish Day School in the Lives of Adults* (Detroit: Wayne State University Press, 2008).

8    Or, Dutch and Hungarian males represent most of those willing to share these experiences with the Shoah Foundation.

9    Conversion, however, failed to protect Jews. According to Nazi racial law, bloodlines, not religion, identified Jews.

10   Hanna Spencer, *Hanna's Diary, 1938–1941: Czechoslovakia to Canada* (Montreal: McGill-Queen's University Press, 2001), xiv.

11   Ibid., 113.

12   Helen Waldstein Wilkes, *Letters from the Lost: A Memoir of Discovery* (Edmonton: Athabasca University Press, 2009), 57–8.

13   Ibid., 126.

14   Ibid., 233.

15   Stanley G. Matthews, "Churches Take Up Task of Aiding Immigrants," *Canadian Churchman*, 12 June 1948.

16   Ibid.

17   Ben Volman, "Rev. Dr. Edward D. Brotsky (1918–2010): A Tribute," *Messianic Insight: Messianic Jewish Perspective of Ben Volman*, accessed 21 July 2010, http://www.messianicinsight.com/2010/05/rev-dr-edward-d-brotsky-1918-2010.html.

18   Reverend Morris Kaminsky, "The Nathanael Institute, Toronto: Resumé of Report to Synod," *Canadian Churchman* 76, no. 16 (18 August 1949), 271.

19   Reverend Morris Zeidman, "Excerpts from 'Jews in Poland Today'" (n.d.), Scott Mission, accessed 13 March 2011, http://www.scottmission.com/designedit/upload/Morris_Zeidman.pdf.

20   Alex Zeidman, *Good and Faithful Servant: The Biography of Morris Zeidman* (Burlington, ON: Crown Publication, 1990), 47.

21   J.B. Salsberg, "The Tug-of-War between Rev. Morris Zeidman and Moyshe Tarnovsky's Chenstochover Society," *The Canadian Jewish News*, 30 December 1982, 5; Former volunteer at the Scott Mission, interviewed by the author, 12 January 2011, Toronto, ON.

22   The same operational standards still apply in many contemporary North American congregations, and remain a point of contention within Jewish circles.

23   George Lysy, telephone conversation with the author, 23 June 2008, Toronto, ON.

24   Anonymous Romanian survivor, interviewed by the author, 16 June 2008, Vancouver, BC.

25   Although contemporary congregations still charge admission for High Holiday services, most institutions waive entrance fees if requested in advance by students, seniors, or other needy Jews for whom the fee poses a hardship.

26   To a lesser degree, Lubavitch Hassidim practised their own form of proselytizing among non-observant Canadian Jews. (No contemporary recognized Jewish community faction actively searched for members among non-Jews.)

27   *Journal of the Incorporated Synod of the Diocese of Toronto of The Church of England in Canada* (Toronto: Parker Bros., 1951), Appendix 1 (g), "Mission to the Jews," 202–7.

28   See Zeidman's *Good and Faithful Servant.*

29   *Journal of the Incorporated Synod of the Diocese of Toronto of The Church of England in Canada* (Toronto: Parker Bros., 1950), Appendix 1(g), 168. In that same report, Kaminsky bemoaned the fact that limited space for the pre-school meant a waiting list of over eighty, resulting in the mission's lack of contact with and influence on the children's parents.

30   *Journal of the Incorporated Synod of the Diocese of Toronto of The Church of England in Canada* (Toronto: Parker Bros., 1952), Appendix 1(f), 206.

31   *Journal of the Incorporated Synod of the Diocese of Toronto of The Church of England in Canada* (Toronto: Parker Bros., 1949), Appendix 1(g), 183.

32   Letter from Manfred Saalheimer, CJC, to Dorothy Shekter, Jewish Social Services of Hamilton, 26 January 1950, in response to letter dated 20 January 1950, Montreal, QC, box 26, Subject Files, CA Hamilton, ON, orphans, UJRA Collection–War Orphans Project, CJCCC, Montreal.

33   "Orphan Boy Placed in Calgary Induced to Changing Religion," CJC I.O.I. Bulletin VI, 14 September 1948, CJC Fonds, CJCCC, Montreal.

34   On orphaned survivors' experiences of uprooting from Jewish life, see Administrative Notes, box 6 ZA/S 1953 6/1A, 1–2, CJC Year Boxes–Supplementary, CJCCC, Montreal, and Akiva Yossef Mandel, interview no. 19050, 1996, SFI.

35   Western Executive Minutes, file 15, box 6 ZA/S 1953, CJC Year Boxes–Supplementary. CJCCC, Montreal.

36   Thomas Kramer, interview no. 45498, 1998, SFI.

37   Ibid.

38   Bob Gosschalk, interview no. 37852, 1998, SFI.

39   Ibid.

40   Neology is most closely aligned with the contemporary North American Conservative movement; Lupovitch, Howard, "Between Orthodox Judaism and Neology: The Origins of the Status Quo," *Jewish Social Studies* 9, no. 2 (Winter 2003): 123–53.

41   Kornel Marten (Szusz) and family immigration papers, in the possession of the author; Vera Gold, interviewed by the author, 21 December 2009, Toronto, ON.

42   Gold, interview.

43   Vera Gold, interview no. 20077, 1996, SFI.

*Chapter Eight: The Final Movement: Israeli Transmigrants and other "Late Arrivals"*

1   Morris Faintuch, interviewed by the author, 24 June 2009, Winnipeg, MB.

2   Canada did not open its embassy in Tel Aviv, Israel, until September 1953.

3   JIAS Immigration Case Files Series CA, Canadian Jewish Congress Charities Committee National Archives (CJCCC), Montreal, and Ontario Jewish Archives (OJA), Toronto; Jewish Public Library Collection, Vaad Ha'ir Assistance Files, 1948–1981, CJCCC, Montreal.

4    The exception to this rule concerns the Czechoslovakian Hassidim and ultra-Orthodox survivors, who arrived in comparable numbers in both waves.

5    House of Commons Debates notice, from a statement by the Honourable W.E. Harris, Minister of Citizenship & Immigration, 29 June 1950, Library and Archives Canada (LAC), Ottawa.

6    Knowles, *Strangers at Our Gates*, 168.

7    Ibid., 169–78; Iacovetta, *Gatekeepers*, 6–14.

8    Previously, Canadian residents and citizens could sponsor only first-degree relatives, including spouses and minor children, except in extraordinary cases.

9    Immigration Act, Statutes of Canada, 1952, LAC, Ottawa.

10    Field Letter no. 127, Director of the AJDC–Paris, Louis D. Horwitz, 16 June 1953, file 417, box 39, CJC Central Files, New Immigrant Regulations 1950–1954, CJCCC, Montreal.

11    Ibid., 2–5.

12    Letter from C.E.S. Smith, director of the Department of Citizenship and Immigration, to Samuel Bronfman, president of the Canadian Jewish Congress, 31 March 1954, 2, file 417, box 39, CJC Central Files, New Immigrant Regulations 1950–1954, CJCCC, Montreal.

13    Minutes of meeting of the Jewish Community Service Committee, 11 January 1952, Montreal, ZA 1952-5-81., CJCCC, Montreal.

14    A few thousand Hassidic and ultra-Orthodox survivors immigrated immediately postwar to Antwerp, Belgium, one of the only remaining pre-war hubs of Hassidism. By the early 1950s, hundreds of these survivors continued on to North America and Israel. To read more about the Belz Hassidims' immigration to Canada via Belgium, see *Chagigas chanukas habayis: Talmud toyre dichaside belz–Montreal* [Rough translation: *The Chronicles of Belzer Institutions in Montreal*] (5 Elul 5757 [1996]), n.p.; and Jacques Gutwirth, "The Structure of a Hassidic Community in Montreal," *Jewish Journal of Sociology* 14, no. 1 (June 1972): 44–7.

15    Esther Friedman, interviewed by the author, 27 October 2009, Calgary, AB.

16    On Holocaust survivors' early years in Palestine, see Boaz Kahana, Eva Kahana, and Zev Harel, *Holocaust Survivors and Immigrants: Late Life Adaptations* (New York: Springer, 2005), and Hanna Yablonka, *Survivors of the Holocaust: Israel After the War* (New York: New York University Press, 1999).

17    See, for example, Shlomo Avineri, *The Making of Modern Zionism: The Intellectual Origins of the Jewish State* (New York: Basic Books, 1981), and Walter Lacquer, *A History of Zionism* (London: Weidenfeld and Nicolson, 1972).

18    Historians and survivors have written about Holocaust survivors' voices and silence in Palestine/Israel, as well as their experiences of self and belonging. These include Orna Kenan, *Between Memory and History: The Evolution of Israeli Historiography of the Holocaust, 1945–1961*, vol. 49 (New York: Peter Lang Publishing, 2003), Dalia Ofer, "Linguistic Conceptualization of the Holocaust in Palestine and Israel, 1942–53," *Journal of Contemporary History* 31, no. 3 (July 1996); Dina Porat, *Israeli Society, the Holocaust and Its Survivors* (Middlesex, UK: Vallentine Mitchell, 2008); and Tom Segev, *The Seventh Million: The Israelis and the Holocaust* (New York: Picador, 2000).

19    Anonymous survivor, interviewed by the author, 18 March 2010, Montreal, QC.

20    Elsa Engler, interview no. 26018, 1997, Visual History Archive, University of Southern California Shoah Foundation Institute (SFI), http://sfi.usc.edu/.

21    Undetermined numbers of Hassidic and ultra-Orthodox survivors also emigrated. Attitudes toward Israel vary, and the politics surrounding their allegiance to the state is the subject

of many books: Zalman Abramov, *Perpetual Dilemma: Jewish Religion in the Jewish State* (Madison, NJ: Farleigh Dickinson State University, 1979); David H. Goldberg and Bernard Reich, "Religion and State in the State of Israel," in *Religion, State and Society: Jefferson's Wall of Separation in Comparative Perspective*, ed. Robert Fatton, Jr., and R.K. Ramazani (London: Palgrave Macmillan, 2009), 215–231; Charles S. Liebman and Eliezer Don-Yehiya, *Civil Religion in Israel: Traditional Judaism and Political Culture in the Jewish State* (Berkeley: University of California Press, 1983); and Jerome R. Mintz, *Hasidic People: A Place in the New World* (Cambridge: Harvard University Press, 1998).

22   For Jewish life in DP camps, see Atina Grossman, *Jews, Germans, and Allies: Close Encounters in Occupied Germany* (Princeton, NJ: Princeton University Press, 2007); Erik Somers and Rene Kok, *Jewish Displaced Persons in Camp Bergen-Belsen 1945–1950: The Unique Photo Album of Zippy Orlin* (Seattle: University of Washington Press, 2004); and Mark Wyman, *DPs: Europe's Displaced Persons, 1945–1951* (Ithaca, NY: Cornell University Press, 1998).

23   Lazer (Lou) Hoffer, interviewed by the author, 20 December 2007, Toronto, ON. See also "Hoffer, Lazer," United Jewish Relief Agencies (UJRA), Series CB, CJCCC, Montreal.

24   Betty Warshawsky, interviewed by the author, 24 June 2009, Winnipeg, MB.

25   There is a vast literature on Israel's War of Independence: Lynne Reid Banks, *Torn Country: An Oral History of the Israeli War of Independence* (New York: Franklin Watts, 1982); David Roy Easton, *No Alternative: Israel Observed* (London: Hutchinson, 1960); Chaim Herzog, *The Arab-Israeli Wars* (New York: Random House, 1982); Dan Kurzman, *Genesis 1948: The First Arab-Israel War* (Middlesex, UK: Vallentine Mitchell, 1970); Netanel Lorch, *The Edge of the Sword: Israel's War of Independence, 1947–1949* (New York: Putnam, 1961); Ze'ev Sharef, *Three Days: An Account of the Last Days of the British Mandate and the Birth of Israel* (New York: Doubleday, 1962).

26   Frieda H, interviewed by the author, 29 April 2011, Toronto, ON.

27   Magda Hilf, interviewed by the author, 5 November 2005, Toronto, ON; "K. Adam," JIAS Immigration Case File Series CA, CJCCC, Montreal.

28   JIAS Immigration Case Files Series CA, CJCCC, Montreal, and OJA, Toronto.

29   This process changed in response to the establishment of a Canadian embassy in Tel Aviv, Israel, in 1953.

30   Letter from Henry L. Levy, director of the AJDC, European Emigration Headquarters, Paris, to Saul Hayes, national executive director of the Canadian Jewish Congress, Montreal, 2 December 1952, box 6 ZA/S, CJC Year Boxes–Supplementary, CJCCC, Montreal.

31   Letter from unnamed caseworker, World Jewish Congress, Rome, to Dr. S. Roth, World Jewish Congress, London, 13 August 1952, box 6 ZA/S, CJC Year Boxes–Supplementary, CJCCC, Montreal.

32   Letter from Dr. Ivo Svarc, chief emigration officer of AJDC's Italian headquarters, to United Jewish Relief Agencies of Canada, Montreal, 4 January 1951, box 2 ZA/S, CJC Year Boxes, CJCCC, Montreal.

33   Manfred Saalheimer, a former German Jewish internee and CJC staff member, offered the following response to Congress representatives seeking information on the ever-changing government guidelines concerning immigration: "New regulations are in force since 4 July, 1952, which restrict immigration almost exclusively to close relatives of Canadian residents." M. Saalheimer, 22 January 1953, box 6 ZA/S, CJC Year Boxes, CJCCC, Montreal.

34   Saul Hayes letter to Mr. J. Klinger, 16 June 1953, box 6, ZA/S, CJC Year Boxes, CJCCC, Montreal.

35   Walter Absil, interview no. 18281, 1996, and Erika Absil, interview no. 18291, 1996, SFI.

36    See Rubenfeld family testimony in Millo, *Voices of Winnipeg Holocaust Survivors*, 304.

37    Regine Frankel, interviewed by the author, 25 June 2009, Winnipeg, MB; Sol and Rachelle Fink, interviewed by the author, 19 October 2009, Winnipeg, MB. Ed Fisch (Erwin) also experienced reunification with loved ones after immigrating to Canada as a war orphan with his brother Leslie (Laszlo). In 1950, Ed helped his mother escape from Budapest to Toronto, and did the same for his grandmother in 1952; Ed Fisch, email correspondence with author, 12 and 20 January 2011.

38    Michael Bienstock, interview no. 6937, 1995, SFI. See also an interview with Eric and Erika Goldfarb, Oral History Collection, Canadian Museum of Immigration at Pier 21, Halifax, NS.

39    *Chagigas chanukas habayis,* 1996.

40    David Weiss, Baron de Hirsch Institute and Jewish Child Welfare Bureau, Montreal, Policy and Procedure Manual: Backgrounds and General Orientation, volume 1, February, 1952, 8,14–15, Fonds PO152, Jewish Public Library Collection, CJCCC, Montreal. See also the testimony of Iberian refugee and JIAS caseworker, Benjamin Schlesinger, interview no. 37516, 1998, SFI, and Iacovetta, *Gatekeepers*, 171–184.

41    The process undertaken to determine eligibility for JIAS services is described in the minutes of meetings of the Jewish Community Service Committee, Montreal, 11 and 18 January 1952, ZA 1952-5-81. CJCCC, Montreal.

42    Minutes of Meeting, 11 January 1952, 1–2, ZA 1952-5-81. CJCCC, Montreal.

43    "David W," JIAS Immigration Case File Series CA, CJCCC, Montreal.

44    Letter from Henry L. Levy to Saul Hayes, Montreal, 2 December 1952, Box 6 ZA/S, CJC Year Boxes–Supplementary, CJCCC, Montreal.

45    Ibid.

46    "Emigrants Stranded in Rome: Canadian Visas Awaited," *Canadian Jewish Chronicle*, 2 November 1952, London correspondence to Montreal.

47    Discussions surrounding fundraising for the United Jewish Appeal (UJA) claimed much space in Canadian Jewish newspapers and Congress bulletins and inter-office Information agendas. Presented daily were various communities' and organizational efforts, dollars raised and provisions collected, the ensuing conflicts with neighbouring Arab nations, and Canadian Jews' personal connections to Israel.

48    For more about traditional Jewish neighbourhoods, see Stephen A. Speisman, *The Jews of Toronto: A History to 1937* (Toronto: McClelland and Stewart, 1987); Gerald Tulchinsky, *Canada's Jews: A People's Journey*; Louis Rosenberg, *Canada's Jews: A Social and Economic Study of the Jews in Canada in the 1930s*; and William Shaffir, Morton Weinfeld, and Irwin Cotler, eds., *The Canadian Jewish Mosaic* (Toronto: John Wiley & Sons, 1981), 13–61.

49    As a rule, "it [is] JIAS policy to grant loans to large families only where the situation is such that it is best economically and socially"; minutes of meeting, 11 January 1952, CJCCC, Montreal.

50    For more information on Canada's labour market in the 1950s, see Michael Hart and Bill Dymond, "Six Stewards of Canada's Economy," *Policy Options/Options Politiques* (June–July 2003): 29–38; J.W. Pickersgill, *My Years With Louis St. Laurent: A Political Memoir* (Toronto: University of Toronto Press, 1975); Dale C. Thompson, *Louis St. Laurent: Canadian* (Toronto: Macmillan of Canada, 1967).

51    European-trained doctors received financial assistance and loans from the JIAS and its affiliated agencies, to support their medical retraining in Canada, to a greater degree than did other

professionals. In exceptional cases, some refugee university students were granted bursaries to cover a portion of their educational costs. JIAS Immigration Case Files Series CA, CJCCC.

52    Fania Wedro, interviewed by the author, 27 October 2009, Calgary, AB.

53    For further discussion on poor adaptation, see Sylvia Endler, "The Prevention of Hard Core Cases Among the Immigrant Displaced Persons" (MSW thesis, McGill University, 1953).

54    We shall return to this subject in Chapter 9.

55    Endler, "The Prevention of Hard Core Cases," 135.

56    Ibid., 136.

57    Alfred Feintuch, executive director, Jewish Vocational Services, "Sheltered Workshops–A Canadian Community's Experience," *Information and Comment: Social and Economic Studies*, no. 11 (October 1951), 2–3. .

58    David Weiss, Fonds PO152, Jewish Public Library Collection, CJCCC, Montreal, 2-4.

59    Sol and Rachelle Fink, interview.

60    Esther Friedman, interview.

61    The development of Hassidic and ultra-Orthodox communities in Canada is discussed in Chapter 5.

62    Yitel Nechamah Bineth, *Omika: The Life of Our Beloved Mother, Lea Paskusz* (Montreal: Self-published, 1999), 157–158. See also Judah Lifschitz, *The Klausenberger Rebbe: Rebuilding* (Southfield, MI: Targum Press, 2007).

63    Vera Gold, interviewed by the author, 14 December 2009, Toronto, ON.

64    An Inter-Office Information (I.O.I.) dated 3 November 1950, cites Winnipeg Jews' willing-ness to provide affidavits for Holocaust survivors seeking entry into Canada: "Recipients of the IOI will recall our references to the Joint Congress-JIAS efforts to obtain individual sponsors for a number of families who were inadmissible hitherto, who, however, could be brought over provided contracts were available for them. The Winnipeg Congress Committee was asked to accept a quota for 17 craftsmen and their families from the list, which was compiled from previous records. The quota was filled and contracts were obtained for the following: 7 tailors, 4 furriers, 4 woodworkers, and two capmakers." It is important to bear in mind that jobs were not more plentiful in western Canadian cities than in the east. Rather, employers and community leaders showed greater empathy and compassion for the survivors' travails than did Canadian Jews elsewhere. Sonja Faintuch, interviewed by the author, 22 June 2009, Winnipeg, MB; Judy Weiszmann, interviewed by the author, 20 October 2009, Winnipeg, MB; Bronia and Sid Cyngiser, interviewed by the author, 27 October 2009, Calgary, AB.

65    Warshawsky, interview; Henny Paritzky, interviewed by the author, 24 June 2009, Winnipeg, MB.

66    Aron Eichler, interviewed by the author, 27 October 2009, Calgary, AB; Gottesman, *Who's Who in Canadian Jewry*, 129.

67    Keith Morgan with Ruth Kron Sigal, *Ruta's Closet* (London: Unicorn Press and the Vancouver Holocaust Education Centre, 2008); David Bogach, interviewed by the author, 30 November 2012, Vancouver, BC.

68    Chaim Kornfeld, conversation with the author, 1 May 2013, Vancouver, BC.

69    Warshawsky, interview.

70    Canadian Jews were among, and remain, the most ardent Zionists in the Western world, raising more funds per capita for Israeli causes than their wealthier neighbours in the United States. For discussions of Zionism in Canada, see David Azrieli, *Rekindling the Torch: The Story*

*of Canadian Zionism* (Toronto: Key Porter Books, 2008); David Goldberg, *Foreign Policy and Ethnic Interest Groups: American and Canadian Jews Lobby for Israel* (Santa Barbara, CA: Greenwood Press, 1990); and Zachariah Kay, *The Diplomacy of Prudence: Canada and Israel, 1948–1958* (Montreal: McGill-Queen's University Press, 1997).

71   Anonymous Canadian Jewish man, interviewed by the author, 5 March 2010, Toronto, ON.

72   Frustrations were expressed by those Israelis who did seek community assistance. See "S., Moshe" and "W., Chana and Motek," JIAS Immigration Case File Series CA, CJCCC, Montreal.

73   Esther Ratz, interviewed by the author, 17 May 2010, Toronto, ON.

74   Martin Gilbert, *The Boys: The Story of 732 Young Concentration Camp Survivors* (New York: Henry Holt & Co., 1997).

75   Sam Wiezenbluth (Sewek Wajcenblith), interviewed by the author, 27 December 2007, Toronto, ON.

76   The '45 Aid Society for Holocaust Survivors is a charitable organization run by the 732 young Holocaust survivors brought to England beginning in 1945, and their descendants, accessed 8 January 2008, http://45aidsociety.co.uk.

77   Morris and Sonja Faintuch, interview.

78   Morris Faintuch, interview.

79   Ibid.

80   Among the approximately 7,000 to 8,000 Hungarian Jews granted entry into Canada in 1956 and 1957, many were also survivors of the Holocaust. However, despite the magnitude of these refugees' wartime trauma, life under communist leadership, and flight from Hungary, their story is not the subject of this study. For more on Canada's role in this refugee crisis, see Peter I. Hidas, "The Hungarian Refugee Student Movement of 1956–57 and Canada," *Canadian Ethnic Studies/études ethniques au Canada* 30, no.1 (1998): 19–49.

## Chapter Nine: Mothers and Misters: Parenting, Work, and Gender

1   For more on marriages between Holocaust survivors in postwar DP camps, and their marriage and childbirth patterns, see Michael Brenner, *After the Holocaust: Rebuilding Jewish Life in Postwar Germany* (Princeton, NJ: Princeton University Press, 1997), Atina Grossman, *Jews, Germans, and Allies: Close Encounters in Occupied Germany* (Princeton, NJ: Princeton University Press, 2009); Zeev W. Mankowitz, *Life between Memory and Hope: The Survivors of the Holocaust in Occupied Germany* (New York: Cambridge University Press, 2002); Mark Wyman, *DPs: Europe's Displaced Persons, 1951–1954* (Ithaca, NY: Cornell University Press, 1998).

2   According to Ada Schein, "Data from the American-occupied zone in Germany indicate a striking rise in the population of infants and children under five during 1946. In January 1946, there were 120 children under the age of five; by September of that year, the number had reached 4,430. According to a report by the American Jewish Joint Distribution Committee (known as the Joint) in late November 1946, out of 134,541 Jewish displaced persons in the American zone, 3.2 percent were infants of up to one year, 3.5 percent were children aged between one and five, and 10.5 percent were children from the ages of six to fifteen. In 1947, the birth rate in the D.P. camps reached 50.2 per thousand, one of the highest in the world, dropping to 31.1 by the summer of 1949." Ada Schein, "She'erit ha-Peletah: Women in DP Camps in Germany," *Jewish Women's Archive: A Comprehensive Historical Encyclopedia*, accessed 1 January 2012, http://jwa.org/encyclopedia/article/sheerit-ha-peletah-women-in-dp-camps-in-germany.

3    Miriam Frankel, interviewed by the author, 6 October 2010, Toronto, ON;  Fania Wedro, interviewed by the author, 27 October 2009, Calgary, AB; Anna (Szczercowska) Holtzman, interviewed by the author, 12 November 2009, Toronto, ON; Liselotte Ivry, interviewed by the author, 8 August 2009, Montreal, QC.

4    Elizabeth Feldman de Jong, interview no. 543, 1995, Visual History Archive, University of Southern California Shoah Foundation Institute (SFI), http://sfi.usc.edu/. On medical experimentation, see Robert Jay Lifton, *The Nazi Doctors: Medical Killing and the Psychology of Genocide* (New York: Basic Books, 2000).

5    For accounts of sexual violence and the Holocaust, see Sonja M. Hedgepeth & Rochelle G. Saidel, eds. *Sexual Violence against Jewish Women during the Holocaust* (Waltham, MA: Brandeis University Press, 2010).

6    Excerpt from Mila (Amalia) B's oral history, recorded by Living Testimonies–Holocaust Video Documentation Archive, McGill University, Montreal, in Yehudi Lindeman, ed., *Shards of Memory: Narratives of Holocaust Survivors* (Westport, CT: Praeger, 2007), 13.

7    JIAS Social Service Department caseload report for January 1952, filed by R. Landua, 1–3, and JIAS Social Service Department caseload report for August 1952, filed by Alfred Rosen, 1–3, file 16, box 5, part 2, JIAS QCB, MAS Joseph Kage Collection, Canadian Jewish Congress Charities Committee National Archives (CJCCC), Montreal.

8    "Social Readjustment of Newcomers," *JIAS Record* (Montreal) I, no. 3, November 1948, 7.

9    Iacovetta, *Gatekeepers: Reshaping Immigrant Lives in Cold War Canada*, 49.

10   "Ilona G.," 2, JIAS Immigration case files series CA, CJCCC, Montreal.

11   Ibid.

12   Iacovetta, *Gatekeepers*, 68–9.

13   Helen Schwartz, interviewed by the author, 5 November 2005, Toronto, ON.

14   Ibid.

15   Judy Weissenberg Cohen, interviewed by the author, 13 December 2005, Toronto, ON.

16   Arthur Birnbaum, interviewed by the author, 11 December 2009, Toronto, ON.

17   Ibid.

18   "Pnina and Isreal G.," JIAS Immigration Case Files Series CA, CJCCC, Montreal.

19   "Hella G.," JIAS Immigration Case Files Series CA, CJCCC, Montreal.

20   Bronia Sonnenschein, interviewed by Dan Sonnenschein, Vancouver, BC, undated (multiple occasions).

21   Bronia Sonnenschein, *Victory over Nazism: The Journey of a Holocaust Survivor*, 3rd Edition, Dan Sonnenschein, ed. (Vancouver: Memory Press, 2013), 58.

22   Dan Sonnenschein, interviewed by the author, 5 June 2013, Vancouver, BC.

23   Sonnenschein, *Victory over Nazism,* 58.

24   Bronia worked for Alaska Pine in various capacities until her retirement, twenty-five years later. Interviews with Bronia Sonnenschein, undated. Courtesy of Dan Sonnenschein.

25   Missionary groups' outreach to Jewish DP mothers is explored in Chapter 6.

26   Mary Palevsky, "Report on Survey of Jewish Refugee Settlement in Canada for the Canadian Jewish Congress," 31, October 1949, file 2, "War Efforts, 1933–1950," CJC Papers, CJCCC, Montreal.

27   Minutes of meeting re: Survey on Refugees, Montreal, 19 April 1949, 1–4, box 1/2, CJC ZC49, CJCCC, Montreal.

28    Undated note on Mothers' and Babes' Summer Rest Home, 3, file 1, Dora Till Collection 1987–1/5, Ontario Jewish Archives (OJA), Toronto.

29    Mothers' and Babes' Summer Rest Home Camp administration operating statement from 5 December 1950 to 11 October 1951, 2–3, file 50, Dora Till Collection 1987-1/5, OJA, Toronto; Rabbi Gail Labovitz, "Multiple Loyalties: A Great-Granddaughter's Reflection on the Life of Ida Lewis Siegel," *Canadian Woman Studies–Jewish Women in Canada Edition* 16, no. 4 (1996), 95–98.

30    Undated note on Mothers' and Babes' Summer Rest Home, 2–3.

31    Untitled memo from E.I. Shapiro, president, to Ben Lappin, Toronto, 4 Mar 1952, 2, file 12, Dora Till Collection 1987-1/5, OJA, Toronto.

32    Letter from David Andrews, managing director of MBH, to Ben Lappin, CJC, Toronto, 15 Oct 1952, 1, file 1, Dora Till Collection 1987-1/5, OJA, Toronto. Formerly independent from Toronto Jewish organizations, the Rest Home joined the Jewish Camp Council in 1951; minutes, Jewish Camp Council–Executive Council meeting, 2 Oct 1956, 1, file 3, Dora Till Collection 1987-1/5, OJA, Toronto.

33    Anonymous survivor, interviewed by the author, 10 January 2011, Toronto, ON.

34    Oral history of Sari G, *CURA: Life Stories of Montrealers Displaced by War, Genocide and other Human Rights Violations,* The Centre for Oral History and Digital Storytelling, Concordia University, Montreal. 2010.

35    Kopel Schmeltzmann, interview no. 46612, Visual History Archive, University of Southern California Shoah Foundation Institute (SFI), http://sfi.usc.edu/.

36    Letter from Herb Weinstein, JFWB, Montreal, to Harold Sharkey, administrative supervisor, Conference Committee for Refugee Rabbis, NY, 3 November 1954, 2, file "M., Berl," JIAS Immigration Case Files Series CA, CJCCC, Montreal.

37    Summary of contact by Sylvia Endler, JIAS social worker, undated, 2, file "M., Berl," JIAS Immigration Case Files series CA, CJCCC, Montreal.

38    Leon Ginsberg, interview no. 30500, 1997, SFI.

39    Ibid.

40    On gender roles in other immigrant communities, see Abigail Bakan and Daiva Stasiulis, *Not One of the Family: Foreign Domestic Workers in Canada* (Toronto: University of Toronto Press, 1997); Marlene Epp, *Women without Men: Mennonite Refugees of the Second World War* (Toronto: University of Toronto Press, 2000); Wenona Giles, Helene Moussa, and Penny Van Estrick, eds., *Development and Diaspora: Gender and the Refugee Experience* (Dundas, ON: Artemis Enterprises, 1996); and Franca Iacovetta, *Such Hardworking People: Italian Immigrants in Postwar Toronto* (Montreal: McGill-Queen's University Press, 1992).

41    Communication between the AJDC, France, and CJC, Montreal, undated correspondence, box 57, JDC Refugee and Relief Program Case Records, UJRA Collection, CJCCC, Montreal.

42    "The Census and the evolution of gender roles in early 20th century Canada," 8 March 2010, 1, *Statistics Canada,* http://www.statcan.gc.ca/pub/11-008-x/2010001/article/11125-eng.htm; "Chart 1: Over the first half of the 20th century, the proportion of household heads who were women increased steadily," Dominion Bureau of Statistics, censuses of population compiled by the Canadian Century Research Infrastructure Project, accessed 15 September 2011 at *Statistics Canada,* http://www.statcan.gc.ca/pub/11-008-x/2010001/c-g/11125/c-g001-eng.htm.

43    On Jewish women and work in the interwar period, see Ruth A. Frager, *Sweatshop Strife: Class, Ethnicity, and Gender in the Jewish Labour Movement of Toronto 1900–1939* (Toronto: University of Toronto Press, 1992).

44   On gender roles in the postwar period, see Joan Sangster, *Transforming Labour: Women and Work in Postwar Canada* (Toronto: University of Toronto Press, 2010).

45   "G., Moshe," JIAS Immigration Case Files Series CA, CJCCC, Montreal.

46   Attractive DP women received public acknowledgment of their wartime activities and survival, and were welcomed into Canada. For an example of a Jewish DP case, see "Pretty Orphan Underground Aide Coming Here," *JIAS Record* (Montreal) I, no. 2, October 1948, 15. For a similar case involving a non-Jewish Czech woman escapee from behind the Iron Curtain, see Iacovetta, *Gatekeepers: Reshaping Immigrant Lives in Cold War Canada*, 36–40.

47   UJRA, Summary of B family, undated, file 53, box 1, RG292, OJA, Toronto.

48   Sangster, *Transforming Labour,* 6.

49   Few foreign-born females ever transcended blue-collar work to enter the professional work-force, spending their entire working careers in low-paying service and manufacturing jobs. Between 1940 and 1950, more than one-third of immigrant women were located in service labour, specifically product fabrications like needlework. Ibid, 54–7.

50   UJRA, Summary of M family, file 491, box 5, RG292, OJA, Toronto.

51   "F., Berco," JIAS Immigration Case Files Series CA, CJCCC, Montreal.

52   Judy Weissenberg Cohen, interviewed by the author, 13 December 2005, Toronto, ON.

53   Mendel and Valerie Good, interviewed by the author, 14 November 2005, Toronto, ON.

54   Ibid.

55   "W., Sonja," JIAS Immigration Case Files Series CA, CJCCC, Montreal.

56   "G., Regina," JIAS Immigration Case Files Series CA, CJCCC, Montreal. Note in original.

57   Ibid., 4.

58   Ibid., 6–7.

59   Ibid.

60   Minutes of meeting re: Conference for Plans for Foster Daycare for DP Millinery Workers Children, 7 September 1949, Montreal, QC, 1, box 1, CJC CZ49, CJCCC, Montreal.

61   This issue was less pressing in smaller communities, which were better equipped to accom-modate the needs of a few nursery school–aged children by integrating them into pre-existing systems. Lesser demands equalled less financial strain on intake agencies.

62   CJC I.O.I. Summary III, 27 July 1949.

63   Letter from David Weiss, executive director of the Family Welfare Department of the Baron de Hirsch Institute and Jewish Child and Welfare Bureau, to Saul Hayes, executive director of the CJC, 26 November 1948, Montreal, QC, box 26, UJRA Collection–War Orphans, JCFW Bureau, 1948–1949, CJCCC, Montreal.

64   Palevsky, "Report on Survey of Jewish Refugee Settlement in Canada for the Canadian Jewish Congress," 21–2.

65   Letter from M.A. Solkin, executive director of the JIAS, to Saul Hayes, 26 November 1948, Montreal, QC, box 26, UJRA Collection–War Orphans Box, JCFW Bureau, 1948–1949, CJCCC, Montreal.

66   Although the JIAS also served the newcomer population, its mandate was limited to survivors' first six months in Canada, and the proposed program would extend beyond that term.

67   Minutes of meeting of Coordinating Committees on Refugee Services, 11 August 1949, Fed-eration of Jewish Philanthropies Office, Montreal, QC, box 1, CJC ZC49, CJCCC, Montreal.

68    Minutes of meeting re: Conference for Plans for Foster Daycare for DP Millinery Workers Children, 7 September 1949, Montreal, QC, 1–2, box 1, CJC CZ49, CJCCC, Montreal.

69    "Survey of Jewish Refugee Settlement, 1949–1950," 4, file 376, box 37, CJC–CENT CA, CJCCC, Montreal.

70    "Special Assistance to Infants and Expectant Mothers Among Refugees to Toronto," CJC I.O.I. Bulletin III, 3 August 1948. CJC Fonds, CJCCC, Montreal.

71    CJC I.O.I. Summary II, 19 April 1949.

72    Ibid.

73    CJC I.O.I. Summary II, 9 May 1949.

74    UJRA, "X Family Case File," file 699, box 6, RG292. OJA, Toronto.

75    "Doctors David and Maria S.," 3, JIAS Immigration Case Files Series CA, CJCCC, Montreal.

76    Ibid., 6.

77    "Doctors Stefan and Mina W.," 2 JIAS Immigration Case Files Series CA, CJCCC, Montreal.

78    For a comprehensive look at her wartime and postwar experiences, see Mina Deutsch, *Mina's Story: A Doctor's Memoir of the Holocaust* (Toronto: ECW Press, 1994).

79    Ibid., 125–6.

80    Dr. Mina Deutsch, interview no. 04.05.24MD, 24 May 2004, Research Department, Canadian Museum of Immigration at Pier 21, Halifax, NS.

81    Ibid. Dr. Mina Deutsch passed away 3 October 2004.

82    Janice Arnold, "Chava Rosenfarb: *Grande Dame of Yiddish Theatre*," *The Canadian Jewish News*, 10 February 2011. Rokhl (Rachel) Korn was another Yiddish writer who achieved notoriety in the postwar Canadian Yiddish scene.

83    Judy Stoffman, "Graduates of Holocaust - Chava Rosenfarb writes in Yiddish, her mother tongue. And she's finding a new kind of literary recognition at age 83," *The Toronto Star*, 17 June 2006, H-09.

84    Announcement by Melech Ravitch to Yiddish writers community (translated from Yiddish), 21 February 1950, Montreal, Chava Rosenfarb File, CJCCC, Montreal.

85    Announcement by Hirsch Hershman regarding Chava Rosenfarb's public speaking event (translated from Yiddish), 25 April 1950, Montreal, Chava Rosenfarb File, CJCCC, Montreal.

86    Born in 1898 in Galicia, and an immigrant to Canada in 1948, Rokhl Korn was part of Montreal's Yiddish writers circle, and the author of eleven volumes of Yiddish poetry and short stories published in pre-war and postwar Europe, North America, and Israel. Unlike Chava Rosenfarb, whose work was thematically linked to the Holocaust and survivors, Korn dealt with issues in nature, and social justice concerns, specifically the global threat of anti-Semitism.

87    Chava Rosenfarb, "Writing in a Language Foreign to Nearly All," *The Montreal Gazette*, 14 August 1999, 11–12. As Goldie Morgentaler related in a lecture on her mother's legacy, even in light of declining readership numbers due to a limited number of Yiddish readers, Rosenfarb continued to write in her venacular until her death in 2011, although translations of her work continue to be published; Goldie Morgentaler, "Teaching Modern Jewish Literature in the Canadian Bible Belt" (paper presented at the Association for Canadian Jewish Studies Annual Conference, Congress for Humanities and Social Sciences, Ottawa, ON, 24 May 2009. More recently, Rosenfarb's life and contributions to Yiddish life and culture have been cited in Rebecca Margolis, *Jewish Roots, Canadian Soil: Yiddish Cultural Life in Montreal, 1905–1945* (Montreal: McGill-Queen's University Press, 2011).

88    Rosenfarb, "Writing in a Language Foreign to Nearly All," 12.

89    Chava Rosenfarb died 30 January 2011.

90    Iacovetta, *Gatekeepers*, 139.

91    "Joseph G.," JIAS Immigration Case Files Series CA, CJCCC, Montreal.

92    Rebeka Bialystok Zloto, testimony no. 27, 1990, The Testimony Project, The Holocaust Centre of Toronto.

93    "Josef and Berta K.," 3, JIAS Immigration Case Files Series CA, CJCCC, Montreal.

94    Ibid., 4.

## *Conclusion*

1    Diary entry, 29 March 1938, 2, MG26-J13, The Diaries of William Lyon Mackenzie King Fonds, Library Archives Canada (LAC), Ottawa, as cited in Abella and Troper, *None Is Too Many*, 17. The Evian Conference, 6–15 July 1938 at Evian-les-Bains, France, unapologetically exposed Canada's position on Jewish refugees: they were Germany's problem, not ours. Even the diminutive Dominican Republic, among the least wealthy nations represented at the conference, extended welcomes to 5,000 refugees. See Ervin Birnbaum, "Evian: The Most Fateful Conference of All Time in Jewish History," *NATIV*, part 1 (November 2008) and part 2 (February 2009); Abella and Troper, *None Is Too Many*, 16–32.

2    Peter Newman, "Are We Doing Enough to Help Our Immigrants?" *The Financial Post* (Toronto), 2 August 1952, 1.

3    Statistics relating to this subgroup of Jewish migrants to Canada are unreliable, and do not take into account the immigrants' or refugees' date and place of birth or wartime experiences. Through the investigation of immigration records and travel logs, this study has arrived at the estimate of approximately 10,000 or more Holocaust survivors among this latter wave.

4    Valerie Knowles, *Strangers at Our Gates: Canadian Immigration and Immigration Policy, 1540–2006* (Toronto: Dundurn Press, 2007),176; Alexandra Zabjek, "How 'the 56ers' Changed Canada," *The Ottawa Citizen*, 15 October 2006, B4.

5    Peter I. Hidas, "Canada and the Hungarian Jewish Refugees, 1956–57," *East European Jewish Affairs* 37, no.1 (2007), 77, 80.

# BIBLIOGRAPHY

## Archives and Libraries

Canadian Jewish Congress Charities Committee National Archives, Montreal, QC

Canadian Museum of Immigration at Pier 21, Halifax, NS

CJC Holocaust Documentation Project, Montreal, QC

Fortunoff Video Archives for Holocaust Testimonies, Yale University, New Haven, CT

The Freeman Family Foundation Holocaust Education Centre, Winnipeg, MB

Jewish Historical Society of Southern Alberta, Calgary, AB

Jewish Historical Society of Western Heritage, Winnipeg, MB

Jewish Museum and Archives of British Columbia, Vancouver, BC

Jewish Public Library, Montreal, QC

Library and Archives Canada, Ottawa, ON

Living Testimonies—Holocaust Video Documentation Archive, McGill University, Montreal, QC

Montreal Institute for Genocide and Human Rights Studies, Memoirs of Holocaust Survivors in Canada, Concordia University, Montreal, QC

Nova Scotia Archives and Records Management, Halifax, NS

Ontario Jewish Archives, Toronto, ON

Rose Library, Strassler Center for Holocaust and Genocide Studies, Clark University, Worcester, MA

Survivors of the Shoah Visual History Foundation, Clark University, Worcester, MA

The Frank and Anita Ekstein Holocaust Resource Library, Toronto, ON

The Testimony Project, Sarah and Chaim Neuberger Holocaust Education Centre (formerly The Holocaust Centre of Toronto), Toronto, ON

United States Holocaust Memorial Museum Digital Archives, Washington, DC

University of Toronto Archives, Toronto, ON

Vancouver Holocaust Education Centre, Vancouver, BC

## Books

Abella, Irving. *A Coat of Many Colours: Two Centuries of Jewish Life in Canada*. Toronto: Key Porter Books, 2002.

Abella, Irving, and Harold Troper. *None Is Too Many: Canada and the Jews of Europe 1933–1948*. Toronto: Lester & Orpen Dennys Publishers, 1983.

Abramov, Zalman. *Perpetual Dilemma: Jewish Religion in the Jewish State*. Madison, NJ: Farleigh Dickinson State University, 1979.

Anctil, Pierre. *Le rendez-vous manqué: Les Juifs de Montréal face au Québec de l'entre-deux guerres*. Montreal: Institut Québécois de Recherche sur la Culture, 1988.

Andlauer, Anna. *The Rage to Live: The International D.P. Children's Center Kloster Indersdorf 1945–1946*. CreateSpace Independent Publishing Platform, 2012.

Armstrong-Reid, Susan E. *Armies of Peace: Canada and the UNRRA Years*. Toronto: University of Toronto Press, 2008.

Aronson, Michael. *Troubled Waters: The Origins of the 1881 Anti-Jewish Pogroms in Russia*. Pittsburgh: University of Pittsburgh Press, 1990.

Avineri, Shlomo. *The Making of Modern Zionism: The Intellectual Origins of the Jewish State*. New York: Basic Books, 1981.

Azrieli, David. *Rekindling the Torch: The Story of Canadian Zionism*. Toronto: Key Porter Books, 2008.

Bakan, Abigail, and Daiva Stasiulis. *Not One of the Family: Foreign Domestic Workers in Canada*. Toronto: University of Toronto Press, 1997.

Banks, Lynne Reid. *Torn Country: An Oral History of the Israeli War of Independence*. New York: Franklin Watts, 1982.

Bartrop, Paul R, ed. *False Havens: The British Empire and the Holocaust*. Lanham, MD: University Press of America, 1995.

Baumel-Schwartz, Judith Tydor. *Kibbutz Buchenwald: Survivors and Pioneers*. New Brunswick, NJ: Rutgers University Press, 1997.

Belkin, Simon. *Through Narrow Gates: A Review of Jewish Immigration, Colonization and Immigration Aid Work in Canada, 1840–1940*. Montreal: Canadian Jewish Congress/ Jewish Colonization Association, 1966.

Ben-Itto, Hadassa. *The Lie That Wouldn't Die: The Protocols of the Elders of Zion*. Middlesex, UK: Vallentine Mitchell, 2005.

Berkovits, Eliezer. *Faith After the Holocaust*. Jersey City, NJ: KTAV Publishing, 1973.

Berman, Judith E. *Holocaust Remembrance in Australian Jewish Communities, 1945–2000*. Crawley, Australia: University of Western Australia Press, 2001.

Betcherman, Lita-Rose. *Ernest Lapointe, Mackenzie King's Great Quebec Lieutenant*. Toronto: University of Toronto Press, 2002.

———. *The Swastika and the Maple Leaf: Fascist Movements in Canada in the Thirties*. Toronto: Fitzhenry & Whiteside, 1975.

Bialystok, Franklin. *Delayed Impact: The Holocaust and the Canadian Jewish Community*. Montreal: McGill-Queen's University Press, 2000.

Bineth, Yitel Nechamah. *Omika: The Life of Our Beloved Mother, Lea Paskusz*. Montreal: Self-published, 1999.

Blakeney, Michael. *Australia and the Jewish Refugees, 1933-1948*. Sydney, Australia: Croom Helm Australia, 1985.

Bogner, Nachum. *At the Mercy of Strangers: The Rescue of Hidden Jewish Children in Poland.* Jerusalem: Yad Vashem, 2009.

Bookman, Max. "Orthodox, Conservative and Reform Congregations." In *Canadian Jewish Reference Book and Directory,* ed. Eli Gottesman. Ottawa: Mortimer Limited, 1963.

Bosworth, R.J.B. *Mussolini's Italy: Life Under the Fascist Dictatorship.* London: Penguin Books, 2007.

Brenner, Hannelore. *The Girls of Room 28: Friendship, Hope and Survival in Theresienstadt.* New York: Schocken Books, 2009.

Brenner, Michael. *After the Holocaust: Rebuilding Jewish Life in Postwar Germany.* Princeton, NJ: Princeton University Press, 1997.

Brown, Michael. *Jew or Juif? Jews, French Canadians, and Anglo-Canadians, 1759–1914.* Philadelphia: The Jewish Publication Society, 1986.

Buber, Martin. *Eclipse of God.* Amherst, NY: Humanity Books, 1988.

Cohen, Beth. *Case Closed: Holocaust Survivors in Postwar America.* New Brunswick, NJ: Rutgers University Press, 2007.

Cohen, Lisa-Catherine. *The Builders: The Fifty-year History of Congregation Habonim.* The Writers Guild of America, 2013.

Cotler, Irwin, William Shaffir, and Morton Weinfeld. *The Canadian Jewish Mosaic.* Toronto: John Wiley & Sons, 1981.

Davies, Alan, ed. *Anti-Semitism in Canada: History and Interpretation.* Waterloo, ON: Wilfrid Laurier University Press, 1992.

De Felice, Renzo. *The Jews in Fascist Italy: A History.* New York: Enigma Books, 2001.

Delisle, Esther. *Myths, Memory & Lies: Quebec's Intelligentsia and the Fascist Temptation, 1939–1960.* Translated from French by Madeleine Hébert. Westmount, QC: Robert Davies, 1998.

———. *The Traitor and the Jew: Anti-Semitism and the Delirium of Extremist Right-Wing Nationalism in French Canada from 1929–1939.* Montreal: Robert Davies Publishing, 1993.

Deutsch, Mina. *Mina's Story: A Doctor's Memoir of the Holocaust.* Toronto: ECW Press, 1994.

Diamond, Etan. *And I Will Dwell in Their Midst: Orthodox Jews in Suburbia.* Chapel Hill: University of North Carolina Press, 2000.

Diner, Hasia R. *We Remember with Reverence and Love: American Jews and the Myth of Silence After the Holocaust, 1945–1962.* New York: New York University Press, 2009.

Dinnerstein, Leonard. *America and the Survivors of the Holocaust.* New York: Columbia University Press, 1982.

Dirks, Gerald E. *Canada's Refugee Policy: Indifference or Opportunism?* Montreal: McGill-Queen's University Press, 1977.

Dove, Richard, ed. *'Totally un-English'?: Britain's Internment of 'Enemy Aliens' in Two World Wars: Yearbook of the Research Centre for German and Austrian Exile Studies.* Amsterdam: The Netherlands: Editions Rodopi B.V., 2005.

Draper, Paula J., and Richard Menkis, eds. *New Perspectives on Canada, the Holocaust and Survivors* (Special Issue of *Canadian Jewish Studies*), Volumes 4–5. Association for Canadian Jewish Studies, 1996–1997.

Dwork, Debórah. *Children With A Star: Jewish Youth in Nazi Europe.* New Haven, CT: Yale University Press, 1991.

Dwork, Debórah, and Robert Jan van Pelt. *Holocaust: A History.* New York: W.W. Norton & Company, 2002.

Easton, David Roy. *No Alternative: Israel Observed.* London: Hutchinson, 1960.

Ehrenreich, John. *The Altruistic Imagination: A History of Social Work and Social Policy in the United States.* Ithaca, NY: Cornell University Press, 1985.

Elazar, Daniel J. *Community and Polity: The Organizational Dynamics of American Jewry.* Philadelphia: The Jewish Publication Society of America, 1980.

Epp, Marlene. *Women without Men: Mennonite Refugees of the Second World War.* Toronto: University of Toronto Press, 2000.

Fackenheim, Emil. *To Mend the World: Foundations of Post-Holocaust Jewish Thought.* Bloomington: Indiana University Press, 1994.

Farbstein, Esther. *Hidden in Thunder: Perspectives on Faith, Halachah and Leadership during the Holocaust,* Volumes I & II. Jerusalem: Old City Press, 2007.

Feldman, Elliot J., and Neil Nevitte. *The Future of North America: Canada, the United States, and Quebec Nationalism.* Lanham, MD: University Press of America, 1984.

Figes, Orlando. *A People's Tragedy: The Russian Revolution 1891–1924.* London: Penguin Books, 1998.

Figler, Bernard. *Lillian and Archie Freiman.* Montreal: The Northern Printing and Lithography Co., 1962.

Frager, Ruth A. *Sweatshop Strife: Class, Ethnicity, and Gender in the Jewish Labour Movement of Toronto 1900–1939.* Toronto: University of Toronto Press, 1992.

Frankl, Viktor. *Man's Search for Meaning.* Boston: Beacon Press, 2006.

Friedman, Saul S. *A History of the Holocaust.* Middlesex, UK: Valentine Mitchell, 2004.

Gafny, Emunah Nachmany. *Dividing Hearts: The Removal of Jewish Children from Gentile Families in Poland in the Immediate Post Holocaust Years.* Jerusalem: Yad Vashem, 2009.

Gilbert, Martin. *The Boys: The Story of 732 Young Concentration Camp Survivors.* New York: Henry Holt & Co., 1997.

———. *The Holocaust: A History of the Jews of Europe During the Second World War.* New York: Henry Holt & Co., 1985.

Giles, Wenona, Helen Moussa, and Penny Van Estrick, eds. *Development and Diaspora: Gender and the Refugee Experience.* Dundas, ON: Artemis Enterprises, 1996.

Gillette, Aaron. *Racial Theories in Fascist Italy.* Routledge Studies in Modern European History. Florence, KY: Taylor & Francis, 2007.

Goldberg, David. *Foreign Policy and Ethnic Interest Groups: American and Canadian Jews Lobby for Israel.* Santa Barbara, CA: Greenwood Press, 1990.

Gottesman, Eli, ed. *Canadian Jewish Reference Book and Directory.* Ottawa: Mortimer Limited, 1963.

———. *Who's Who in Canadian Jewry.* Montreal: The Canadian Jewish Literacy Foundation for the Jewish Institute of Higher Research of the Central Rabbinical Seminary of Canada, 1965.

Grobman, Alex. *Battling for Souls: The Vaad Hatzala Rescue Committee in Post-Holocaust Europe.* Jersey City, NJ: KTAV Publishing House, 2004.

Grossman, Atina. *German, Jews, and Allies: Close Encounters in Occupied Germany*. Princeton, NJ: Princeton University Press, 2009.

Harney, Robert, and Harold Troper. *Immigrants: A Portrait of the Urban Experience*. Toronto: Van Nostrand Reinhold, 1975.

Hecht, Thomas O., as told to Joe King. *Czech Mate: A Life in Progress*. Jerusalem: Yad Vashem, 2007.

Hedgepeth, Sonja M., and Rochelle G. Saidel, eds. *Sexual Violence against Jewish Women during the Holocaust*. Waltham, MA: Brandeis University Press, 2010.

Helmreich, William. *Against All Odds: Holocaust Survivors and the Successful Lives They Made in America*. New York, NY: Simon & Schuster, 1992.

Henry, Marilyn. *Confronting the Perpetrators: A History of the Claims Conference*. London: Vallentine Mitchell, 2007.

Herzog, Chaim. *The Arab-Israeli Wars*. New York: Random House, 1982.

Holborn, Louise W. *The International Refugee Organization: A Specialized Agency of the United Nations, Its History and Work, 1946–1952*. London: Oxford University Press, 1956.

Iacovetta, Franca. *Gatekeepers: Reshaping Immigrant Lives in Cold War Canada*. Toronto: Between the Lines, 2006.

———. *Such Hardworking People: Italian Immigrants in Postwar Toronto*. Montreal: Institute for Research on Public Policy, 1993.

Iacovetta, Franca, Roberto Perin, and Angelo Principe, eds. *Enemies Within: Italian and Other Internees in Canada and Abroad*. Toronto: University of Toronto Press, 2000.

Iggers, Wilma, and George Iggers. *Two Lives in Uncertain Times: Facing the Challenges of the 20th Century as Scholars and Citizens*. New York: Berghahn Books, 2006.

Jennisen, Therese. *One Hundred Years of Social Work: A History of the Profession in English Canada, 1900–2000*. Waterloo, ON: Wilfrid Laurier University Press, 2011.

Kage, Joseph. *With Faith and Thanksgiving: The Story of Two Hundred Years of Jewish Immigration and Immigrant Aid Effort in Canada, 1790–1960*. Montreal: Eagle Publishing, 1962.

Kahana, Boaz, Eva Kahana, and Zev Harel. *Holocaust Survivors and Immigrants: Late Life Adaptations*. New York: Springer, 2005.

Kangisser Cohen, Sharon. *Child Survivors of the Holocaust in Israel: "Finding Their Voice": Social Dynamics and Post-War Experiences*. Brighton, UK: Sussex Academic Press, 2005.

Kaplan, Marion A. *Dominican Haven: The Jewish Refugee Settlement in Sosua, 1940–1945*. New York: Museum of Jewish Heritage–A Living Memorial to the Holocaust, 2008.

Kay, Zachariah. *Canada and Palestine: The Politics of Non-Commitment*. Jerusalem: Israel Universities Press, 1978.

———. *The Diplomacy of Prudence: Canada and Israel, 1948–1958*. Montreal: McGill-Queen's University Press, 1997.

Kelley, Ninette, and Michael J. Trebilcock. *The Making of the Mosaic: A History of Canadian Immigration Policy*. Toronto: University of Toronto Press, 1998.

Kelly, Orr. *Meeting the Fox: The Allied Invasion of Africa, from Operation Torch to Kasserine Pass to Victory in Tunisia*. Hoboken, NJ: Wiley, 2002.

Kenan, Orna. *Between Memory and History: The Evolution of Israeli Historiography of the Holocaust, 1945–1961*. New York: Peter Lang Publishing, 2003.

King, Joe. *From the Ghetto to the Main: The Story of the Jews of Montreal.* Montreal: Jewish Publication Society, 2001.

Klein, Ruth, and Frank Dimant, eds. *From Immigration to Integration. The Canadian Jewish Experience: A Millennium Edition.* Toronto: Institute for International Affairs of B'nai Brith Canada, 2001.

Kluger, Ruth. *Still Alive: A Holocaust Girlhood Remembered.* New York: The Feminist Press of the City University of New York, 2001.

Knowles, Valerie. *Strangers at Our Gates: Canadian Immigration and Immigration Policy, 1540–2006.* Toronto: Dundurn Press, 2007.

Koch, Eric. *Deemed Suspect: A Wartime Blunder.* Halifax: Goodread Biographies, 1985.

Krell, Robert, ed. *Childhood Survivors: Memories and Reflections.* Victoria, BC: Trafford Publishing, 2007.

Kurzman, Dan. *Genesis 1948: The First Arab-Israel War.* Middlesex, UK: Vallentine Mitchell, 1970.

Lacquer, Walter. *A History of Zionism.* London: Weidenfeld and Nicolson, 1972.

*Land of Promise: The Jewish Experience in Southern Alberta.* Calgary: Jewish Historical Society of Southern Alberta, 2006.

Lappin, Ben. *The Redeemed Children: The Story of the Rescue of War Orphans by the Jewish Community of Canada.* Toronto: University of Toronto Press, 1963.

Levine, Allan. *Coming of Age: A History of the Jewish People of Manitoba.* Winnipeg: Heartland Associates, 2009.

Levitt, Cyril H., and William Shaffir. *The Riot at Christie Pits.* Toronto: Lester & Orpen Denys, 1987.

Levy, Richard S., and Binjamin W. Segel. *A Lie and a Libel: The History of the* Protocols of the Elders of Zion. Lincoln: University of Nebraska Press, 1996.

Lewin, Izaak. *Przez Pryzmat Historii.* Warsaw: Jewish Historical Institute, 1994.

Liebman, Charles S. and Eliezer Don-Yehiya. *Civil Religion in Israel: Traditional Judaism and Political Culture in the Jewish State.* Berkeley: University of California Press, 1983.

Lifschitz, Judah. *The Klausenberger Rebbe: Rebuilding.* Southfield, MI: Targum Press, 2007.

Lifton, Robert Jay. *The Nazi Doctors: Medical Killing and the Psychology of Genocide.* New York: Basic Books, 2000.

Lindeman, Yehudi, ed. *Shards of Memory: Narratives of Holocaust Survivors.* Westport, CT: Praeger, 2007.

Lipinsky, Jack. *Imposing Their Will: An Organizational History of Jewish Toronto, 1933–1948.* Montreal: McGill-Queen University Press, 2011.

Lipschitz, Chaim U., with Sonia Winter, Hallie Cantor, and Judy Bendet, eds. *The Shanghai Connection.* New York: Maznaim Publishing Corp., 1988.

Lipschitz, Max A. *The Faith of a Hassid.* New York: Jonathan David Publishing, 2003.

Lorch, Netanel. *The Edge of the Sword: Israel's War of Independence, 1947–1949.* New York: Putnam, 1961.

Mankowitz, Zeev W. *Life between Memory and Hope: The Survivors of the Holocaust in Occupied Germany.* New York: Cambridge University Press, 2002.

Margolis, Rebecca. *Jewish Roots, Canadian Soil: Yiddish Cultural Life in Montreal, 1905–1945*. Montreal: McGill-Queen's University Press, 2011.

Martz, Fraidie. *Open Your Hearts: The Story of the Jewish War Orphans in Canada*. Don Mills, ON: Véhicule Press, 1996.

Mayer, Jack. *Life in a Jar: The Irena Sendler Project*. Middlebury, VT: Long Trail Press, 2011.

Medres, Israel. *Between the Wars: Canadian Jews in Transition*. Translated from Yiddish by Vivian Felsen. Montreal: Véhicule Press, 2003.

Millo, Belle, ed. *Voices of Winnipeg Holocaust Survivors*. Winnipeg: Jewish Heritage Centre of Western Canada, 2010.

Mintz, Jerome R. *Hasidic People: A Place in the New World*. Cambridge, MA: Harvard University Press, 1998.

Morgan, Keith, with Ruth Kron Sigal. *Ruta's Closet*. London: Unicorn Press and the Vancouver Holocaust Education Centre, 2008.

Mosse, Werner Eugen. *Second Chance: Two Centuries of German-speaking Jews in the United Kingdom*. Tübingen, Germany: J.C.B. Mohr, 1991.

Ogilvie, Sarah A., and Scott Miller. *Refuge Denied: The* St. Louis *Passengers and the Holocaust*. Madison, WI: University of Wisconsin Press, 2006.

Palmer, Howard. *Patterns of Prejudice: A History of Nativism in Alberta*. Toronto: McClelland and Stewart, 1982.

Pickersgill, J.W. *My Years With Louis St. Laurent: A Political Memoir*. Toronto: University of Toronto Press, 1975.

Polen, Nehemia. *The Holy Fire: The Teachings of Rabbi Kalonymus Kalman Shapira, the Rebbe of the Warsaw Ghetto*. New York: Jason Aronson, 1994.

Porat, Dina. *Israeli Society, the Holocaust and its Survivors*. Portland: Vallentine Mitchell, 2008.

Rabinowitz, Dorothy. *New Lives: Survivors of the Holocaust Living in America*. New York: Avon Books, 1977.

Ramati, Alexander. *Barbed Wire on the Isle of Man: The Wartime British Internment of Jews*. NewYork: Harcourt, Brace, Jonavich, 1980.

Robinson, Ira. *Rabbis and Their Community: Studies in the Eastern European Orthodox Rabbinate in Montreal, 1896–1930*. Calgary: University of Calgary Press, 2007.

Rosenberg, Louis. *Canada's Jews: A Social and Economic Study of the Jews in Canada in the 1930s*. Ed. Morton Weinfeld. Montreal: McGill-Queen's University Press, 1993.

Rubenstein, Richard L. *After Auschwitz: History, Theology, and Contemporary Judaism*. Baltimore: Johns Hopkins University Press, 1992.

Rubin, Israel. *Satmar: An Island in the City*. Chicago: Quadrangle Books, 1972.

Rubinstein, Robert Eli. *An Italian Renaissance: Choosing Life in Canada*. Jerusalem: Urim Publications, 2010.

Rutherdale, Robert. *Creating Postwar Canada: Community, Diversity, and Dissent, 1945–75*. Vancouver: University of British Columbia Press, 2008.

Sachar, Abraham Leon. *The Redemption of the Unwanted: From the Liberation of the Death Camps to the Founding of Israel*. New York: St. Martin's Press, 1983.

Sangster, Joan. *Transforming Labour: Women and Work in Post-war Canada*. Toronto: University of Toronto Press, 2010.

Schild, Erwin. *The Very Narrow Bridge: A Memoir of an Uncertain Passage*. Toronto: Adath Israel Congregation/Malcolm Lester, 2001.

Schneiderman, S.L. ed. *The Diary of Mary Berg: Growing up in the Warsaw Ghetto*, 2nd ed. Oxford: Oneworld Publications, 2006.

Schnoor, Randal F. and Alex Pomson. *Back to School: Jewish Day School in the Lives of Adults*. Detroit: Wayne State University Press, 2008.

Segev, Tom. *The Seventh Million: The Israelis and the Holocaust*. New York: Picador, 2000.

Shaffir, William. *Life in a Religious Community: The Lubavitcher Chassidim in Montreal*. Montreal: Holt, Rhinehart and Winston of Canada, 1974.

Shaffir, William, Morton Weinfeld, and Irwin Cotler, eds. *The Canadian Jewish Mosaic*. Toronto: John Wiley & Sons, 1981.

Shahar, Charles, Morton Weinfeld, and Randal F. Schnoor, eds. *Survey of the Hassidic and Ultra-Orthodox Communities in Outremont and Surrounding Areas*. Montreal: Coalition of Outremont Hassidic Organizations, 1997.

Sharef, Ze'ev. *Three Days: An Account of the Last Days of the British Mandate and the Birth of Israel*. New York: Doubleday, 1962.

Shulman, Abraham. *Case of Hotel Polski: An Account of One of the Most Enigmatic Episodes of World War II*. New York: Holocaust Library, 1982.

Somers, Erik and Rene Kok. *Jewish Displaced Persons in Camp Bergen-Belsen 1945–1950: The Unique Photo Album of Zippy Orlin*. Seattle: University of Washington Press, 2004.

Sonnenschein, Bronia. *Victory over Nazism: The Journey of a Holocaust Survivor*. 3rd ed. Ed. Dan Sonnenschein. Vancouver: Memory Press, 2013.

Speisman, Stephen A. *The Jews of Toronto: A History to 1937*. Toronto: McClelland and Stewart, 1987.

Spencer, Hanna. *Hanna's Diary, 1938–1941: Czechoslovakia to Canada*. Montreal: McGill-Queen's University Press, 2001.

Stevenson, Garth. *Community Besieged: The Anglophone Minority and the Politics of Quebec*. Montreal: McGill-Queen's University Press, 1999.

Stingel, Janine. *Social Discredit: Anti-Semitism, Social Credit and the Jewish Response*. Vol. 6. Montreal: McGill-Queen's University Press, 2000.

Thompson, Dale C. *Louis St. Laurent: Canadian*. Toronto: Macmillan of Canada, 1967.

Thornton, Martin. *The Domestic and International Dimensions of the Resettlement of Polish Ex Servicemen in Canada, 1943-1948*. Wales, UK: Canadian Studies, Edwin Mellen Press, 2000.

Troper, Harold. *The Defining Decade: Identity, Politics, and the Canadian Jewish Community in the 1960s*. Toronto: University of Toronto Press, 2010.

Troper, Harold, and Morton Weinfeld. *Old Wounds: Jews, Ukrainians and the Hunt for Nazi War Criminals in Canada*. Toronto: Penguin Canada, 1989.

Tulchinsky, Gerald. *Branching Out: The Transformation of the Canadian Jewish Community*. Santa Rosa, CA: Stoddart, 1998.

———. *Canada's Jews: A People's Journey*. Toronto: University of Toronto Press, 2008.

————. *Taking Root: The Origins of the Canadian Jewish Community*. Toronto: Stoddart Publishing, 1997.

Waldstein Wilkes, Helen. *Letters from the Lost: A Memoir of Discovery*. Edmonton: Athabasca University Press, 2010.

Weiner, Anita. *Expanding Historical Consciousness: The Development of the Holocaust Educational Foundation*. Skokie, IL: Holocaust Educational Foundation, 2002.

Weinfeld, Morton. *Like Everyone Else but Different: The Paradoxical Success of Canadian Jews*. Toronto: McClelland and Stewart, 2001.

Weisser, Michael R. *A Brotherhood of Memory: Jewish Landsmanshaftn in the New World*. New York: Basic Books, 1985.

Wenocur, Stanley. *From Charity to Enterprise: the Development of American Social Work in a Market Economy*. Urbana: University of Illinois Press, 1989.

Werner, Hans. *Imagined Homes: Soviet German Immigrants in Two Cities*. Winnipeg, MB: University of Manitoba Press, 2007.

Wiesel, Elie. *Night*. New York: Bantam Books, 1982.

Wistrich, Robert S. *A Lethal Obsession: Anti-Semitism from Antiquity to the Global Jihad*. New York: Random House, 2010.

Wyman, Mark. *DPs: Europe's Displaced Persons, 1951–1954*. Ithaca, NY: Cornell University Press, 1998.

Yablonka, Hanna. *Survivors of the Holocaust: Israel after the War*. New York: New York University Press, 1999.

Zeidman, Alex. *Good and Faithful Servant: The Biography of Morris Zeidman*. Burlington, ON: Crown Publication, 1990.

Zertal, Idith. *From Catastrophe to Power: Holocaust Survivors and the Emergence of Israel*. Berkeley: University of California Press, 1998.

Zoltak, Sidney. *My Silent Pledge: A Journey of Struggle, Survival and Remembrance*. Toronto: MiroLand, 2013.

Zuccotti, Susan. *The Italians and the Holocaust: Persecution, Rescue and Survival*. Lincoln, NE: University of Nebraska Press, 1996.

Zuckerman, Yitzhak, and Barbara Harshav. *A Surplus of Memory: Chronicle of the Warsaw Ghetto Uprising*. Berkeley: University of California Press, 1993.

Zweig, Ronald W. *German Reparations and the Jewish World: A History of the Claims Conference*. London: Routledge, 1987.

## Articles and Book Chapters

Abella, Irving, and Harold Troper. "'The Line Must Be Drawn Somewhere': Canada and Jewish Refugees, 1933–39." In *The Canadian Jewish Mosaic*. Eds. William Shaffir, Morton Weinfeld, and Irwin Cotler. Toronto: John Wiley & Sons, 1981. 178–209.

Anctil, Pierre. "Interlude of Hostility: Judeo-Christian Relations in Quebec in the Interwar Period, 1919–1939." In *Anti-Semitism in Canada: History and Interpretation*. Ed. Alan Davies. Waterloo, ON: Wilfrid Laurier University Press, 1992.

Baron, Leib. "Origins of Yeshivas in Canada." In *Canadian Jewish Reference Book and Directory*. Ed. Eli Gottesman. Ottawa: Mortimer Limited, 1963.

Birnbaum, Ervin. "Evian: The Most Fateful Conference of All Time in Jewish History." *NATIV,* part 1 (November 2008) and part 2 (February 2009). Shaarei Tikva, Israel: Ariel Center for Policy Research.

Dasberg, Haim. "Children of the Holocaust: Now and Then." In *Childhood Survivors: Memories and Reflections.* Ed. Robert Krell. Victoria, BC: Trafford Publishing, 2007, 55–60.

Draper, Paula Jean. "The Accidental Immigrants: Canada and the Interned Refugees: Part II. *The Canadian Jewish Historical Society Journal* 2, no. 2 (Fall 1978): 80–120.

Gellman, Irwin F. "The *St. Louis* Tragedy." In *American Jewish History-America, American Jews, and the Holocaust Edition,* Volume 7. Ed. Jeffrey S. Gurock. New York: Routledge, 1998, 57–69.

Goldberg, David H. and Bernard Reich. "Religion and State in the State of Israel." In *Religion, State and Society: Jefferson's Wall of Separation in Comparative Perspective.* Ed. Robert Fatton, Jr., and R.K. Ramazani. London: Palgrave Macmillan, 2009, 215–231.

Gutwirth, Jacques. "Hassidim et Judaicite à Montreal." *Recherches Sociographiques* 14 (1973): 291–325.

———. "Hassidism and Urban Life." *Jewish Journal of Sociology* 38 (1996): 105–13.

———. "The Structure of a Hassidic Community in Montreal." *Jewish Journal of Sociology* 14, no. 1 (June 1972): 44–7.

Hart, Michael and Bill Dymond. "Six Stewards of Canada's Economy." *Policy Options/Options Politiques* (June–July 2003): 29–38.

Haska, Agnieszka. "Adam Żurawin, a Hero of a Thousand Faces." *Holocaust Studies and Materials,* no. 1 (2008): 123–46.

Hidas, Peter I. "Canada and the Hungarian Jewish Refugees, 1956–57." *East European Jewish Affairs* 37, no. 1 (2007): 75–89.

———. "The Hungarian Refugee Student Movement of 1956–57 and Canada." *Canadian Ethnic Studies/études ethniques au Canada* 30, no. 1 (1998): 19–49.

Kage, Joseph. "The Jewish Immigrant Aid Services of Canada (JIAS)," in *Canadian Jewish Reference Book and Directory,* ed. Eli Gottesman. Ottawa: Mortimer Limited, 1963, 249.

Labovitz, Gail. "Multiple Loyalties: A Great-Granddaughter's Reflection on the Life of Ida Lewis Siegel." *Canadian Woman Studies-Jewish Woman in Canada Edition* 16, no. 4 (1996): 95–8.

Lapidus, Steven. "The Forgotten Hasidim: Rabbis and Rebbes in Pre-war Canada." *Canadian Jewish Studies* 12 (2004): 1–30.

Martin-Nielsen, Janet. "An Engineer's View of an Ideal Society: The Economic Reforms of C.H. Douglas, 1916–1920. *Spontaneous Generations* 1, no. 1 (2007): 95–109.

Menkis, Richard. "Anti-Semitism in the Evolving Nation: From New France to 1950," in *From Immigration to Integration. The Canadian Jewish Experience: A Millennium Edition.* Ed. Ruth Klein and Frank Dimant. Toronto: Malcolm Lester, 2001, 31-51.

Palevsky, Mary. "Report on Survey of Jewish Refugee Settlement in Canada for the Canadian Jewish Congress." October 1949, file 2, "War Efforts, 1933–1950," JCC, CJC Papers, CJCCC, Montreal.

Pfeiffer, Julius. "From Amsterdam to Montreal for $1.25." *Jewish Life* (Montreal), July 1973, 38–49.

Rosenberg, Louis. "Two Centuries of Jewish Life in Canada," In *Canadian Jewish Reference Book and Directory*. Ed. Eli Gottesman. Ottawa: Mortimer Limited, 1963, 81–89.

Rosenfarb, Chava. "Writing in a Language Foreign to Nearly All." *The Montreal Gazette*, 14 August 1999, 11–12.

Schein, Ada. "She'erit ha-Peletah: Women in DP Camps in Germany," *Jewish Women's Archive: A Comprehensive Historical Encyclopedia*. http://jwa.org/encyclopedia/article/sheerit-ha-peletah-women-in-dp-camps-in-germany.

Schnoor, Randal F. "Traditions and Innovation in an Ultra-Orthodox Community: The Hasidim of Outremont." *Canadian Jewish Studies* 10 (2002).

Sheftel, Anna and Stacey Zembrzycki. "'We Started Over Again, We Were Young': Postwar Social Worlds of Holocaust Survivors in Montreal." *Urban History Review/Revue d'histoire urbaine* 39, no. 1 (2010): 20–30.

Speisman, Stephen. "Anti-Semitism in Ontario: The Twentieth Century," in *Anti-Semitism in Canada: History and Interpretation*. Ed. Alan Davies. Waterloo, ON: Wilfrid Laurier University Press, 1992. 113-133.

Stoffman, Judy. "Graduates of Holocaust—Chava Rosenfarb writes in Yiddish, her mother tongue. And she's finding a new kind of literary recognition at age 83." *The Toronto Star*, 17 June 2006, H-09.

Tweed, Jean. "Security, Not Paternalism, Behind Aid to Immigrant." *Saturday Night*, 13 March 1948, 6.

*Vaad Hatzala (Committee for Rescue): Major Jewish Orthodox Organization for rescue, relief & religious rehabilitation among war-torn Jewry*. 1946. Vaad Hatzala Committee for Rescue, 1943–1948, CJC Box 23, CJCCC.

Weinfeld, Morton. "Quebec Anti-Semitism and Anti-Semitism in Quebec." *Post-Holocaust and Anti-Semitism*, no. 64 (2008). http://jcpa.org/article/quebec-anti-semitism-and-anti-semitism-in-quebec/.

Zabjek, Alexandra. "How the '56ers' Changed Canada." *The Ottawa Citizen*, 15 October 2006, B4.

## Unpublished Material

Abrams, Percy. "A Study of the Jewish Immigrants in Hamilton and Their Relationship with the Jewish Community Centre." MSW thesis, University of Toronto, 1955.

Banauch, Eugen. "'Home' as a Thought Between Quotation Marks: The Fluid Exile of Jewish Third Reich Refugee Writers in Canada 1940-2006." PhD dissertation, Universität Wien, 2007.

Craft, Kenneth. "Canada's Righteous: A History of the Canadian National Committee on Refugees and Victims of Political Persecution." MA thesis, Carleton University, 1987.

Draper, Paula Jean. "The Accidental Immigrants: Canada and the Interned Refugees." PhD dissertation, University of Toronto, 1983.

Endler, Sylvia. "The Prevention of Hard Core Cases Among the Immigrant Displaced Persons: A Study of 77 Immigrant DP Families Served at the Jewish Immigrant Aid Society, July 1, 1951 to February 29, 1952 Who Required Further Service After a Six Months' Period." MSW thesis, McGill University, 1954.

Gerber, Jean. "Opening the Door: Immigration and Integration of Holocaust Survivors in Vancouver, 1947–1970." MA thesis, University of British Columbia, 1989.

Giberovitch, Myra. "The Contributions of Montreal Holocaust Survivor Organizations to Jewish Communal Life." MSW thesis, McGill University, 1998.

Gordon, Ross. "The Historiographical Debate on the Charges of Anti-Semitism Made Against Lionel Groulx." MA thesis, University of Ottawa, 1996.

Kogen, David C. "Changes in Jewish Religious Life." MA thesis, University of British Columbia, 1951.

Petrovsky-Shtern, Yohanan. "Jews in the Russian Army, 1827–1914." PhD dissertation, Brandeis University, 2001.

Reed, Patrick. "A Foothold in the Whirlpool: Canada's Iberian Refugee Movement." MA thesis, Concordia University, 1996.

Weiner, Miriam. "Case Work Services for Displaced Persons Immigrating to Canada." BSW thesis, McGill University, 1952.

## Newspapers and Magazines

*Canadian Churchman*

*Canadian Jewish Congress Inter-Office Information Bulletin*

*Halifax Herald*

*Health*

*Jewish Bulletin*

*Jewish Life*

*JIAS Record*

*Le Patrie*

*Saturday Night*

*The Canadian Jewish Chronicle*

*The Canadian Jewish Review/The Canadian Jewish News*

*The Financial Post*

*The Jewish Western Bulletin*

*The Montreal Star*

*The National Post, Toronto*

*The New Life*

*The Ottawa Citizen*

*The Toronto Star (Toronto Daily Star)*

*Y.M.H.A. Review*

# INDEX